RAHNER AND METZ

Transcendental Theology as Political Theology

Titus F. Guenther

UNIVERSITY
PRESS OF
AMERICA

Lanham • New York • London

Copyright © 1994 by
University Press of America®, Inc.
4720 Boston Way
Lanham, Maryland 20706

3 Henrietta Street
London WC2E 8LU England

Library of Congress Cataloging-in-Publication Data
Guenther, Titus F.
Rahner and Metz : transcendental theology as political theology /
Titus F. Guenther.
p.   cm.
Includes bibliographical references and index.
1. Christianity and politics—Catholic Church—History—20th century.
2. Man (Christian theology)—History of doctrines—20th century.
3. Theology, Doctrinal—History—20th century.   4. Rahner, Karl.
5. Metz, Johanes Baptist.   6. Catholic Church—Doctrines—
History—20th century.   I. Title.   II. Title: Transcendental theology
as political theology.
BX1793.G83   1993   261.7'0904—dc20   92–44976 CIP

ISBN 0–8191–9033–0 (cloth : alk. paper)

The paper used in this publication meets the minimum requirements of
American National Standard for Information Sciences—Permanence
of Paper for Printed Library Materials, ANSI Z39.48–1984.

To

Karen

Acknowledgments

Naturally, a publication of this kind is never only an individual effort. The many people who, in one way or another, have made it possible for me to complete this book are gratefully remembered. Although I cannot list everyone, I wish to name a few of the obvious people and institutions, whose assistance has been invaluable. There is first the patient but most efficient direction of my advisor, Dan Donovan, professor of systematic theology at the University of St. Michael's College, Toronto. Besides his many helpful comments concerning content, I am also indebted to professor Donovan for valuable suggestions about style.

Second, I found much encouragement in the positive response by professors Johann Baptist Metz and Karl Rahner to my thesis proposal (cf. chapter 4, n.#32). During a visit to Münster in 1984 I enjoyed a friendly reception by professor Metz and he made available to me a number of his as yet unpublished essays. Throughout the time of research and writing I have been in regular, friendly conversation with professor Metz concerning the themes and position of my book--which does not necessarily mean agreement on all points.

Third, my deep appreciation goes to professors Francis Schuessler Fiorenza, Leo O'Donovan, Margaret O'Gara, and Harry McSorley, and Michael Fahey, respectively. Their correspondence and other written or spoken comments were always encouraging and helpful in bringing this study better into focus. I am also very pleased to be able to include the **Foreword** by professor Leo O'Donovan in this book.

Fourth, I fondly remember the helpful conversations with the librarian of the University of Freiburg, Albert Raffelt, who generously made available to me materials relevant to my investigation. Fifth, in the accumulation of research materials, I

Rahner and Metz

am indebted to the Interlibrary Loans system of the Association of Commonwealth Universities, through the National University of Lesotho (Africa) during my work there as Protestant Chaplain and part-time lecturer in theology from 1981 to 1984.

Sixth, the contribution of my wife Karen, in a variety of ways (but typing my manuscript is not one of them!), simply defies description. She courageously took over, for extended periods, much of our shared job as Conference Youth Ministers, which freed me to concentrate on writing. In her unqualified support, Karen consistently generated new strength for me to press on in my project when morale flagged.

Furthermore, I am indebted to the Doctoral Fellowship of the Social Sciences and Humanities Research Council of Canada for its Research Award toward what was to become this book. Likewise, I am grateful to the Commission on Overseas Mission and the Mennonite Board of Missions, respectively, for paying off portions of my student loan debt while serving under these agencies in Lesotho and Chile in turn. A word of thanks goes to all authors and publishers who kindly granted permission to publish quoted materials in this book. Next, the present version of the book owes much to Terry Cambias, former superior of the Maryknoll Order in Chile, whose bold-yet-sensitive editorial touches made the text more readable. Finally, the technical assistance from Gottlieb Hauser in manuscript formatting and producing an index is gratefully acknowledged.

Table of Contents

Foreword

As a reader for Titus Guenther's doctoral thesis, on *Rahner and Metz: Transcendental Theology as Political Theology*, I strongly encouraged the author to consider publishing his work. It is thus with great pleasure that I welcome its appearance in print. The book offers a highly competent and persuasive treatment of two outstanding theologians of our century. Reading it again, I believe the following points merit special appreciation.

In the first place, Guenther's investigation is of intrinsic interest, not only because of the two authors he investigates but also because of its methodological implications for the conversation (rather than opposition) of different contemporary theologies. In a highly pluralistic situation, culturally and religiously, authors are often played off against one another when they might more productively be brought into dialogue. Without superficial harmonization, Guenther has revealed a deep complementarity and interdependence between the writings of Karl Rahner and Johann Baptist Metz. At the same time he recognizes an irreducible distinction between them. A careful reading of his analysis, I suggest, will lead one to a still more careful reading of his major subjects.

As I understand his book, Guenther basically asks whether Karl Rahner's theology may be said to represent a true version of what Johann Baptist Metz has for some twenty years termed a political theology. To approach the issue as exactly as possible, the author first exposes the intention and scope of Metz's work. His first chapter thus offers a clear and sympathetic interpretation of Metz's relation to modern secularity, his dialogue with Marxism and critical theory, and the development of his own special themes. I am impressed by Guenther's treatment of Metz on existence as a political problem and on discipleship christology. He likewise summarizes his subject author well on the truly Christian meaning of solidarity, the difference between evolutionary and eschatological understandings of time, and the relation of the "eschatological proviso" to critical theory. I applaud still more his argument that narrative theology should be seen as a corrective to doctrinal theology rather than as a substitute for it. This introductory chapter on Metz is well positioned, leading to a fresh review of Rahner.

Guenther next turns to the basic dynamism of Rahner's thought. His presentation is clearly appreciative, at times even enthusiastic--but not uncritical. He situates Rahner well in the context of his time and wisely selects the most appropriate evidence for answering his main question. Rahner's indebtedness to modern transcendental philosophy and his difference from it, his development of a theology of human subjectivity and freedom, his ringing incarnationalism and pastoral commitment all stand out in bold relief. Likewise, the new range of questions that came to the fore with the Second Vatican Council and his searching concern for the church's role in the world. As chapter 2 presents the original lines of Rahner's thought and chapter 3 its developing social dimension at the time of the Council and thereafter, the reader finds more and more reason to agree with Guenther that it contains the critical power and apologetic potential to warrant being called something like "political."

But in his final chapter Guenther becomes more nuanced, and most effectively so. Taking a valuable clue from David Tracy, he sees Rahner and Metz as theologians who manifest a unity in difference, the fundamental paradigm for which comes from the Gospels' witness to Christ. His earlier pages justify an insistence that Rahner meets the demands of a political theology through his concern for contemporary experience, his call for a deprivatized theology, his reflections on solidarity, his conviction of the interrelation of theory and practice, and his own version of "remembering narrative theology." At this point, one might say that Rahner's theology has shown the inner resources to incorporate the themes of political theology, while Metz appears as the theologian who most obviously prompted that development.

Yet Guenther analyzes a still deeper reason for a fruitful difference between the master and the master student. Not just systematic comprehension differentiates the former from the latter's historical preoccupation with human suffering. Rather, two contrasting theological temperaments are in evidence, the one sustained by a pervasive incarnational and sacramental sense, the other more apocalyptically keyed. As a result, Rahner, deeply influenced by Metz's thought, could deny that he was directly writing political theology and yet remain in fundamental harmony with it. And Metz, perhaps influenced by the dialogue even more than Rahner, can continue to ground his apocalyptic eschatology in the memory of Jesus which is celebrated in the sacramental church.

The book thus represents a dialectically refined treatment of this subject. The author might perhaps have stated his own position more clearly at times; as it stands the reader must often infer it from his use of both original and secondary sources-- which are indeed masterfully employed. I welcome all the more, therefore, the inclusion of Guenther's careful discussion on evangelical nonviolence in the various parts of the book.

Some further observations--rather than proposing "weaknesses" in this work--may indicate how effectively it can generate further inquiry on its subject. Guenther's central argument is quite convincing, but his basic thesis might be strengthened by further reflection on the following developments in Rahner's thought. First, in Rahner's later theology increasing attention is given to the cross and its place in history. While his thinking was indeed strongly incarnational throughout his career, the cross nevertheless figures prominently from the beginning with *increasing* emphasis in the final years, as a number of critics have observed.

Second, there is the question of Rahner's treatment of sin and death. (The theme, of course, is not absent from the book; the issue is whether more direct exploration could further strengthen the author's central argument.) It has frequently been noted that the first of these topics receives much less attention in Rahner than the second. A sensitive reading on Rahner's tendency in this area can yield evidence for a deeper recognition of negativity in human experience and its systematic implications. (Metz himself wrote a variation on Rahner's treatment of concupiscence when he approached the problem of unbelief.) Where, in an obvious way, has Rahner addressed the darkness which figures so prominently in Metz's thought?

Third, considering the sacraments somewhat more concretely, there may be further evidence for the "practicality" of Rahner's theology in his treatments of penance and the Eucharist. Was he not an early champion of the view that reconciliation with the neighbour (in the church) symbolizes our reconciliation with God? Were his views on the Eucharist ever stated without primary reference to the cross of Christ and our hope to pass through it to the resurrection of the body? Can there really be a sacramental life in the church that is called to serve the world unless the freedom of church and world are served by those sacraments?

Finally, is it necessary to call Rahner's thought a "political theology" in order to show that it complements (or supplements) rather than ignores Metz's programme? I believe the central issue is whether Rahner's twofold method, transcendental and historical, has intrinsically and genuinely social and public dimension. There are of course other ways to put that point: Can it satisfy the requirements of practical fundamental theology (in consort with a systematic theology)? Does it offer a theology of practical human solidarity before God? Is it simultaneously doxological and socio-critical? With its own particular themes and emphases, is it genuinely a constant call to personal and corporate conversion for the sake of the kingdom?

In terms increasingly common on our continent, one might ask whether Metz's programme does not lead us inevitably to see how profoundly public Rahner's theology really was. I myself am inclined to say that as his sense of time and history developed, he became increasingly aware of how dialectical his intention had been from the start, and of how profoundly he had been wrestling with the question of eternity germinating in time, through the joys and sorrows, the inevitable catastrophes and occasional triumphs of the human spirit that is called to union with God's own Spirit. His life's journey, his human concerns, his theological method were all markedly dialectical, struggling to affirm God's way in a world that we poor creatures so readily distort and disclaim.

However we answer such questions of interpretation, Titus Guenther's readers will be truly indebted to him for helping us to raise them and to realize how concretely they affect our lives of witness and discipleship.

Leo J. O'Donovan, S.J.
President
Georgetown University
Washington, D.C.

Author's Preface

The initial idea for this book came as a by-product of a research essay I wrote on the anthropological theology of Karl Rahner. This led to the discovery of the catalogue of critical questions raised by Johann Baptist Metz early in his theological career about Karl Rahner's work. Did Metz's political theological critique constitute a radical break with his mentor's thought? Or might his "new political theology" rather be seen as a radical continuation of that transcendental theology, in which the human spirit is perceived as fundamentally world-directed for its true realization, and in which the "hearers of the word" must listen within their history for God's revealing word? This book wrestles with this question, leaning towards the latter alternative, even though the question may not allow for a clear either/or answer.

The development of the book can be summarized as follows. Using the categories of Metz's "new political theology" (elaborated in chapter 1), it investigates Rahner's theology (with its dialectically related transcendental and historical moments) to see if it does not in fact function as a new political theology in its own right. In spite of his general reticence on this point, Rahner himself on one occasion makes the qualified claim that his theology is indeed such a political theology.

After situating this controversial claim in the current theological debate, the early chapters set the stage for testing the validity of the book's thesis by elaborating the relevant ideas in the theologies of Metz and Rahner, respectively. It becomes evident that Rahner's thought, intrinsically and from the beginning, tends toward the world-directedness that was later developed formally in the work of Metz. Moreover, already in parts of chapter 2 we find evidence suggesting that Rahner frequently theologized in the context of his practical commitments which had a notable political theological impact.

The stage being set, chapter 3 proceeds to analyze the life and writings of Rahner for their actual implicit and explicit political theological performance. Measured against the central criteria of Metz's thought, Rahner's theology seems to do well indeed. It is deeply praxis oriented in its responsiveness to the concrete modern situation; is a "narrative theology" par excellence, and requires that the universal solidarity of Christian love include solidarity with the apparently socially "useless" individual, thus serving as the "interruptive" force against modern progressivist ideologies that would sacrifice the imperfect present for an ideal future.

In parenthesis, it could be objected that this interpretation (of Rahner's theology as a superb "biographical," "narrative theology," for instance) is based to a large extent on Metz's interpretation of Rahner and not Rahner himself, and is thereby weakened. However, against such an objection we may note that, besides the extensive primary evidence given below, considerable secondary evidence is also offered from notable interpreters of Rahner's work who would not call themselves "political" theologians. Moreover, I consider it to be significant that Karl Rahner never did object to this interpretation by Metz. When Metz said that Rahner's work met political theological criteria, Rahner apparently did not feel that his thought was being distorted or coopted. He did object, however, when on other occasions his work was said not to meet these criteria (cf. my Introduction).

The final chapter (4) closely compares these two major Catholic systematic thinkers, revealing a deep complementarity and interdependence between them. At the same time, an irreducible distinction between them clearly remains. This unity-in-difference appears to be a matter of "theological temperaments" rather than a significant theological contradiction. Metz's new political theology reveals a "prophetic-apocalyptic" temperament and Rahner's political theology is marked by an "incarnational-sacramental" temperament. Both their theologies, however, are rooted in the same original gospel narratives, although each stresses a different dimension. Therefore, both theologies may be deemed "orthodox." And both theologies enrich one another.

Perhaps the reader will ask why this book does not include a section on the relation of its thesis to the political theology of the historic peace churches--the author's background. Would the book not be richer, had it included a more sustained dialogue between the sociopolitical teachings of its theological subjects (Rahner and Metz) and the theology of the "peace churches" that grew out of the Radical Reformation? After all, the practice in these churches of baptizing adult believers[1] initially constituted no less than "an act of civil disobedience" (Klaassen [1989]: 251)--not to mention their (almost) consistent rejection of participating in armed violence for over four and a half centuries. I am desisting from doing so for two reasons. First, to enter upon such a dialogue with sufficient care would deserve a study all its own. Second, because of my present teaching responsibilities at the Evangelical Theological Community of Chile, I am unable to carry out such an expansion, even in a shortened form. Thus I needed to make the choice between broadening my manuscript (and probably not publishing it) and/or submitting it in its more limited, specialized form, making only minor changes in the original text. I have chosen the latter alternative.

I am thus submitting the "thesis" of the book for discussion and scrutiny. This book has no pretences of being a definitive word on its subject. It wants rather to present a modest argument about the relationship between the theologies of two important authors of our century on the vital subject of "political theology" versus "transcendental theology" (as defined below), and what each has to offer to a world in crisis, in order that readers may

---

[1] For an authoritative study of this position, cf. D.F. Durnbaugh, *The Believers' Church: The History and Character of Radical Protestantism*, (Herald Press: 1968 and 1985).

be enriched by it or challenged and moved to respond to the argument presented here. The manuscript cannot claim to be up to date, since Metz is still writing, and scholarship on both Rahner and Metz continues. My hope is that the research presented here is nevertheless worth the reader's consideration.

Titus F. Guenther
Santiago, Chile, 16th February, 1992

A Personal Note

Born in 1946, I grew up in a German-speaking Mennonite community in Paraguay and completed my teacher training in a predominantly Catholic school in Paraguay's capital, Asunción, before leaving for university studies in Canada in 1971. During my undergraduate studies at a Mennonite theological college in Winnipeg, our school took notice of the "new openness" wrought in the Catholic world as a result of the Second Vatican Council. Thus, when after a year of studies in secular anthropology at University of Manitoba I felt irresistibly drawn back to theology, I turned to the University of St. Michael's College, member of the federation of colleges which forms the renowned Toronto School of Theology. During the course of my Masters and Ph.D. programmes at this school--in the diverse company of fellow Mennonite, other Protestant and Catholic students--I thoroughly enjoyed the open, "ecumenical" atmosphere at this center of learning.

In the area of liturgy, however, St. Michael's College was less "open." I remember our disappointment when the Advanced Degree Student Council received an answer from the Dean to the effect that he was not at liberty to announce openly that non-Catholic students were "invited" to participate fully in the mass celebrated by the academic community during the week. We were never turned away when we attended, of course. By contrast, the academic atmosphere was accommodating and deeply rewarding.

In this setting, as I became familiar with the "anthropological theology" of Karl Rahner and the *"christliche Anthropozentrik"* of Johann Baptist Metz, I discovered that I did not have to choose between the study of theology and anthropology but could study both at the same time. The theological anthropology I now pursued was cast in a rather different key, of course, from the discipline commonly evoked by the term anthropology. My lasting interest in anthropology had been awakened by the constant interaction between Mennonites and indigenous people of the Central Paraguayan Chaco during my childhood and youth. Their vastly different way of life was often perplexing and constantly challenging to our own cultural identity. When the gifted missionary-anthropologist, Jacob Loewen, visited these communities and made the culture of our aborigine neighbours come alive before our eyes, I became fascinated by anthropology.

With respect to the present study, the reader will quickly notice that I am not writing as an "insider" of the Catholic tradition. Perhaps this is a strength and a weakness at the same time. My perspective is rooted in the Anabaptist-Mennonite tradition. Historically, this branch of Christianity derives from the "radical wing" of the Reformation[1] and belongs to the historic peace churches. Though seldom put in the foreground, the reader will sense this "radical orientation" as present throughout the book, but more especially when the question of the appropriate means for sociopolitical engagement on the part of Christians is dealt with.

---

[1] Cf. G.H. Williams, *The Radical Reformation*, (Westminster Press, 3rd. Printing, 1975); Spanish, *La Reforma Radical*, (México: FCE, 1983). For an artistic portrait of this movement in its initial stages, cf. *The Radicals* (produced by Sisters and Brothers, Goshen, Indiana, 1990), based on the historical novel by M. Augsburger, *Pilgrim Aflame* (Herald Press, 1967). The film is focused on the life and martyrdom of the Anabaptist leader, Benedictine ex-Abbot Michael Sattler. A good representative work about the Anabaptist-Mennonite story is C.J. Dyck, ed., *An Introduction to Mennonite History: A Popular History of the Anabaptists and the Mennonites*, (Herald Press, 2nd ed. 1981); Spanish, *Cuadernos Menonitas: Una Introducción a la Historia Menonita*, Tomos I & II, (Edición SEMILLA, 1984-1985). For scientific inquiry, cf. *The Mennonite Encyclopedia*, 4 Volumes, H.S. Bender, *et al*, eds., (Mennonite Publishing House, 1957; Supplementary Volume 5, C.J. Dyck and Dennis Martin, eds., (Herald Press, 1990); contains circa 1,000 new articles on important topics and updates materials in the first 4 volumes..

A Personal Note

My inquiry is therefore an "ecumenical" exercise by definition, if more implicitly than explicitly. The reason for not placing my personal position in the foreground of the discussion is twofold. First, to discuss the question of the appropriate means for Christian witness and involvement in modern society with the care and sensitivity it deserves would require a sustained, separate study.[2] Second, this book was first a Ph.D. dissertation. As such its specific focus was to investigate how these two leading thinkers of the Catholic community discern and propose to carry out the church's responsibility toward the individual and society in today's world. Given the natural limitations that such an investigation entails, I had to bracket out other possible ramifications in order to keep the project manageable. The reader will nevertheless be able to detect easily what position I am inclined to adopt.

The pacifist way of life does not need to lead to isolationism from the world's problems, as some critics fear it must. One need only point to the relatively strong social outreach program of the

---

[2] The interested reader will find good examples of peace church thinking on the "just war doctrine", and topics like Christians and power, Christians and violence, Christian political engagement, and church versus state in the following books: John H. Yoder, *When War is Unjust: Being Honest in Just-War Thinking*, (Augsburg Publishing House, 1984); W. Klaassen, *The Just War: A Summary*, (Dundas: Ontario, 1978); Spanish, *La Guerra Justa: Un Resumen*, (Ediciones CLARA - SEMILLA, 1991); J.H. Yoder, *The Politics of Jesus. Vicit Agnus Noster*, (W.B. Eerdmans, 1972); Spanish, *Jesús y la Realidad Política*, (Buenos Aires: Ediciones Certeza, 1985). According to Ted Koontz, this book by Yoder is **"the most important modern Mennonite interpretation of the political orientation of Jesus and the early church,"** (ME V: [1990] p.162). R.J. Sider, *Christ and Violence*, (Herald Press, 1979); Spanish, *Cristo y la Violencia*, (Ediciones SEMILLA - CLARA, 1991); Ted J. Koontz, "Church-State Relations," in: *The Mennonite Encyclopedia* [ME], Vol. V (1990), pp.159-162 (cf. ME IV: [1957] pp.611ff.)

Mennonite constituency around the world throughout this century[3] in order to allay such fears. At the same time, it cannot be denied that as a matter of historical fact Mennonites have sometimes given way to the temptation of becoming withdrawn in quietism.

It has been exhilarating for me to discover in this study that the worldwide post-conciliar Catholic church--a thousand times larger than the Mennonite community--boldly and widely takes the offensive in giving an account of its Christian faith and hope before the modern world. This concern has also been central, historically, to the Anabaptist-Mennonite church. Furthermore, to find that Mennonite and Catholic Christians (at least the main protagonists of this book) hold a growing number of central convictions in common is truly inspiring. Both stress that the criteria for sociocritical teaching and action need to be grounded in the gospel, and that only a discipleship lived in community can offer genuine Christological knowledge and a solution to the faith crisis in the church, as well as an effective Christian witness to post-Enlightenment modern society.

The author

---

[3] C. Redekop and S. Steiner's commentary is instructive on this point, when they report: "Simultaneously while developing this new respectable, scholarly identity, Mennonites in the post World War II era entered the larger North American society in an unparalleled fashion. Alongside renewed creativity in the historical, theological, psychological, biblical and aesthetic disciplines, **the Mennonite church exploded into the social arena with large mission, relief and service programs. Peace and service activism became identity symbols especially for younger Mennonites.** The Mennonite Central Committee (MCC) became identified as a small but very respected worldwide relief agency. Two or three year voluntary service assignments became commonplace for young Mennonites. By the 1980s almost half the Mennonite population worldwide was non-white." *Mennonite Identity: Historical and Contemporary Perspectives, Ibid.,* eds., (University Press of America, 1988), p.267 (emph. added). (Actually MCC began its relief program already in response to the post W.W.I calamities.)

On Procedure

A few logistical things need to be clarified. The reader will find some inconsistencies in the spelling of certain words. For example: the word "realization" also appears as "realisation," when quoted from a British translation; the word "neighbour" also appears as "neighbor," when cited from a US translation; the word "fulfillment" is spelled "fulfilment" by some translators. My policy has been to leave the spelling in citations as found, while using the Canadian spelling in my own text--which at times still leaves one to choose between two equally acceptable alternatives, e.g. enquiry and inquiry.

In my own writing I have tried to be sensitive in using inclusive language. But when citing other sources, my policy has been to leave the respective author's formulations intact, even if these represent "exclusive" language.

In terms of footnoting, I use a combination of the social sciences style (of an abbreviated reference to the source plus page numbers in brackets) and regular footnoting. The former seems to be much more practical when a simple reference to the page number is needed. The latter I reserve mainly for references where further commentary is required.

Finally, when using original German sources, only my translations appear in the text. Any untranslated German citations (kept to a minimum) appear in the footnotes. Otherwise I believe my procedure is self-evident.

Introduction

Numerous dissertations, books and articles have been written to explore the wide-ranging significance of the great work of Karl Rahner.[1] These studies treat the philosophical, methodological, spiritual, pastoral or ethical aspects of his work, to name but a few.[2] Surprisingly, however, hardly anyone has paid any attention to whether or not his work, commonly characterized as transcendental and anthropological theology, may yield anything in terms of sociopolitical significance.[3]

---

[1] On the European scene, cf. "Verzeichnis der Schüler Karl Rahners und ihrer Dissertationen," and A. Raffelt, "Bibliographie der Sekundärliteratur 1948-1978," in *Wagnis Theologie*, H. Vorgrimler, ed., (Freiburg i.Br: Herder, 1979), pp.577f. and pp.598-622; in North America the scholarship on Karl Rahner is also considerable.

[2] A handy "topical survey" of Rahner's theological work is Leo J. O'Donovan, ed., *A World of Grace: An Introduction to the Themes and Foundations of Karl Rahner's Theology* (N.Y: Seabury, 1980). The editor writes: "The sequence of our own chapter topics is designed as a running introduction to *Foundations [of Christian Faith]*, with an essay devoted to each of the topics there, and in the same order....To highlight **the inherently practical and ethical dimension of this theology,** an essay has been added (chapter 12) to reflect on **Rahner's contribution to contemporary and future Christian ethics**" (p.xi; my emph.).

[3] In German, I could mention: K. Fischer, "Der 'praktische' Impuls in K. Rahners Konzeption vom Menschen als Geheimnis," *Der Mensch als Geheimnis*, (1974), pp.389-399; N. Mette, "Zwischen Reflexion und Entscheidung. Der Beitrag Karl Rahners zur Grundlegung der praktischen Theologie," *Trierer Theologische Zeitschrift* 87 (1978), pp.26-43, pp.136-151; and as a major work, K. Neumann, *Der Praxisbezug der Theologie bei Karl Rahner*, (Herder, 1980).

The most comprehensive work in this area is undoubtedly Neumann's. His inquiry into the *Praxisbezug* (reference to praxis) in Rahner, obviously overlaps with, but does not pre-empt my project. He specifically states that his point of departure is "a wider concept of praxis," so as to include in his treatise the "uncontrollable religious processes" such as prayer, contemplation, worship, listening and silence, for example. My investigation is more modest and more ambitious at the same time: more modest in not focusing on everything in Rahner's work that may legitimately be claimed to have "practical" significance; more ambitious in its claim that Rahner's transcendental theology produces results that meet political theology's ideals.

Some commentators claim that a transcendental theology is inherently incapable of addressing matters of public life effectively. Their position has been succinctly summarized by Leo O'Donovan as follows:

In English, I may cite Leo J. O'Donovan's essay, "Orthopraxis and Theological Method in Karl Rahner," *CTSA Proceedings* 35 (1980) 47-65; also the unpublished M.A. Thesis by E.R. John, *Political Themes in the Thought of Karl Rahner*, (U. of St. Michael's College, Toronto, 1983). While this thesis is similar in some ways to my project and contains valuable insights, it differs in that the political theological dimension is not as central as in my investigation.

Neumann confirms my observation, when he states: "Detailed studies concerning the philosophical dimension in Rahner's work and about the central themes of his theology are available. **But the practical aspect and the practical impulses of his theology have sofar hardly been studied indepth**" (p.16). Yet, says Neumann, the more knowledgeable students of Rahner (naming Metz, Vorgrimler, and Lehmann) have amply attested that "**the relation of Rahner's work to the praxis of life and faith [Lebens- und Glaubenspraxis] plays a decisive role and that, ultimately, it has to be understood from there;**" Rahner himself "confesses": "'Underlying everything I did was a very immediate pastoral and spiritual concern.'" Neumann adds rightly: "**It is all the more noteworthy that this [practical] dimension of Rahner (to my knowledge) has not been the subject of a major inquiry**" (pp.15f.; my tr. and emphs.).

His [Rahner's] approach is said to yield an appreciation not so much of contingent history as of generalized historicity. As a result, the argument goes, the method is insensitive to social problems and ineffectual in the realms of policy and social change.[4]

Theologians who subscribe to this interpretation, he says, are conveniently disregarding the fact that Rahner has never allowed himself to be hemmed in by one particular method. Rather, from the beginning, he has used a "twofold method" with transcendental and historical moments which are "dialectically [inter-]related."[5]

Furthermore, even if it is admitted that "there can be no doubt of Rahner's starting point; it is the individual subject and his experience of transcendence," as Daniel Donovan does in his review of Rahner's *Foundations of Christian Faith*, one should not overlook the fact that his starting point is inherently world-directed. For, Donovan points out, the fact "that the transcendental is always mediated through the historical follows upon his understanding of man as spirit in the world."[6]

---

[4] Leo O'Donovan, "Orthopraxis...," *op. cit.*, p.48. As a specific example, cf. R. Johns, who contends: because of its "transcendental" starting point, "Rahner's theology lacks a world relation...," has no "political ethic" and no "ontology which takes account of the material, biological, social and technological reality in which man lives." R.D. Johns, *Man in the World: The Political Theology of Johannes Baptist Metz*, (1976), p.46, also p.47.

[5] O'Donovan, *op. cit.*, p.49. As an example the author cites a statement from 1952, in which Rahner was "outlining his view on human dignity and freedom, [and wherein] he expressly said that for a genuine knowledge of human nature, including a concrete knowledge of the possibilities which human nature freely realizes, we **'must rely...on a twofold method: on a transcendental method...[and] the reflection on the historical experience humanity has of itself'**." O'Donovan goes on to show that Rahner, in subsequent writings, has frequently insisted upon this "twofold method" (my emph.).

[6] Daniel Donovan, "Rahner's 'Grundkurs': Frankly Pastoral," *The Ecumenist* 16 (July-August, 1978), p.68. What is meant by this focus on the transcendental experience of the person is more sharply defined by Metz who,

In light of the above, it would seem justified to examine the question of the relationship of Rahner's theology to the fast-growing discipline of the "new political theology." This idea occurred to me as a result of certain specific critical comments by Johann Baptist Metz (student and friend of Rahner) concerning some possible shortcomings of his mentor's transcendental theology, which defines the human individual fundamentally as "a being of absolute transcendence toward God." These words occur in what is perhaps the most concentrated criticism by Metz of Rahner's transcendental and anthropological method in his "Essay on Karl Rahner" that appears as the "Foreword" to SW. The penetrating questions presented there merit quoting in full. (It should however be remembered that these questions appear at the end of an essay of superlative praise of Rahner's achievement.) Thus concludes the essay:

> Yet questions remain unanswered and new questions arise, and these latter
> must begin at as deep a level as Rahner's approach itself. For example,
> does not such a transcendental-existential approach (which defines man *a
> priori* as that being characterized by absolute transcendence towards God)
> concentrate the necessarily historically realized salvation of man too much

---

in commenting on "the fundamental anthropological definition that is present in [Rahner's] transcendental theology," says, **"This can be expressed concisely in the following way: man exists as an anticipation of God and this anticipation conditions the possibility of his knowledge and behaviour."** J.B. Metz, *Faith in History and Society*, (N.Y: Seabury, 1980; hereafter: FHS), p.65; *Glaube in Geschichte und Gesellschaft*, (1977, 3. Aufl. 1980), p.61.

The following comment by Donovan (in the above review) with regards to strengths and weaknesses of different theological methods is relevant here as well:

"There are many conceivable starting points for theology, each having its own possibilities and its own dangers. To pit starting point against starting point tells us little of the value of a particular theology or of the achievement of its author. Much more significant is what a theologian does with the possibilities that are his through his starting point, and of how and whether he is sensitive to, and is able to compensate for, its limitations."

on the question of whether the individual freely accepts or rejects this constitution of his being? Is there not danger that the question of salvation will be made too private and that salvation history will be conceived too worldlessly, breaking too quickly the point of the universal historical battle for man? Anthropologically oriented theology places the faith quite correctly in a fundamental and irreducible relationship with the free subjectivity of man. However, is the relationship of this faith to the world and history sufficiently preserved (*aufgehoben*)? This relationship to the world certainly cannot be renewed in the classical sense of a cosmology, since the faith is not in a cosmological sense worldly. But the faith is and remains (in the light of its biblical origins and its content of promise) in a social and political sense worldly. Therefore, should not the transcendental theology of person and existence be translated into a type of "political theology"? And finally, does not a radical transcendental-existential theology undervalue the rank of eschatology? Can the eschatology really be extrapolated out of the existential approach of theology? Or does not every anthropologically oriented theology which does not want to leave the world and history out of the sight of operative and responsible faith flow into an eschatologically oriented theology? Is [**not in fact only**] the eschatological horizon broad enough to communicate (*vermitteln*) unabridged the faith and the historically arising world?[7]

---

[7] J.B. Metz, "Foreword: An Essay on Karl Rahner," W.V. Dych, tr., in: *Spirit in the World*, N.Y: Herder & Herder, 1968, p.xviif. (my emph.). The crucial importance of this criticism for my enquiry warrants that the same text be given here in the original German--the more so as the English rendering is faulty at one point (cf. square brackets). It reads:

"Dennoch bleiben Fragen, entstehen Fragen, Fragen, die nun freilich ebenso tief ansetzen müßten wie Rahners Ansatz selbst. Wird durch einen solchen **transzendental-anthropologischen Ansatz, der den Menschen vorweg als das Wesen absoluter Transzendenz auf Gott bestimmt,** das geschichtlich zu realisierende Heil der Menschheit nicht zu sehr auf die Frage konzentriert, ob der einzelne diese seine Wesensverfassung frei annehme oder ablehne? Entsteht damit aber nicht die Gefahr, daß die Heilsfrage zu sehr privatisiert wird, die Heilsgeschichte zu weltlos konzipiert und dem universalen geschichtlichen Streit um den Menschen zu rasch die Spitze abgebrochen wird? Die anthropologisch gewendete Theologie bringt zwar mit vollem Recht den Glauben in eine fundamentale und unaufhebare Relation zur freien Subjektivität des Menschen. Sind darin aber Welt- und Geschichtsbezug dieses Glaubens hinreichend 'aufgehoben'? Gewiß kann dieser Weltbezug des Glaubens nicht im klassischen Stil der Kosmologie erneuert werden. Denn der Glaube ist nicht in einem kosmologischen Sinne welthaft. Aber er ist und

In this catalogue of questions, I believe, all the elements of criticism of the transcendental theological approach that will emerge in Metz's subsequent writings are contained already, at least in germ.[8]

The purpose of my inquiry, however, is not primarily to examine the validity of these criticisms, but rather to advance the positive argument that the work of Rahner does have far-reaching political theological implications. To put it more sharply: **the central argument of my book is that Karl Rahner's transcendental theology is inherently** *also* **"political theology," in the good sense of the word.** [Rahner himself, as we will see presently, has on one occasion made this guarded claim.] This is obviously a controversial claim that needs qualifying. We need to know what is meant here by "political theology." By using this term, I want to suggest that transcendental theology, while able

---

bleibt--vor allem wenn seine biblischen Ursprünge und seine Verheißungsinhalte ins Auge gefaßt werden--in einem gesellschaftlich-politischen Sinne welthaft. Müßte darum nicht die transzendentale Theologie der Person und Existenz in eine Art "politische Theologie" umgesetzt werden? Wird schließlich in einer radikal anthropologisch gewendeten Theologie der Stellenwert der Eschatologie nicht doch unterschätzt? Kann die Eschatologie wirklich aus dem anthropologischen Ansatz der Theologie extrapoliert werden? Oder gründet nicht vielmehr jede anthropologisch gewendete Theologie, die Welt und Geschichte nicht aus den Augen einer operativen Glaubensverantwortung verlieren will, in einer eschatologisch gewendeten Theologie? Ist **nämlich nicht erst** [omitted from translation] der eschatologische Horizont umfassend genug, daß in ihm Glaube und geschichtlich entstehende Welt unverkürzt vermittelt werden können?" J.B. Metz, "Karl Rahner [Porträt]," in: *Tendenzen der Theologie im 20. Jahrhundert. Eine Geschichte in Porträts*, H.J. Schultz, ed., (1966, 2. Aufl. 1967), pp.517f.

[8] Cf. for instance his FHS, especially pp.60-70, pp.154-168.

to perform the principal functions of political theology, is not reducible to political theology.[9]

We look to the work of Johann Baptist Metz for an authoritative definition of "political theology." Metz is renowned as one of the founders of this relatively new discipline and claims to have developed it along the lines of a fundamental theology. Metz's "new political theology" (new in contrast to the conventional political theology of the Constantinian age which has largely prevailed throughout the history of Christendom), supplies the essential categories needed to develop the central claim of this book. These categories must be used critically, lest they predetermine the results of my inquiry.

Using Metzian categories as a heuristic tool to read Rahner is promising for good reasons. Metz is regarded as "certainly Rahner's most speculatively gifted student,"[10] and is known to have criticized Rahner's theology substantively, precisely from the standpoint of political theology. Rahner has acknowledged: **"Metz's critique of my theology (which he calls transcendental) is the only criticism which I take very seriously."**[11]

My claim is validated if it can be demonstrated--even against specific criticisms by Metz of Rahner's transcendental theology-- that Rahner can and does indeed largely meet Metz's

---

[9] I am aware that this statement is problematic, considering Metz's claim that the "new political theology" is a fundamental theology and not a mere branch of theology, claiming to encompass the whole theological edifice (cf. n.#17 below). Given that claim, a theology (including transcendental theology) would have to either be political theology or nothing, i.e., it could not be anything else besides political theology. This claim would seem to be at odds, however, with our age of pluralism which affects even theology--unless one were to posit a pluralism even within the new political theology itself.

[10] H. Vorgrimler, *Karl Rahner: His Life, Thought and Work*, E. Quinn, tr., (1965), p.25.

[11] Karl Rahner, "Introduction" in: J.J. Bacik, *Apologetics and the Eclypse of Mystery*, (U. of Notre Dame Press, 1980), p.ix.

requirements for political theology. This I intend to demonstrate. This is not to deny that significant differences exist between these theologians. Rahner, for instance, simultaneously acknowledges, even vigorously defends(!), the basic "orthodoxy" of Metz's political theology and expresses reservations about its possible incompleteness. Consider for example his "public letter" in defense of Metz, occasioned by the refusal of certain authorities to appoint Metz as Professor of Fundamental Theology at Munich.[12]   Rahner rejects the notion that *"the* **political theology, which Metz has founded and represents within Catholic theology...,"** could be proper grounds for the refusal. To the contrary, if Metz's theology were unorthodox, asks Rahner, how could it be, **"that no serious questioning has arisen with respect to his orthodoxy in his many books and articles and in his public international ministry?..."**

In the same letter, however, Rahner admits that there are differences between him and his former student when he says that "Metz and I are not at all of the same opinion on the matter [regarding political theology], for Metz has already attacked my own theology vigorously."

Elsewhere, Rahner is more specific about their agreements and differences.[13]   Commenting on **"the relationship between my theology and the political theology...of Johann Baptist Metz**, my student and friend," Rahner first states the critique FHS makes of his theology, namely:

> Metz insists on going beyond my own theology to a societal situation of man and the Christian praxis, precisely because this praxis is not merely the carrying out of an abstract Christian theory.

---

[12] Cf. Karl Rahner, "Ich protestiere" (Offener Brief...), in: *Publik-Forum* 8 (1979), pp.18f.; my tr.).

[13] Cf. his "Introduction" to J. Bacik, *op. cit.*, (1980), pp.ixf. Rahner's critique is made here with particular reference to Metz's latest book at that time, *Faith in History and Society* (FHS, 1979; German 1977; emphs. are mine).

Rahner then expresses general agreement with the "positive contribution in Metz's book," which apparently consists in "the critique" that **"every concrete mystagogy must...from the very beginning consider the societal situation and the Christian praxis to which it addresses itself."** If he did not do justice to this aspect in his "theory of mystagogy," Rahner admits, "then this theory must be filled out."

But after having admitted this, Rahner turns around to defend his work as being, in effect, such a **"political theology from its inception"**: If his theology might have needed "filling out," "it is not therefore false."

> For it has always been clear in my theology that a 'transcendental experience' (of God and of grace) is always mediated through a categorical experience in history, in interpersonal relationships, and in society. If one not only sees and takes seriously these necessary mediations of transcendental experience but also fills it out in a concrete way, then one already practices in an authentic way political theology, or...a practical fundamental theology.

Finally, Rahner points out that political theology may be just as incomplete without transcendental theology as vice versa:

> ...such a political theology is, if it truly wishes to concern itself with God, not possible without reflection on those essential characteristics of man which a transcendental theology discloses.

Rahner then ends on a conciliatory note when seeing these theologies as complementing rather than opposing each other: "Therefore, I believe that my theology and that of Metz are not necessarily contradictory. However, I gladly recognize that a concrete mystagogy must, to use Metz's language, be at the same time 'mystical and political'."[14]

---

[14] Other instances of such cautious acceptance by Rahner of the unique dimensions in the new political theology could be adduced. E.g., K. Rahner, "Rede des Ignatius von Loyola an einen Jesuiten von heute," *Schriften zur Theologie* (STh) XV, pp.373-408; cf. esp. p.107; and *Glaube in winterlicher Zeit*, P. Imhof, H. Biallowons, eds., (1986), p.128.

Considering the sort of critical questions Metz's political theology asks of Rahner, and Rahner's response to these questions (as just presented), the following points merit special attention: a) Is there an inherent and necessary limitation (to an individualistic soteriology) in the transcendental and anthropological starting point? b) What stature does transcendental theology accord to historical or categorial reality? c) Can the anthropological starting point encompass a proper eschatology and does this, in fact, happen in Rahner's work? d) To what extent is Rahner's radically transcendental and anthropological theology able to give an account of the faith before the historically emerging secularized world, as demanded by the "new political theology"? In short, we may slightly alter Metz's rhetorical question and state it as an open question: "must [omitting the word "not"] the transcendental theology of the person and existence be transposed into some sort of 'political theology'," if the Christian faith is to remain "worldly" in a "social-political sense" as was the case in its biblical origins?[15]

In order to answer these questions, I need to establish briefly what is at the heart of Metz's political theology. The plea for **deprivatizing Christianity** is certainly central. In the post-Enlightenment "secularized" world the tendency of Christianity has been to retreat from the world and to withdraw into the privacy of the individual's interior life.[16]

---

[15] Cf. Metz, "Karl Rahner [Porträt]," *Tendenzen...*, p.518. For Engl. tr., by W.V. Dych, cf. "Foreword: An Essay on Karl Rahner," by J.B. Metz, in: *Spirit in the World*, (N.Y: Herder & Herder, 1968), p.xviii.

The "political theology" into which Metz would have transcendental theology "transposed" is, as the immediate context reveals, a political theology with a strong **eschatological colouring**. Furthermore, as I will argue below, the "eschatological horizon" in question is quite certainly already here tending towards an **apocalyptic eschatological** undertone, although this dimension would be developed more fully in Metz's subsequent writings.

[16] Cf. J.B. Metz, "Kirche und Welt im Lichte einer 'politischen Theologie'," in: *Zur Theologie der Welt*, (1968, 4. Aufl. 1979), pp.99-116.

Another equally central tenet of "political theology," is its **redefinition of the relationship between theory and practice.**[17] It aims to accomplish this through a critical combination of the gospel message with the standpoint of "critical reason."[18] This dialogical confrontation of the gospel with critical theory allows the "new political theology" to rediscover the Christian call to a life of discipleship (*Nachfolge*) as both "mystical" and "political" at the same time.[19]

---

[17] Cf. J.B. Metz, "Political Theology," in: K. Rahner, ed., *Encyclopedia of Theology: The Concise Sacramentum Mundi*, (1975), p.1239. Metz argues here that **"all theology must be of itself 'practical,' oriented to action;"** that **"theological truth" cannot be discovered apart from praxis within society.** Furthermore, unlike the Social Gospel movement, political theology is not simply a branch in theology called "applied theology," Metz contends. Rather, **"political theology claims to be a basic element in the whole structure of critical theological thinking"** (my emph.). Only if this holistic claim, which makes it into a "fundamental theology," is overlooked, could the "new political theology" "be mistaken for a theology dabbling in politics, i.e., in direct contact with sociopolitical public life, which would be wrong." Nothing could be farther from its interest, explains Metz: new political theology, in "its society-directed thinking," aims precisely to "prevent the Church and theology being saddled as it were unwittingly with this or that political ideology."

[18] *Ibid.*, pp.1239f. Metz proposes to avoid the pitfall of supporting political structures unwittingly by assessing "everything in the light of the eschatological message of Jesus," but within the framework of "the new standpoint provided by the critical reason" which resulted from the Enlightenment and found articulation from Hegel and Marx onward. What is central to "the new starting-point," says Metz, "is the fundamental relation between reason and society, the society-directed character of critical reason, the compulsion felt by the critical reason to consider itself in the light of society and the impossibility of critical reason's justifying its claims 'on the level of pure reasoning'." For Metz, "pure theology" is no more possible than "pure reason."

[19] This is captured well in J.B. Metz, *Zeit der Orden?*; the subtitle expresses it succinctly: ***Zur Mystik und Politik der Nachfolge*** (Herder, 1977). (The title for the English translation, *Followers of Christ: The Religious Life and the Church*, (Search Press, 1978), unfortunately, does not convey as clearly the direction of the book as does the original German.) As can be

There are other essential emphases or categories in Metz's "new political theology." There is his **narrative-practical** theology, as a critique of transcendental-idealistic theology. Also important is the concept of the **dangerous memory** or *memoria passionis et resurrectionis*, which reads history from the perspective of victims rather than of the victors. While not wanting to neglect the individual subject, it places a high premium on **intersubjectivity** as the "subject of history;" as, for example, when it interprets prayer as an act of human solidarity with ages past, present and yet to come.[20] And finally, it offers an **apocalyptic-eschatological** reading of time that sees **religion as interruption,** as a critique of the widely-held evolutionary interpretation of time as an endless stream of sameness.

My main task in this book is to demonstrate that Rahner's fundamentally transcendental and anthropological theology is able to perform negative and positive functions in the modern world, similar to those of the "new political theology." Obviously, it cannot be a question of finding identical terminology in Rahner's work, since much of the "new" political theological terminology emerged only from the middle of the 1960s onward. Nor is it a matter of looking for identical functions, but rather what might be called functions that "approximate" one another. For instance, it is quite clear that Rahner has not developed a formal "narrative" theology. But it can be argued (with Metz) that his whole empirically-based dogmatic is really a narrative theology

---

inferred from the table of contents, the act of following after Christ, and not orthodox doctrine, is seen as the mark of true Christianity: e.g., "Following Christ as a criterion of identity and faithfulness," reads one subheading (pp.22-27).

[20] On this point, cf. J.B. Metz's little spiritual treatise, which he co-published with Rahner, *The Courage to Pray* (Crossroad, 1980; German original, 1977), pp.1-28. The matter is of course dealt with at greater length (and more "scientifically") in Metz's major work, FHS (1980).

in its own right as it introduces the individual "subject" into traditional dogmatic theology.[21]

The first chapter gives a brief outline of Metz's "new political theology"--showing how it develops as the historical context evolves.[22] The second chapter presents aspects of Rahner's work relevant to this book, e.g., his methodology, his concept of freedom, his eschatology, and his treatment of the love of God and love of neighbour. As with the summary of Metz's theology, the chapter shows the original context in which Rahner's theology emerged, how it develops internally and adjusts to tasks presented by the historical context. Lehmann, for example, says one may "conditionally" postulate "three phases" in Rahner's theology. And he argues that the last of these phases shows a marked shift towards the historical and categorial, or "the 'a posteriori' elements in theology," and that this clearer

---

[21] Karl Lehmann, *Rechenschaft des Glaubens*, pp.36*f. Lehmann gives here a summary of Metz's "Karl Rahner--ein theologisches Leben. Theologie als mystische Biographie eines Christenmenschen heute" (1974). In this essay (in English, adapted, in FHS, pp.220-228), Metz describes Rahner's theology as consisting of a creative interplay between dogmatics and biography in that it introduces the "subject" into traditional dogmatic theology. But the subject in question is not a "transcendental subject." Rather, "**'subject'...is man involved in his experiences and history and capable of identifying himself again and again in the light of those experiences**" (FHS, p.220; my emph.).

It is therefore not a question of a 'new theological subjectivism' in Rahner, but (as Metz is careful to elaborate) of **narrative theology** in this qualified "biographical" sense:

"Theology is biographical when the mystical biography of religious experience in the concealed presence of God is written into the doxography of faith. It is also biographical if it is not a derived theology that is exclusively preoccupied with one concern and ultimately tautological in its search for irrefutability, but is rather a concentrated and shortened narrative of biography in the presence of God" (FHS, p.220).

[22] For a careful examination of how the various central categories of Metz's "new political theology" relate to the overall development of his thought, cf. N. Ancic, *Die 'Politische Theologie' von Johann Baptist Metz als Antwort auf die Herausforderung des Marxismus*, (Frankfurt am Main - Bern: Verlag Peter D. Lang, 1981, pp.271-284.

"differentiation of his transcendental point of departure" has probably resulted from his exchange (*Gespräch*) with Metz. But at the same time, Lehmann asserts that "the transcendental and the historical-categorial moments," are not merely juxtaposed to each other in his work but, in their strict unity, form "the very foundation [*Grundansatz*] [which] permeates the entire theology of Karl Rahner."[23]

The chapter on Rahner is presented in two parts. Part one concentrates more on establishing the inner theoretical dynamic of his work. Part two focuses more on the actual contents of his theology as it relates to the theme of this book. Even if the theoretical foundation and methodology of Rahner's theology would allow it to fulfill some of the same functions as political theology, in actual fact it might not do so. Conversely, even if his transcendental starting point were ill-suited for the agenda of political theology, his actual work could nevertheless show a remarkable ability to furnish the same services to humankind as

---

[23] Cf. K. Lehmann, "Einführung: Karl Rahner. Ein Porträt," in: *Rechenschaft...*, pp.39*f.; my tr. According to Lehmann, the **first phase** runs until roughly the mid-1950s, and in it Rahner's "transcendental thought" moves still largely within a classical theological framework. But in the **second phase**, during the next decade, the *Transzendentaltheologie* becomes the formal *leitmotiv* of his theology, somewhat at the expense of historical-categorial reality. Perhaps that is why critics began to feel that **"Rahner, in his transcendental starting point, passed over the intersubjective, personal and above all sacramental dimension, while, at the same time, he lost sight of raw factual reality, the political, and especially the more inclusive social rootedness [of things]"** (p.39*; my tr. and emph.). Finally, seemingly sensitive to such criticism, Rahner entered a **third phase** (in the late sixties) in an attempt to rectify, or "fill out," these perceived shortcomings in his theology.

does political theology.[24] Assessing Rahner's work in this two-step manner allows us to establish our claim more forcefully.

The third chapter considers whether or not Rahner's work is significant from the viewpoint of political theology. Put differently, the chapter answers the question of what kind of "political theology" did Rahner develop, and how it differs from that of Metz. This raises the question whether there exists today a pluralism of equally valid, i.e., equally biblically or traditional-theologically based, "new political theologies." If the answer to this question is yes, then the question has to be asked whether or not Rahner and Metz are tapping different parts of the one vast Christian tradition, and if so, whether or not both their theologies may claim to be "political theologies" with equal validity.

---

[24] That the latter is indeed the case, has been suggested by O'Donovan, when he observes that Rahner's theology "was not produced...according to some preconceived scheme or method." Instead, O'Donovan reminds us, it emerged mainly "in the form of occasional essays addressed to what he considered pressing issues in the life of the Christian community." The writer warns that one can easily make too much of Rahner's use of a transcendental method, as it can lead us to overlook investigating the actual historical experience which Rahner wishes to address. He continues: "There is often more history in [Rahner's] very choice of topics than many critics recognize. Above all, there is always an emphasis that adequate treatment of any question must include fuller historical analysis." Therefore, he concludes, "the critical method of current political and liberation theologies are producing just that necessary embodiment," at least to a certain extent. However, the question that Rahner would ask of these theologies is whether their method has "an interpretative sense with which to read history"? For **"there are no facts, whether of oppression or of liberation, without the commitment which interprets them."** There is then in Rahner a **"polarity of historical concreteness and historical openness [which] gives Rahner's thought great flexibility, richness--and incompleteness"** (cf. O'Donovan, "Preface," in: *A World of Grace...*, *op. cit.*, pp.ixf.; my emph.).

If this represents a sound reading of Rahner's work, it supports the claim of this book--as do the above comments on Rahner by Lehmann and Metz, respectively (cf. notes 21 and 23).

Chapter 1

"Political Theology" as Practical Fundamental Theology

1. Johann Baptist Metz: Biographical Notes

Johann Baptist Metz is the founder of a "political theology" within Catholicism.[1] He was born 5 August 1928 in Auerbach in the Upper Palatinate region of Germany. He studied in Bamberg, Innsbruck and Munich. Metz earned his doctorate in philosophy in 1952, was ordained a Catholic priest in 1954, and received his doctorate in theology in 1961. He has been professor of fundamental theology at the University of Muenster since 1963. From 1966 to the present, Metz has been involved in various initiatives: co-founder and member of the Bi-confessional Research Institute at the University of Bielefeld and member on the Science Council of the Center for Interdisciplinary Research at the same university. He is co-founder and co-editor of the international theological journal *Concilium* and director of its section for dogmatics; co-editor of various series of academic publications, as well as member on advisory committees of several international journals. Moreover, Metz served as Consultant to the Vatican Secretariat for Unbelievers from 1968-

---

[1] Concerning Rahner's defense of the "orthodoxy" of Metz's "political theology," cf. my Introduction, p.8. Rahner attests that his student's theology stands solidly "within Catholic theology."

1973, and from 1971-1975 as Consultant to the Synod of German dioceses.[2]

Metz did his doctoral work in theology under Karl Rahner in Innsbruck. His dissertation concentrated--like Rahner's own dissertation in theology--on the thought of Aquinas: *Christliche Anthropozentrik*.[3] Metz aspired to a prestigious teaching post at Munich in the late 1970s, which Rahner thought he amply deserved to occupy, as is evident from a protest letter by him on behalf of Metz, but it was denied him on account of his "political theology."

Several important clues about Metz the theologian emerge from his biographical data. First, his student experience at Innsbruck under Karl Rahner was a decisive one that was to accompany him for the rest of his life, even though he, in turn, became the founder of his own "fundamental theology." Metz states in 1984, the year of Rahner's death: "'Karl Rahner has renewed the face of our theology. Nothing is quite as it was before him....Even those who criticize or reject him still live on his insights, his acute and sensitive perceptions in the world of life and faith'."[4]

---

[2] The information for this biographical data is based mainly on the *Bio-bibliographische Notiz* (unpubl.), received through Werner Kroh, Metz's *Assistent*, via personal correspondence.

[3] The subtitle reads: *Über die Denkform des Thomas von Aquin* (Munich: Kösel Verlag, 1962). With "Einführender Essay" by K. Rahner.

[4] J.B. Metz, *Den Glauben lernen und lehren. Dank an Karl Rahner*, (Munich: Kösel, 1984), p.13 (as cited in H. Vorgrimler, *Understanding Karl Rahner*, cf. "Preface"). Metz's words of dedication in this booklet are instructive: "Karl Rahner, dem Achtzigjährigen: Lehrer meiner Theologie, Vater meines Glaubens" ("To Karl Rahner, the eighty-year-old: teacher of my theology, father of my faith," my tr.). Elsewhere, Metz expresses his total indebtedness to Rahner even more strongly when, after criticizing "the transcendental theology of the subject developed by my teacher, Karl Rahner," he adds: "The questions of a political theology of the subject have been evoked by Rahner's theology, [and] they have remained captive in it even in contradiction to it" (FHS, p.65; tr. emended. Cf. the original: "An ihr haben

Second, his ordination to priestly service in the church stands in between his two doctoral degrees. This, I believe, may have symbolic meaning, namely, a profound dedication to scholarship, but always (critically) in the interests and service of the church--the wider church--which stands at the center of his work.

Third, his work reveals a constant and keen sense for ecumenism, not only towards other Christian denominations, but also non-Christian religions, e.g. the Jewish and Islamic faiths.[5] Fourth, this openness towards other denominations/religions has an academic, even secular counterpart, viz. his involvement in and support for interdisciplinary research, and his respectful concern for unbelievers (cf. also his *Theology of the World*, henceforth ThW).

Finally, Metz's biographical data display a tremendously wide range of interests, from a deep international involvement (through the founding and editing of theological journals, his writings on Third and First World church relations, his worldwide lecture tours) to a constant availability on the national church scene. The data also suggest an amazing balancing act between a passion for a new church orientation--expressed in the phrase "church **of** the people" instead of a "church **for** the people."[6] --and an actively

---

sich auch die Fragen einer politischen Theologie des Subjektes entzündet, ihr bleiben sie noch im Widerspruch verhaftet." *Glaube in Geschichte und Gesellschaft*, 1977; 3. Aufl. 1980, p.61.) (For a summary of what sort of questions Rahner's theology provoked from political theology, cf. my Introduction, p.4f.)

[5] Cf. J.B. Metz, *Im Angesichte der Juden. Christliche Theologie nach Auschwitz*, (unpub., undated essay, 1984?), p.21.

[6] J.B. Metz, "Base-church and bourgeois religion," *Theology Digest* 29:3 (Fall, 1981), pp.203-206. The opening caption states this succinctly: "The Third World, says Metz, has become part of the First World's history and horizon. Transition from a bourgeois church for people (providing services) to a base-community church of people must begin with First World repentance" (p.203). We have here, in effect, a translation of the doctrine of solidarity into ecclesiology.

committed allegiance to the existing institutional church while
calling it to repentance; between a passion for the church in the
poor hemisphere and a critical adherence to his own well-to-do
church, which stands for the church in the rich industrialized
world.

All of these aspects of Metz's life and thought are noteworthy
insofar as they shed light upon the ethos of his new political
theology. Since actual practice is all important for this theology,
it follows that its author's way of life should offer us valuable
insights about its nature. And if other theologians should
manifest similar attitudes and actions, they may then to that
extent also be regarded as political theologians.

Another biographical detail must be added before we turn to
study the emergence of political theology more closely, a detail
to which Metz himself (albeit in retrospect) accords tremendous
importance for his entire theology. It relates to his experience as
a young soldier near the end of W.W. II, an experience which
Metz shares with a friend who had been a Russian prisoner of
war. He titles the private letter: "Dangerous Memories: A Short
Letter on a Large Topic" (my tr.). The "dangerous memory" in
question, says Metz, "has fixed the tracks of my God-question
[*Gottesfrage*, in the sense of theodicy] and molded the contours

---

Cf. also Metz, "Transforming a Dependent People: Toward a Base-
Community Church," *The Emergent Church* (henceforth EC), (Crossroad,
1981), pp.82-94.

Metz, in fact, far from rejecting the institution as destroying human
freedom, "inverts" the negative attitude of the modern age ("the social
criticism initiated by the Enlightenment and provoked by Marx in a
revolutionary way, as a criticism of existing institutions and their political
power relationships") into a positive attitude. Metz counters that today's
"criticism of society is...again...in need of an institution"; that "it is not only
a question of whether and how critical freedom and constant enquiry can
maintain itself permanently within the existing institutions, but rather whether
and how critical freedom is at all possible without institutionalization, if it is
to gain the maximum force and efficacy for its task of criticizing society." Cf.
Appendix IV, "On the Institution and Institutionalization," ThW, pp.131-136;
quote p.133.

of my understanding of God." This is how he relates his "memory":

Toward war's end, only 16, I was forced to leave school and pressed into the military.... On the front...the company consisted of nothing but young people, mainly 17-year-olds, more than 100 of us. One evening the company commander sent me with a message to battalion headquarters. The entire night I wandered about through burning villages in ruins and farm yards. When I returned to my company on the following morning, I found only dead people, nothing but dead people, destroyed by a combined attack of bombers and tanks. I could only stare at all of them--only the day before I had shared children's fears and youthful laughter with them--stare at their dead faces. I remember nothing but a soundless cry. Devastated, I wandered about in the forest alone for several hours more....Nothing but a soundless cry. I can still see myself as I was that day, and behind this memory all my childhood memories have crumbled. I was never able to reconcile myself to this memory, never have I been able to look upon it as an adventure which had a happy ending after all.[7]

On the surface, this experience may hardly seem to be of the caliber to furnish the very key to, and foundation of, the theological work of a lifetime, though undoubtedly it was a very traumatic experience for a young soldier. This is, however,

---

[7] J.B. Metz, *Gefährliche Erinnerungen. Kleiner Brief zu einem großen Thema* (unpub., undated), pp.1f.; (my tr.). In German:
"Gegen Kriegsende wurde ich, 16jährig, aus der Schule herausgerissen und zum Militär gepreßt...an der Front...die Kompanie bestand aus lauter jungen Leuten, meist 17jährigen, weit über 100. Eines Abends schickte mich der Kompanieführer mit einer Meldung zum Bataillonsgefechtsstand. Ich irrte die Nacht über durch zerschossene, brennende Dörfer und Gehöfte, und als ich am Morgen darauf zu meiner Kompanie zurückkam, fand ich nur noch Tote, lauter Tote, überrollt von einem kombinierten Jagdbomber- und Panzerangriff. Ich konnte ihnen allen _____ nur noch ins erloschene tote Antlitz sehen, ihnen, mit denen ich tags zuvor noch Kinderängste und Jugendlachen geteilt hatte. Ich erinnere nichts als einen lautlosen Schrei. Verstört irrte ich noch stundenlang allein im Wald umher....Nichts als einen lautlosen Schrei. So sehe ich mich heute noch, und hinter dieser Erinnerung sind alle meine Kindheitserinnerungen zerfallen. Nie konnte ich mich mit dieser Erinnerung versöhnen, nie habe ich sie als ein schließlich doch glücklich bestandenes Abenteuer begriffen."

precisely such a pivotal "memory" of a concrete event which serves Metz as an illustration of how memory functions as a category, and how all political theological categories influence one another and are all always present. All the central categories that penetrate Metz's entire theological work are rooted in this episode. To be sure, as can be seen in other contexts, this small-scale "dangerous memory" actually merges with the infinitely more horrid memory of the holocaust of the German concentration camps, which for Metz takes on apocalyptic proportions: it "interrupts," and marks the end of Christian theology as known until then.[8] For here, as his brief elucidation in the remainder of the letter shows, was born Metz's insight--however dim--**into the need to deprivatize** religion (salvation

---

[8] J.B. Metz, *Im Angesichte der Juden...*, *op. cit.*, the entire essay is to the point, but it reaches a certain climax on pp.9f., where we read among other things: Christian theology has reached a "phase" in which, "'*Auschwitz*-as-the-end' is taken seriously in theology, and this not just as the end to a certain phase in Jewish history, but rather as the end to the type of Christendom which resists elaborating its own identity in the face of, and together with, the Jews. Finally, what is at issue--in the face of *Auschwitz*--is not merely a revision of the Christian theology of Judaism, but rather a revision of Christian theology as such.... We Christians can never return to a pre-*Auschwitz* situation; and we can get beyond *Auschwitz*, strictly speaking, not by ourselves, but only together with the victims of *Auschwitz*. This is in my view the basis for Jewish-Christian ecumenism" (my tr.).

As the same essay reveals, the "dangerous memory" of *Auschwitz*, and the demands it poses on Christian theology, is in Metz's thinking really **paradigmatic for all oppression and suffering in the world**, for the unavoidable need to read history from the perspective of the victims rather than that of the victors. Thus he states in another recent essay: "*Auschwitz* is here representative of the crisis of the modern age" (my tr.). "Theologie im neuen Paradigma: politische Theologie," (unpubl., 1983?), p.6.

For a slightly earlier treatment of Jewish/Christian relations by Metz, cf. "Christians and Jews after *Auschwitz*: Being a Meditation also on the End of Bourgeois Religion," EC, (1981; a speech of 1978), pp.17-33. The above essay, says Metz, puts his thesis even more provocatively than did this earlier statement.

can never be a private matter), and **universal solidarity** (Christian hope has to be hope for all or it is not hope).[9]

This solidarity, in contrast to its basically utopian Marxist counterpart, extends also into the past, assuming into itself the memories of the suffering and unfulfilled hopes of those who lived before us. Thus since the lives of all the other young soldiers had been tragically snuffed out, Metz was unable to count his own individual survival as a happy ending. With them an essential part of Metz had also died. No one can be saved alone.

Metz also recounts this memory when he wants to explain to his students:

---

[9] Metz, *Gefährliche Erinnerungen. Kleiner Brief...*, pp.2f. This experience, says Metz, teaches him that, as a "fundamental theologian," he may not ask: "What saves me?, but rather: Who saves you? I do not start with the question: What happens to me in suffering, what happens to me in death?, but rather: What happens to you--to you [pl.]--in suffering, in death?"

In the same way, he continues, this memory has molded "the fundamental contours of Christian hope" for him: "The question: What may I hope for? changes for me into the question: What can I, what may I hope for you [plural]?--and thereby finally also for myself?" (My tr.)

In order to spell out this idea a bit more, Metz gives the following quote from the "Synod Text, 'Our Hope'..." ("Synodentext 'Unsere Hoffnung': "Ein Beschluß der Gemeinsamen Synode der Bistümer in der Bundesrepublik Deutschland" #18)--essentially drafted by Metz himself:

"'The hope, which we profess, is no vague and nebulous confidence, is no innate optimistic view of existence (*Daseinsoptimismus*); this hope is so radical and so demanding that nobody could hope it for himself or herself alone and only with reference to him or herself. With reference to ourselves alone: were we finally left with more than melancholy, barely hidden despair or blind egotistic optimism? **Daring to hope for God's kingdom--always means hoping for it in view of others and therein for oneself.** Only when our hope includes the others, when it quietly adopts the dynamics of love and of the 'communio,' does it cease to be small and fearful and to mirror our egotism that is devoid of promise'" (my tr. and emph.).

It is significant that in this way the essentially political-theological interpretation of Christian hope has the backing, formally at least, of the whole German Catholic Church.

why at the center of my theological inquiry stands the contentious theological-political treatise of the God-question as theodicy-question: the cry to God in the face of the stories of suffering in the world; and why in doing so I always start with the question about the suffering of others, with the suffering of the immediate past.[10]

Finally, implicit in Metz's telling of the memory of this tragic personal experience is an extremely important principle of political theology: the greatest insights of this theology, its deepest truths, must be grounded in the memory of a concrete story and not in abstract systematic conceptualization. What this means and how important this is to Metz becomes more evident when he extends this prototypal use to the tragic memory of the German concentration camps in the above-mentioned essay. He opens the essay by paraphrasing Kierkegaard approvingly: **"In order to experience and understand what this means, namely being a Christian, an assessment of a specific historical situation is always necessary."** For his native Germany, Metz asserts, this "situation" could only be characterized by the expression "after *Auschwitz*".[11] *Auschwitz* is not meant here in

---

[10] *Ibid.*, p.2; (my tr.): "Davon erzähle ich auch meinen Studenten, wenn ich ihnen zu erläutern suche, wieso im Zentrum meines Gottesinteresses die streitbare, theologisch-politische Behandlung der Gottesfrage als Theodizeefrage steht: der Schrei nach Gott angesichts der Leidensgeschichten in der Welt; und wieso ich dabei immer bei der Frage nach dem Leid der anderen, nach dem unmittelbar vergangenen Leid einsetze."

It may be noted here already, and will become more obvious below, that Metz's use of the category of "dangerous memory" has a built-in safeguard against a random use of memory: not all human stories may claim the same worth. Rather it is the stories of suffering victims which are given a certain priority over others.

[11] Metz, *Im Angesichte der Juden...*, p.1; (my tr.) He continues: "The situation, of which Christian theology must absolutely be aware, must always also or even first be characterized--at least for our country--as: 'after *Auschwitz*'" (my tr.).

Regarding this insistence that an analysis of the situation is a necessary part of doing theology, it could be suggested that Metz has learned this as much from Karl Rahner as from the school of critical theory (cf. O'Donovan's

a narrow sense; Metz states this explicitly in another essay: "*Auschwitz* is here representative of the crisis of the modern age."[12]

It is also clear from the essay on Christian-Jewish relations that even Metz's Christology[13] --actually an inversion of the more conventional Christology-from-above (or from-the-past) into a Christology-from-below (and from-the-present)--is deeply grounded in the frighteningly contemporary concrete history of human suffering. In Metz's Christology, Matthew 25, about Christ being embodied in the least of those among us, becomes palpitatingly alive. Here, also, is grounded his notion of the praxis of discipleship. In fact, he coins the word *Nachfolgechristologie* (discipleship-Christology), in which the

---

comments on Rahner and "historical analysis" as cited in the Introduction, n.#24).

[12] J.B. Metz, "Theologie im neuen Paradigma: politische Theologie," (Unpubl., 1984?), p.6; (my tr.); In German: "Auschwitz stehe hier für die Krise der Moderne." (Engl.: "Political Theology: A New Paradigm of Theology?" *Civil Religion and Political Theology*, L.S. Rouner, ed., (Notre Dame, IN: Univ. of Notre Dame Press, 1986).

[13] In light of this and other explicit statements by Metz on Christology, Francis Schüssler Fiorenza's categorical claim that "Metz has produced no Christology" is noteworthy indeed. (Cf. F. Schüssler Fiorenza, "Critical Social Theory and Christology: Toward an Understanding of Atonement and Redemption as Emancipatory Solidarity," *CTSA Proceedings* 30 (1975) pp.63-110; quote p.79.) If such a claim was indeed justified at the time, it could not be so since the appearance of *Followers of Christ* (Engl. 1978; German 1977). There, although urging every religious order to start by telling its own story, Metz would always have them authenticate their stories, their way of life by "continually scrutiniz[ing] their way of life and their traditions by the touchstone of following Christ." (cf. pp.22-26; quote p.25.) Does Schüssler Fiorenza perhaps mean that Metz does not have a "high" Christology?

As Metz sees it, the doctrine and practice of discipleship is implicit practical Christology: "When the history of the religious life is understood as a collective biography, as the family chronicle of a community engaged in following Christ, then this history itself has a theological status. **In this history of following Christ there is recounted a portion of that practical knowledge concerning Jesus the Christ that belongs to the heart of christology**" (my emph.).

praxis of following Christ and knowledge of Christ are inextricably bound together.

This starting point in Christology, which gives priority to the praxis of discipleship, leads to the insight that was already proclaimed by the Anabaptists of Reformation times, namely, that true knowledge of Christ is only attainable through following after him, through walking in his footsteps.[14] It leads Metz (as

---

[14] For Metz's development of a *Nachfolgechristologie*, cf. *Im Angesichte der Juden...*, pp.16-20. The argument of the whole essay is generally based on Romans 9-11 (cf. p.2), where Paul reminds the young Christian church (among other things) of its indebtedness to the Jews for its salvation. Metz applies this in several ways, one of them being that we today must re-learn the Old Testament Jewish *Glaubensweise* (way-of-faith), which is marked by a greater awareness of "being-on-the-road" than is the case with us bourgeois church members with our tendency to sit back and "meditate" on the meaning of our salvation. Metz states that he uses the term *Glaubensweise* in order "to highlight the intertwined-ness of faith-content and faith-realization, of subject and object,...of faith-theory and faith-praxis, of theory and praxis" (p.16; my tr.).

With regards to the Anabaptists, two references may suffice here: First, there is the saying of the 15th century Anabaptist/ Spiritualist leader Hans Denck, (which among Mennonite, Amish and Hutterite descendants of Anabaptism is a commonplace): "**'No one can know Christ unless he follow him in his life'.**" W. Klaassen, *Anabaptism: Neither Catholic nor Protestant*, (Waterloo: Conrad Press, 1973), p.47. This emphasis may not be seen as a prejudice against "theology, theologizing or theologians," says Klaassen. Anabaptists, when asked what they believed "often...simply repeated the Apostolic Creed," and wrote a good deal of theology themselves. What they insisted upon was merely that theologians were not exempt from "obedience to Christ and the path of discipleship. For only there does true learning take place.... There is no genuine apprehension of truth [according to Anabaptists] except in the school of Christ which is the life of discipleship. There God constantly reveals himself through the Spirit to learned and unlearned alike," the measure being one's openness and "abandonment to God and his will."

Nor was the ethos of Anabaptist religion one of "privatization," but of **individual and societal transformation precisely through the practice of discipleship,** as our second reference illustrates: Harold S. Bender, one of the pioneers in reviving studies of Anabaptism in our century, makes this claim: "**First and fundamental in the Anabaptist vision was the conception of the essence of Christianity as discipleship. It was a concept which meant the transformation of the entire way of life of the individual believer and society so that it should be fashioned after the teachings and example of Christ.** The Anabaptists could not understand a Christianity which made regeneration, holiness, and love primarily a matter of intellect, of doctrinal belief, or of subjective 'experience,' rather than one of transformation of life....[For them] repentance must be 'evidenced' by newness of behavior....**The whole life was to be brought literally under the lordship of Christ in a covenant of discipleship...**" *The*

it did the Anabaptists over 450 years ago) to a certain preference for the Jesus of the gospels who calls for "imitation," over against the Christ of Paul's epistles who died for us and whose saving grace is obtained by faith (alone).[15]

Anabaptist Vision, (Scottdale, Pa.: Herald Press, 1944), p.44.

For a more recent and thorough application of this central tenet of Anabaptism to present-day sociopolitical problems, the reader may be referred to the essay "The Original Revolution," by Mennonite theologian, John H. Yoder, in his: *The Original Revolution*, (Herald Press, 1971), pp.13-33, esp. pp.27-31.

[15] Metz does not advocate this preference for the "synoptic way-of-faith" (*Glaubensweise*) to the exclusion of the "way-of-faith with a Pauline accentuation," but only **as a corrective** to an historic one-sidedness or omission, which robbed us of the "Jewish Old Testament way-of-faith" that is constitutively present in the synoptic Gospels. Therefore: "Precisely because in the course of the history of Christianity this synoptic way-of-faith has receded in favour of the way-of-faith with a Pauline accent, it is imperative today to remember precisely that synoptic way-of-faith and to identify it as the 'Christian way-of-faith'" (*Im Angesichte der Juden*, p.17).

Metz is careful to note, however, that this does not mean abandoning the New Testament in favour of the Old: "This way-of-faith of a Jewish character" is not here derived from the Old Testament, but it belongs "to the fundamental situation of the Christian faith;" it stems "precisely from the New Testament itself" (p.17). **This "Jewish God-mysticism" [*Gottesmystik*] is embodied, above all, in Jesus himself.** This is why Metz asks: "Have not we Christians far too quickly left behind the Jewish God-mysticism and devotion [*Gebetsfrömmigkeit*] as we actually encounter it in the God-experience of the Jesus of the synoptic gospels?" (p.20; my tr.).

For a discussion of a similar preference for the synoptic Gospels (also not exclusive) on the part of Anabaptists, cf. R. Friedmann, *The Theology of Anabaptism*, (Herald Press, 1973), pp.21f., *et al*. While Friedmann can speak of the Anabaptists having an "implied...theology of the Gospels"--presumably because they were attracted by its **narrative** nature: Jesus spoke mainly in parables--their testimony to their faith, nevertheless, is "graphically described" as presenting "nothing but a beautiful mosaic of Scripture texts."

A fitting example is found in Ridemann's 240-page *Rechenschaft unsrer Religion, Lehre und Glauben*. (Von den Brüdern, die man die Huterischen nennt.) (First published in 1545 and reprinted last by Verlag der Hut. Brüder Gemeine, Cayley, Alberta in 1962.) Friedmann (p.129) writes: "Its margins contain close to three thousand Bible references..." Moreover, the book shares the very concern that is so central to Metz (as we will see below) as its motto expressly states: **"Seid allezeit erbietig zur Verantwortung Jedermann, der Grund fordert der Hoffnung, die in euch ist. 1. Pet. 3,15"** ("Always be prepared to give an answer to everyone who asks you to give the reason for the hope that you have." NIV). As for the book's concrete addressee, Friedmann comments: "Riedemann's *Rechenschaft* was intended in part to inform the Landgrave Philipp of Hesse [and by extension, the surrounding

Finally, because the praxis of discipleship is inherent within this starting point, so are the concomitant categories of "dangerous memory" and theology as "narrative." For all of these are intertwined in Metz's thought:

> This Christology of discipleship makes it clear that...Christianity contains, before all systematic knowledge [*Systemwissen*], narrative and memory knowledge. Narrative and memory are the cognitively corresponding categories to a faith that understands itself as walking, as a being-on-the-road, as a constitutional form of homelessness.

The insights concerning the significance of "memory" and "narrative," says Metz, he has learned from the Jews, believers and unbelievers.[16]

---

larger society] about the content of the Anabaptist faith, and in part to give the brethren at home in Moravia a clear and scriptural formulation of what they believed." (p.129).

[16] Metz, *Im Angesichte der Juden*, p.18; (my tr.): "Diese Nachfolge-christologie macht deutlich, daß auch das Christentum vor allem Systemwissen ein Erzähl- und Erinnerungswissen enthält. Erzählung und Erinnerung sind die kognitiven Entsprechungen zu einem Glauben, der sich als ein Gehen, ein Unterwegssein, als eine konstitutionelle Form der Heimatlosigkeit begreift." Metz says, he learned the significance of "memory" and "narrative," "not only from G. Scholem but also from W. Benjamin, not only from M. Buber but also from E. Bloch, not only from F. Rosenzweig but also from E. Fromm, not only from N. Sachs but also from F. Kafka" (my tr.).
These people, however, have not taken Metz away from, but more deeply into the New Testament: "**Christianity also and from its very roots remains ultimately a remembering and narrating community** [*Erzählgemeinschaft*]." As a look at the "synoptic way-of-faith of a Jewish type" shows, at the center of Christianity "stands...not an entertaining story but a dangerous story, and it invites us not simply to meditate on but to follow after or reenact [it];" "the Christian faith is a corporeal, in a certain sense sensory, happening..., which cannot be spiritualized into a purely attitudinal faith [*Gesinnungsglauben*]." But Metz fears this spiritualization is precisely what has taken place: "has not discipleship become for us too much an attitudinal discipleship, love an attitudinal love, suffering an attitudinal suffering, exile an attitudinal exile, persecution an attitudinal persecution?" (pp.18f.; my tr.)

Thus Metz has come full circle. He began by telling his own tragic experience or memory. This gave rise to all the other interconnected categories on which his political theology is built. He ended with the renewed call for remembering and telling the stories of the sufferings of his fellow men at home (the Jews) and the world over (the poor parts of the globe). Since the memory of suffering is not a private matter, his story ties in with that of his fellow soldiers and inevitably broadens to include the infinite number of stories, or the collective story, of human suffering.

Thus Metz attempts to take seriously the insight of "critical theory" that all truth must be grounded in praxis. He verifies this contention by examining the Jewish tradition and the Christian gospel, and arrives at the same conclusion. Or does he? Is the solidarity which he discovers here the same as that advanced by his secular dialogue partners, or does it contain "a twist" in its extension into past suffering and only via the past into an eschatological future? Will this approach make a difference for the present?

After this brief synopsis of the dynamics of Metz's political theology--based on a couple of his later statements in relation to his life--we now turn to a closer, more systematic analysis of some of the more central categories of this theology and their development. Although all his key concepts clearly emerge from, or can be channelled through, one crucial experience or memory, what Metz offers us in the *Kleiner Brief* is really a heuristic interpretation of an event that lies several decades back in history. Thus, even though he is indeed grounding his theological concepts in concrete practical experience, he does so by using certain theoretical tools, an intellectual framework that he developed later in life in response to impulses from the Frankfurt School, Rahner, Vatican II and from the post-W.W.II German context in general.

2. Critical Affirmation of Modern Secularism

Although Metz claims that his traumatic war experience has molded and shaped his whole theology, we also know that his earlier endeavours have to do with making theological sense of modernity--and this in a rather "theoretical," intellectual way. This is most evident in the themes and argumentation of two earlier books, *Christliche Anthropozentrik* and *Theology of the World*, which together represent much of the key research done by Metz from the late 1950s up to 1967 when the latter was published. Before looking at these works briefly, however, it will be helpful to first touch on some of the central traits of the modern period of history, to understand better what it is that Metz critically affirms.

Ernst Tröltsch identified the Enlightenment "as the beginning of the really modern period of European culture."[17] The Enlightenment can be described as the 18th century European intellectual movement which

> ...saw in human reason the actual essence of the human being. It sought to liberate culture from the tutelage of the church and from mysticism and superstition, advocated tolerance and believed in the progress of humankind through the organization of life according to rational-natural principles and through scientific research.[18]

This movement reached Germany partly from England (in the form of empirical philosophy and Newton's physics) and partly from France (Voltaire, Encyclopaedists). Leading German representatives were Lessing and Kant. Kant defined the Enlightenment "as man's emergence from his self-imposed

---

[17] H. Raab, "Enlightenment," *Encyclopedia of Theology: A Concise Sacramentum Mundi*, K. Rahner, ed.; J. Cumming, exec. ed. of Engl. tr., (London: Burns & Oates, 1975, 1977, 1981 & 1986), p.428 (henceforth, *Concise SM*).

[18] F.A. Brockhaus, ed., *Der Volksbrockhaus von A-Z*, 14. völlig neu bearbeitete Auflage, (Wiesbaden: F.A. Brockhaus, 1969), p.58 (my tr.).

tutelage and the resulting demand to use his reason directly,"[19] both in one's personal life and publicly in society.[20] Politically, the Enlightenment took the form of "enlightened absolutism," as opposed to the absolute sovereignty of princes or kings, and prepared the way for the French Revolution. The ultimate aim of the French Revolution (as well as the American Revolution) was to share political power equally among all citizens.

Thus the Enlightenment was the beginning of a total transformation of all areas of life, in the West at first, but eventually also beyond. A modern world, a human-made world, was built on Enlightenment presuppositions. The process of modernization would deeply affect both the sovereignty of the state and the authority of the church. With the advent of modernity, history was entering an era of rapid revolutionary change in the areas of politics and technology as well as religion. Christianity experienced a deep crisis in its relation to this world. The apparent total unity between religious and social life in the Middle Ages had gradually, yet radically, been torn apart by the merciless critique of Enlightenment rationalism. It rejected Christianity's claim to universal validity. Christianity largely responded by withdrawing from a public confrontation (or dialogue) into the "private" sphere of existence, defending religion from within the church or the individual's interior life. But around 1900 the spirit of modernity began to penetrate the church to such an extent that it had to take issue with it in an unprecedented way. The crisis which this confrontation brought upon the life of the church stands at the center of what is referred to as modernism.

---

[19] K. Rahner/H. Vorgrimler, *Concise Theological Dictionary* (2nd ed. 1983), p.148. The writers add that this "definition...can only be interpreted as a criticism of Christianity if the latter is held to be among the powers which promoted and exploited this ignorance and antagonism to criticism."

[20] Cf. Metz, "The Church and the World in the Light of a 'Political Theology'," ThW, where he picks up this point (esp. pp.108f.).

In Martin Marty's division of church history, the "modern" era represents the last of four major segments: "Early-Medieval-Reformation-Modern."[21] The concept "modernism" should be understood here as referring to the whole of the multifarious movement with its positive and negative dimensions.

Roger Aubert points out that the term "modernism" was used since Reformation times and designated the "tendency" to think more highly of the modern age than antiquity. He adds that in the 19th century, Protestantism came to speak of "the anti-Christian tendencies of the modern world and also ne radicalism of liberal theology"[22] in terms of modernism. It is therefore not surprising that the Catholic church also used this term to describe the movement around the turn of the century that called for reforming the church and its teaching in the light of the needs of the time.

Pius X condemned this multifaceted movement in his encyclical *Pascendi*, calling it the synthesis of all heresies. Aubert argues that the modernists' concerns were in themselves quite legitimate but that the movement suffered from imprudence and was given to "wild exaggerations." Because of its diversity in form, modernism cannot be defined beyond some generalities. Theologically speaking, Aubert says it points to "the manifold crisis in the doctrine and discipline of the Church at the end of the 19th and the beginning of the 20th century." But it is less "a set of definite doctrines" than a certain "direction" or

---

[21] M. E. Marty, *A Short History of Christianity*, (Philadelphia: Fortress Press, 1959; 3rd. Printing 1986), p.9.

Following different criteria, Metz (adopting Rahner's outline) divides church history into three "epochs," of which the third one starts with Vatican II when the church truly begins to be a world church. Cf. "Theologie im neuen Paradigma: politische Theologie," *op. cit.*, p.8 and p.14, n.26.

[22] R. Aubert, "Modernism," *Concise SM*, p.969.

"tendency".[23] He adds that at first the movement wanted to stay in the church while adopting and using the new thought patterns of the modern world for a better ministry to modern-minded people. The modernists seemingly perceived no danger that the spirit of Christianity might be suppressed in their one-sided approach. Besides attempting to change the discipline and tradition of the church, many modernists claimed "almost absolute freedom for Catholic scholars with regard to the magisterium." And these modernist "tendencies" of the late 1800s became particularly pronounced, writes Aubert, in the fields of "exegesis, philosophy of religion, apologetics, political and social action."[24]

Rahner and Vorgrimler similarly define modernism as "a collective term for certain false or distorted theological views" that emerged around the turn of the century. They agree with Aubert's judgment in seeing in the modernists' motivation--"to proclaim the Christian faith to the men of that time in an adequate manner"--a "legitimate desire (indeed the abiding duty)." They also note that in the movement (although proposing "wrong solutions to many problems it had grasped aright") "numerous adherents...were embittered by clerical intrigues and driven out of communion with the Church" and that until the present day "modernism" remains a label applied too readily by arrogant church people who fail to understand "how difficult faith is in our time."[25]

---

[23] *Ibid.*, p.969; cf. also Brockhaus, *op. cit.*, p.604. Brockhaus, in defining "modernism," concentrates entirely on the movement's clash with the Catholic Church, stating that it is "that movement within the Catholic Church, condemned by Pope Pius X in 1907, which tried to reconcile the Catholic faith and modern thought." He adds: "The anti-modernist oath was prescribed for all Catholic priests from 1910-1967" (my tr.).

[24] Aubert, "Modernism," *Concise SM*, p.970.

[25] Rahner & Vorgrimler, "Modernism," *Concise Theological Dictionary*, Engl. tr. by R. Strachan, *et al*, (London: Burns & Oates, 2nd ed. 1983), pp.312f.

This empathetic, though critical, identification with the faith crisis that follows for the modern believer in the wake of the Enlightenment will also determine Metz's pastoral concern for and relation to nonbelievers today, when he points out that "the question of unbelief is first and foremost a question put by the believer himself" and not, as formerly held, by a merely "extrinsic" atheism. This, he notes, was recognized by Vatican II in saying "how weighty are the questions which atheism raises."[26]

What Aubert says about the modernist movement[27] in Italy applies to the movement in general: "It was a legitimate but insufficiently mature effort to react against the backwardness of ecclesiastical sciences in Italy and to build a bridge between Catholicism and the pretensions of the modern world."[28] The interpretive statement of Rahner and Vorgrimler is a bit more specific about the "errors" of modernism. They say:

> the following errors came to light in France, England and Italy: that theology is a matter of feeling; that religion is a product of the subconscious; that neither of these must be constrained by reason, which has only a very minor role to play in religion; that revelation is awareness of an interior religious need; that these objectifications, when ossified, become Tradition; that dogma is only a symbolic expression of these objectifications, which like them must change with the progress of civilization; that there is a natural need to communicate one's own

---

[26] J.B. Metz, "Apologetics," *Concise SM*, p.24.

[27] Some of the leading figures in the modernist crisis were: A. Loisy (France) and G. Tyrrell (England), both famous for their involvement in the controversies of modern exegesis; R. Murri (Italy) and Fr. Poels (Holland), who attempted to organize society around "Christian-democratic ideals" (independently of "all control from the hierarchy")--theirs was a vision of "social modernism"; F.X. Kraus (Germany), where modernism took the form of a *Reformkatholizismus*, mainly opposing the so-called "ultramontane tendencies" of Rome. (Cf. Aubert, *op. cit.*, p.972.)

[28] Aubert, *op. cit.*, p.972.

objectifications of religion to others, and that when this is done the Church results. These were coupled with biblical criticism.[29]

What all of these "errors" clearly have in common is a thoroughly anthropocentric basis. The human being, and not God, is the one who decides about matters of ultimate authority, including religious form and its content.

The Catholic church of that time considered modernism to be a "great menace" to its life, and its response, as we have noted, was accordingly harsh. Rather than discerning whether the modernist demands might have any validity to them, it introduced the "anti-modernist oath" as a screening device by which total conformity to conservative church teaching and discipline was to be enforced among its clergy. While legitimate and necessary to a certain extent, this reaction succeeded in suppressing serious attempts to deal with the genuine problems raised by modernity.[30]

In the modernist crisis Christianity felt the cumulative effects of the critical rationalism of the Enlightenment. Because of its concern with the human individual's fulfillment, education, culture, and with humanity and civilization generally, modernism eventually rejected supernatural revelation and grace as unimportant (if not untenable before the court of reason and feeling). It sought a solution to individual and social problems

----

[29] Rahner & Vorgrimler, *op. cit.*, p.312; Aubert, *op. cit.*, elaborates on many of the same "errors" at greater length.

[30] Obviously, Metz's goal is to rectify this historical mistake, first, by admitting that it was a mistake as seen in this rhetorical question: "Have we not here, as it were, failed to recognize our own child, so that it ran away from us at an early age and now confronts us in a form that is secularistically alienated from us? Did not Christianity hesitate too much at the beginning of the modern period to embrace this new approach to the world?" And second, by countering it in saying: "It is not the secularization of the world that is a misfortune for the Christian faith, but...the attitude which we Christians had towards it (and largely still have today)." J.B. Metz, ThW, p.39.

It is, of course, Metz's ongoing ambition to engage in an affirmative-yet-critical dialogue, in a "fruitful conflict," with modernity.

from innerworldly sources, above all human reason. According to Heribert Raab "the anthropocentrism of the Enlightenment strove for the *regnum hominis* (instead of the *regnum Dei*),...aiming at the perfect happiness of mankind (the welfare state of enlightened absolutism)." The rejection of the supernatural order was accompanied by "the progress of secularization" (the latter being varied from place to place). There was then, according to Raab, a definite "tendency to rationalize religion (Kant, *Religion within the Limits of Pure Reason*), to humanize it as ethical deism, to reduce the confessions to a common denominator of 'natural religion', and to dissolve theology into a philosophy of history."[31]

The church's attempts to eradicate the modernist tendencies were unsuccessful in the long run. The Western world still today is moving steadily toward ever greater secularization. But the situation to which Metz addresses himself is by no means an unmediated legacy from the turn of the century. As the world has grown more secular (marked not by militant atheism, but rather by a postatheistic attitude), the Catholic church's posture (and Christianity's in general) has been deeply altered. This is most evident in Vatican II's declaration on the church in the modern world. The Enlightenment and modernism provide the perspective for understanding Metz's critical theology about the modern secular world.

In his early books, Metz continues the critical but positive dialogue between the Christian theological tradition and the post-Enlightenment secularized world begun by his teacher Karl Rahner and others.[32] His first book presents the thesis that

---

[31] H. Raab, "Enlightenment," *Concise SM*, pp.428f.

[32] Karl Rahner, *Geist in Welt. Zur Metaphysik der Endlichen Erkenntnis bei Thomas von Aquin*, (Kösel, 3. Aufl. 1964), p.9. In the "Vorwort zur Zweiten Auflage," Rahner states his own objective for the book thus: "What I have tried to achieve above all was this: to get away from much of what is called 'neo-scholasticism,' back to Thomas himself, precisely in order to penetrate more deeply the challenge of present-day philosophy" (my tr.). This attempt at building a bridge between traditional philosophy and the modern

Thomas Aquinas represents the beginning of a far-reaching shift in our human self-perception (and therefore of the world) that reached a certain climax with the Enlightenment: from a **cosmocentric** to an **anthropocentric** understanding of ourselves and our world.

This **anthropocentricity** has nothing to do with the ontological ranking order of pre-Thomistic times, which places human beings on the highest rung of the ladder of creaturely being (which remained partly present with Thomas). Rather, says Metz, it represents a total change of the philosophical-theological *Seinsverständnis* (understanding of being) as such. In this anthropocentric ontological perception, human beings gradually realize that in everything they articulate about the world, be this about material or spiritual beings, they are invariably also saying something about themselves, their intersubjectivity and [their] transcendentality. In other words, "anthropology can in no way be an arbitrary discipline beside others, but is rather a fundamental discipline, which runs through and explains itself in all philosophical-theological articulations."[33] The first major point of this work, then, consists in the elaboration of the fundamental shift that has taken place in Western thought, starting with Thomas Aquinas and reaching a certain peak with the Enlightenment.

The fact that Metz finds evidence that links modernity's concept of being to the work of Aquinas (not by accident in the

---

situation also describes much or all of Rahner's theological work.

[33] J.B. Metz, "Nochmals: Christliche Anthropozentrik," *Theologische Revue* Nr.1, 61 (1965), pp.14f.; (my tr., a bit expanded): Metz explains the anthropocentric "*Seinsverständnis*" as being led by the insight, "daß dem Menschen dies alles [knowledge about other creatures or being] nur gegeben und offenbar ist in seinem 'Seinsverständnis' (theologisch: in seinem Glauben), und daß er deshalb in all diesen Weltaussagen immer auch etwas von sich, seiner Intersubjektivität und von seiner Transzendenz aussagt, daß also, anders formuliert, die Anthropologie gar nicht eine beliebige Disziplin neben anderen sein kann, sondern eine Fundamentaldisziplin ist, die sich in allen philosophisch-theologischen Aussagen durchhält und expliziert." (My emph.)

"expressly ***theological*** sections of his work"),[34] is helpful for the second important point of the book, namely, that this post-Enlightenment anthropocentric understanding of reality is not opposed to Christianity. Moreover, it is not only compatible with, but actually and fundamentally inherent in the Christian doctrine of the incarnation, a point also made by Protestant theologians like Heinz Zahrnt and Dietrich Bonhoeffer.[35]

Both these points, if correct, are obviously of great importance. On the one hand, if in our knowledge about any and all things or beings, the knowing human subjects are always included (*mitgewußt*), if we (rather than a "natural" cosmos) thus unavoidably stand at the center of being ("being" is here primarily identified with *Seinsverständnis*), then major consequences flow from this for our human freedom and responsibility. A certain, far-reaching emancipation comes with this significant shift in world-view. Human beings (certainly Christians) are charged in an unprecedented way with the

---

[34] *Ibid.*, p.19; (my tr., expanded): "Nicht zufällig mußte ich dabei [in this demonstration] die Ansätze und Belege den ausgesprochen *theologischen* Partien seines [Thomas's] Werkes entnehmen" (his italics).

[35] *Ibid.*, p.19. What I call his second major point, Metz describes as "the central point of my book." In his own words it is this:
"The aim was to characterize the 'anthropocentric mode of thought'...[always in contrast only with a 'cosmocentric' one; it cannot be contrasted here with the 'theocentric mode of thought'] precisely as the interpretation of existence that corresponds to the biblical-Christian *Logos*, and to identify its emergence as an effective mode of thought in history as the epochal influence of Christianity upon the history of Western thought. Thomas seemed to me to be that high point [*Topos*] in this process at which this mode of thought first breaks through. At the same time, this circumstance shows him to be an original Christian thinker who points more towards the modern age than to Aristotle" (my tr.).
Cf. also Albert Keller, "Secularization" *Concise SM*, pp.1554-1561, where he points out how Protestant theologians, like Dietrich Bonhöffer (who led the way) and Heinz Zahrnt, argue the same point. The latter is cited as claiming that secularization "'results directly and authentically from the kernel of Christian revelation itself'" (p.1560).

freedom and responsibility for planning and constructing the world in which to live.

As we have seen, in this modern self-understanding--along with a deeply transformed relation to the world, as world--Metz detects a significant change in the perception of our being together as human beings. Metz argues that along with the new conception of the world as "surrounding world" or "co-world" (*Welt als Mitwelt*, formally not yet fully developed even in Aquinas) comes the notion of "intersubjectivity."[36] We have already met this important political theological category under the name of "solidarity." This concept will be further explored below.

The thesis that modern secular anthropocentricity is profoundly rooted in, and is a consequence of Christianity itself, is equally momentous. For if the incarnation of the *Logos* ultimately means that God affirms the world in its "worldliness" and human beings in their humanness, or rather that God sets the world free **to become** truly "secularized" and humankind **to become** fully "humanized," then the least that follows from this is that the trend of the pre-Vatican II church towards a defensive ghetto existence and privatization of religion must be stopped and reversed. Metz describes the ghetto attitude as follows:

> For a long time the Church has observed this process [of secularization] only with resentment --to some extent even up to the recent council-- regarding it exclusively as a falling away and a false emancipation and only very slowly finding the courage to let the world become secular in this sense and see this process not just as an event which is against the historical intentions of Christianity, but also as something that is partly determined by the innermost historical impulses of Christianity itself and its message.[37]

The Christian message must be "deprivatized" and, in a sense, "secularized." It must be brought to bear upon the present-day

---

[36] *Ibid.*, pp.14, 15.

[37] Metz, ThW, p.143.

"emancipated" world order and must be articulated in a way that can be grasped by the modern "anthropocentric" philosophy of life. However, this has to be a cautious "dialogue." For if, on the one hand, modern Christian theology "cannot but strive to explain itself in terms relevant to its historical situation," there are, on the other hand, "the intrinsic limits of this apologetical effort to communicate the Christian faith [which] must not be blurred or disregarded. Apologetics is not adaptation or accommodation," but a "dialogue".[38]

Since modern anthropocentric philosophy centers around the concept of **intersubjectivity**, Metz concludes that the only theological mode suited for this changed milieu is a "new political theology," in the widest sense of the term. Present-day theology "must now expound above all the social implications of the Christian faith and promise."[39] This calls for both a negative and a positive function of theology, as Metz explains in another context:

> I understand political theology, first of all, to be a critical correction of present-day theology inasmuch as this theology shows an extreme privatizing tendency (a tendency...to center upon the private person rather than 'public,' 'political' society). At the same time, I understand this political theology to be a positive attempt to formulate the eschatological message under the conditions of our present society.[40]

We cannot properly appreciate how crucial Metz's concept of "anthropocentricity" (in the sense of *Mitsein* and "intersubjectivity") really is for his theology in general, without noting how it relates to Rahner's anthropological theology of the subject. This point will be developed below, but a few comments are in order here. In a general way, of course, Karl Rahner had

---

[38] Metz, "Apologetics," *Concise SM*, p.21, cf. also p.24.

[39] *Ibid.*, p.24.

[40] Metz, ThW, p.107. On the society-directedness of political theology and its claim to be inherent to all theology, cf. my Introduction, p.11, n.#17.

already laid the groundwork in creating an anthropocentric framework of thought in philosophy and theology.[41] Rahner's theological contribution, known as *anthropologische Wende* (anthropological turn), is well known. In a word, it consists of a shift or reorientation which deeply transforms objective scholastic theology by making the human subject the starting point of theological reflection, rather than objective dogma.

Metz builds upon and develops further this notion. However, since there was continual interaction and dialogue between them, and since Metz thoroughly revised and supplemented Rahner's early foundational works (to such an extent that in the case of *Hearers of the Word* "Metz almost becomes a 'co-author' [with Rahner] in this revision"),[42] the exact degree of his contribution is not easily established.

------

[41] In the area of philosophy, a good example is found in Peter Eicher's *Die anthropologische Wende. Karl Rahners philosophischer Weg vom Wesen des Menschen zur personalen Existenz* (Freiburg / Schweiz: Universitätsverlag, 1970). The title speaks for itself, attributing to Rahner a certain pioneering position.

In the area of theology, Josef Speck's *Karl Rahners theologische Anthropologie* (München: Kösel, 1967), based on an analysis of Rahner's foundational works and the early volumes of his *Theological Investigations*, serves a similar purpose.

[42] R.D. Johns, *Man in the World:...*, p.73. In Chapter III, subsection: "Revisions of Rahner's Works" (pp.72-78), Johns offers a minute analysis of the changes and additions undertaken by Metz in the second editions of Rahner's foundational works. E.g., in *Hearers of the Word*, Metz deleted 886 and added 142 lines, and "In the first edition there was only one footnote. In the second there are 121 for a total of 878 lines. This would amount to about twenty-five pages of text...Of the total of ninety-nine alterations in the text, sixty-five are subtractions" (p.74). The longest subtractions are much longer than the additions (which are less than ten lines each), says Johns.

In light of this, and the fact that Metz wrote his own *Christliche Anthropozentrik* about the same time he carried out these revisions, it seems nearly impossible to establish who influenced whom. However, when Rahner expressly employs in the mid-1960s the category of "anthropocentricity" as a key category for evaluating philosophical and theological traditions, arriving at similar results as Metz above, he refers the reader to this foundational work of Metz. (Cf. K. Rahner, "Theology and Anthropology," *Theological Investigations*, IX (TI henceforth) (Herder & Herder, 1972), p.38, n.18.

Metz clearly takes the concept of anthropocentric theology to another plane, precisely by stressing its dimension of **intersubjectivity** so heavily. According to some theologians, this is where Metz has most deeply influenced Rahner's work. Thus Francis Schüssler Fiorenza states that "Rahner tends to incorporate some of Metz's own criticisms into the development of his own position," viz. he "attempts to take over the notion of **intersubjectivity** which he really got from Professor Metz."[43] More on this subject will be said below.

In *Christliche Anthropozentrik*, Metz has laid the "theoretical" foundation for his theology in a way similar to Rahner's early foundational works. According to Metz's profound theological analysis of Christian and modern history, anthropocentricity is grounded originally in the doctrine of the incarnation itself, emerging gradually in scholastic thought, and coming into its own (in a more recognizable way) in the philosophical climate of the Enlightenment.

In *Theology of the World*, Metz critically affirms the philosophical legacy of modernism. Much of what was at the heart of the turn-of-the-century confrontation with the modernist movement is taken for granted as acceptable, even necessary, in the milieu in which Metz writes the book. At the same time, the church's (critically) coming to terms with the modernist challenges is far from being accomplished, and Metz endeavours in fact to carry the modernist agenda even further, albeit in a more nuanced and balanced way.

Metz states boldly at the beginning of this book that "today's world has become secular" (even if the process is not complete), and therefore theology must be "concerned with the question of a 'secular' starting point and the point of reference of the theological responsibility of the believer."[44] This novel starting point is elaborated from an attitude of basic affirmation of

---

[43] Francis Schüssler Fiorenza, in a personal letter to me (March 18, 1981).

[44] Metz, ThW, cf. p.13 and p.9, respectively. Numbers in brackets are from this source, unless otherwise indicated.

modern secularity: "This work marks a first attempt to give a positive interpretation of this permanent and growing secularity of the world in the light of Catholic theology" (p.13). Although Metz displays an affirmative approach, the phrase "in the light of Catholic theology" provides the actual criterion for both Metz's criticism and affirmation of modernity.

Metz is working from a number of fundamental assumptions in his theology. First, he speaks of "the historically irreversible process of secularization" (p.16). Second, he submits "that the 'spirit' of Christianity is permanently embedded in the 'flesh' of world history and must maintain and prove itself in the irreversible course of the latter." This view has a solid Christological foundation: "the process of history is 'accepted' in the Christian *logos* and remains so" (p.16; also pp.66f.). Herein lies the reason why theology can no longer allow the concrete history of the world (often assumed to be essentially "unchristian" on account of its "secular" nature) to be separated from the history of salvation.

Despite this positive valuation of modern secular history, however, Metz does not propose to facilely proclaim modern secular history as Christian. Far from it. He knows too well about "the sign of the constant protest within the world against God" under which modern history (and all human history) stands. How, then, asks Metz, "does this irreversible secularization (which we cannot take seriously enough) still stand beneath the 'law of Christ' (1 Cor. 9:21)?" (p.17). The final and positive answer to this question can be had only in light of the incarnation and the cross. Even though the coming of the *logos* into the world is the certain promise of God's "acceptance" of human or world history, Metz knows "that the Christian understanding of history stands beneath the sign of the cross" since it continues to rebel against God (p.17). Theology can only "seek out and testify to this constant if always hidden and crucified 'marriage' between salvation and world history" (p.16).

It is clear from these statements that Metz's affirmative treatment of the one world history as salvation history is cast entirely in an eschatological mold. Hence, as will be seen below, we would profoundly misunderstand his concepts of history and of freedom in history if we were to overlook this point. For it is in this eschatological openness toward the future, which alone (when based in the messianic "past" or ministry of Jesus Christ) guarantees that something truly new can happen in history. It alone makes true freedom for human beings possible.

Metz is deeply convinced that in the incarnation God has definitively assumed the history of the world as his own history, and that this "assumption" is provisional or ambiguous. This conviction leads him to ask the following "eschatological" questions:

> In what way is what happens *within* history still an advent, a future in terms of the Christian past, a coming upon us of what took place in Jesus Christ? How is he himself still active, as the Lord who reigns within and throughout history, not merely as its transcendent guarantee?...How is his spirit still poured out over the face of our secular world? How does that which forces itself upon us ever more urgently still come *historically* from the 'hour of Christ'? (p.17; italics his).

The task of present-day theology, according to Metz, is to seek answers to these questions (assuming that they can be answered).

In offering this positive interpretation of the modern "emancipated" world, Metz is not merely trying to "infiltrate" the secular realm so as to cover it over with a Christian veneer. This world is more than the negative side in the "dialectic" of history. It is "ultimately also something that is positive for a Christian," it is not only a negative mirror of God's "acceptance" (in its rejection of it) but manifests this "acceptance" of the world also positively (p.19). From the following words we see how far Metz is prepared to take this affirmative interpretation of the world of today in relation to Christianity: "The secularity of the world should not reveal itself to us primarily as a dethroning of Christ within the world, in an historically intensified protest against him, but as the decisive point of his dominion in history" (p.19). Such a view--admittedly, the perspective of 'faith'--is tenable only on the "theological basis of secularization" which Metz presents in the following "thesis":

The secularity of the world, as it has emerged in the modern process of secularization and as we see it today in a globally heightened form, has fundamentally, though not in its individual historical forms, arisen not against Christianity but through it. It is originally a Christian event and hence testifies in our world situation to the power of the 'hour of Christ' at work within history (pp.19f.; italics his).

To demonstrate the meaning and prove the accurateness of this thesis is the burden of the rest of the book. To be sure, this thesis has a solid basis in Scripture: "'For the Son of God, Jesus Christ,...was not Yes and No; but in him it is always Yes. For all the promises of God find their Yes in him. That is why we utter the Amen through him to the glory of God' (2 Cor. 1:19f.)" (p.21). God's Yes to us, "our standing in Christ," our being sealed with the Spirit (verses 21f.), (which Metz extends so as to include "the world"), is to be seen as having "eschatological definitiveness" (p.21).

If God's Yes to the world, however, were the fully "realized" Yes, Metz argues in effect, then the church would not have come into being: "If the world had not been accepted in protest and refusal, there would be no Church.... Rather, the world would be undialectically the actuality of this acceptance, and its history itself would be the unveiled representation of the nearness of God, given once and for all." But what we have in actuality is "the guilty rejection by the world of the accepting *logos*," says Metz, and therefore the church came into being: "The Church which he founded is the historically tangible and effective sign, the sacrament of the eschatologically final acceptance of the world of God" (p.21; also p.50, n.51).

Does this admission of the world's guilty rejection of God's grace not invalidate Metz's thesis that exactly today's secularized world is profoundly rooted in Christianity itself? Or how can this claim be defended in the face of reality? Are we not back to the position that only a certain segment of the world--co-extensive with "the church," responding in obedience--belongs to salvation history? In order to clarify this problem, it is necessary to take a closer look at Metz's understanding of "secularity" and how it is rooted in the incarnation.

His understanding of secularity can be summarized as follows: Insofar as the modern world has become truly secularized, i.e., has accepted the challenge to be precisely "worldly" as distinct from God, it is but fulfilling its creator's intent for it. The historical church has very often not understood this and has in this sense acted like parents who may drive away their own child through lack of understanding towards the emerging secular world. Hence Metz asks: "Have we not here, as it were, failed to recognize our own child, so that it ran away from us at an early age and now confronts us in a form that is secularistically distorted and alienated from us? [and now can]...be itself before us only with a bad conscience?" (p.39).

Thus, for Metz, what is wrong with the secular world is not that it is too secular, but that it is not secular enough. Hence, the first thing the church must do in its relation to this world is to "catch up" with the genuine degree of secularization that can be found in the world, and second, the church must continue on the path of its own (and so the world's) total secularization. Metz in fact equates Christianization and secularization: "we may say that 'to Christianize the world' means fundamentally 'to secularize it'," in the sense of "bestowing on it...its own worldly being" (p.49).

Here we touch upon the fundamental problem of the nature of authentic secularization. Metz has suggested that the world's distorted secularity may be "partly" Christianity's fault for "releas[ing] the world far too hesitatingly," but it also relates to "its [the world's] *hubris* and false will to autonomy" (p.39). Ultimately, the total and genuine secularization which Metz envisions for the world is unattainable if the world is left to its own resources. Genuine secularization can only be grounded in God's initiative and the liberating power of his grace. This must not be seen as just another attempt to subjugate the world or rob it of its rightful liberty. Rather, there is no other way of achieving true secularity but through faith. In Metz's own words: "where there is no faith in a transcendent creator, there is also no genuine secularization of the world and no genuine availability of this world to men." This was precisely the problem of the ancient Greeks, according to Metz. They never truly "desacralized" the world, and hence their world could never fully come into its own, nor become fully available to human beings (cf. p.65).

It is different when the Christian gospel is taken seriously, wherein

> [humanity] stands inescapably before the face of...the absolutely transcendent God, the *[Deus] semper ma[i]or*, who dwells in 'unapproachable light' (1 Tim. 6:16), who...is infinitely higher than the created world and constantly places it at a distance in its own finitude. But [humanity's] attachment in faith to this God of absolute transcendence...actually liberates the world....Faith itself, therefore, produces a fundamental secularity of the world (p.64).

This insight is crucial. It is precisely this faith which safeguards our view of the world from a false absolutization or from becoming an "ideology." Without this faith, human beings invariably fall prey to the ancient temptation of absolutizing certain inner-worldly realities, and thus not allowing the world to be secular in its genuinely finite, creaturely way. Likewise, where there is no transcendence in faith, and no releasing the world into its own secularity, there cannot be any true human freedom. And without human freedom there can be no real history. This bringsus to another crucial point of Metz's theology, namely, the question of the relationship between the "anthropocentricity" described earlier and the irreversibly and increasingly secularized world? What is the place of the human being in a worldly world which fulfills its creator's intent to the extent it truly and genuinely becomes "worldly"? Metz answers this question profoundly and extensively in a chapter entitled "The Future of Faith in a Hominized World." He demonstrates on the basis of Christology that the human being is pivotal in a process of genuine secularization. For Metz, this view is rooted directly in the gospel. There we learn that the *"Verbum homo factum est."* Metz interprets:

> For in the incarnation of the eternal Word it was not the world itself that was immediately divinized. The final turning of God towards the world

took place, rather, in man. He and only he is the place where God has forever accepted the world and its history. God's relation to the world and to history is mediated and perfected in man. Its divinization takes place via its hominization (pp.66f.).

Metz further elaborates his concept of anthropocentricity with the claim that apart from human beings the "world" has neither genuine history nor freedom, nor, indeed, proper being. From the perspective of the gospel the world is not a pre-existent cosmos holding humankind in a controlling embrace. Rather, it is the "material" at our disposal for our "becoming [human] in history before God and of the latter's turning to us in Jesus Christ." In fact,

> All the world's being has its 'anthropocentric apex' in the Gospel of scripture. It is not simply the untouchable framework and horizon within which the drama of human freedom is played. The world 'exists,' rather, for the sake of human freedom: it becomes a hominized world. It appears as a world in the process of coming to be, which acquires its own nature through the freedom of man bestowed by God, throughout his sinful involvement with himself and his flights of grace (p.66).

The fact that this hominization process is grounded in the incarnation makes it unexplainable from a dialectical materialist point of view.

Metz takes the same care to ground (in reference to Karl Rahner) his definition of history in the transcendent "God of history," who himself appears in it; "in his Son," history becomes "the actual destiny of the unchanging God." "Transcendence itself has become an event....God is no longer merely 'above' history; he is himself 'in' it, in that he is also constantly 'in front of it' as its free, uncontrolled future" (pp.22f.). It is of the greatest importance to Metz that the unique relation of Jesus Christ to history be understood. He is the very beginning of history as well as its eschatological end; the world (and history), according to Colossians and Ephesians, "has its 'foundations' and its 'goal' in Christ" (p.51). Metz asserts about Christ and history:

He is of decisive importance for the reality of history itself....He does not simply claim it retrospectively, for it belongs to him from the beginning, inasmuch as he founded it as genuine history, and the presence of his kingdom *in* history, the Church, is the symbolical re-presentation of this eschatological founding of history (p.23; for further grounding in Scripture, cf. n.13).

What Metz says here concerning history proper applies also to "the world" by extension, since he defines "the world as history"--and finds convincing biblical evidence for it (cf. pp.51-55). But he rejects the "dialectical" theological reading of history, which sees it basically as a succession of moments of salvation and damnation, considering it counter to the gospel. For Metz, "the world is not simply the place where there is a dialectical unity of salvation and damnation," which would not allow for anything really "new" in history. Rather, the gospel holds that an essential part of the world's "nature" is an open "future in which the world is either the one thing or the other, the world of absolute self-encapsulation or the world as the place of the presence of the promise."

The concept of a truly future-oriented history--which alone makes human free and responsible action possible--emerged only slowly in the Western world. The so-called "anthropological turning point" was finally ushered in with the advent of the modern era. In it the world was no longer regarded as a static, finished entity, but rather as potential building material which human beings can shape and transform in freedom and responsibility. Thus Metz can speak of "the world as an anthropological world of history," which "in its being [appears as] the expression of the most various free historical actions and interpretations" of human beings (p.55). But when read theologically, history always bears the marks both of human fallenness and of the saving act of Christ.

Such an anthropocentric understanding of the world and history also brings changes with respect to the conception of eschatological salvation. According to Metz, "the 'future world,' which is promised finally and irrevocably in Jesus Christ, as the eschatological city of God, as the heavenly Jerusalem, is not something without a history, finished, and independent of the believer's life, but is always 'coming into being' in the historical movement of faith." If we were told earlier that God's acceptance of the world is an "anthropocentric" acceptance, now we learn that human beings actively participate in that process: "the believer acts not only 'within' the world, but he changes it, he transforms it himself within the framework of this divine promise...given and...present to him as an individual only in the solidarity of the covenant" (p.55). The "intersubjective basis" of the Christian life envisaged here is perhaps stated more concretely in the following words: "The experience of the world and behavior in relation to it take place...within the framework of human community, and this not simply in the 'private' sense of the I-thou relationship, but in the 'political' sense of social togetherness" (p.54). More will be said about this below.

Several things have become clear in our discussion thus far. First, Metz's affirmation of the irreversible and increasing intensity of the secularization process is always qualified by his Christology. The actual model for genuine secularization is found only in the incarnation itself. Second, measured against that touchstone, the modern world has barely begun its true secularization process; it appears much more bent on self-absolutization than on obedient creaturely self-realization. For Metz, the actual level of secularization remains vague and opaque (cf. his summary p.41). But, third, in spite of the fact that the worldliness of the world seems far more like an idolatrous falling away from God than a coming into its own being, God, in his irreversible act in the *Logos*, has given the world the eschatological promise, imperfectly but indelibly embodied in the church. God promises that he has lovingly accepted forever the world and that in the end the world as a whole will accept the summons to become truly secular (and so distinct from God) and thereby precisely realize the will of God.

Fourth, it has become evident that human beings have a crucial role to play in the responsible transformation or secularization of the world, even though this is ultimately achievable only as a response to God's initiation of the process in Jesus Christ. **But**

only if we believe in the transcendent mystery which manifested itself in Christ do we gain the liberty which frees us for creative action in the world and prevents our vision or our program from becoming ideological.

Fifth, seeing anthropocentricity as intersubjectivity implies that the transformation of the "world as history" into a genuinely "worldly" history and human beings into truly "earthly" citizens involves every individual but cannot be carried out by any individual alone. This transformation must be done in solidarity with others, and not only in the private but also in the public sphere. This emphasis on the public, political dimension also has a solid Christological foundation for Metz (cf. pp.113f.)

The survey thus far leaves no doubt about Metz's position towards modernity. In simplified terms, Metz holds that the Christian theologian has no choice but to embrace modernity in its world-directedness, because it is the (wayward) child of Christianity. But this affirmative stance toward the world in the process of secularization may not be mistaken for a blind "incarnational optimism" (*Inkarnationsoptimismus*) on his part (cf. *ZThdW*, p.26; Engl: ThW, p.29). Rather, Metz's critical affirmation represents an act of faith in the abiding (eschatological) "acceptedness" of the world by God in spite of the "secularistic *hubris*" of which it is guilty (cf. pp.31f.).

Before leaving Metz's somewhat "theoretical" theological analysis of the modern situation, it is important to indicate briefly what practical implications he attaches to his findings for Christian life today. For Metz the precondition for knowing what "being a Christian" means is to assess one's "historical situation." In a sense this whole book is such an assessment, and the result, stated often, is that our situation is marked by an extreme and growing secularism. But when Metz, in certain sections of the book (cf. pp.70-77; pp.141-155), becomes more concrete in his practical application, his assessment becomes more condensed and focused.

The first of these two references offers us the more poignant example. It forms the final subsection to the chapter entitled "The Future of Faith in a Hominized World," and is focused on the question: "How can the believer concretely accept this world situation, and how can the accepted experience of the hominized world become the beginning of an original experience of faith?" (p.70). That this challenge is formidable is evident when it is remembered that the secular hominized world situation can be seen as an "accepted" world only under the sign of the cross. In order not to lose sight of the eschatological character of God's acceptance of this world, Metz takes a close look at the world, as it were, and summarizes its main features under four categories: this hominized world is a "pluralistic world," a world in the process of becoming (*Werde-Welt*), a "world without miracles" and a "dehumanized world."

The pastoral question that concerns Metz in this crisis situation is "how [this] world-experience can be communicated at all as the beginning of a genuine Christian experience of faith" (p.70).

Metz's answers to these questions show a similar approach in each case. Hence one answer can represent the others. He begins by an honest, realistic examination of these crisis areas. For example, today's hominized world actually looks like an increasingly "dehumanized world." Humans have manipulated not only the material world but other human beings as well (p.74). (For a closer description of the subtlety and degree of this "dehumanization" process, Metz borrows sizable passages from Karl Rahner; cf. pp.144f). If the human being seems to become more the object of the hominization process than its controlling subject; if, indeed, "the process of hominization seems...to reveal itself as a total threat to what is human" (pp.74f.), Metz admits, it would be easy to lose courage and reject it altogether, including its inherent "possibility (entrusted to us as a task to realize) of a deeper humanization of human life" (p.75).

When this "task" is willingly accepted (and without the *hubris* of false self-absolutization), this hominized world holds out, according to Metz, not only the continued possibility of faith in God, but actually offers to us the possibility of a deepened experience of God precisely in our fellow men and women. In his own words:

Is it not the case that human relations such as marriage, friendship, and fraternity are in extreme danger in a hominized world, but also that only in it can they come to their full flower, into their absolute uniqueness, admitting of no dehumanization, no outside exploitation, no tribalization, no institutionalization? Does not the hominized world provide...the opportunity for extensive humanization, for more radical attention to other individuals, for an acuter sense of individual responsibility? Would it not therefore seem that [human beings] in a hominized world would more fully experience in every human encounter (according to a central idea of our faith) God himself? Would [they] not more intensely understand that in the affirmed and accepted fact of the absolute and unexploitable individuality of the other, in the accepted mystery of [their] own unique [selves], the transcendental mystery of God himself is present? Would [they] not then see that the other, [their] brother-[sister], is the topos of his numinous experience? (pp.75f.)

The key here, for experiencing the creator in the creature, is again a Christological one. Since Metz's theology largely understands itself as a dialogue (or a "fruitful conflict") with Marxist thought, this statement about the inviolability of the individual human subject takes on a heightened significance.

3. Metz's Relation to Marxism and Critical Theory

We need to comment briefly on the relationship between Metz's thought and Marxist-critical philosophy, i.e., the more central points held in common by Marxists among themselves, critical theorists among themselves, and (to some extent) among representatives of both Marxism and critical theory, despite the differences within each camp, and between the camps. Matthew Lamb, for instance, argues that "certain common characteristics of critical theory can be delineated," namely, "the challenge *of* critical theory [which] is to face squarely the radical critique of society provided by Marxist perspectives," on the one hand, and on the other, "the challenge *to* critical theory is to elaborate an understanding of praxis capable of genuinely transforming contemporary social relationships."[45]

Technically, the expression "critical theory" refers to the Frankfurt School of Social Research and the critical philosophical position it pioneered. This school "came into existence in the mid-1920s as an association of Left intellectuals," and was privately funded. In terms of its intellectual rootage, "The concept of 'critical reason' derives from the traditions of Kantian critical philosophy and of Marxian critique of ideology."[46]

The school thus described covers virtually all areas of study, and can be defined as follows: "Critical theory is a fundamental methodological enterprise not only concerned with sociology and philosophy but also with such diverse fields as epistemology, psychology, literary criticism, economics, aesthetics, education, anthropology, political science, and theology."[47] We want to very briefly relate Metz's theology to critical theory's most central features: its expressly critical function and its emphasis on the priority of criticism in relation to discovering truth.

Critical theorists share a certain future orientation. Ernst Bloch, from whom Metz says he has learned much in this regard, is an outstanding example.[48] The catastrophic events of our century

---

[45] Matthew Lamb, *Solidarity with Victims: Toward a Theology of Social Transformation*, (N.Y: Crossroad, 1982), p.29; his italics. Lamb adds that "Both of these challenges are...common to most work in critical theory."

[46] Paul Piccone, "General Introduction" to: *The Essential Frankfurt School Reader*, (N.Y: Urizen Books, 1978), p.xi.
This Introduction provides a succinct history of critical theory, including its dissemination to North America.

[47] Lamb, *op. cit.*, p.29.

[48] J.B. Metz, *Unterbrechungen. Theologisch-politische Perspektiven und Profile*, (Gütersloh: G. Verlaghaus Gerd Mohn, 1981), cf. especially p.59, where Metz says he met Bloch only relatively late in Bloch's life, in personal discussions after public debates, adding: "...I, the young theologian, always came away from him with gratitude and more reflective." But their talks represented open two-way communication and not "proselytism," as is evident

have exposed the vestiges of what Lamb calls "the innocent faith of the Enlightenment in pure reason" or "pure theory" as a fallacy.[49]

This optimism was sobered by the man-made disasters of our century, especially the two World Wars, including the Nazi death camps. Moreover, critical theorists realized painfully that human reason per se easily tends towards reproducing what exists in society rather than critically shaping it. Thus, even though they do not have a common methodology, these critical theorists seem to agree on the need for a critique of the critique, or a "negative dialectics." Matthew Lamb holds that Susan Buck-Morss' description of the critical stance developed by Adorno, represents "the spirit in which it [the Frankfurt School] was undertaken," and that it is applicable "as well to the other critical theorists," namely:

> 'The whole point of his relentless insistence on negativity was to resist repeating in thought the structures of domination and reification that existed in society, so that instead of reproducing reality, consciousness could be critical, so that reason would recognize its own nonidentity with social reality, on the one hand, and material nature's nonidentity with the categorizing consciousness that passed for rationality, on the other.'[50]

The critical theorists had become convinced that somewhere along the way the (originally correct) critical intention of Karl Marx's analysis of history had been lost. His intent had been "the

---

from this comment by Metz: "In the course of time [our] differences became indeed less significant--and more essential at the same time" (my tr.).

[49] Lamb, *op. cit*, p.28. In Lamb's own words: "The innocent faith of the Enlightenment in pure reason has crumbled under the devastation of two world wars, the holocaust, nuclear arms races, environmental pollution, iatrogenic disease, and dwindling confidence in democracy on the part of both capitalist and socialist 'experts'."

[50] *Ibid.*, p.37, as quoted by Lamb from *The Origin of Negative Dialectics*, by Susan Buck-Morss.

liberation of human destiny,"[51] precisely by "realizing" thought in society through the class struggle. Marx had wrongly assumed a quasi-automatic self-correcting dynamic in history: the capitalist system of production would bring upon itself its own undoing by further exasperating the alienated working class. The latter would then set up the kind of "relations of production" conducive to harmonious relations towards nature and between fellow workers. The workers would develop a working atmosphere marked by "intelligent openness and critical responsibility."[52]

Historically, the critical theorists realized, things did not work out that way. Whether Marx himself had not entirely overcome the fallacy common to both idealism and empiricism, namely that "reason is identical with [social] reality,"[53] or whether his followers soon lapsed into this fallacy again, may be left open here. What is certain is that the revisionist Marxists or critical theorists became convinced that the very dialectics of Marx

---

[51] *Loc. cit.*. Lamb here argues that the critical theorists discovered from the "tragic destiny of Marxism" that "it too was not immune from the fatal flaw" of assuming a social or historical identity with reason and hence engaging directly in the categorial aspects of reason. This insight posed the challenge to them (not least on the basis of "fidelity to dialectics as initiated by Marx") that they unmask "the guilt of criticism innocent of its own presuppositions." Hence it was a matter of rehabilitating Marx's teaching (and example) by changing and adapting it so that it becomes effective in the present situation.

[52] *Ibid.*, p.39.

[53] *Ibid.*, p.38. Lamb contrasts critical theory with idealism and empiricism as follows: The latter two views only appear to be different; both "take for granted that reason is identical with reality. Idealism and empiricism differ only in how that identity is known." By contrast critical theory is convinced of the continued nonidentity between historical reality and thought. Therefore, its "basic methodological presupposition...is that there should be a continued effort to realize reason in social reality."

Incidentally, according to Lamb, modernity suffers from the same illusion (*Schein*) as idealism and empiricism, when the "modern is supposed to be the new." But in reality, says Lamb, only when it is realized "how modernity is in fact an ever-identical archaism [is it] possible to discover what is different and new" (p.38).

"demanded that they go beyond Marx." And this was not only a matter of faithful interpretation but of "chang[ing] his theory" in such a way that it might better approximate the goal which critical theory holds in common with Marx: its commitment to the emancipation of humanity.

It should be noted, however, that critical theory envisions this "humanized" liberated state entirely in the Marxian frame of thought, i.e., in an "ever more adequate realization of reason in reality," or what Horkheimer has called "an obscure harmony between being and thought, understanding and sense perception," out of which "there will emerge in the future age the relation between rational intention and realization." This harmonious relation is to be seen in the context of society and "work-processes," as Horkheimer's explanation shows.[54]

This intimate relatedness to original Marxism notwithstanding, these words contain at the same time a radically new element. Perhaps it might be called the element of greater realism expressed in a **"not yet"**: "The effort to realize reason in society

---

[54] *Ibid.*, p.38. Horkheimer's words merit repeating: "critical theory 'is motivated today by the effort really to transcend the tension [of the non-correspondence between reason and reality] and to abolish the opposition between the individual's purposefulness, spontaneity and rationality, and those work-process relationships on which society is built. Critical theory understands man as in conflict with himself until this opposition is removed. If activity governed by reason is proper to man, then existent social practice, which forms the individual's life to its least details, is inhuman, and this inhumanity affects everything that goes on in society'" (as cited by Lamb). Metz accepts this definition of the individual in his relation to society (in its general descriptive terms at least) and uses it in his critique of the contemporary "personalist and existentialist theologies," which may in fact miss the individual if they fail to consider his social entanglement. In his words:
"it is our contention that theology, precisely because of its privatizing tendency is apt to miss the individual in his real existence. Today this existence is to a very great extent entangled in societal vicissitudes; so any existential or personal theology that does not understand existence as a political problem in the widest sense of the word, must inevitably restrict its consideration to an abstraction" (ThW, pp.110f.).

means that critical theory is committed to the imperative value of truth. Truth as a correspondence between reason and reality is [however] *not yet* attained--they are [still] nonidentical..."[55] Truth, therefore, is seen here as a task that is always before us. This critical orientation toward the future (and through that future to the present) is one aspect of critical theory where Metz freely admits having learnt from thinkers like Ernst Bloch. Of course, this "learning" should be qualified: Metz's comment on his discussions with Bloch is to the point: he says he always came away grateful and more reflective and that with the passing of time their differences had indeed decreased--and become more substantive at the same time.[56] This type of "learning" is likely to characterize Metz's relation to critical theory generally, as it does his relation to the secularized world.

Critical theory is profoundly characterized by the conviction of an ongoing nonidentity between reason and reality. This tenet it also shares, to an extent at least, with the original Marxian emphasis on the primacy of praxis over theory. In his reaction against idealist philosophy, Marx protested that it merely "interpreted" the world without changing it. According to Ancic, Marx proposed (in effect) to correct this exercise in abstraction not by creating a counter philosophy but by "suspending" (*aufheben*) philosophy in a process of realizing what it theorizes

---

[55] *Ibid.*, p.38; his italics. Marx was in one way also deeply aware of how Hegel's idealist system clashed against the brokenness of the real world when he asserted: "'The world, that confronts a total, self-sufficient philosophy, is...a torn one'" (my tr.). But rather than being led by this insight to an "ongoing critical theory," he wished to deal with this clash, so to speak, by "eliminating" (*aufheben*) philosophy through its immediate concrete realization, i.e. making it correspond to reality. Or in Ancic's words (*op. cit.*, p.84): "Aus dieser prekären Konstellation der geistig-politischen Wirklichkeit zog Marx die praktische Konsequenz: die radikale Aufhebung der traditionellen Philosophie, die zugleich ihre eigene praktische Verwirklichung bedeutet."

[56] Metz, *Unterbrechungen*, p.59. Cf. n.#48 above for the quote.

about.[57] This meant giving decided (if not exclusive) preference to praxis over theory. The tacit assumption seems to be that the criteria for a proper realization of thought in social reality were somehow self-evident. The goal was to overcome human alienation in all its aspects, from the self, work-products, the work-process, fellow humans and nature.

The critical theorists noted that Marx's "iron laws of social history," if not proven wrong in both socialist and capitalist countries, were at least shown to be slower to take effect than previously thought. However, this did not prevent them from sharing Marx's values, goals and methodological approach. These center around the truth of a non-alienated, liberated human being. The way to achieve this "project" is to engage in praxis and not (at least not first of all) to theorize abstractly on this "obscure harmonious" relation.

Thus it would seem that the only major difference between Marx and the critical theorists is the latter's realization that a more critical, and hence more "philosophical" approach is called for, because the project of a classless harmonious human society is less imminent and less automatic in coming about than Marx had assumed.

Metz basically assumes the same critically affirmative position in his relation to Marxism and "critical reason" as he displayed towards modern secularism--and for the same reason. Critical reason, as a fruit of the Enlightenment, must also be fundamentally derived from Christianity. In his definition of "political theology" as fundamental theology, Metz argues that "all theology must be of itself 'practical', oriented to action," and that "theological truth" cannot be discovered apart from praxis within society. Clearly that claim is a reference to, and an affirmation of the "society-directed thinking" of Marxism and neo-Marxism. He shares with critical theorists the insight that there is a need for an ongoing critical attitude. But while admitting that theology cannot be "spared the [ongoing] questionableness of [human] existence and the hazards of the

---

[57] Ancic, *op. cit.*, p.85. Cf. #55 above.

future," he counters that theology "need not fall into the other
extreme, the barren cult of questioning everything."[58]

How can theology accept and employ the Marxian category of
praxis and critical reason's notion of ongoing criticism, without
suffering the same fate as the founders of these categories? A
brief analysis of a relatively early (1966) essay,[59] read by Metz
as part of the Christian-Marxist public dialogue series (sponsored
by the Paulus Society, in which Karl Rahner also participated)
will answer this question. The essay shows how Metz's theology
relates to both Marxism and critical theory generally. It is also
entirely consistent with his treatment of modern secularism in
general.

The essay deals explicitly and frankly with all central points
on which Christians and Marxists traditionally differ most
strongly. In it we see the "new political theology" at work as
Metz does precisely what he proposes all theology must do: he
takes seriously "the new standpoint provided by critical reason."
But he also wants to critique "everything in the light of the
eschatological message of Jesus."[60]

In this essay we witness how Metz "deprivatizes" the
inherently "societally provocative message of Jesus" as he
engages in critical dialogue with the Marxist Garaudy. The
mandate to do so is itself derived from this Christian message.
For did not the cross stand outside the city walls and the

---

[58] Metz, "Apologetics," *Concise SM*, p.24.

[59] J.B. Metz, "Nachwort," *Der Dialog. Oder ändert sich das Verhältnis
zwischen Katholizismus und Marxismus?*, Roger Garaudy, J.B. Metz, K.
Rahner, eds., (Rowohlt, 1966) pp.119-138. From here on referred to as *Der
Dialog*.

[60] Cf. Introduction. Ancic (*op. cit.*, pp.103-110) also shows how Metz
wishes to harness these two models of thought (*Denkmodelle*), the praxis
category and the critique category, with the help of the "eschatological
proviso."

religious sanctuary: "outside" "in the profanum of the world, a scandal, a foolishness and--a promise for it"?[61]

This text from Hebrews is the basis of Metz's conviction that the Christian faith oriented by the central biblical promises must necessarily concern itself with issues of social and world responsibility. And this includes entering into dialogue "with the big political-social utopias" of today. Doing this, Metz stresses, "has nothing to do with a suspect neo-politicization of Christianity and the church." On the contrary, only if it takes seriously its "social-critical" task, can Christianity avoid giving ideological sanction to a given social order (p.138). Some further examples of how Metz responds to his Marxist dialogue partner, Roger Garaudy, are in order here.

For Metz, this dialogue aims not at easy compromises but at frank yet open "fruitful conflict," "in which theology seeks to remain faithful to the message it is charged with precisely by resolutely sharing the problems and questions of its surrounding world [*Mitwelt*]."[62] He then proceeds to analyze such central questions as the mythologization of human existence by Christianity (as Garaudy alleges); modern society's obsession with the "novum"; human alienation or the struggle concerning the human individual; the adequacy of the Marxian concept of the "whole person" (or of the sources of alienation); the relation between the eschatological promises and innerworldly society; and others.

Metz consistently admits that the historical church has often evoked suspicion of mythologizing and/or privatizing its message. For example, about the actual historical church he asks in the rhetorical negative:

---

[61] Metz, *Der Dialog*, p.138. Bracketed numbers in the text are taken from this source until further notice. Quotations from this source were translated by me from German.

[62] *Ibid.*, pp.121f., quote on p.121. We have met this thought also in Metz's article, "Apologetics" (cf. n.#58).

Has it actually realized in a credible way, that the promises it proclaims, the hope to which it testifies, is not a hope in the church, but rather in the kingdom of God as the future of the world: for a reign of universal peace and righteousness (cf. 2 Pet. 3:13), which knows no more tears and in which 'there will be [no more death,] no more mourning or sadness' (Rev. 21:4; from JB)? And has it dedicated itself in creative-aggressive expectation to these promises, to the promise of the Sermon on the Mount, that makes it [the church] continually into the church of the poor and oppressed? (pp.128f.)

On these matters, Metz says, we will need to allow ourselves to be questioned "to the roots of our Christian existence," and adds that "without a painful turnabout, we will not be able to advance" from this state of affairs (p.129).

After that admission and a call to repentance, he proceeds to criticize the Marxist position. Metz shows on the basis of Scripture and historical analysis that in its reductionistic assessment of the human being, Marxism's "whole person" is far from whole. The concept fails to deal adequately with such alienating factors as evil, guilt, concupiscence and death, by reducing them to economic alienation only (cf. p.134).

Specifically, Metz objects to the Marxian concept of death (cited by Garaudy) as the person's "dying into the totality of future humankind." Is this not a greater "mythologization" of death than the one it accuses Christianity of? Metz recognizes the intended solidarity, but holds it does not take as seriously the "radical alienation" of the human being (in death for example) as does Christianity. "The Christian...hopes to overcome [this threat to existence] only in solidarity with Jesus, the crucified and risen one..." (p.134). Those elements rightly emphasized by Marxism-- that the experience of death must be deprivatized; it is essentially related to other people--are found in the conception of death contained within the horizon which "the message of Jesus" offers to the Christian.[63] But Metz emphasizes, it must be a matter of

---

[63] Metz, *Der Dialog*, pp.134f. On p.135 Metz elaborates further on this idea: "For even the Christian attitude towards death may not be narrowed down to something individualistic and world-less. Even this attitude is realized

"**deprivatizing**," not "**depersonalizing**" death, and by extension all other dimensions of life. This means raising consciousness toward the fact, "that I can realize my hope only in that I seek to make room for such a hope in others; that I can realize my freedom only as a concrete commitment for the freedom of others--against all forms of subjugation of the human being" (pp.135f.).

Metz further responds to Garaudy's famous "alternative to religion," consisting in the Marxian projection not so much of an existence *against* God, but rather of an "offer of a positive possibility of existence, a total humanity *without* God" (p.136). The manner in which Metz responds is as significant as the content of his response. First he points out that he finds this sort of "postatheistic" orientation no less disquieting than more militant atheism. Then he responds, not by arguing (at least not directly) for the need of faith in God, but rather by saying that the place where the merits or hazards of belief and unbelief must be decided will be "the endangered human being: this human being could be the locus where the truth between belief and unbelief proves itself today...[or] becomes visible" (p.136). In other words, Metz takes up the challenge of Marxism's call to praxis. For only in its practice may the church of Vatican II (expressly claiming to be the 'church of the poor and oppressed'), along with all of Christianity, prove its credibility, i.e., if it takes up (and persists in) "its historical responsibility for the human being which issues out of its trust-in-the-promises [*Verheißungsglauben*]" (cf. pp.136f.).

This point is also made earlier in the essay when Metz contrasts orthodoxy and orthopraxis as follows: As "co-workers" towards a "new world" of universal peace and righteousness, Christians must not argue but practically demonstrate the veracity

---

with a view to the world, to the world of our brothers [and sisters]: it is realized in the selfless emptying of ourselves in love for the others, the 'least among us', is realized in our selfless commitment for *their* 'hope'" (italics his; my tr.). He grounds this thought in 1 John 3:14: "We know that we have passed from death to life, because we love our brothers."

of their faith. "The orthodoxy of [their] faith must constantly 'make itself true' [*bewahrheiten*] in the orthopraxis of [their] eschatologically oriented action upon the world; for the promised truth is a truth, which has to be 'done', as John (cf. 3:21) emphasizes very clearly" (p.128). However, while Metz agrees with the Marxian stress on the primacy of praxis in establishing truth, the very eschatological promises, which Christians must help usher in, enable Metz to avoid the utopian pitfall into which Marxism falls in its attempt to "suspend" philosophy by its direct realization in a classless society. Because Christians must themselves create the conditions which, as it were, validate the eschatological promises, because they must themselves transform their world, states Metz, "the Christian understanding of the end times is not therefore a "presentistic" [*präsentische*] eschatology, in which all passion for the future becomes transposed into a world-less representation of eternity within the individual moment of existence" (p.128). And quite obviously, if Christians must be involved in the realization of the reality held out by the eschatological promises, properly understood Christian eschatology can be no "passive expectation" and the world a disengaged "waiting room," says Metz. Rather, "Christian eschatology must be understood much more as a productive and aggressive [*kämpferische*] eschatology." Or (borrowing from Bloch), Metz adds, Christian hope is a hope which does "not only offer us something to drink, but demands that we also cook something." Therefore, he concludes, "eschatological faith and earthly engagement do not exclude but include one another" (p.128).

This engagement is of course no blind and militant "world-optimism." The promises made visible in Christ, says Metz, urge us on in our efforts about the future but they are also a scandal, critically resisting our striving "in the name of the oppressed and offended human individual." Because,

In view of the scandal of the cross, the Christian trust in the promises [*Verheißungsglaube*] can never become a simple ideological paraphrase of the modern aggressive [*kämpferische*] attitude toward progress; can never simply canonize the technological, economic and social progress, rightly brought about by us (p.129).

This Christian faith and hope--an aggressive hope against all hope--is and remains always "essentially 'untimely'" in a productive sense, which in relation to our future related efforts has "a critical-liberating power and task." Metz then borrows a lengthy quote from Rahner in order to illustrate this "critical task of the church." In it Rahner says that it is not an extrinsicistic criticism, but rather one stemming "from one's own experience on the road into one's own innerworldly future." Rahner goes on to say that this criticism must explain (to the human individual striving towards the future of his own creativity):

'that the increase of the planned [reality] always also evokes an increase in the unplanned and unforeseen; that the sacrifice for the future of the coming generations loses its meaning and dignity, and thus also its power in the long run, if this sacrifice considers the people living at this present moment merely as material and means for the construction of the future without regard for the absolute worth, right and dignity of the presently living individuals.... The church must warn against those utopias, which are not the beginning of the real future, but are the program for the construction of a future that is unrealistic...' (p.129f.).

Thus, rightly understood, Christian faith based on biblical promises has a "critical-liberating power and task" both against itself (preventing it from becoming ideological) and against what Metz calls "a forced attitude towards progress." It knows not more but less about the future than both Eastern and Western conceptions of the future (cf. p.130). In the light of this faith based on God's promise (which has always also a "negative theology" in it), Metz criticizes Garaudy's concept of the "total person," by which the latter characterizes the Marxist conception of the future, as "a problematic abstraction" and at the same time as asking too much of the future. Metz continues his critique:

Does not every vision of the future as autonomously fulfilled humanism falter in the face of the human being himself or herself?....Do we not clearly experience that the **hominization** of the world resulting from our technological arrangements, that the process-like transposition [*prozessuale*

Überführung] of its [the world's] possibilities into given realities does not by any means create a growing **humanization** (and *does not precisely in the attempt at paralleling these two processes lie the dangerous illusion of Marxism*)? Do we not know all too clearly, that even as human beings in an extremely hominized world we will always continue to ask for the yet unfulfilled *Humanum*, even as it is asked in Isaiah: 'Watchman, what time of night?...The watchman answers: Morning is coming, then night again. If you want to, why not ask, turn around, come back?' (Is. 21:11f.; JB)? (p.131; my emphs.)

We have encountered these thoughts already in the above discussion of hominization versus humanization. But in this statement we note that Metz agrees with the Marxian call to establish truth through praxis, yet rejects its tendency toward immanentist reductionism. What, however, is his source for criticizing what might be called the Marxist "praxis-critique" of social and historical reality? It might be suggested that Metz is simply borrowing from critical theorists in applying something of an ongoing critique or a negative dialectic. Quite clearly, Metz agrees with critical theorists on the need for continued critical thought. But in light of the above description of the extreme negativity (almost for its own sake) of critical theory, his position shows also a crucial difference, perhaps more hinted at than elaborated: the "negative theology" (mentioned twice in this essay; pp.123, 131), which, according to Metz, has always been part of Christianity and which is always a dimension in the *Verheißungsglaube* (faith that is based on the promise) is both similar and dissimilar to a negative dialectics.

The similarity is found in the critical function of the negative theology which consists in what Metz elsewhere calls the "eschatological proviso" (or *eschatologischer Vorbehalt*).[64] Like

---

[64] Metz, ThW, p.114. Cf. also Ancic, *op. cit.*, p.109: Ancic gives this interpretation of Metz's "eschatological proviso": "God preserves for himself the right to establish his universal, definitive rule, which is not like any worldly rule and does not bestow definitive legitimacy on any such rule. The eschatological proviso has the character of the end times and serves as theological basis for the fact that there can be no inner-worldly identifiable political subject of the totality of history" (my tr.).

the negative dialectics of critical theory, so the eschatological proviso criticizes every social and historical reality, as well as all humanly conceived visions of such realities, as not yet corresponding to the ultimate truth. Hence all realities and all human visions of realities are at best "provisional" realities in need of criticism until the end of time. That is why, as we have seen in Metz's definitions of the new political theology, he defines its primary task as a permanently critical task.

The dissimilarity between this proviso and negative dialectics is fundamental, however. The negative or critical function of the former is one dimension of an otherwise positive program. The critical eschatological proviso is firmly rooted in the positive eschatological future, which according to Metz is the God of the Bible. The most poignant Old Testament report of God's revelation, he says, is found in the book of Exodus (3:14). God is here described as our future, "but as *our* future, insofar as it possesses *itself*, is founded in itself and is not simply a correlation of our own wishes and strivings: 'I will be what I will be' [NEB],... [This] defines the divinity of God as a free 'power of our future' possessing itself, and not primarily as a 'being above us' in the sense of a hereafter that can be experienced detached from history." The God so understood is neither the projection of our own wishes (Feuerbach) nor the product of our resignation over the infeasibility of our limitless striving. Says Metz: "he does not appear as the quenching of the historical initiative of [human beings], but precisely as the liberation of this initiative" (p.123).

In the New Testament (as has already been intimated earlier), the anchor of the critical power of the eschatological proviso is

----

Quoting from Metz, he adds: "'Wherever a party, a group, a nation or a class seeks to identify itself as this subject, and thereby aims to make the totality of history into the horizon of its political activity, it must, of necessity, become ideologically totalitarian'." Aside from this "relativizing function of the eschatological proviso, which subjects all false absolutizations, the stately and ideological "totalitarianism," to its critique," it functions also as a "stimulant" towards a persistent "critical-liberating" engagement in the present situation (cf. pp.109f.; my tr. and emph.).

the life and message of the crucified and risen Jesus Christ (the *"Verbum caro factum est"*). In this regard, i.e., in its incarnate positivity, the eschatological proviso is fundamentally different from the self-defeating negative dialectics of critical theory. This judgment of critical theory does not minimize its correct diagnosis of the need for ongoing criticism of church and society. Metz's (often implicit) dialogue with critical theory is therefore never self-righteous, but is rather meant as a fellow seeker for the truth sharing in their experience while holding out an alternative answer. Metz does not hesitate to draw attention again to revelation as the source of an answer, where negative dialectics has no answer. But he is deeply conscious of the fact that in a pluralistic age, and after a long history of malpractice, only the lived truth of praxis will have credibility.

There is another fundamental dissimilarity: while critical theory by definition lacks a concrete social agent, Metz's *Verheißungsglaube* has no shortage of real and prospective agents. There is, obviously, the worldwide Christian church, which is the imperfect but concrete historical embodiment of God's irreversible salvific acceptance of the world in the act of incarnation. It needs to be remembered that Metz gives the whole so-called "Christ event" (incarnation, life, teaching, death and resurrection) above all an eschatological interpretation. Thus, even though each of the named salvific aspects of the life of Jesus Christ represents the historical realization of God's promise to humankind, to Metz they seem to represent even more strongly (renewed) eschatological promises of the final salvation of the world.

This eschatological perspective also marks his view of the Christian church: on the one hand, the church is the embodiment in history and society of God's irrevocable salvation of the world in Christ, and in this sense might be termed "realized eschatology." On the other hand, it is but the tangible promise of the "not yet" aspect of salvation history (which is the one world history). The church is the provisional body which came into existence only because much of humankind has yet to believe in God's acceptance of the world in its creaturely distinctness in obedience. That church will only cease to exist when the unchangeable promise of the whole world coming under the lordship of Christ is realized in the eschaton. Some critics feel that Metz emphasizes the "provisional" dimension of soteriology at the expense of actualized salvation in history.[65]

Implied in this actual (though provisional) agency of the church is what I would call the prospective or potential agency of all humankind. Metz holds "that the 'spirit' of Christianity is permanently embedded in the 'flesh' of world history...," and the "process of history is 'accepted' in the Christian *logos* and remains so," even though in our temporal existence it is a matter of a "constant if always hidden and crucified 'marriage' between salvation and world history."[66] Thus, if the incarnation of the *logos* and the church founded by him are the eschatological promise of the salvation of the whole world, then clearly everyone is a potential agent summoned to place his or her life under the continual criticism of this promise. Everyone is also summoned to claim as free grace the positive salvific contents of the promise, which humankind is to bring about in free and obedient self-actualization. In another context, Metz specifically names these promises when he says: "It is impossible to privatize the eschatological promises of [the] biblical tradition: **liberty, peace, justice, and reconciliation.** Again and again they force us to assume our responsibilities towards society."[67]

This assessment of world history by Metz does not claim a self-righteous superiority over an unrealistic Marxian "world-optimism" in its goal of establishing the innerhistorical identity

---

[65] Ancic (*op. cit.*, p.117), says these critics express concern over the absence of what might be called the actualized dimension of salvation in Metz's theology. Specifically, the criticism relates to a supposed "lack of a firm anchoring of political theology in Jesus Christ and in God's saving act of redemption that is proclaimed and actualized in him" (my tr.).

[66] Metz, ThW, p.16; cf. also FHS, p.188.

[67] Cf. "The Church and World in the Light of a 'Political Theology'," ThW, p.114.

of thought and society in the classless society, wrought solely by human agency. Nor does it claim to be superior to the historical pessimism of critical theory, which, although longing for the same humanly achieved identity or harmony between thought and social reality, has to resign itself to the ultimate unachievability of this noble goal purely on the basis of a negative dialectics. Metz is too keenly aware of the humbling failings of the historical church to point a finger at others. He fully agrees with both Marxism and critical theory that truth must be ascertained through praxis and prevented from becoming ideological through ongoing criticism. But, as we saw in his critical affirmation of modern secularism, Metz knows (in the light of biblical revelation) that aside from faith and hope in the transcendent God, who has become identified with history in Christ, this is not possible. In other words, through faith Metz's hope has a positive source of power enabling humanity to become a world transforming agent. And as part and parcel of this revealed and incarnated source of power is the built-in critique of the cross, under the sign of which all of history continues until the eschatological consummation.

In short, as with modern secularism, what Metz finds troublesome about Marxism and critical theory is not that they are too humanistic, but that they are not humanistic enough; not that they make too much of human alienation but that they do not take it seriously enough; not that they make too much of human agency but that they do not avail themselves of the only means which can set the full human potential free; not that they demand too much freedom (emancipation)[68] for human beings

---

[68] In his references to and critical affirmation of practical human freedom as emancipation, Metz is appropriating a fundamental Enlightenment category. For as Ancic (*op. cit.*, p.6) points out, Kant, in his famous essay "Was ist Aufklärung?" defined "the Enlightenment as the 'exodus of the human person from his or her self-inflicted dependency'" (my tr.).

In ThW, Metz refers to Kant's definition of the emancipated state as the ability to make use of one's reason in all things, including in public. He says, Kant held that "a man is enlightened only when he has the freedom to make public use of his reason in all affairs...[and] only he is enlightened who, *at the*

but that it is withheld from some in the name of a program which is given priority over people; not that they are too critical of ideological tendencies but that their immanentist approach is impotent in avoiding its own "ideologization."

For Metz, then, there can be no other fuller measure of the truly human than Jesus Christ, nor can human alienation be effectively dealt with without Christ. That is why he considers the act which risks itself in "brotherly love toward the least among us" (an act by which Christian hope pre-empts and overcomes death; cf. 1 John 3:14) a matter of following after Jesus (*Nachfolge Jesu*) in his "life for others", and not an autonomously achieved human feat (cf. p.135). For what Metz holds with regard to death, namely, that the Christian who views it as the most "radical 'self-alienation',...hopes to conquer [it] **only in solidarity with Jesus the crucified and risen one...**" (p.134), surely extends to the other sources of alienation and how he would deal with these.

It is important to at least mention some of the criticisms made by theologians of Metz's political theology,[69] since they relate

---

same time, fights to realize those sociopolitical suppositions that offer the possibility of publicly using reason" (p.112).

But whereas modern philosophical conceptions of freedom largely criticized institutions and relied upon their subjective reason for their authority, Metz suggests that the rightfully sought-after emancipation is too vulnerable to be defended by individual thinkers. It may need safeguarding through its institutionalization. He suggests that the church might be such an institution of freedom in the sense of being "the bearer of the criticism of social practice." (ThW, cf. pp.131-136) This idea is also advanced on p.116, when he writes: "The hope she announces is not a hope for herself but for the kingdom of God. As institution, the Church truly lives on the proclamation of her own proviso. And she must realize this eschatological stipulation in that she establishes **herself as the institution of critical liberty**, in the face of society and its absolute and self-sufficient claims."

[69] In view of Metz's definitions of political theology (presented above), it should not come as a surprise if I designate the critical dialogical theology here outlined as political theology--especially in view of its constant and strong eschatological dimension. All these aspects are intimately and

to his openness towards modernity generally and Marxism and critical theory specifically. These criticisms lead us into the next political theological category of narrative theology and dangerous memory.

The criticism from the right is familiar. Johns lists Josef Ratzinger and Hans Maier among those who fear that Metz does not do justice to God's acts of salvation within past and present history because of an excessive preoccupation with the eschatological future (Ratzinger),[70] and that Metz is dabbling in a revival of "a dangerous form of the politization [sic] of theology" (Maier).[71]

Since Metz's eschatology-oriented critique is intended to be a corrective of the traditional concept of history which he believes to be oriented excessively toward the historical "past," his counterpart emphasis of "future" may well be (or appear to be) extreme. But a cursory look at even a relatively early statement shows clearly that his concept of the eschatological bears powerfully upon the present, not to mention the fact that the whole foundation of these promises lies solidly in the historical

---

inextricably intertwined for Metz as the following statement shows: "*Every eschatological theology...must become a political theology, that is, a (socio)-critical theology.*" (ThW, p.115; italics his.)

[70] Cf. Johns, *op.cit.*, pp.158-159. "Ratzinger says that in the Theology of Hope (which he uses to refer to Metz's theology as well as that of J. Moltmann) history is conjugated so radically in the future tense that the past is disregarded." A look at the highly critical quote from Ratzinger on Metz (as given by Johns) makes clear that a substantial part of the difference has to do with widely differing understandings of history. Whereas Ratzinger's is a more positive-objectivist, Metz's is a more "modernist" dialectical conception of history. Johns, in this instance, is surely right in admitting that Ratzinger's critique of the "neglect of the past in contemporary eschatological theology," may be partly justified, but that in the case of Metz it certainly overstates its case. For "in his *memoria*-thesis is an attempt to give his theology a means of appropriating the past creatively. It helps him achieve a balance in his use of temporal categories."

[71] *Ibid.*, p.158; cited by Johns from Maier.

"past" of the gospel.[72] Against Maier's suspicion of a repetition of the classical theological justification of the status quo by Metz, the latter can be shown to have made numerous explicit disavowals. For example:

> No doubt, these [eschatological] promises cannot simply be identified with any condition in society....The history of Christianity has had enough experience of such direct identification and direct "politifications" of the Christian promises. In such cases, however, the "eschatological proviso," which makes every historically real status of society appear to be provisional, was being abandoned (ThW, p.114).

He obviously wants to avoid this mistake. But "provisional" does not mean "arbitrary": "This eschatological proviso does not mean that the present condition of society is not valid. It *is* valid, but in the 'eschatological meanwhile'. It does not bring about a negative but a critical attitude to the societal present."[73]

Metz also has critics on his left. Johns would probably place himself among them. His criticism of Metz's political theology is that it fails to supply a concrete, specific "theological praxology"; that Metz "has been more successful in incorporating insights from Enlightenment critical philosophy than he has from the Marxist sociopolitical critique," and this apparently "because of a residue of scholastic content in his thought."[74] It would appear from his demand for "concreteness and specificity...for a definitive theological and ecclesiastical stance on social, ethical and political issues," that Johns has hardly grasped the meaning of the "eschatological proviso," so central to Metz's political theology. The function of this proviso is precisely to remind all the overly concrete and specific "praxologists" of the perpetual

---

[72] Metz, ThW, cf. pp.114f.

[73] *Ibid.*, p.114; his italics. If the last sentence is aimed at critical theorists, the subsequent ones are surely directed at Marxists: "Its promises are not an empty horizon of religious expectations; neither are they only a regulative idea. They are, rather, a critical liberating imperative for our present times."

[74] Johns, .*op. cit.*, cf. pp.vif.

need to remain open to our humanly uncontrollable future. This negative theological function is at the same time also its most positive function, since it alone allows the actual contents of the future promises to enter into our ongoing "present" existence.

This is not to deny entirely the validity of Johns' point about Metz's "ecclesiology" being inadequate. However, Metz has done considerable work in that area since then (cf. *The Emergent Church*, among other things).

Space does not allow for discussing Metz's critics mentioned by Ancic in his book, save the "fundamental question" raised by Karl Lehmann, namely, what in the philosophical framework of Metz's political theology gives it a specifically and distinctly "Christian" content.[75] This question is surprising in light of the clear Christological foundation of Metz's theology. Is this criticism made because Metz's Christology is always presupposed but seldom elaborated in great detail? This is true especially of his works that preceded Lehmann's work referred to by Ancic. It was still several years before Metz was to develop his *Nachfolgechristologie* (discipleship-Christology) in FoC, *et al*.

4. Narrative Theology and the Role of Dangerous Memory

Ancic argues that although Metz never responded directly to the various critical voices questioning his political theology, they nevertheless caused him to employ the name "political theology" more sparingly (because of its historically negative connotations) as well as to move on to introduce the further category of "dangerous memory" into his theology.[76] This category served, on the one hand, to balance out the dimension of the past which stands under the primacy of the "future" dimension in his

---

[75] Ancic, *op. cit*, p.117.

[76] *Ibid.*, pp.113-122, esp. pp.113 and 116.

political theology, and on the other, to respond to a problem which Metz felt was besetting the present world and society, namely, a growing loss of historical consciousness and memory.[77] This addition, however, did not represent a discontinuity, but a corrective in the sense of broadening the general ethos of Metz's new political theology.

Metz introduced the concepts of "memory" and "narrative" (as categories that correspond cognitively to the practical pilgrim life of discipleship) for other reasons besides those already mentioned, namely, balancing his temporal tenses, and averting the present societal loss of remembering. An even more important "pastoral" reason is his concern about the present identity or faith crisis within the church itself. He speaks of a silent but wide-spread slipping away from the church among the common church membership, because the subtle theological answers from the "elitist" leadership in the church to the modern problems of the laity leave them confused. According to Metz, the crisis is rooted in the intuition of lay people "that the living identity of the Christian body with Jesus has become lost in later Christianity, that Christianity cast off its conformity to Christ a long time ago and that Jesus' intentions were long ago successfully taken over by other historical movements." Thus

---

[77] *Ibid.*, p.119. On the latter point, Ansic's quote from Metz is particularly relevant. According to it, we are witnessing "the development of an increasingly history-less and memory-less society, so that in it traditions are increasingly preserved, and translated into the present, only by way of institutions and their formulated self-understanding, that is, by way of formulated creeds." To this quote Ansic adds a significant comment: "In view of this problematic situation of today's world and society, the Christian faith-understanding as memoria must be interpreted from the perspective of content and dogma" (my tr.).

This quotation (and comment) may also serve to allay Ratzinger's concern over "an abandonment [by Metz] of any reference to tradition in order to turn to the projection of that which must be done [in the future]" (as cited by Johns, *op. cit.*, p.159), and to show that Metz is possibly beginning to take into account, and incorporate, some of the criticisms about an excessive emphasis of the eschatological dimension in theology (as the quote in question stems from 1969).

they developed the slogan "'Yes to Jesus, no to the Church'" (FHS, p.165f.; cf. p.93). This crisis, contends Metz, will not go away through "a more scholarly form of hermeneutics and a more critical reconstruction of the history of Christianity. It can only be diminished by providing evidence of the spirit and power of Christianity in consistent imitation of Christ, in other words, by practical conformity to Christ."[78]

This critical-practical idea is basic to all of Metz's works from about 1970 onward.[79] For the church to have identity, it has to have a living memory of the "story" on which it is founded.[80]

---

[78] Metz, FHS, p.154. In this chapter (pp.154-168) Metz contrasts his "narrative and practical Christianity" with Rahner's "transcendental and idealistic" (and to some extent with Pannenberg's *et al.* "historicist") Christianity (cf. p.158).

Metz describes "memory and narrative as categories of practical reason that have the function of saving identity." Because of the primacy of the "practical" dimension, he sees them as a "post-idealistic" concept of Christianity. In contrast, he considers Rahner's "transcendental theory of anonymous Christianity" an "idealistic concept" (cf. pp.157f.). The latter, in spite of Rahner's otherwise consistent aversion to all "elitism," strikes Metz as "an idealist elitism," because it reserves "full and explicit (!) knowledge of the faith" to the philosophers, whereas in his view it should be "the arcanum of Jesus...the practical arcane knowledge of the imitation of Christ" (cf. pp.159f.).

[79] The idea of solving the Christian identity crisis through narrative practical Christianity (which we will discuss below) can be seen as increasingly basic to most of Metz's writings from about 1970 on. By far the major portion of FHS is dedicated to elaborating this concept. Although this work appeared as a book (in German) only in 1977, many of its key chapters on memory and narrative represent journal articles from the early 1970s. Other works by Metz in which the categories of memory and narrative (in conjunction with the concomitant category of "discipleship") are dealt with are the German synod document *Our Hope: A Confession of Faith for Our Time* (which was chiefly drafted by Metz), FoC--the latter cites extensively from the former, of which it is a further elaboration--and EC.

[80] The following statement by Metz makes clear both Christianity's basic tendency to reach out into its given spiritual environment and its solid rootedness in one concrete but unique historical event: "Christianity has penetrated the space of the Greek *logos* and its metaphysics as a community

This requires telling or "narrating" the story ever anew to each generation. Neither the original story nor stories of individual believers[81] are only or primarily told to quiet down listeners; they are not passive entertainment, but they need to arouse their audience to action. There is a connection here between the dangerous remembered stories within Christian history and sacramental theology. According to Metz, one can view "the story as an effective sign and...the narrative aspect of the

---

of memory and narrative. It is aware that its memories are related to a single historical event in which man has been irrevocably redeemed and set free in the eschatological sense by God." (FHS, p.188).

Metz evidently has in mind "the dangerous memory of the freedom of Jesus Christ," as his thesis defining the church reveals: "the Church must understand and justify itself as the public witness and bearer of the tradition of a dangerous memory of freedom in the 'systems' of our emancipative society." The basis for such a thesis?: the *memoria Jesu Christi*, including his suffering death and resurrection (FHS, pp.89f.; cf. also p.111).

[81] FHS, cf. pp.164f. Here Metz explains the advantage of "narrative" over against "pure discourse or argument" in terms of the relation between universal vs. individual salvation history: "narrative makes it possible to discuss the whole of history and the universal meaning of history in such a way that the idea of this universal meaning is not transferred to a logical compulsion of totality or a kind of transcendental necessity, as a result of which the mystical-political histories of individuals would be of secondary importance in comparison with the saving meaning of history as a whole and could only be incorporated subsequently into the framework of a definitive history dissociated from the subject. In the narrative conception of Christian salvation, history and histories--the history of salvation and the many histories of salvation and the absence of individuals--merge together without diminishing each other. The individual histories do not take place without regard to the previously narrated history of salvation and the history of salvation is able to assimilate the individual histories." In practical terms "the narrated (and remembered) universality and definitiveness of the meaning of history," says Metz, "mean that the historical praxis of opposition to meaninglessness and the absence of salvation is not superfluous, because it is transcendental or historical, but indispensable."

sacrament as a sign."[82] The telling of these stories has a saving aspect to it, just as narration of the eucharistic formulae ('on the night that he was betrayed...') can be called "a saving narrative" (FHS, p.208).

In Metz's understanding, memory and narrative is a matter of re-enacting the Christian experience by telling it so that it becomes an invitation to imitate this story in our lives today. He is convinced of the merits of this approach because the church from the beginning did "not primarily form an argumentative community, but a storytelling community" in which "the exchange of experience of faith, like that of any 'new' experience, takes the narrative form" (FHS, p.209). In order to prevent misunderstanding, Metz hastens to add that storytelling and narration do not replace argument and reasoning: "there is a time for storytelling and a time for argument." Nor does narrative "withdraw into the purely private sphere or the aesthetic sphere of good taste." Metz makes his strong plea for narrative theology "with a practical and socially critical effect," because he feels "for too long, we have tried to suppress the narrative potential of Christianity..." (FHS, p.209). Hence this plea for narrative has to

---

[82] FHS, p.208; on pp.207f. Metz, as an illustration of the quasi-sacramental practical event-like quality of storytelling, retells one of Martin Buber's Hassidic stories (with introductory comments):

"'The story is itself an event and has the quality of a sacred action....It is more than a reflection--the sacred essence to which it bears witness continues to live in it. The wonder that is narrated becomes powerful once more....A rabbi, whose grandfather had been a pupil of Baal Shem Tov, was once asked to tell a story. 'A story ought to be told', he said, 'so that it is itself a help', and his story was this. 'My grandfather was paralyzed. Once he was asked to tell a story about his teacher and he told how the holy Baal Shem Tov used to jump and dance when he was praying. My grandfather stood up while he was telling the story and the story carried him away so much that he had to jump and dance to show how the master had done it. From that moment, he was healed. This is how stories ought to be told.'"

be understood as a corrective to and not a substitute for an (one-sided) argumentative-intellectual theology.[83]

Although he advocates a storytelling approach to Christian proclamation--religious groups are to begin by telling their own stories[84] --Metz does not by-pass either tradition, the institutional dimension or the Christological center of Christianity. As a closer look at his discussions on memory and narrative reveals, the content of the dangerous Christian memory is none other than the body of Christian dogmas, at the center of which stands "the *memoria passionis, mortis et resurrectionis Jesu Christi.*" And since Christians "remember [in faith] the testament of Christ's love, in which the kingdom of God appeared among men by initially establishing that kingdom between men..." (FHS, p.90), "institutionalization" or a historical, visible structuring inherently belongs to Christian existence. What became apparent in ThW above (specifically in Metz's critique of a predominant Marxian criticism of institutions), is reinforced in FHS at various points, namely, that the Christian church is indispensable "as the institutional bearer of this Christianity and its memory," (FHS, cf. p.92). The church is indispensable because only by way of an institution can "the historical identity and continuity of the church and its mission" (FHS, p.94) be secured. The individual Christian alone, in contrast, is far too vulnerable.

---

[83] On how Metz thinks that "such corrections are often exaggerations," cf. his opening comments to his "thirty-five [apocalyptic] theses" in FHS, p.169. It may be well to consider this insight of Metz also in connection with other central "corrective" points of his theology, e.g., his stress on "deprivatization" of a too individualistic, privatized theology.

Metz's recognition of a need for "scientific theology" is stressed explicitly also in his *Unterbrechungen* (Gütersloher Verlagshaus, 1981), p.24: "Certainly, scientific theology is indispensable for the Christianity of our time, if it does not (from the outset) wish to fall into the cognitive loneliness of a sect" (my tr.).

[84] Cf. FoC, p.25. (Cf. n.#13 in this chapter.)

But in making this assertion, the definition of the church is rather important. Continuity is not basically a question of "apostolic succession" (FHS, p.93), but rather of a practically lived continuity, because "Church in this instance means above all: we Christians who try to live in the memory of Christ and for whom the idea of a tradition of this memory which is completely free of the Church as an institution and which entrusts this memory exclusively to the private individual is an illusion" (FHS, p.94). Implicit in this definition is the highly important concept to Metz's theology of a communal "imitation of Christ." This imitation or discipleship becomes for him the medium both for solving the church's internal identity crisis, and for publicly and critically witnessing in society in an effectively liberating way.

As an example of the former, the church may not hope to repair the internal faith crisis resulting from its deficient past performance "by providing a better or more subtle interpretation of the Church's past history. It can only be solved by a painful process of change involving proof of the spirit and strength of a new praxis" (FHS, p.93; cf. p.166). This can only be achieved through the two-dimensional mystical-political practice of Christian discipleship, in which the "alternative of prayer and action" is not acceptable.[85] The thoughts on how the church serves as a public witness within modern emancipatory society, are familiar from Metz's earlier writings referred to above. Although presented now in relation to memory, the content of

---

[85] Prayer and action are not opposites but complement each other. The importance of prayer to Metz's theology can be seen from his argument that only in prayer can the church equip itself for discharging its societal responsibility. In his words, the church "tries to gain from prayer the freedom that it needs from the plausible structures of social mechanisms and prejudices and the strength to be independent enough to take liberating action in the interest of others, the 'least of the brethren'." On the other hand, only "in this action" can prayer "set itself free from the suspicion that it is no more than an opium of the people..." FHS, p.95.

This emphasis on the mystical-political dimension of Christianity is also found throughout FoC.

that "subversive" or "challenging memory" is, in effect, the same Christocentric eschatological promise of freedom, rooted in the cross and resurrection of Jesus, as we met in earlier discussion.[86]

And again, as in earlier discussions, Metz shows himself to be a well-informed sympathetic dialogue partner to the demands of modernity for full human emancipation which humankind must actively strive for in solidarity. But the necessary empowerment for achieving this worthy goal lies for him in the dangerous memory of a specific past historical event,[87] rather than in a mere theoretical future project, as envisioned by critical reason. (It should be mentioned at this point that, according to Metz, certain leading critical theorists are realizing the liberating merits of the narrative of remembered story and are turning towards its use as they discover the ultimate sterility of critical reason per

---

[86] FHS, cf. pp.90f. His definition of the church is clearly addressed to the central concerns of modern society, but these concerns are criticized and modified by the eschatological memory: "The Church acts as the public memory of the freedom of Jesus in the systems of our emancipative society. It reminds us of an indebted freedom, God's eschatological history of freedom which is gained in the cross and resurrection of Jesus and which cannot be absorbed into the ideal of man's coming of age that is contained in the middle-class history of the Enlightenment or into the apotheosis of the history of liberation by revolution."

Rather than exonerating us from "the responsibility to take care of the history of freedom," says Metz, it "initiates us into it: 'All things are yours...the world or life or death or the present or future, all are yours, and you are Christ's and Christ is God's' (1 Cor 3: 22-23)." It is here that the church derives both its relativizing and liberating power: "In this sense...the Church is an emancipative memory, liberating us from all attempts to idolize cosmic and political powers and make them absolute." (Quotes from p.90.)

[87] FHS, cf. p.188. Thus the source of power through which human freedom is ultimately achieved is not some immanentist vision of a harmonious society, but for Metz it lies in the remembrance and retelling of the "single historical event" of Jesus Christ on which Christianity is centrally built (cf. n.#80 above).

se).[88] However, Metz's category of memory is not to be seen as "a purely archaeological repetition backwards" (as he says Kierkegaard described the *anamnesis* of Plato). Instead "memory is, in its eschatological orientation, a repetitive memory forward" (FHS, p.188).

Included in this category of remembering, whereby "memory represents the connecting link between reason and history," and in which "history and freedom are determined by eschatological recollection,"[89] is a practical "future" orientation which deeply affects our relation to the present world situation. For although it is fundamental for the Christian community to narrate verbally its central story, "recalling the historically unique event of the salvation irrevocably offered to man in Jesus Christ," this interpretation of memory according to Metz's political theology is at the same time not so narrow as to be limited to remembering the "historical Jesus" alone; it also includes the memory of the history of the church as his body, as the following statement indicates: "The memory of Christ's passion and of the sufferings of mankind as the basis for freedom-oriented action and the history of liberation passed on by word of mouth becomes the legitimate prerequisite for critically argumentative reason."[90] The validity of this interpretation by Rahner and Vorgrimler of Metz's theology hardly needs demonstrating at this point (cf. FHS, p.195).

It is important to note that the categories of memory and of narrative have a formal character for Metz. It is not a matter of "a mere subjective recollection," but, as in the central salvific events of both testaments (remembered in the Passover and

---

[88] Cf. FHS, pp.192-194. Here Metz argues that critical theorists have also begun to realize the crucial importance of the categories of memory and narrative in the human search for emancipation, citing evidence from the works of Benjamin, Marcuse, Adorno and Habermas.

[89] Rahner & Vorgrimler, "Memory," *Concise Theological Dictionary, op. cit.*, p.304.

[90] *Loc. cit.*

Eucharist, respectively), memory or "anamnesis may be theologically defined as the ceremonial re-presentation of a salutary event of the past, in order that the event may lay hold of the present situation of the celebrant." Rahner and Vorgrimler continue their Metzian explanation of memory by pointing out that while the foundational event retains its historical uniqueness in the "Judeo-Christian anamnesis..., it is at the same time present, that is, remains in force as an accomplished fact," and the human being "is able to actualize the effectual presence of this event in his own time in a manner that is superior to a mere subjective recollection."[91]

The content of the "memory" cannot be an idealistic or abstract concept but an "event" that is accomplished in "a personal act" which affects the salvation of believers in the present and "must commemorate in advance their future salvation."[92] Thus this "sacramental" reading of the categories of memory and narrative (which we already found in Metz himself) serves to answer a number of challenges both internally and externally: 1) Inner-theologically, it answers the contention that Metz has failed to recognize the acts of salvation which God has realized in history because of an excessive preoccupation with the "future promises." These promises are really but the consequences or the extension of God's historical action. 2) It also answers the "external" challenges of Marxism and critical reason: e.g., a) the event remembered is not a philosophical idea but a historically tangible human/divine act; b) because this concrete act may not be reduced to a mere distant memory but must constantly be "re-presented" or re-enacted in the present, it fulfills the requirements of true praxis; c) at the same time, memory/narrative contain in themselves a "natural" dynamism towards a future in which truly "new" things can and will happen (but without becoming a mere idealistic projection into a utopian future) as they inspire those who remember to "realistic"

---

[91] Rahner & Vorgrimler, "Anamnesis," *Ibid.*, p.10.

[92] *Loc. cit.*

transformative action; d) through these categories, too, genuine human "emancipation" is achieved because they mediate the concretely and historically lived freedom of Jesus Christ (and of all those who became free in following him), and this not at the expense of the present or past generations but in solidarity with them. Because as Rahner and Vorgrimler explain: "The salutary event [in Christ] envisages all mankind; and consequently authority to re-enact it is vested not in the individual but in the Church which represents humanity and was herself founded by that event."[93]

Some comments about the category "narrative theology" are in order before moving on to Metz's concept of "solidarity." After introducing the category of narrative theology in its "practical and performative" dimension (in a fairly "theoretical" discussion) as being particularly appropriate for mediating experience (cf. FHS, pp.205-218), Metz inserts an "excursus" on "theology as biography" (FHS, pp.219-228). Metz considers memory and narrative as the cognitive categories that correspond best to a Christianity of discipleship. In this excursus (surprisingly in the light of his criticism elsewhere of Rahner's "idealistic concept" of Christianity), Metz declares Rahner's theology to be an outstanding "paradigm" of a theology that narrates the life story of every ordinary Christian today (in Europe and beyond), and of the church in our century, and indeed, of all humanity. In Metz's words:

> What should by now be clear, then, from this consideration of Rahner's theological approach as a paradigm, is the type of theology to which the narrative structure of Christian faith most closely corresponds. In struggling with the neoscholastic tradition and evolving a dogmatic theology that is basically a concentrated and shortened biography of human history in the presence of God, Rahner has contributed to the history of the identity of modern theology that can no longer be ignored. He has, in brief, produced a mystical biography with a dogmatic intention (FHS, p.227).

---

[93] *Loc. cit.*

A closer look at the details of this excursus would reveal that in Metz's estimation Rahner closely embodies the sort of double-structured Christianity of practical discipleship which Metz elaborates at length in FoC (he often refers to this source throughout FHS) and the German Synod text *Our Hope*.... The complementary aspects of the praxis of Christian discipleship are shown there to be "mystical" and "political," respectively. And like the sections on memory and narrative in FHS, these other works are deeply concerned with how to remedy the growing identity crisis of present-day Christianity. The solution that Metz consistently proposes lies not in a more refined theology; the solution is obtainable only when the church prayerfully and publicly remembers and retells her own story--always evaluating it against the dangerous story on which the church itself is founded. However, although this "retelling" certainly entails verbal reiteration, it decidedly also means proclamation through the re-enactment of the praxis of a living imitation of Christ. According to this "excursus," Metz holds that Rahner has in an exceptional degree succeeded in giving such a practical/verbal account of the Christian faith, with a remarkable effect on both believers and unbelievers alike. For Metz, narrative and argumentative theology are not opposed but rather complement each other. And in Rahner's work the ideal balance is apparently nearly achieved, since in it, "doxography and mystical biography are merged into one another." Metz adds: "This unity is reinforced by Rahner's distinctive understanding of theology as study, initiation, mystagogy and the induction of life into the experience of mystery" (FHS, p.226).

It is evident, even from our limited discussion of the categories of memory and narrative, that far from representing a discontinuity with the ethos of Metz's new political theology, they rather deepen and reinforce its basic direction as defined above. In his elaboration of these theological concepts, Metz continues to be a sensitive dialogue partner with modern thinkers, but his own remembrance of and rootedness in the Christian tradition provides him with answers to the questions that beset believers and nonbelievers alike in our time, answers that are markedly different from those provided by secularist Marxism, for example, concerning the value of the human person and the role of the institution in human history. This will become even more obvious when we examine Metz's concept of intersubjectivity or solidarity. For although there is a degree of solidarity-thinking in the utopian concept of a classless society, it is only a form of collective egoism and remains a far cry from the Christian political theological understanding of a universal solidarity which literally cannot leave out any "class" or member of society past, present or future.

The discussion of intersubjectivity will also illuminate some further aspects of the categories of memory and narrative theology, since they are interrelated with "solidarity."

5. Intersubjectivity as Solidarity in History

Metz's understanding of solidarity is solidly rooted in his "discipleship Christology." As Jesus chose to live in solidarity with the poor and marginalized, so we must show solidarity with the "least among us." Metz says so expressly: "The Christian praxis of solidarity will always be directed towards the imitation of Christ" (FHS, p.235). The "least among us" in postwar Germany, Metz contends, are prototypically the victims of the concentration camps, in particular those who did not survive them. This means, by extension, that the Christians of the rich hemisphere must practice solidarity with the people who are not allowed to be free subjects of the history of humankind.[94]

In *Christliche Anthropozentrik*, Metz found that "solidarity" was implicit in the modern notion of "anthropocentricity." The notion demanded a general "solidarity" with its "surrounding world" (*Mitwelt*) and, more specifically, a solidarity in terms of socially "shared being" or "intersubjectivity" (*Mitsein*). Consistent with his way of relating to modern thought in general, Metz

---

[94] FHS, cf. pp.229f.

critically affirms the modern anthropocentric notion of intersubjectivity, since it too is directly implied in the Christian tradition.

Even a cursory overview of Metz's statements on "solidarity" readily shows that they are meant as a critique of both the Marxian and the capitalist middle-class concepts of solidarity. Both of these share the idea of endless evolutionary time and progress, and solidarity for them really means mutuality between equals (cf. FHS, pp.230, 233). Incidentally, according to Metz, solidarity, in the privatizing theology of the church, also represents at best an "interpersonal, I-Thou syndrome" (FHS, p.230). Such forms of solidarity are not based on Christian values but belong to a rationalized consumer society whose ultimate values are exchange, profit and endless progress. The Christian concept of solidarity, based on unselfish love is (like memory and narrative) a dangerous concept that is bound to clash with such a society. Because,

> it is very difficult if not impossible to unite the process of rationalization based on the theory of evolution that is taking place in the modern world with the Christian religion that is based on the commandment of love. A form of solidarity not only with men of reason, but also, even more radically, with those in need would seem to have little chance of survival in a rationalized society based on exchange (FHS, p.231).

Metz's fundamental theological concept of solidarity is not an "idyllic" idea which people may accept for themselves if they so choose; it boldly confronts those who misread it as "a sympathetic contact between allies or partners" and those who "systematically reject it." For these basically selfish alliances, "the logic of the Christian idea of solidarity will eventually result in a counter-alliance that is expressed in the partisanship of the imitation of Christ," asserts Metz (FHS, p.231). What this "partisanship of the imitation of Christ" means more concretely, becomes evident in his discussion of the "evangelical counsels" of poverty, chastity, and obedience in FoC. There Metz explains that these evangelical virtues, perfectly embodied in the Jesus of the gospels, are not values for their own sake. For instance, choosing to be poor is not virtuous in itself but its virtue lies precisely in our choosing it as an act of solidarity with those who have no choice in the matter--as Jesus did. The same thing holds true, suggests Metz, with regard to chastity or celibacy. This too is a virtue only if we do it for the sake of solidarity with those who either have no one to share life with or those whose marriages have crumbled for a variety of reasons.

An important aspect in Metz's discussion on solidarity relates to the tension between universal and partisan (or particular) solidarity. To begin with, Metz has no illusion that this tension can ever be definitively resolved within history (cf. FHS, p.232). I have already cited evidence of Metz's position on solidarity from some of his unpublished essays, solidarity particularly with those people from the underside of history: his fellow soldiers, the Jewish victims, in short, all people to whom rightful active participation as subjects in the one history of humankind was denied. Metz insists that Christians may not hope for themselves except in solidarity with the "victims" of triumphant history of all times. The unfulfilled hopes of the suffering and the dead become the charge to us who are alive today.

The following highly representative statement by Metz (universal and partisan at once) is clearly a powerful critique of the modern-futuristic orientation concerning human togetherness. This critique is clearly based on the Christian hope in a transcendent God of the resurrection of the dead:

> Solidarity here should be understood in a strictly universal sense as a solidarity that has to justify itself not only with regard to the living and future generations, but also with regard to the dead. In this hope, then, the Christian does not primarily hope for himself--he also hopes for others and, in this hope, for himself. The hope of Christians in a God of the living and the dead and in the power of that God to raise men from the dead is a hope in a revolution for all men, including those who suffer and have suffered unjustly, those who have long been forgotten and even the dead (FHS, p.76; cf. also p.229).

Underlying this powerfully "revolutionary" critique of the one-dimensional modern attitude towards progress--which has a concept of history that differs from the historical outlook of the conquerors only in that it would replace the "victors" with the "victims" of progress--is unmistakably the same "eschatological proviso" that we saw at work in our discussion of Metz's relation to Marxism and critical theory. Thus the hope that underlies this solidarity with all humankind--but with a certain primacy towards the little ones in history--far from offering false and pacifying consolation, serves precisely as an activator and as the criterion for the type of action to be taken to truly humanize historical social structures. Hence Metz can claim: "This hope does not in any sense paralyze historical initiatives or the struggle for the state of all men as subjects. On the contrary, it acts as a guarantee for the criteria which men use again and again to oppose, in the presence of the accumulated sufferings of those who have been unjustly treated, the prevailing unjust structures and relationships" (FHS, p.76).

Although Metz advocates a universal solidarity with all humankind, he holds that this inclusiveness must never hinder us from a certain preferential solidarity with the needy and suffering, those who are prevented from becoming the real subjects of their history. His own understanding of human solidarity is based on a reading of history that is biased towards suffering humanity. This does not mean that he takes a narrow view of the world. On the contrary, it is the result of an analysis of "the world situation...and the global structures determining man's fate today" in the opening chapter of FHS, made in the light of "the Word of the God who calls all men to be subjects in his presence" (FHS, cf. p.234). We cannot accept "the theological truth that all men are created in the image of God" in isolation "from the deep inequalities which exist today in the world and make it impossible for so many men to become subjects" (FHS, p.234). It is also this doctrine of creation that provides theology with the means to unmask and criticize all ideologies of equality, seeking only private gain in a de facto world full of inequalities.

His analysis of the world situation has taught Metz that a worldwide perspective is required if Christians (and the church) are to live up to the full potential of the concept of human solidarity. For it is "only now, when people are more fully present to each other as men (not simply intellectually, but in their interdependence, suffering and need)," that we may discover all it implies to say all people are equal before their creator (FHS, p.234). He welcomes these developments and argues that theology may no longer avoid facing up to the challenges contained therein.

Metz is aware that there are dangers in, e.g., "the fundamental socialist notion of international solidarity with the working class and...the demand to achieve worldwide solidarity in this way," since in reality it represents to a large extent one of those "ideologies of equality" (FHS, pp.234f.). He urges Christians to simply uphold a genuine concept of solidarity against a false concept. For Metz, "The Christian praxis of solidarity will always be directed towards the imitation of Christ." It is not and may not pretend to be neutral in failing to be "partisan" in the sense of the "political" act of identifying with the least among us. What this means is that Christianity is "not able to remain neutral in the struggle for a worldwide solidarity for the sake of the needy and the underprivileged. It is compelled, with its emblem proclaiming that all men should become subjects in solidarity in the presence of God and its refusal to regard the already existing subject in society simply as the only valid religious subject, to take part in that struggle" (FHS, p.235).

Metz, however, not only criticizes the modern understanding and practice of solidarity in the name of a "Christian" solidarity; he also has some challenging questions for the de facto Christian church. "One particularly urgent question in this context is, for example, how the one world Church should react to its own class problem, that is, the great contrast between the Church of the North and that of the South? How should it reconcile this antithesis with its own understanding of itself as the one community at the Lord's table and the sign of eschatological unity?" (FHS, p.235).

The implied message is clear, especially if we recall what Metz has stressed not only throughout FHS but also and even more emphatically in his *The Emergent Church*, namely, "that the

Church will only become a Church in solidarity when it ceases to be a protectionist 'Church for the people' and becomes a real 'Church of the people'" (FHS, p.231). If we combine the two statements in view of his "imitation theology," according to which Christianity can only hope to become credible insofar as it embodies the contents of the gospel, then the message is this: unless the church repents of its past failings, when it largely internalized the social inequalities of the outside world, and unless it strives ever anew to be that united body of Christ that allows all members to play their rightful role, it will only reinforce the suspicion "that religion and the Church are pure superstructures of that society" (FHS, p.235).

A further comment with respect to the tension between universal and particular solidarity in Metz's thinking is in order here, insofar as it concerns the "means" for our engagement towards achieving solidarity. Metz does not accept that our rightful universal solidarity excuses us from partisan "political" commitment in solidarity with the disadvantaged. We will also recall Metz's saying that the Christian hope, on which our universal solidarity is based, always provides the "criteria" for how to oppose unjust structures and relationships. Although one could wish for a clearer and more detailed treatment of the means for partisan Christian engagement in the struggle for genuinely universal solidarity, the following closing statement about Christian solidarity from a worldwide perspective is courageous and significant:

> When Christianity takes its place in the movement towards the development of worldwide community it will be able to express, in and for that great community, **its understanding of a solidarity that is free from violence and hatred.** Love of one's enemies and opposition to violence and hatred do not, however, dispense Christianity from the need to struggle for the state when all men will be subjects. If it does not do this, it will fail in its task to be the home of hope in the God of the living and the dead who calls on all men to be subjects in his presence (FHS, p.236).

This quote seems to imply a criticism of the "militant," partial (i.e. class) solidarity of a Marxian type, that is willing to sacrifice the present generation and forget the dead for the sake of progress towards "a *Utopia*" that is really "a paradise of the conquerors" (FHS, cf. pp.236f., n.8). Metz's words imply that a Christian solidarity that wishes to include all humanity would be self-defeating if it left room for violence and hatred.

On other occasions, however, his comments on the subject of "means" for our Christian engagement in the struggle are more ambiguous. We witness this, for instance, in his short excursus on peacemaking, "The Christian's Participation in Political Peace Work," (ThW, pp.137-140), centered around "the eschatologically promised peace of Christ...open to all men and especially the poorest, the last" (p.137). Despite its sensitivity, the excursus is ambiguous when speaking about the realistic, gradual humanization of conflicts. Metz writes: "This realistic attitude towards peace helps us then to criticize war passionately and to prevent it from arising--not because every fight and every conflict could be avoided, but because modern war is seen to be an inhuman and totally inappropriate means of resolving conflict" (p.139). Depending on how the words "every fight and every conflict" are meant, this statement might still be seen as allowing for some instances of the conventional "just wars" to be acceptable, because they are supposedly unavoidable. And ultimately, is modern war rejected as "totally inappropriate" primarily because it is too ghastly to contemplate, or because the Prince of Peace has commanded love of all human beings, including the enemy?[95]

In *Unterbrechungen*, Metz argues in a peculiar fashion that Ernesto Cardenal's sanction of the revolution is legitimate, even in the face of the Sermon on the Mount with its specific love commandment. Metz admits that the relation between religion and revolution stands under the reservation of "the protest of love

---

[95] Arthur Cochrane formulates these alternative criteria poignantly, asking, in effect: Is it the **"fear of the Lord"** or merely the **"fear of the bomb"** that moves many people in our day to reject (especially nuclear) war as a means for conflict resolution? Cf. *The Mystery of Peace* (Elgin, IL: Brethren Press, 1986), in his introductory chapter.

against revolutionary violence," and asks "Can violence, seeing how completely contrary to love it appears to be, ever serve the cause of peacemaking?" He adds: "Christians stand here in a real dilemma..." Metz then elaborates an affirmative answer by splitting up the love command into its twofold structure of love of God and love of neighbour. Thus if love of God compels Christians to accept their own powerlessness and to suffer wrong, it is different with the love of neighbour: "As love of neighbour, however, it cannot accept the powerlessness and oppression of the 'least of the brothers', and seek to love God, as it were, with its back turned on the suffering ones" (my tr.).

Metz's exegesis turns into **eisegesis** when he paraphrases Matthew 5:39 as follows: "In the language of the Sermon on the Mount this means: It is expected of the Christian to turn the other cheek also, if someone strikes him (or her) on the right cheek; but he (or she) is not at liberty to admonish the other, who receives blows on the right cheek, to also offer the left one (cf. Mt.5:39)" (my tr.). One wonders where he gets the authority to overrule the words of the giver of this unequivocal "eschatological" love command. If Jesus demanded this absolute and universal love of his followers (many of whom definitely belonged to "the least of the brothers and sisters" in their community), how can we dispense our neighbour, even the victimized ones, from it? Was the oppressive situation perhaps less extreme in Jesus' day than in ours? Hardly![96]

Metz takes this further, however. For him, love and nonviolence are not necessarily inseparable. **"Because nonviolence can be masked cowardice and because it can bear the traits of opportunism, it cannot unambiguously identify the face of love. Love can--momentarily, and never intentionally, always of necessity--adopt the dark face of violence as an expression of desperation; [only] in that way, of course, can love always know how much it is injured by all**

---

[96] Cf. Martin Hengel, "'Politische Theologie' und neutestamentliche Zeitgeschichte," *Kerygma und Dogma* 18 (1972) pp.18-22.

violence." [97]   At the basis of this reasoning is the assumption
that, ultimately, the only real alternative to the sin of omission of
"allowing" our poor neighbours to suffer is to adopt as
permissible violent intervention on their behalf. But such an
assumption comes as a surprise ever since Mahatma Gandhi,
Martin Luther King and Dom Hélder Camara. What gives us
today the right to presume to decide whether people should
overcome suffering and oppression by means other than
nonviolent love, if it was the standard assumption throughout the
New Testament that such love should be the means, even if it led
to martyrdom? Thus, for instance, Rev. 12:11 (JB) says: "They
have triumphed over [the dragon, i.e. (in part at least) the
persecuting Roman empire] by the blood of the Lamb and by the
witness of their martyrdom, because even in the face of death
they would not cling to life." John Howard Yoder (to cite but
one theologian of the historic peace churches) concludes his
careful study of the New Testament, saying: **"A social style
characterized by the creation of a new community and the
rejection of violence of any kind is the theme of the New
Testament proclamation from beginning to end, from right to
left. The cross of Christ is the model of Christian social
efficacy, the power of God for those who believe. [And adds:]**
***Vicit agnus noster, eum sequamur.* Our Lamb has conquered;
him let us follow."** [98]

This latter position is one which Metz would mostly share.
Even in the same *Unterbrechungen* (p.23) he contends: **"In my
opinion, the only resistance that is admissible is the resistance
of practical discipleship, 'following after' the one who has
called the God of his way of life his and our 'Father'."** Or
again (p.27), he describes **"discipleship as a praxis,
which...begins with the assumption that the violent negation
of the individual, including the bourgeois individual, means**

[97] *Unterbrechungen* 1981, pp.76f.; my tr.

[98] John H. Yoder, *The Politics of Jesus. Vicit Agnus Noster*, (Grand
Rapids: Michigan: W.B. Eerdmans, 1972), p.250.

that barbarism is breaking out....And for this reason, precisely, [this practical discipleship] seeks a hate-free solidarity for everybody..." (my tr. and emph.).

What is perfectly clear is that Metz's concept of solidarity in nonviolent love (as he treats of it) has nothing whatever to do with a bland passivity. Rather, he expects there to be ongoing "conflict." The church will always need to exercise a critique of society through its proclamation, in word and in action, based on the foundational eschatological values and promises. In this regard, Christian solidarity is for Metz of a piece with his political theology in general. His political theology presupposes this solidarity, as the following comment shows: "'Political theology' is in the service of the Church's work of criticism. But this critical attitude does not spring from any spirit of resentment and fault-finding, but from a spirit of freedom and hope for all. It describes the way in which in our society faith seeks to keep both itself and its own universal future open for the sake of that society." (ThW, p.140).

In conclusion, Metz's theological category of Christian solidarity is entirely consistent with his treatment of memory and narrative, with which it is in fact inextricably intertwined for obvious reasons. It is also a fine blend of "internal" and "external" criticism of thought and social praxis in our times. It is a "dangerous" solidarity for the same reason that memory and narrative are described as dangerous. It is disturbing to unilinear evolutionary progress for the same reason that the new political theology is so profoundly disturbing to modern sociopolitical structures. Namely, it remembers and is motivated by the same eschatological story of Jesus Christ which forms the basis of memory and narrative and which is at the center of his entire political theology. Unsurprisingly, the proclamation and living out of such a Christian idea of solidarity in a world which can only strive forward--and thereby leaves most of humankind and all the dead behind--entails a dangerous and deeply disturbing "interruption."

6. Evolutionary Time versus Apocalyptic Time

Metz gives a great deal of attention to the problem intimated by these "contrasting" categories. Here we present a relatively simple summary. The essence of the problem is already implicitly present in all of his eschatology-centered political theology. His concern with the eschatological-apocalyptic dimension of theology appears to intensify somewhat in his later works. One of these bears the title *Unterbrechungen* (interruptions). This is Metz's most succinct definition of the essence and function of what Christian eschatology is all about. It "interrupts" the endless flow of sameness of the evolutionary concept of time.

In *Unterbrechungen*, Metz continues his dialogical "fruitful conflict" with the familiar modern ideologies, as well as further challenging Christian bourgeois religion to struggle against its tendency to become the mirror image of the surrounding society. The trump card here as before remains the counter-challenge of a radical praxis of an obedient discipleship (*Nachfolge*) of Jesus (cf. pp.24-28) as the only convincing answer or apologia open to Christianity. And this radical discipleship is of course precisely a matter of practicing the eschatological values of the kingdom of God inaugurated by Jesus Christ. This always was and remains a grand interruption amid the progress-oriented ways of the world.

In *Unterbrechungen*, Metz advocates a threefold "interruption." First, the ideals that are ingrained in a consumer society's attitude towards progress call for an "anthropological revolution."[99] Second, the book aims at interrupting a Christianity that stands under the spell of bourgeois religion. Christianity must cease being a superstructure of middle-class society and start interrupting and changing it, in the spirit of the

---

[99] Cf. Metz's "Vorwort" to *Unterbrechungen*; also EC, pp.34-47. In this Chapter, Metz advances the thesis that the Lord's Supper represents the bread of survival and is the anticipatory sign of this "anthropological revolution," advocated in these pages.

gospel, "from below," from the grass roots. Third, the conventional mode of theologizing, whether conservative or progressive, which shows signs of having capitulated to what Metz describes as an evolutionary concept of history or time, must be interrupted by an apocalyptic understanding of history.

In order to understand better what Metz means by these contrasting concepts, it will be helpful to look at what he considers to be the symptoms of the evolutionary conception of time which in his view holds sway so widely today, and see how he thinks a radical "interruption" through an apocalyptic concept of history can help us gain freedom from it. A couple of definitional statements from among the thirty-five theses on apocalyptic versus evolutionary philosophies of life (cf. FHS, pp.169-179) will be helpful here. Then we will briefly look at some of Metz's practical considerations on how the Christian life can serve as a redemptive interruption.

Metz contends that ours is "the age of timelessness." He illustrates this with the following example: "Catastrophes are reported on the radio in between pieces of music. The music continues to play, like the audible passage of time that moves forward inexorably and can be held back by nothing." This feeling is strangely coupled with our modern technological omnipotence which has given rise to "a cult of the makable--everything can be made." The shadow side of this absolute self-sufficiency is that "everything can be replaced."

We moderns have lost the ability to wait, because our increasing scientific and technological control of nature has resulted in a conception of "time as a continuous process which is empty and evolving towards infinity and in which everything is enclosed without grace. This understanding of reality excludes all expectation and therefore produces that fatalism that eats away man's soul." Or again: the present "fiction of time [is] an empty infinity, which is free of surprises and within which everyone and everything is enclosed without grace" (FHS, pp.170, 172). The "social signs" for this range from apathy to "unreflecting hatred;" from fatalism to fanaticism.

According to Metz, this perception of time and reality is given mythic status in the modern world: "its myth is evolution" (p.172). And neither Marxian thought nor Christian theology are exempt from the spell of this evolutionary consciousness. "Revolutionary consciousness in the grip of evolutionary consciousness: Marx, who praised revolutions as the locomotive of world history," says Metz's thesis XII. He cites Walter Benjamin as suggesting that revolutions, on the contrary, are the hand of the human race pulling the "emergency brake," because for Benjamin the great modern tragedy is that everything simply continues endlessly. As Metz sees it, "it is not utopias that can break the grip of timelessness, but the eschatological consciousness that does not let its apocalyptic sting be drawn by evolution" (p.175); the grip of timelessness can be forced open only by "the memory of the apocalyptic vision."

As an example in modern theology, where the apocalyptic idea of time has been sacrificed to an evolutionary timelessness, Metz points to R. Bultmann, who maintained that "the problem of mythical eschatology had been solved by the simple fact that Christ's parousia had not, as the New Testament expected, taken place, but that world history had continued and would--as every person of sound judgment knew--continue on its course" (p.173). This is symptomatic of what has happened widely to theology. It did not wish to be suspected of "unsound judgment" and hence it sought refuge in the embrace of historical evolutionism. As Metz sees it, this "evolutionary logic" is deadly, for it cannot conceive of "the God of the living and the dead, the God who does not let the past, the dead, rest in peace." It is worse than negating atheism (p.173).

The grip of this evolutionary, timeless history, Metz proposes, can and must be broken by the Jewish-Christian apocalyptic vision of the Bible, which is the very source of Christian theology. That vision firmly expects that God's messiah has and will continue to "interrupt" life in history. He observes further that the question that concerns Christian theology in its view of time and history is not about "the relationship between eschatology in the present and eschatology in the future...but rather of the relationship between an eschatological and an evolutionary consciousness of time." Put differently, the problem is not above all a question of "how much we have already been saved and to what extent have we not yet been saved;" rather it is: "How much time do we (still) have?" That is how eschatology asks about time in a "non-evolutionary" way (FHS, p.177).

This is, in Metz's view, the consciousness of the Bible and specifically of the gospel. It expects God to interrupt the course of history by the inbreaking of his kingdom. It is moreover the only time-consciousness that corresponds to the imitation of Christ. While an evolutionary reading of reality "paralyzes the imitation of Christ," the imminent and "passionate expectation of the day of the Lord" does not allow the following after Christ to be postponed. The time to follow after Christ in "a practical solidarity with the least of the brethren" (as described in the apocalyptic chapters in Matthew) is always now. An apocalyptic conception of time is not overcome or paralyzed with fear of disaster but is strengthened and driven by a hope that courageously faces persecution and cannot be stilled until the eschatological promises are realized (FHS, cf. pp.176f.).

The category of practical discipleship, so central to Metz's political theology, thus turns out to be conditionally related to an "apocalyptic vision" of time. As he puts it: "The Christian idea of imitation and the apocalyptic idea of imminent expectation belong together. It is not possible to imitate Jesus radically, that is, at the level of the roots of life, if 'the time is not shortened'. Jesus' call: 'Follow me!' and the call of Christians: 'Come, Lord Jesus!' are inseparable" (FHS, p.176). Such a consciousness is neither cowardly nor fanatical; it does not flee from but absorbs death and suffering: "Imitation in imminent expectation: this is an apocalyptic consciousness that does not cause, but rather accepts suffering--defying apathy and hatred" (p.176).

This, in short, is the kind of religion that Metz sums up in the single word, "interruption," which alone can break into the emptiness of endless evolutionary time. Whereas the latter has only room for activity that helps its forward march of progress, this "apocalyptic" religion resolutely pulls the emergency brake, not by violent revolution, but by making time for constructive acts that do not "pay." Its "first categories of interruption," according to Metz, are "love, solidarity, which...takes time, memory, which remembers not only what has succeeded, but also what has been destroyed, not only what has been achieved, but also what has been lost and in this way is turned against the victory of what has become and already exists. This is a dangerous memory. It saves the Christian continuum" (FHS, p.171).

But what is the bread on which this utterly simple yet so "revolutionary" time consciousness feeds? It is this that Metz discusses in his chapter, "Bread of Survival" in *The Emergent Church* (EC, pp.34-47). There he shows how in the "modern age" we have developed a Nietzschean "anthropology of domination" (p.35), which bears all the marks of a behaviour governed by the evolutionary time consciousness. "In it," says Metz, "man understands himself as a dominating, subjugating individual over against nature; his knowledge becomes, above all, knowledge via domination, and his praxis is one of exerting power over nature. In this dominating subjugation, in this activity of exploitation and reification, in this seizing power over nature, man's identity is formed. Man *is* by subjugating." By contrast, "all non-dominating human virtues such as gratitude and friendliness, the capacity for suffering and sympathy, grief and tenderness, recede into the background. They are deprived of social and cultural power or...they are entrusted to women, who are deprived of power anyway in this dominating male culture" (EC, p.35).

This anthropology based on subjugation, claims Metz, is by now permeating our sociocultural existence to the very roots, resulting in extreme egoism and a disconnectedness for human individuals, making it impossible for them to see or judge themselves from the standpoint of the victim (EC, pp.35f.). The church, he adds, is by no means exempt from this perception of reality, as it often speaks cynically of "so-called underdeveloped peoples,"--really "often a question of peoples whose cultures we have subjugated, devastated and exploited" in the process of colonialism in which the church was usually no innocent bystander (EC, p.36).

This critical analysis of the roots and consequences of the pervasive Western anthropology of subjugation, Metz assures us, does not intend to eliminate the natural sciences and large-scale technology in general. Rather, the intention is to humanize them by critically unmasking their anonymous pressure, their ethos, which is a kind of survival at all costs, be it on the individual or social, political or economic levels. Its long-term effects of apathy, resignation and fearful panic are all too evident today as "our dominating dreams of progress have collapsed into contagious fears of survival [overnight]" (EC, p.37). But what is the source of true life, since the approach in which "life only aims at survival" has evidently failed?

Metz's revolutionary answer to the anguished question "What does [modern] man live on?..." is a reference to the memory, central to the eucharistic community: "the passion, death, and resurrection of him who...said of himself: 'I am the bread of life'" (Jn 6:35, 48). The secret nourishment of the life offered by Jesus is, in turn, made evident when he says 'My food is to do the will of him who sent me' (Jn 4:34). There is a drastic contrast here to Nietzsche's will to power (EC, p.37). But Metz warns that a progress-oriented society will respond with hostility to the "ingestion" of the true "bread of life." Because the introduction of those banned qualities of "death, suffering, love, fear, and grief" into an atmosphere that knows only a striving for pure survival, represents a fantastic interruption. And the nourishment of the sacrament, properly understood, gives us precisely the power "in the midst of our life of domination...to take these [qualities] into ourselves," says Metz (EC, p.37).

In simplified terms, through the eucharistic "bread of life" we become a) "receptive to death," so that death is allowed its place in life, since we realize it is not death as such but the suppression of death that alienates us from ourselves; b) receptive "toward suffering and those who suffer," making us courageous toward suffering and even allowing the sufferings of others to become our own, and helping us to realize the scandal of "class oppositions between the rich and poor churches" that are supposed to be united around the one Lord's table; c) open to love, bringing it back into and thus provoking the prevailing economic "attitude of grasping and struggling for advantage" through the new "praxis of sharing among [our]selves and with others;" d) able again to mourn and to have fears and to become vulnerable or assailable, which again is a grave affront to a society in which mourning, melancholy and grief bear the stigma of being "an unbecoming, helpless sentimentality," since these emotions are thought to be useless to the march of progress (EC, cf. pp.37-41).

Such, then, are the values which, if believers allow them to be nursed back to health in themselves and their communities through re-enactment of the eucharistic vision and values, will precipitate a veritable "anthropological revolution." It amounts to nothing less than "a revolutionary formation process for a new subjectivity," liberating us not from poverty and misery, but from excessive wealth; not "from what we lack, but from our consumerism in which we are ultimately consuming our very selves" (EC, p.42). It is therefore a revolution that, although sharing certain aspirations with it, is fundamentally different from that revolution which Marx thought of as the locomotive of world history. This anthropological revolution, by reintroducing and bringing to power "the non-dominating virtues," serves as the emergency brake which interrupts the incessant flow of world history.

What concrete shape could this anthropological revolution take? According to Metz, it is to some extent embodied in the so-called "basic communities" of Latin America, which do "combine together prayer and political struggle, the Eucharist and work for liberation" (EC, p.46). This model could and should be emulated also in other parts of the world so that these committed grass roots communities, "nourished by the power of the Eucharist," would become the "motive force and the manifestation of the anthropological revolution" described here (EC, p.46). But Metz is well aware how impossible this challenge seems; that it looks as though we do not have enough time left to turn the deeply entrenched evolutionary direction of history around before humanity destroys itself. He is convinced, we will only dare to try if we have the sober apocalyptic Christian hope, that would still "plant a tree in my garden" (Martin Luther), even if we knew the world would end tomorrow (EC, pp.46f.).

Much of what we have discussed in the last three subsections (memory-narrative, solidarity, evolutionary versus apocalyptic time) finds a kind of summary in Metz's discussion of "discipleship of Jesus" in his debate with Walter Jens.[100] It becomes evident in this debate that Metz does not have in mind a literalist discipleship: "Imitation of Jesus is not [literal] imitation or admiration, but it is a way of opening oneself up to new situations in his 'spirit', in his 'direction'."[101] When he proceeds to illustrate what specific reactions true discipleship will provoke in specific situations, it is immediately clear that he is speaking about the same type of apocalyptic "interruptions" that he envisaged in his anthropological revolution discussed earlier. Thus he predicts:

> In times of nationalistic thinking, for example, it [discipleship] leads to the suspicion of national betrayal. In situations of a socially proclaimed racism, it becomes subject to the suspicion of betraying the race. And in times of outrageous social contrasts in the world, suspicion of class betrayal against the supposedly plausible interests of the 'haves'.

But when this happens, the Christian may draw strength from the example and experience of Jesus:

> Did not Jesus himself fall into the suspicion of being a traitor? Did not his way [of life] lead him to that? Was he not crucified as a traitor against apparently generally accepted values? His road, at the end of which everything--all dignity and all respectability, even of the powerless suffering

---

[100] Metz, "Warum ich Christ bin. Ein Brief an Walter Jens" (Why I am a Christian: a letter to Walter Jens), *Unterbrechungen*, pp.20-28.

[101] *Ibid.*, p.25, (my tr.): "Nachfolge Jesu ist nicht Imitation oder Bewunderung, sondern ein Sicheinlassen auf neue Situationen in seinem 'Geist', in seiner 'Richtung'."

love of solidarity--was taken from him, was the road of his obedience, with which he suffered of God [*an Gott litt*] and his [God's] powerlessness in the world.[102]

Metz adds that the obedience of our discipleship should have the same proportions as did Jesus' obedience to the will of the Father. And he warns that "The following [*Nachfolge*] of the obedient Jesus forbids us to confuse the mystery of God's will with the mystery-less will to preserve our familiar lifestyles; discipleship can also make us look like traitors to our bourgeois way of life."[103]

In summary, what is new here is that Metz boldly unmasks and confronts the modern rationalistic time consciousness. However, the means by which he proposes to break the tightening stranglehold of the evolutionary philosophy of life is the retelling and the re-enactment of the same dangerous memory that we have met before. The short formula for it is: the praxis of Christian discipleship, i.e., the unpretentious practical living of the central Christian virtues as these are rooted in the eucharistic memory.

---

[102] *Ibid.*, p.25f.; (my tr.): "In Zeiten nationalistischen Denkens z.B. führt sie [die Nachfolge] in den Verdacht der Ehrlosigkeit. In Situationen eines gesellschaftlich proklamierten Rassismus zieht sie den Verdacht des Rassenverrates auf sich. Und in Zeiten der himmelschreienden sozialen Gegensätze in der Welt den Verdacht des Klassenverrats an den vermeintlich plausiblen Interessen der Besitzenden."

Because, "War nicht Jesus selbst in den Geruch des Verräters geraten? Hatte ihn sein Weg nicht dorthin gebracht? Wurde er nicht als Verräter an scheinbar allgemein akzeptierten Werten gekreuzigt? Sein Weg, an dessen Ende ihm alles genommen war, auch jede Hoheit und jedes Ansehen ohnmächtig leidender solidarischer Liebe, war der Weg seines Gehorsams, mit dem er an Gott litt und dessen Ohnmacht in der Welt."

[103] *Ibid.*, p.26; (my tr.). In Metz's words, "Nachfolge des gehorsamen Jesus verbietet uns, das Geheimnis des Willens Gottes mit dem geheimnislosen Selbsterhaltungswillen der uns vertrauten Lebensformen zu verwechseln; sie kann auch uns wie Verräter an unserem bürgerlichen Leben aussehen lassen."

In conclusion, then, Metz's new political theology is a "practical fundamental theology," in the sense that for it "the discipleship of Jesus [is] the actual foundational praxis [*Begründungspraxis*] of Christianity."[104] His political theology is not a branch of theology as a whole, because all theology must prove its orthodoxy by orthopraxis and all theology must be "apologetic" theology--as Metz's political theology is from beginning to end--in the sense of giving an account about the Christian hope that is within its subjects.[105] Therefore, it lays claim to being a fundamental theology in that it attempts to address critically the challenges of modernity both inside and outside Christianity, always on the basis of the central eschatological promises contained in the life, death and resurrection of Jesus Christ--and in our practice of "imitating" it.

We have already answered to an extent some of the criticisms of Metz's theology as being too sporadic and not offering sufficiently detailed and concrete proposals for changing society. There is no need here for further elaboration on the matter, except to say that if he were to develop concrete plans for the remaking of society, he would in a sense become untrue to his own central theological principle, according to which Christianity stands under the eschatological proviso.

If a critique of the ethos of the new political theology as outlined above were to be warranted, viz. a lack of concreteness in ecclesiastical and social planning, it would have to come from a different angle than that from which Johns' objections come. For instance, Metz's increasing emphasis on the "apocalyptic" dimension (the prophetic, the critical, the role of "interrupting") in the Jewish-Christian tradition, while appropriate and even necessary as a corrective for countering the modern evolutionist consciousness, can hardly avoid incurring a deficit in regard to the "incarnational" dimension (the ontological, the cultic life of

---

[104] *Ibid.*, p.24; (my tr.): "...**die Nachfolge Jesu [ist] die eigentliche Begründungspraxis des Christentums...**" (my emph.).

[105] Cf. FHS, p.3, *et passim*; and "Apologetics," *op. cit.*

the church). In this regard, there may be a certain imbalance, even though the latter dimension is not by any means absent in his work. Certainly, in his earlier ThW, the incarnational dimension receives considerable emphasis, as does the institutional church. In his subsequent writings, the growing stress on religion as "interruption" finds a degree of counterbalance as he demonstrates the importance of the active memory and narrative of the Christian tradition, to be re-enacted in the celebration of the Lord's Supper and the praxis of Christian discipleship. To be sure, these categories are also marked as standing in the interruptive mode of being dangerous memory and narrative. But their interest is directed at the concrete church in its concrete surrounding world.

To add another critical observation, Metz's sometimes strident approach can result in superficial treatment of rather weighty theological issues that borders on the arbitrary (resulting in inconsistency within his own theology), as noted above in his interpretation of Jesus' love commandment and its relation to the use of violent strategies towards achieving social change. There can however be no doubt that as an "apologetic" theology before the modern secular age, and as a critique from the inside of the Christian church, Metz's new political theology is most impressive both in its sympathetic openness towards his audience and in the frankness with which he confesses the generally solid Christocentric foundation of his practical fundamental theology. It is to the credit of his theology that it does not pretend to know all the answers but rather shows an openness to learn--a posture perfectly suited to a theology centered on a Christology of discipleship, on being "on the road."

Further critical questions of the new political theology will arise at a later point in this book in connection with the evaluation of transcendental theology's political theological properties and performance (chapter 3), after assessing Rahner's theological work.

Having identified the major categories and the dynamics of Metz's new political theology in this chapter, the subsequent chapters will examine Rahner's transcendental and anthropological theology in order to establish the validity of the claim that Rahner's theology is also a political theology in a sense that approximates Metz's definition of the same.

Chapter 2

Characteristics and Dynamics of Rahner's Theology

The first chapter presented the central categories in Metz's political theology. The rest of this book will examine Rahner's transcendental and anthropological theology in the light of these categories. To ensure the openness of the investigation, it will be helpful and necessary to first develop some understanding for Rahner's theology in terms of the times in which it was written, what its motivation was and how it operates. In other words, before considering in some detail (in the third chapter) the claim that Rahner's theology may rightfully be considered a political theology, in this chapter we inquire into how his work relates to the historical setting in which it developed, and whether his methodology is at all congenial to producing a theology that might exhibit sensitivities to the sociocritical motif. Also, since the concepts of freedom and eschatology figure strongly in both the new political theology and transcendental theology, the chapter will end with a test run on the ethos of Rahner's method, with a brief discussion of how he applies it to the notions of freedom and eschatology.

This chapter, then, is of a more "theoretical" nature, while the next one will be concerned more with the actual political theological "content" and performance of Rahner's work. Even this "theoretical" discussion, however, in terms of depth and the choice of detail, is streamlined in the direction of our overall focus on political theology. Thus the deliberations here, in examining the characteristics and dynamics of Rahner's work, have as their primary goal to provide a theoretical foundation for our overall project, rather than to offer a comprehensive academic analysis of his methodology as such.

1. The Early Historical Context of Rahner's Theology

A proper understanding of any work of culture or scholarship is of course contingent upon the consideration of when it was produced and under what circumstances. Rahner's theology is no exception to this rule. An assessment of its political theological performance requires taking into account the historical context in which he wrote his theology.

Today, one takes for granted the world-directedness of the Catholic church, symbolized, for example, in the Second Vatican Council's decree on the church in the modern world. Similarly, it is now a matter of course that Catholicism embraces a multiplicity of theologies within one worldwide church, such as liberation theology, political theology, feminist theology, existentialist and transcendental theologies, to name only a few. And the historical-critical method is widely, if critically, applied by Catholic biblical scholars. The situation in the same church was, however, very different during the 1930s, when the first of Rahner's major scholarly works started to appear. The church had not yet transcended its narrow, defensive position,[1] described in the discussion of the modernist crisis above. Vatican II and what it stands for in terms of the renewal and modernization (in the

---

[1]Herbert Vorgrimler's characterization of the holder of the Catholic Chair of Philosophy in Freiburg in the 30's, Martin Honecker (who rejected Rahner's dissertation), as "a naive, narrow-minded representative of...rationalistic neo-scholasticism" surely had application beyond the immediate person so described. Cf. *Karl Rahner: His Life, Thought and Work*, E. Quinn, tr., (Montreal: Palm Pub., 1965), p.21.

sense of bringing its teaching and practice "up to date") of the "monolithic"[2] Catholic church lay still well in the future.

Karl Rahner's major role in making the watershed event of Vatican II possible through his incisive theological writings, as well as his achievements as a theological advisor during the council itself, are familiar.[3] It is simply quite unthinkable that anyone could have written an explicit "new political theology" in the pre-conciliar atmosphere within which Rahner began and lived a good part of his life, without having been silenced by the official Catholic church. The time of theological pluralism, and hence of "political theology" as such had not yet come.

Rahner had to begin somewhere else. He began working from the inside out, by what Metz calls "reintroducing" the human "subject" (in the broad sense) into "the dogmatic consciousness of scholastic theology."[4] Rahner seems to have moved as fast

---

[2] On a description of the Catholic church of that time as "monolithic," cf. n. #8 below.

[3] Karl Lehmann, "Karl Rahner," *Bilanz der Theologie im 20. Jahrhundert. Bahnbrechende Theologen,* H. Vorgrimler & R. Vander Gucht, eds., (Freiburg i.Br.: Herder, 1970), p.178. (Henceforth simply: *Bilanz.*) Lehmann claims: "There is no question that [Rahner] (along with others, of course) was decisively involved in the actual, i.e., long range preparation of the Second Vatican Council" (my tr.). For details substantiating this claim, cf. H. Vorgrimler, *Understanding Karl Rahner: An Introduction to His Life and Thought,* J. Bowden, tr., (N.Y: Crossroad, 1986), pp.94-109; pp.141-184. (From here on cited as: *Understanding Karl Rahner.*)

[4] J.B. Metz, "Karl Rahner--ein theologisches Leben. Theologie als mystische Biographie eines Christenmenschen heute," *Stimmen der Zeit* 192 (1974), pp.306f.; my tr. In the (expanded) graphic words of Metz: "Rahners Theologie hat 'das Subjekt' ins dogmatische Bewußtsein der Schultheologie erhoben. Sie hat es herausgebrochen aus dem Fels eines scholastischen Objektivismus, in den diese Schultheologie allenthalben eingeschlossen war." That this is not a matter of a trendy subjectivism of internalized, privatized feeling is clear from Metz's qualifying comment: "To insert the subject into dogmatic theology means therefore, among other things, to make the human being with his or her religious history of life and experience into an objective theme in dogmatics (again!); means to bring dogmatics into life and life into

as he could at introducing moderate changes into the theology
and life of his church. His principle for "modernizing"
theological teaching was to differentiate between the abiding
"nucleus" and its temporal "clothing," or between "what was
eternally valid [and] the historically conditioned" in the
formulations of dogmatic statements. While fully defending the
"nucleus" in a dogma, Rahner saw nothing sacrosanct in its
formulation. The latter can and has to be adapted to every age in
order to be understood.[5]

A good illustration of a "typical" reinterpretation by Rahner of
a troublesome dogma would be that on the (bodily) Assumption
of Mary. Even though he thought it pastorally untimely that this
dogma was promulgated by Pius XII (modern people had enough
problems of belief without adding relatively unimportant
dogmas), he accepted it and studied it for its true meaning. He
looked for its nucleus by examining its historical beginning and
development and found that although it originated from legends
of the fifth century, it had potential theological significance for
today in that it conveys a holistic view of the human being, of
spirit and body, and while applying to Mary in particular, it
"clearly indicates the **positive implications for all human beings**
to be found in this reference in dogma to the corporeality of
humanity and our consummation."[6]

---

dogmatics (again!); it means, in short, to reconcile dogmatics and the reality
of life [*Lebensgeschichte*] with one another, means finally to merge theological
doxography with mystical biography,...as the realization of scholastic theology
and its own systematics itself" (p.307; my tr.).

[5] Vorgrimler, *Understanding Karl Rahner*, p.91.

[6] *Ibid.*, p.89. Although the following insights will be met also in
connection with Rahner's theological method, it may be noted now already:
the first relates to his concern with the whole human being and the second to
his concern **with all humanity through the individual**. With regard to the
first, Vorgrimler says: "Rahner attempts to think in terms of a total view of
man, though governed by the spirit, in light of the possibility of the total
consummation of man in death, including his bodily consummation--now, and
that means not just at the last day." But, and this is the second point, Mary is

Rahner's attempts at renewal, coupled with frank criticism of his church, made him rather "unpopular" in official church circles from the early postwar years onward, and he remained so until his death, according to Herbert Vorgrimler.[7] Certain measures were taken against Rahner, such as prohibiting publication of certain of his writings (e.g., his study on Mariology, 1951); restriction of topics on which he could speak publicly (e.g., concelebration, 1954). In 1962, a preliminary censorship was imposed from Rome on all further writings by Rahner, aimed at

---

here seen not as "an individual case, but every dead person would be taken up by God into a state of consummation which also involved corporeality--though in an inconceivable and utterly changed form." This view can even summon biblical support (cf. Mt 27:52f.).

Incidentally, Rahner's examination of the doctrine of the "virgin birth" for its original intention yields a similar universal result: "the intention of all the ancient writers who had said anything about the virginity of Mary was certainly not to express the biological or anatomical aspects." Rather the nucleus or "religious and theological content" of "virginity" is that "a person is virgin who is wholly orientated on the fulfilment of the will of God, who is 'at God's disposal'." Vorgrimler adds: "Of course in this deeper sense married people, too, can be virgin." Besides, "with this solution Rahner succeeded in solving all the problems which arise from the mention in the Bible of the brothers of Jesus" (p.91).

[7] Herbert Vorgrimler, *Understanding Karl Rahner*, p.87. For details on "measures" taken against Rahner, cf. Vorgrimler's chapter, "Difficulties," pp.87-94.

Vorgrimler summarizes the situation in *Karl Rahner. Bilder eines Lebens*, P. Imhof & H. Biallowons, eds., (Benziger/Herder, 1985), p.50, saying: "Already from the late 1940s, Karl Rahner had drawn the attention of the church authorities to himself for two reasons: on the one hand, and precisely in order to make the church credible, he had laid bare its negative aspects using open, honest and even cutting language. On the other hand, he had tried to examine certain dogmas in order to determine, what in them belonged to the time-conditioned husk and what made up the transtemporal content, the kernel of a dogmatic formulation. In doing so, he had regularly translated these dogmas into the language of our time. These efforts towards the renewal of theology and the church were met with a variety of 'measures' from the church's authorities..." (my tr.).

silencing him just before the council began. This measure was silently dropped later.

Another aspect of Rahner's work during the postwar years is instructive about those times, and about his theologizing procedure in general. It relates to Rahner's development of a moral theology shortly after the war, in which the freedom and responsibility of individual Christians was strongly stressed. Closer analysis shows, according to Karl Neumann, that Rahner's motive for emphasizing individual ethical behaviour so strongly was to correct a particular imbalance. The situation around the middle of this century, was, on the one hand, that in the "monolithic church" with "totalitarian" tendencies, the individual Catholic Christian sought to hide behind a certain collectivist morality.[8] On the other hand, a certain brand of situation ethics, with a strong existentialist flavour, had just come into vogue, which allowed individuals to make their own rules for each occasion.

Rahner opposed both tendencies with equal vigour. In 1946, in an article, "The Individual in the Church," he spoke against an "ecclesiastical collectivism" in Catholicism in which the individual was assumed to have no Christian duties beyond willingly and obediently marching along with the "masses" of the church membership. In an excessively rules-oriented church, Rahner tried to carve out a space of freedom, of emancipation

---

[8] Karl Neumann, *Der Praxisbezug der Theologie bei Karl Rahner*, (Freiburg i.Br: Herder, 1980), p.376. What is meant by this "monolithic church" with "totalitarian" tendencies is likely the sort of self-righteous mentality Vorgrimler says Rahner encountered right after the war: "There were many in office who thought that a new beginning was quite superfluous. For them the church was the only authority to have remained intact in the Nazi barbarism, and they proudly flaunted this view. They thought nothing was necessary for rebuilding other than strict, uncritical obedience towards the hierarchy." Rahner countered this view with public lectures like "Church of Sinners" (1946), "Do not Stifle the Spirit" (1962), and others. *Understanding Karl Rahner*, p.88.

and responsibility for the individual Christian.[9]   Rahner also opposed the one-sided claims of situation ethics, that held it to be impossible to establish universally valid and abiding ethical norms, by his counter claim that such norms can be reached and that in fact ethical norms for the individual can exist only within a generally normative ethics.[10]

These examples illustrate that Rahner's writings are the result of a careful analysis of the situation--a point upon which Metz's political theology also places great emphasis. And on the basis of this analysis, Rahner evidently found that what was called for in an age where Christians fluctuated between the extremes of either an irresponsible "herd" mentality or an arbitrary situation ethics, was to raise consciousness towards a healthy balance between individual and communal freedom and obligation. Again, as in his reading of Mariology, Rahner discerned and preserved the "nucleus" in both existentialist situation ethics and ecclesiastical authority via generally binding norms.[11]

This clearly shows that Rahner employed careful situation analysis in his theology from early on. Nor was this analysis

---

[9] Neumann, *Ibid.*, cf. pp.377-378. Neumann mentions another essay on the topic, "On the Question of a Formal Existential Ethics" (1963; *Theological Investigations*, TI II, pp.217-234; the German text was published in 1955). The essays, "Freedom in the Church" and "The Dignity and Freedom of Man" (also in TI II) speak to this topic as well.

[10] *Loc. cit.*, n.10. In connection with situation ethics, Neumann mentions two essays, "Situationsethik und Sündenmystik," and "Der Apell an das Gewissen" which were published jointly in 1950 under the telling title: "Gefahren im heutigen Katholizismus."

[11] *Ibid.*, cf. p.378. Thus Neumann states: "...his aim is to insert the genuine kernel in situation ethics into Catholic moral theology: the existentialist ethics or individual ethics....There is a domain in the morality of the individual which cannot be encompassed by universal norms. The Church, with its universal laws, cannot preoccupy itself with this sphere. [However:] This domain is not therefore left to arbitrariness. There is a divine will-for-the-individual [*Individualwillen Gottes*], which is aimed precisely at the individual and which is therefore just as 'binding' as the universal norms. To insert this again into the Christian consciousness has been one of Rahner's most important goals from then (1946) until now" (my tr.).

merely a happenstance. That Rahner consciously used this method can be seen, for instance, in his 1954 lecture, "Theological Interpretation of the Position of Christians in the Modern World."[12]   In this lecture, as well as in his post-conciliar book, *The Shape of the Church to Come* (SCC),[13] his systematic approach is to ask: "Where do we stand?", "What are we to do?", and what will the church of the future be like? In light of this and other evidence, Leo O'Donovan clearly is correct in asserting that there is often more "history" in Rahner's very choice of lecture topics than his readers frequently realize. O'Donovan rightly adds: "there is always an emphasis [by Rahner] that adequate treatment of any questions must include fuller historical analysis."[14]

If Rahner has not, and perhaps could not have, produced a formal political theology in the pre-conciliar Catholic church (given its degree of openness), one should not therefore conclude that he did not concern himself with "practical theology" in a way that approximates the post-conciliar meaning of "praxis" (at least in the Metzian sense). Rahner initially conceived of and developed his "practical theology" as "pastoral theology" in the 1950s and 1960s. In it he challenged "the church as a whole in the midst of the world today," both officials and lay members, to accept the responsibility of giving a "concrete account of the

---

[12] K. Rahner, "A Theological Interpretation of the Position of Christians in the Modern World," *The Christian Commitment: Mission and Grace*, Vol. I, (London & Sydney: Sheed and Ward, 1963), pp.3-55. Lehmann comments on this 1954 public lecture: in it "each given situation in which Christians find themselves in any particular present moment is seen..., in principle, as fundamentally co-determining the realization of their salvation. Over the years this idea leads then to a new approach in practical theology as a scientific discipline in the framework of the theological subject areas" (*Bilanz*, p.173; my tr.).

[13] Karl Rahner, *The Shape of the Church to Come*, E. Quinn, tr., (N.Y: Seabury, 1974; German origl. 1972). About this booklet Neumann states: "The little volume, *Strukturwandel der Kirche*, is a succinct practical theology. After part one 'Where do we stand?' follows, as part two, 'What shall we do?'" (*op. cit.*, p.385, n.49; my tr.).

[14] Cf. n.#24 of the Introduction.

faith"[15] in that world. This notion is familiar to us from the work of Metz.

Lehmann characterizes Rahner's conception of "practical theology," as follows: a) in contrast to dogmatic ecclesiology, concerned with the essential, abiding nature of the church, practical theology is interested in the church insofar as it is a concrete historical entity whose practical principles of action for the realization of its message of salvation at every moment in history must be worked out through sociological and theological analysis; and b) the formal perspective of this practical theology is that all realization of the church's life is conditioned by the present moment. But what is indispensable for this practical theology is that the situation analysis should always be a careful **theological** analysis.[16] Metz, too, made his critical-affirmative evaluation of modern secularism "in the light of Catholic theology."

Metz's definition of "political theology" claims that all theology must necessarily be practical theology. Rahner offers a similar inclusive definition of "practical theology:" "Practical theology is that theological discipline which is concerned with the Church's self-actualisation here and now--both that which is and that which *ought* to be." And further on: "*Everything* is its subject-matter; i.e. the Church's self-realisation in all its dimensions...homiletics, catechetics, the study of mission and welfare work are partial fields within practical theology as

---

[15] Karl Lehmann, "Sorge um die praktische Theologie," *Bilanz*, pp.172-174. Quotes are from p.174. Lehmann gives here a succinct overview of the development and the chief characteristics of a "practical theology" in Rahner's work. He claims that Rahner shows an ongoing preoccupation with the relation between 'theory' and 'praxis' that found a first expression in his 1959 *Sendung und Gnade. Beiträge zur Pastoraltheologie.* The primary aim of this volume, says Lehmann, was to render "a service to praxis, and not least of all to its theory, that derived originally from the center of theology." These early scattered, actual and implicit elaborations, adds Lehmann, would subsequently take on more and more the caliber of a "scientific-theoretical conception of a pastoral theology" in the multi-volume *Handbuch der Pastoraltheologie,* published during the 1960s (my trs.).

[16] *Ibid.,* cf. p.174.

such...."[17]   Although this is a relatively late formulation, this perspective was evident in Rahner from the beginning, as Lehmann has observed.[18]

By way of summary, then, considering that much of Rahner's career falls chronologically well before the Catholic church allowed for a plurality in its theology, and before political theology in fact emerged with its terminology and categories, one may obviously not expect Rahner's work to resemble an explicit political theology. Nevertheless, Rahner's work has doubtlessly played an invaluable part in helping to open up the defensive church from the earlier part of this century and in making it receptive to a pluralism of theological expression. Thus the church came to abandon its ghetto mentality of self-preservation and turned instead into a true world church that exists for the salvation of this world. In view of this, the claim that it is largely due to Rahner's pioneering theological efforts that the new political theology (along with other theologies) became viable at all, may be justified.[19]

---

[17] Karl Rahner, "Practical Theology within the Totality of Theological Disciplines," TI IX, G. Harrison, tr., (N.Y: Herder & Herder, 1972), pp.102 and 104, respectively; italics are his.

[18] Lehmann, *Bilanz*, cf. pp.172f. On Rahner's preference to calling his "pastoral theology" "practical theology," cf. Vorgrimler, *Understanding Karl Rahner*, p.84.

[19] Lehmann, *Bilanz*, p.180. In this age of short memory, observes Lehmann, people are apt to overlook former achievements in order to declare them to have been "superseded." His comment with respect to the "charismatic" element in Rahner's theology is surely relevant also in regard to "political theology:" "One overlooks e.g. foundational statements concerning the charismatic dimension in Karl Rahner's current theological work, without remembering any more, that such talk, to a certain extent at least, is possible at all only because there have previously been the pioneering and at that time risky advancements by Rahner in this direction (summarizingly then: *The Dynamic Element in the Church*, (QD 12) Herder, 1964; German original, 1958)" (my tr.).

This assessment is confirmed by Vorgrimler when he says in Part II of his recent "biography" of Rahner, that everything he did and wrote shows "that Karl Rahner was deeply involved in serving people in the church, in church praxis and in the discipline of pastoral theology. He also understood his own activity as a dogmatic theologian primarily in terms of such practical service and as a service to those involved in practice."[20]

We get a good indication of how seriously Rahner took the development of a "systematic" practical theology from the relatively large number of writings he produced in the so-called area of "pastoral theology." While indeed all his theology is marked by a deep "pastoral" concern for the individual in modern society, his more explicitly pastoral theological work is found in *Mission and Grace* (1959) and the ambitious four-volume *Handbook of Pastoral Theology* (planned and produced from 1960 onward). According to Vorgrimler, "The *Handbook* was to cover two enormous areas: first, it was to show how the church had come to have its present form, and secondly, it was to show in detail what the church should really be about today (what is 'historically appropriate')."[21]   Again, this demonstrates unmistakably that Rahner was profoundly sensitive to the historical situation.

The following topics of Rahner's own important articles in the *Handbook* are instructive concerning his balanced approach between the dogmatic and the practical theology:

> on the foundation of pastoral theology as practical theology, the basic nature of the church,...the presence of God's communication of himself; on the vehicles of the church's self-realization, the whole church as subject, ministry and charisma, the members of the hierarchy, the sacraments (Vol.I); also, among others, on theological anthropology, the situation of the

---

[20] Vorgrimler, *Understanding Karl Rahner*, p.83.

[21] *Ibid.*, p.84.

church in the present (II.1); mission, church and world (II.2); times of life
(III); and the sacrament of penance and priestly training (Vol.IV).[22]

It is obvious, then, that even in Rahner's early work there is an
undeniable predisposition towards, if not an anticipation of, the
sort of theological dynamic that would be formalized in the "new
political theology" that was to emerge in the 1960s, above all in
the work of Metz, Rahner's student. In order to determine if
Rahner's theology can indeed be shown to be, and function as a
"new political theology," we now turn to his theological method.

2. Motivation, Characteristics and Dynamics of Rahner's Transcendental and Anthropological Methodology

The purpose of discussing Rahner's approach to theology in
this chapter is to demonstrate that his theological method is in
itself conducive toward meeting the requirements of the new
political theology, outlined above--or at least is not inherently
incompatible with them. A common designation of Rahner's
work is to call it a **transcendental** theology, because at the
center of it stands "the individual subject and his experience of
transcendence."[23] What this ultimately means can be seen from
Metz's interpretive summary of *Spirit in the World* (SW),
according to which Rahner

---

[22] *Ibid.*, pp.84f.

[23] Cf. Daniel Donovan, *op. cit.*, p.68. The author is, however, aware that
Rahner's is no one-sided transcendentalism, for he says in the same context:
"That the transcendental is always mediated through the historical follows
upon his understanding of man as spirit in the world."

define[s] man as that essence of absolute transcendence towards God **insofar as man in his understanding and interpretation of the world respectfully "preapprehends"** (*vorgreift*) **towards God.**[24]

As is evident from this statement, Rahner's understanding of the human person as essentially transcendental inevitably includes the equally essential **historical** dimension in the human subject by which the transcendental dimension is in fact always mediated.[25] We shall say more below about Rahner's conception and use of the "transcendental" and its dialectical relatedness to the historical aspect of reality.

Furthermore, Rahner's theology is also often called an **anthropological** theology, because he starts his reflections with the human person rather than with dogmas about God. While this describes his work accurately, misunderstanding will be avoided only if it is realized that its human-centeredness is in turn enveloped in a radical God-centeredness. The following comparative statement on the matter by Rahner is most explicit and instructive:

---

[24] J.B. Metz, "Foreword: An Essay on Karl Rahner," in Karl Rahner, *Spirit in the World* (SW), William Dych, tr., (N.Y: Herder & Herder, 1968), p.xvi (emph. added).

[25] On the inextricable relatedness between the "transcendental" and "historical" moments in Rahner's theological methodology, cf. Leo O'Donovan's extensive discussion, including his response to criticisms of the supposed one-sidedness of the transcendental method, "Orthopraxis and Theological Method in Karl Rahner," *op. cit.*, especially pp.48-52. (From here on this source is referred to as "Orthopraxis.")

For primary evidence, cf. Rahner's "Reflections on Methodology in Theology," TI XI, pp.68-114; particularly pp.84-101. For instance, he writes: "transcendental theology neither can nor will constitute theology as such, but is rather an element in it, because theology (...) [is] always intended to express that which is concrete and historical in its irreducibility, and in this must precisely render intelligible the fact that this concrete element in history can really affect man at the ultimate level of his existence and his subjectivity" (p.100).

As soon as man is understood as the being who is absolutely transcendent in respect of God, "anthropocentricity" and "theocentricity" in theology are not opposites but strictly one and the same thing, seen from two sides. Neither of the two aspects can be comprehended at all without the other. Thus, although anthropocentricity in theology is not the opposite of the strictest theocentricity, it is opposed to the idea that in theology man is one particular theme among others,...or that it is possible to say something about God theologically without thereby automatically saying something about man and vice versa; or that these two kinds of statements are connected with one another in respect of their object, but not in the process of knowing itself (TI IX, p.28.).

Although this statement clearly implies that for Rahner there is no purely "empirical" anthropology, separate from "theology," it also demonstrates how seriously Rahner takes the modern anthropocentric philosophy of life, discussed in chapter one.

This perspective of a "mutuality" between the human and the divine can be recognized already in Rahner's 1937 lectures in the area of philosophy of religion (published in German in 1941 and eventually translated under the title *Hearers of the Word*). Even though he writes there that "a positive [kerygmatic] theology" exists "not because man thinks but because God has spoken," Rahner hastens to add: "Nonetheless,...there would be no word of God were there no one who was at least intrinsically capable of hearing it." Furthermore, although in these lectures "human nature" is ultimately measured against the standard revealed in the God-man, the human being does not constitute a mere subordinate "part" of theology. In Rahner's words:

...there is a theological anthropology, not just in the specific or strict sense that God himself in his *Logos* reveals to man the ultimate structure of his own human essence, so that a theological anthropology is a part of the *content* of theology; but in the sense that an unreflective, perhaps naive, self-understanding by man is the condition of the possibility of theology at all.[26]

---

[26] Karl Rahner, *Hearers of the Word*, J.B. Metz, 2nd revised ed.; M. Richards, tr., (N.Y: Herder & Herder, 1963), p.168.

We will return to the theme of the unity-in-difference of "anthropology" and "theology" in Rahner's thought later on.

The concrete reason--which needs to be seen above all as a "pastoral-apologetic" reason[27] --why Rahner chose and developed a transcendental and anthropological method for his theology is found in his conviction that neoscholasticism with its "objectivist" dogmatic starting point in theology was highly inadequate in responding to the faith crisis in the modern world. After the vast changes in the modern horizon of thought,[28] this approach and its conceptualization from a different age had to seem alien to the way reality had come to be perceived and experienced in modern times. The modern shift from a cosmic world order to an anthropocentric order, revolving not around a fixed "cosmic" constellation but around the human subject, had to be addressed constructively by the gospel message of

---

[27] On the all-pervasive "pastoral" motif in Rahner, cf. K. Lehmann, *Rechenschaft*, p.49*:
"All efforts have as their only goal to introduce [the reader] as authentically as possible to the spirituality and thought of Karl Rahner in all its nuances, and--what is more important to Karl Rahner as well--to predispose the susceptible reader for his or her encounter with the living God: 'All subtle theology, all dogma, all Church law, all adaptation and all "No" of the Church, all institution, all office and all authority, all holy liturgy and all mission have as their single goal: faith, hope and love of God and humanity. All other plans and actions of the Church would become absurd and perverse, if they tried to circumvent this task and to seek only themselves'" (my tr.).
(Lehmann's quote is from Rahner's "Das Konzil--ein neuer Beginn," p.24f.) Lehmann has also commented on the subordinate role of Rahner's methodology from the very beginning in *Bilanz*, p.163.

[28] Among the weighty changes in the modern horizon of thought, diagnosed by Rahner in his situation analysis, are the following: "Pluralism in convictions, both philosophical and religious..., the great extension of man's knowledge in the present century, and the calcification of theological concepts, which have either changed in meaning in the course of history or no longer correspond to the changed conditions of life--these are, in Rahner's view, the three most important factors in the present crisis of faith." Karl-Heinz Weger, *Karl Rahner: An Introduction to his Theology*, D. Smith, tr., (N.Y: Seabury Press, 1980), pp.5 & 7.

Christianity. Since the conventional theological approach was not equal to the challenge, Christian theology would have to respond creatively by constructing a method that would allow it to make its age-old message intelligible to the modern human subject. In Rahner's own words: "we must say that today's *contemporary situation* demands a transcendental anthropological programme and method." Theology "*cannot* and must not return to the stage before modern philosophy's transcendental anthropological change of direction since Descartes, Kant, German Idealism...." Such a return to premodern times is not required by the profoundly atheistic tendency towards a self-absolutizing human autonomy in modern philosophy, because a closer look reveals that, paradoxically,

> ...this same philosophy is also most profoundly Christian..., for according to a radically Christian understanding man is not ultimately one factor in a cosmos of things,...but the subject on whose freedom as subject hangs the fate of the whole cosmos: otherwise salvation-history and profane history could have no cosmological significance, and Christological cosmology would be infantile concept-poetry (cf. TI IX, pp.38f.).

What follows from this affirmative-critical reading of the modern situation and its way of thinking, so reminiscent of Metz's response to modernity, is that Rahner does not conceive of the human subject, its freedom and Christology in isolation from the concrete process of humanity's history of self-realization, both as salvation history and profane history. This is obviously highly significant for the thesis of this book.

Before exploring further the structure and inherent dynamics of Rahner's theological method in relation to political theology, it is imperative to examine its religious and philosophical "roots" briefly. With respect to the religious roots, the importance of Rahner's "experience of God"[29] for his entire work can hardly be overemphasized, including his early foundational philosophical

---

[29] For Vorgrimler's comments on Rahner's personal Ignatian "experience of God," which is "foundational" for Rahner's "theological life," cf. chapter 3, n.#1.

works. Leo O'Donovan's interpretive comments are surely relevant here when he holds it to be unlikely that "the original inspiration" of Rahner's theology was "in the first place of a philosophical character." He suggests that even "Rahner's method...is not a theological method erected on a philosophical foundation but rather, from start to finish, a religiously inspired theology which has generated a philosophy within itself in order to foster its own further development."

The extent to which O'Donovan takes this assertion is apparent, when he argues that even Rahner's "philosophy of religion," *Hearers of the Word* (HW) ought to be seen in the light of this antecedent spirituality. This work is normally seen to be a text that "prepare[s] for, rather than presuppose[s], a possible revelation from the Lord of the history in which...we must look for a saving word if it is to be given;" an effort "to pursue a purely rational analysis of the conditions of possibility for a genuine revelation of God's own self;" or its "whole plan" is thought to be "analogous to the late neoscholastic apologetics which prepared its readers for recognizing a God who revealed his purposes through a divine legate who founded a church with its visible center in Rome."

While this interpretation of HW is "defensible" in some ways, O'Donovan continues,

> ...it can be more plausibly argued that the lectures comprising this book were not written as an explanatory argument to ground the intellectual conviction that human beings are open to a possible revealing word from God in their history. **Rather, an argument is developed from the lived conviction that God's word heard in history opens us to new clarity about the possibilities of our true natures.**

O'Donovan submits further that HW "does not prescind from faith in order to inquire into its foundations; instead it asks what understanding of reality (general ontology) and what correlative understanding of the human world (metaphysical anthropology) theology can appropriately use in its reflection on faith."

The plausibility of this reading of HW is reinforced not only by "the thrust of the text itself," but also by the considerable number of Rahner's explicitly spiritual-mystical publications by 1937, listed by O'Donovan. Moreover, even if Rahner had not yet developed his concept of the "supernatural existential" in the 1930s, many of his essays in the opening volumes of TI, the writer notes, "document Rahner's thesis that the world we experience is touched from the start by the gracious presence of God..."[30] We may sum up then by saying that we shall fail to grasp both the motive for creating and the dynamics of Rahner's transcendental and anthropological methodology, if we are not conscious of his concern for enabling the modern individual, every individual, to experience God in his or her everyday existence. Thus in an interview occasioned by the appearance of *Foundations of Christian Faith*, Rahner himself states most succinctly and unmistakably the central motive of all his theological efforts:

> I really only want to tell the reader something very simple. Human persons in every age, always and everywhere, whether they realize it and reflect upon it or not, are in relationship with the unutterable mystery of human life that we call God. Looking at Jesus Christ the crucified and risen one,

---

[30] "Orthopraxis," pp.57f.; my emphs.

Klaus Fischer argues similarly that HW is based on the Ignatian spirituality, which is not one of the "pure spirit" but an "incarnational" spirituality: "Naturally, a mysticism that derives ultimately from Ignatius, and thus also Rahner's [mysticism], can be no mysticism of the pure spirit. Instead, it is originally an incarnational mysticism, of seeking God in all things. It pushes towards overcoming a pure inwardness and is thus also for Rahner fundamentally a mysticism of 'Spirit in the World,' pushing beyond the modern subject-object split and even more beyond the supposed opposition between the transcendence of the spirit and history, which [opposition] it works to overcome." *Der Mensch als Geheimnis. Die Anthropologie Karl Rahners* (Freiburg i.Br: Herder, 2. Aufl. 1975), pp.29f.; my tr. Although the immediate reference of these words is to HW, Fischer, too, holds this spirituality to be the very foundation or origin of all Rahner's theology. (For his mention of the "Ignatian legacy" cf. p.47, n.45; and for his evidence of Rahner's personal experience of God, cf. p.31.)

we can have the hope that now in our present life, and finally after death, we will meet God as our own fulfillment.[31]

And precisely because Rahner was convinced that every individual experiences herself or himself to be fundamentally a being of transcendence, and because transcendentality is for him another name for God,[32] he has chosen to develop a transcendental theological method in order to help individuals to experience consciously or thematically what they inevitably experience already, if unconsciously and unthematically, by the mere fact of being human. It will become apparent presently why it matters to experience consciously what one already "knows" unreflexively.

In terms of its background in the history of modern philosophy, Rahner's transcendental and anthropological theology has a two-fold source.[33] It is rooted both in classical-Medieval, especially Thomistic, philosophy, and in modern philosophy, centered around the "idea of turning towards the subject," which originated with Descartes and was developed further by Kant.[34] Transcendental Thomism enabled Rahner to avoid certain shortcomings which he perceived in the Kantian epistemology in relation to the human subject. Before discussing the role of transcendental Thomism in Rahner's evaluation of, or conversation with modern philosophy, a few things need to be

---

[31] *Karl Rahner in Dialogue: Conversations and Interviews 1965-1982*, P. Imhof & H. Biallowons, eds.; H.D. Egan, tr., (N.Y: Crossroad, 1986), p.147 (henceforth: *Conversations*).

[32] Weger (*op. cit.*, p.31) says for instance: "Rahner regards transcendental experience and experience of God as materially the same." More will be said about this presently.

[33] On the "philosophical structures of [Rahner's] theology" being built on "these two [philosophical] traditions," cf. William V. Dych, "Theology in a New Key," *A World of Grace*, p.8.

[34] Weger, *op. cit.*, p.22.

understood about the conception of human transcendence in modern philosophy.

As for the relationship between Rahner's "philosophy of transcendence" and modern (especially Kantian) transcendental philosophy, we may limit ourselves to a simplified outline here, based on other more detailed discussions on the subject.[35] As stated earlier, modern philosophy is marked by its increased focus on the individual subject. But what does this mean? "This so-called 'turn to the subject' in modern philosophy," explains William V. Dych, "refers to the fact that in modern, transcendental philosophy it is the inquiring subject itself which has become the object of inquiry." In other words, in this "anthropocentric" rather than "cosmocentric" approach to reality, human existence provides the "basic paradigms" for understanding all reality, which is the reason why former impersonal categories give way to personal ones like "self-presence, freedom, transcendence" in speaking of "human existence" and reality generally.[36]

The modern philosophical inquiry into the subject reached a certain high point with Kant. Most centrally, it led Kant to his famous "question about the conditions of the possibility--or the presuppositions--that have to be present in the knowing subject for man to be able to know and judge at all, especially in cases where a datum of knowledge or judgment contains more than can be mediated by sense-perception" (Weger, p.23).

---

[35] The similarities and the differences between Kant's and Rahner's understandings of transcendent subjectivity and their correlative epistemologies are discussed in some detail, for instance, by Weger (*Ibid.*, pp.18-34) and by Francis Schüssler Fiorenza, "Introduction: Karl Rahner and the Kantian Problematic," Karl Rahner, *Spirit in the World*, W. Dych, tr., (N.Y: Herder & Herder, 1968), pp.xix-xlv.

A succinct and helpful introduction to Rahner's epistemology, although not explicitly contrasted to that of Kant, is found in William V. Dych, "Theology in a New Key," *op. cit.*, pp.1-16.

[36] Dych, "Theology in a New Key," *op. cit.*, pp.8f.

Simply put, it was Kant's view that the conditions that make knowledge in the human subject possible amount to an *a priori* transcendental structure in the subject. Kant held that "whatever object man observes, he automatically makes a connection between it and certain 'categories' or previously existing structures of his capacity to know. It is only in this way that it is possible for him to know and to judge." Kant called these judgments "synthetic judgments *a priori*," which form the context proper for his use of the concept "transcendental." He said: "'I call all knowledge that is concerned not with objects, but with our ways of knowing objects, insofar as [this is] possible, *a priori* transcendental'" (cited by Weger, p.23).

The 'transcendental' subjective structures, then, become to some extent separated from the "objective" reality to be known as they are "situated" within the knowing subjects. "Knowledge" in a sense is "trapped" in, or limited by, the always antecedent structures that constitute the knowing subjects. Thus all knowledge is modified by the subject's *a priori* mental construct, while "knowledge" of metaphysical entities is limited to an interhuman level. Kant was able to affirm an *a priori* "horizontal transcendentality" in the subject with respect to empirical data that allows all human beings to draw identical conclusions from the same data, because all have an *a priori* "transcendental" subjective structure of knowledge that functions alike in relation to the same type of empirical data.[37] However, he could not, on the basis of his understanding of the transcendentality of the human subject, affirm at the same time a "vertical transcendentality," i.e., a metaphysical knowledge of God.[38]

One might say crudely that Kant takes the human individual's transcendental subjectivity too seriously and not seriously enough at the same time. What this means will become apparent in the

---

[37] Weger, *op. cit.*, p.24.

[38] While Kant's critique of reason does not imply a denial of the existence of God, says Schüssler Fiorenza, "it appears...to have destroyed all theoretical knowledge of God" (cf. "The Kantian Problematic," pp.xxviiif.).

discussion of Rahner's treatment of the transcendental human subject. But if we may oversimplify here, it means that Kant seems to assign an exaggerated importance to human subjectivity in giving it too decisive a role in the process of "generating" ("horizontal") metaphysical knowledge--a role it cannot possibly fulfill on its own. Paradoxically, however, in so doing, Kant is in fact underrating the real potential of transcendental subjectivity, because in his too narrow and exclusive focus on the subject he fails to consider the true dimensions that belong to the person, thanks to his or her inextricable interconnectedness with "objective" reality, with all of reality, as a genuinely transcendent being.

Rahner follows the modern philosophical "turn to the subject" in making the reality of human existence the measure for understanding all of reality. He thereby agrees that the human subject is fundamentally a transcendental being, but has a conception of human transcendentality rather different from Kant's. The difference has to do, in part, with the fact that Rahner views the relationship between the *a priori* transcendental essence of the knowing subject and the object of knowledge differently than Kant. While in Kant's "synthetic judgments *a priori,*" the emphasis is clearly weighted in favour of the "previously existing structures" or mental "categories," Rahner is careful not to underemphasize the pole of "objective reality" in the process of knowing. In Rahner's epistemology, the transcendental "knowing" human subject is unavoidably grounded (or immersed) in the "objective" reality that is to be apprehended, while in Kant the same subject remains "suspended" in a rationalism of "pre-existent," "special innate idea[s]" or in "a special and immediate intuition"[39] which forms the condition

---

[39] *Ibid.* For a more detailed discussion of how Rahner's philosophy is really "both a revision and an assimilation of Kant's [critical] thought," cf. pp.xxxv-xlv; quote, p.xxxvii.

Concerning the matter of Rahner's "transcendental understanding of being," Schüssler Fiorenza states: "Since he is aware that all human knowledge is related to sense intuitions, he rejects those philosophical positions which

for grasping reality (which can, however, never be known "in itself"). While for Kant the "prevenient," special mental "categories" of knowledge in the subject form the "conditions for the possibility of knowing" objects, for Rahner these "conditions" consist above all in the actual existence of both the object to be known and the knowing subject. Thus Dych aptly says: "One must first be in existence before one can reflect on it" (calling this "a very important principle" in Rahner's thought).[40]

In order to understand what is meant by this Rahnerian "principle," one has to consider his background in transcendental Thomistic philosophy. Rahner's unique valuation of "objective" reality in relation to the transcendent human subject and his or her knowledge is rooted in that philosophy. What this involves concretely can be seen in Rahner's philosophical work, SW, which may be viewed as "a serious dialogue with Kant's critical philosophy." In that dialogue, according to Schüssler Fiorenza, Rahner examines Aquinas' *Summa Theologiae* I, 84, 7 "in the perspective of Kant's question concerning the possibility of metaphysics." The central question of the book is, therefore: "How is metaphysics possible when all human knowledge is necessarily referred to sensible intuition?" In Aquinas' thought, "All human knowledge occurs through a *conversio intellectus ad phantasma*."[41] In Rahner's own (if retrospective) interpretation of this key phrase in Aquinas' epistemology, this means the

---

maintain that a metaphysics of transcendence is possible because of a special innate idea or because of a specific and immediate intuition of a metaphysical object, be it an eternal truth or an objectively conceived absolute being." This would be to reduce God to the level of one "object" among many. "Instead he proposes a transcendental understanding of God, who is not known by man as an object of reality, **but as the principle of human knowledge and reality**" (emph. added). Schüssler Fiorenza then goes on to spell out briefly how "This fundamental nonobjective transcendental knowledge of God as the principle of knowledge and reality is central to Rahner's whole theology." (pp.xliiif.)

[40] Dych, *op. cit.*, p.3.

[41] Schüssler Fiorenza, "The Kantian Problematic," *op. cit.*, p.xxxvi.

human subject, as a spiritual being in the world, gains conscious self-possession (or, by extension, knowledge of any sort) strictly and exclusively through the **turning toward worldly reality.** But as Rahner himself says explicitly, the *conversio ad phantasmata* "may precisely not be translated as 'turning to the sensorial' but as 'turning toward history, toward [one's] free self-realization, toward fellow men and women'."[42]   (This would represent a corrective, then, to Schüssler Fiorenza's reading of the central phrase of SW as referring the subject to "sensible intuition" as a condition for self-knowledge; and also a "correction" of the Marechalian interpretation of transcendental Thomism, as Rahner notes in the same context.)

In Rahner's (Thomistic) understanding of human subjects, therefore, the condition for the possibility of knowledge by human persons is not an isolated "previous subjective structure" but the fact that they must **exist** precisely in active self-transcendence toward the interpersonal reality within history. The ultimate "presupposition" for this is, however, the "existence" of absolute being, i.e. absolute transcendence, which alone makes possible the conscious act of self-transcendence in the individual human subject. In the end, then, it is transcendence as such, which "exists objectively and independently of man" (Weger, pp.26f.), that forms the condition of the possibility of all transcendent activity in the subject. The human subject can only "exist" (i.e. transcend itself), as a result of a radical groundedness in, or orientation towards, absolute transcendence. The transcendental subject is both inseparable from and never identifiable with transcendence as such. As Weger states:

> Man participates in it and is directed towards it, but never in fact has it. Neither man's origin nor his destiny can, in Rahner's opinion, simply be the void, nothingness or nonbeing; nor can they be no more than a projection of the human spirit that is not in accordance with objective reality. Transcendence is reality and man is only a transcendental subject because this transcendence exists. In a word, this transcendence is another and more original name for God (Weger, p.27).

---

[42] My tr. For the German original, cf. n.#8 in the Conclusion.

This epistemological "presupposition" has a far-reaching significance in relation to the question of the metaphysical possibility of knowing God, for in every act of self-transcendence on the part of the subject by which self-knowledge is acquired, much more is involved. For when the subject knows itself as a finite being, Rahner says, it "has already transcended its finiteness. It has differentiated itself as finite from a subjectively and unthematically given horizon of possible objects that is of infinite breadth."[43]   In other words, the subject could not possibly be conscious of itself, know itself as an individual subject, if this horizon of absolute transcendence (another word for reality as such) against which to "project" itself did not (pre)exist. Therefore, the limitations of the particular subject not withstanding, all self-transcendence involved in human knowledge inevitably leads to God. That is why Rahner can say: "...man is a being of transcendence towards the holy and absolutely real mystery" (F, p.21; G, p.32), for "all other understanding, however clear it might appear, is grounded in this transcendence. All clear understanding is grounded in the darkness of God" (F, p.22; G, p.33).

If one considers this insight about all particular knowledge to be *ipso facto* rooted in and tend toward a consciousness of infinitely transcendent reality, and recalls at the same time Rahner's epistemological interpretation of *conversio ad phantasma* in the sense that all knowledge in the subject requires that it turn toward concrete innerhistorical reality, then it becomes evident that in his metaphysics of knowledge the human individual is seen both as a spirit of infinite transcendentality and a spirit of a radically concrete groundedness in space and time. As a result of its radically transcendent nature the human subject defies all efforts at giving it a proper definition (cf. F, p.216; G, p.215).

---

[43] Karl Rahner, *Foundations of Christian Faith*, (Seabury Press, 1978), p.20, my emph.; *Grundkurs des Glaubens*, (Freiburg i.Br., 1976, 1978), p.31. (From here on "F" and "G" in brackets stand for these two works, respectively.)

The transcendental subject in Rahner's epistemology, therefore, is seen to be more objectively concrete and more transcendent at the same time; it is taken less seriously and more seriously than in Kant. The reason for this is that for Rahner "knowledge of the knowing subject...is always at the same time a knowledge of the metaphysical--and therefore **in an objective sense transcendental**--structures of the object itself."[44]

It is noteworthy that while Rahner, in his "serious dialogue" with modern philosophy, is engaged in a consistently philosophical discussion, he makes no attempt to hide a "previous," personal "religious" conviction that God "exists." In other words, Rahner's "conversation" follows the logic of philosophy to its logical conclusion, but his conclusion is clearly influenced by his "experience of God" (which he in fact had prior to writing SW and HW). This experience of God enabled him to avoid short-circuiting his logical thought, because his mystical "knowledge" of God accompanied his philosophical thought and continued where the latter reached its limits. Weger also speaks to the importance of Rahner's 'experience of God' for his epistemology: "Again and again Rahner's anthropological approach breaks through and discloses new depths because of Rahner's own experience" (p.25).

The following comment by Daniel Donovan is instructive on how, in summary, transcendental Thomism enabled Rahner to adopt the central insights from the modern philosophy of transcendence, without however falling into the same pitfalls (e.g., with regards to possible metaphysical knowledge of God), when he says:

> [Rahner's] involvement...in the tradition of transcendental Thomism has been marked from the beginning by an acute sense of its religious possibilities. The turn to the subject in modern philosophy presented Christianity with a new cultural context within which and to which to speak. It also created an agonizing problem, because the understanding of many of its most influential representatives seemed to cut off the subject from God. **Transcendental Thomism attempted to follow the turn to the**

---

[44] Weger, *op. cit.*, p.26; emph. added.

subject while avoiding its negative religious implications. It understood human subjectivity as radical openness to the absolute mystery.[45]

To be sure, this human subjectivity of "radical openness to the absolute mystery" is seen by the same transcendental Thomism as radically "world-directed" and always "mediated through the historical," *a posteriori phantasmata*.

We have briefly presented the background of Rahner's philosophical concept of the transcendental human subject within the history of philosophy. We turn now to the practical possibilities of such a transcendental and anthropological approach to theology.

It will be remembered from the discussion of Rahner's "practical-pastoral theology" in the preceding section that in his opinion all theology must be "practical theology." By this he means above all that all theology is co-determined by the concrete historical situation in which it operates as it searches for truth--an understanding closely related to critical reason's concept of *praxis*. Part and parcel of this understanding of "practical theology" is Rahner's constant "pastoral" concern that underlies all his theological work (cited in his words in this section), namely, to help modern individuals to realize that they always stand before, or are on the way towards, an absolutely loving God, whether they are aware of it or not. And since the "situation" plays a vital role in the theological search for truth, Rahner, by extension, had to take very seriously the experience modern individuals have of their human existence in seeking to determine the ultimate meaning for their lives. For example, these individuals' experience of living in a highly scientific, technological and increasingly demystified[46] world necessarily

---

[45] Daniel Donovan, *op. cit.*, p.66; my emph.

[46] Rahner's resolute theological struggle against the "demystification" of the modern scientific age is attested by Metz, for example, in *Den Glauben lernen und lehren. Dank an Karl Rahner*, (Munich: Kösel, 1984). Cf. especially "Mystik, konkret" (p.20), and "Aufstand gegen die Geheimnislosigkeit der Moderne" (pp.21-23).

had to become a crucial factor as theology sought to impress upon them that they were actually and inevitably standing before a personally loving God. What method was needed, Rahner asked himself, in order to show human subjects living in this modern milieu that they can nevertheless have an "honest" faith[47] in God-as-absolute-mystery, if this God is apparently totally incompatible with the scientific world-view of today? How can one enable people who live in a demystified world to believe in the "ultimate mystery" without thereby reducing this "God" to being an "object" among objects?[48] It was Rahner's burden to make it plain to modern individuals that the seemingly unfathomable and distant mystery was really palpably near, nearer than anything else, and that they can and do experience this mystery constantly in life, that

> ...God himself as the abiding and holy mystery, as the incomprehensible ground of man's transcendent existence is not only the God of infinite

---

[47] The primary motive of Rahner's method consisted in what he calls the "responsibility to the man of today required of me, so that he might be soberly critical and a Christian at the same time." Cited by R. Kress, *A Rahner Handbook*, (Atlanta: John Knox Press, 1982), p.12.

This "pastoral" motivation can be found often in Rahner's writings and interviews, as well as in his prefaces to several major works. With respect to the latter, cf. Vorgrimler, *Understanding Karl Rahner*, p.78, citing words to that effect from the Preface to Vol. I of *Sacramentum Mundi*. The same kind of practical considerations (to reach and equip the working priest, the student priest, or "the much-cited lay person with his often urgent theological questions," cf. p.80) can be found as Rahner's leading motivation for embarking on such major works as, e.g., the *Quaestiones Disputatae*, or his *Theological Investigations* series. (On the latter, cf. TI I, p.xxii; STh I, p.8.)

[48] Rahner deliberately tries to avoid the mistake he perceived in R. Bultmann's otherwise legitimate and necessary demythologization efforts, in which the latter ran the risk of overlooking the genuinely mystical dimension in the modern individual and thus appeared to be "remythologizing" this "transcendent" individual by "confin[ing] him within the single dimension of the existential." Cf. K. Rahner and H. Vorgrimler, "Demythologization," *Concise Theological Dictionary*, (London: Burns & Oates, 2nd. ed., 1983), pp.118f.

distance, but also wants to be the God of absolute closeness in a true self-communication, and he is present in this way in the spiritual depths of our existence as well as in the concreteness of our corporeal history (F, p.137).

What was needed in order to achieve this, Rahner was convinced, was a transcendental and anthropological methodology, based squarely upon the personal, yet universal, experience of modern human existence. This method would enable the theologian to analyze the modern individual's experience of his or her existence in a way which would prepare him or her for an encounter with God in the things of everyday life, similar to the way in which Rahner himself had been taught by "Ignatian spirituality" to find God in all things.[49] In concrete, practical terms, how did Rahner elaborate his method from this modern experience of human existence? We have already discussed his understanding of human transcendentality in general terms as it relates to the modern transcendental philosophy and to transcendental Thomism. However, a closer analysis of how his metaphysical anthropology is rooted in concrete human experience is still required for a fuller understanding of his methodology.

It is imperative to realize from the beginning that the category "experience" at the center of the transcendental and anthropological method is of a specialized, technical nature--though it is inevitably related to all particular, categorial human experiences. It is the *a priori* experience of human

---

[49] Vorgrimler gives some excerpts from Rahner's writings in which Rahner professes to have experienced God directly. Vorgrimler adds, this "experience of God" can happen to anyone, "in the midst of specific, ordinary everyday experiences, in particular events in which people suddenly find themselves torn away from dealing with quite ordinary matters and tasks and thrown back on themselves; they can no longer escape, yet feel an inward motive force which comes from elsewhere, supporting and urging on." Then follows the lengthy statement from Rahner, which offers examples like aloneness, responsibility, experience of personal love, facing death, *Angst*, etc., and concludes: "this single basic experience of man is present in a thousand different forms, and in this experience it is borne in upon him that his existence is open to the inconceivable mystery." *Understanding Karl Rahner*, pp.11-14.

existence itself, which is the presupposition for all *a posteriori* experiences. The former is not to be identified with the latter, although it can only be actualized through it. The category refers, in simplified terms, to the experience of that dimension within the subject which enables it to consciously experience itself or empirical objects (knowledge); to experience the ability to shape its environment and itself (freedom); and to experience that the categorial reality of time and space cannot contain the conscious subject completely (transcendence). This primary experience is not the result of the person's "association with the world of experience" but "precedes that association;" it is "not constituted by the *a posteriori* reality and categorial experiences and objectivizations," but rather it is the presupposition for the person's human knowledge and free activity and for experiencing one's everyday existence (cf. Weger, pp.18f.).

The viability of Rahner's methodology depended on whether or not this primary experience could indeed be shown to be present in all human beings across educational, cultural, religious and historical boundaries. To demonstrate this, Rahner approached the matter from several angles. Hence it will be helpful to discuss briefly how, in practice, Rahner develops a universalizable philosophy of human existence, and what role he assigns in it to the *a priori* experience by the subject.

1. Rahner, in his epistemological analysis of the human subject, established that it never simply and purely experiences the world of objects, but also experiences always and at the same time itself. The self-awareness, present in all our knowledge of categorial reality, may be indirect or "unreflective," but it is always given as the consciousness that is indispensable for empirical knowledge. This self-presence is analogous to the light which is both the condition for seeing the object of our attention and is "seen" at the same time, whether we think about it or not (cf. Weger, 29).

Knowledge, therefore, is a two-way process: "In knowing an object the subject is aware of itself; knowledge encompasses both the knower and the known" (Dych, 5). It is this consciousness of the self, implicit in all our knowledge, that makes us capable of being "present to ourselves" and certifies our human existence to be a "spiritual existence." Likewise, in this residual (self)-consciousness that accompanies all concrete knowledge, we have clear evidence that we cannot be totally contained by the world of things. In the experience of our constant "self-presence," even as we become conscious of a world of objects, we experience our conscious subjectivity or spiritual personhood.

2. Next, we learn about our subjectivity from a different, if analogous, angle; we know ourselves to be "determined" by certain genetic and environmental factors. We do not experience ourselves at all as only a product of our own making, but **also** very much as "the product of what is not ourselves." Still, in spite of these determining factors, "we experience ourselves as responsible for ourselves" (Dych, p.6). We realize that we are subjects of radical freedom, including the freedom to shape our physical and social environments and ourselves. This fundamental freedom, which goes always "beyond" the ability to decide to do this or that particular act, is the "condition" in the subject for being able to make particular choices. As with our *a priori* spiritual self-presence, so this experience of the *a priori,* enabling freedom in us tells us that our existence as free subjects transcends the tangible world with its natural laws and scientific explanations.

3. The experience of ourselves as self-present, free subjects naturally raises the question: "Where, then, do we come from, if not entirely from the world, and where does our transcendence take us, if the world does not entirely define our limits?" Dych continues: "All the knowledge we acquire always gives rise to further questions. When pushed far enough, all of our clarities trail off into obscurity; the chain of scientific logic hangs loose at both ends" (p.6). As human questioners, therefore, in following this open-ended logic of our knowledge, we will ultimately experience our basic transcendentality in the fact that we do not only have questions, but we are, each of us, a question that leads us towards an "obvious" horizon which, nevertheless, we can

never reach or embrace.[50] This ongoing questioning brings us finally face to face with the incomprehensible "known unknown" (Dych, p.6). Likewise, the realization that comes with the experience of our inescapable freedom, a freedom to realize or refuse to realize ourselves in a world of determinants, raises in us the question of how far this transcendent freedom takes us. Does our unavoidable freedom bring with it responsibilities only to ourselves and for the present, or are we responsible to someone else, and do our decisions have a meaning that endures beyond the limits of time? These and other questions, which we experience due to our essential self-presence and freedom, demonstrate to us that we also experience ourselves as fundamentally transcendent beings, that we transcend ourselves and our temporal existential situation.

As Rahner's strictly anthropological analysis of our experience shows, we discover that as self-conscious, free and transcendent subjects, we elude any attempts at adequate definition. We experience ourselves as being ultimately a mystery to ourselves.

This brief outline of Rahner's philosophical analysis of human existence, on the practical level of human experience which is universally accessible to human beings, confirms the accuracy of his understanding of human transcendentality as presented earlier. What is significant in this is that these aspects, all of which

---

[50] Anne Carr, in her sketch of Rahner's transcendental method, also elaborated on the concept of subjectivity as radical human questioning as follows: "The experience in which we become conscious of ourselves as selves is one of radical questioning....We know ourselves as the product of numerous forces outside ourselves and yet as more than the sum total of ethnic origins, parental relationships, or social backgrounds. Our questioning of each single explanation we can find leads us to a place in which we stand outside ourselves. In opening ourselves to the unlimited horizons of such questioning, we have already transcended or gone beyond ourselves, and beyond the limits of any particular question or explanation. In a sense, this power of transcendence is infinite, never-ending in our experience...The power of radical questioning, which is not so much something we have as it is that which we *are*, is the meaning of subjectivity." A. Carr, "Starting with the Human," *A World of Grace, op. cit.*, pp.19f.

confirm the human subject as essential transcendentality, are comprehensible to the subject not as something imposed from outside, but as its own innermost experience. Obviously, most individuals usually do not "thematically" think about the fact that their every conscious experience or free action (no matter how trivial) is also and unavoidably an experience of their basic transcendental, "spiritual" nature, which infinitely transcends all categorial experience. Nevertheless, Rahner has shown, everybody has this primary experience of this *a priori* transcendentality, even if it is only on the nonconceptual, nonexplicit, nonsystematized and nonreflective level of knowing (cf. Weger, pp.27f.). This universal *a priori* experience of being a fundamentally self-transcendent subjectivity (as made evident through self-presence or freedom) becomes for Rahner the most central mark of our humanness. This is the subject's "original" experience of its own existence, original in that it is not injected (or "indoctrinated") by words or lessons from the outside world but rather springs up from its own deepest depths (cf. Dych p.4). And this "original" experience or knowledge can be raised to the reflective, conceptual, systematic, thematic level of communication. In fact, since we are not isolated but "social beings," there is something of an "innate" need to conceptualize and communicate our "original" experience to others. However, and this underlines our basic transcendentality once more, our primary or original experience or knowledge can never be fully captured and communicated in our conceptualization of it. A simple example helps to illustrate the point. Everybody knows basically about sorrow, joy or happiness, because all have experienced it in life. But if we try to explain its meaning in words, it soon becomes evident how inadequate these words are for recapturing the actual experience itself, because the experience, all experience, eludes us into the sphere of absolute transcendence.[51]

---

[51] Weger (*op. cit.*, pp.29f.) says on the incongruous relationship between primary experience and its conceptualization that, according to Rahner, "there can be reflection about experience at the transcendental level of objective

Some practical results flow from Rahner's transcendental and anthropological methodology. First, with his philosophical method he created a universally intelligible language for theology as a tool for "translating" the theological message (with its claim to universal validity) into modern thought. Beginning with the individual's own experience of human existence, and interpreting it strictly within the horizon and language of metaphysical anthropology--universally understandable--Rahner was able to demonstrate convincingly the subject's essential and inextricable relatedness to the mystery of absolute transcendence. Philosophy, strictly speaking, is not competent to say exactly what significance the absolute mystery has, as experienced by the subject at its very core as an unanswerable question. Metaphysical anthropology can only tell the subject that, in virtue of its own infinite transcendentality, it not only *has* but fundamentally *is* an unanswerable question to itself. If there is to be an attempt at answering this question, for good or for ill, it will need to come from Christian faith and theology. But the philosophical analysis can serve as the "empirical" framework upon which theology can base its proposed answers to the human question.

Second, if theology could demonstrate that this absolute mystery as such is not only (as our experience of absolute transcendence seems to suggest) unmeasurably far off but actually, intimately near, that it is not a void or nothingness or a mere human projection (as rationalist philosophy would claim), but is in fact the ever greater God of Christian faith and theology, then this metaphysical-anthropological method would provide a great advantage indeed. For then the modern individual might become convinced of the veracity and salvific meaning of the Christian message not from an extrinsic indoctrination via the communication of a system of doctrinal concepts

---

knowledge; and that that experience can be presented systematically and conceptually and even made an explicit objective of knowledge; but that this can only take place within the transcendental sphere, and that sphere can never be systematic." Cf. W.V. Dych, *op. cit.*, pp.4f., making the same point.

(neoscholasticism), but from the more immediate intrinsic experience of his or her own existence as a transcendent mystery.

The main goal of Rahner's transcendental theology was precisely to "thematize" for (and with) modern individuals what they already experience unthematically; to tell readers that "human persons in every age, always and everywhere, whether they realize it and reflect upon it or not, are in relationship with the unutterable mystery of human life that we call God."

Third, the metaphysical anthropological approach to theology offers the advantage that even the reason why it is important for the subject to reflect upon and acquire more understanding of the absolute mystery is inherently obvious and thus need not be artificially superimposed. Since the transcendental subject (on account of its profoundly mysterious nature) is deeply intertwined with the absolute mystery, it simply cannot truly know itself without considering this relatedness to the mystery traditionally called God. And since it is a constituent characteristic of self-conscious subjectivity to want to "know" itself more fully, it follows naturally that it should want to reflect on its relation to God. Nor is such an endeavour to consciously clarify a person's relation to the transcendental mystery beneficial for the individual alone. It has also a decidedly social or public significance.[52]

----

[52] Vorgrimler explains why Rahner felt compelled to "disclose to others these possibilities of experiencing God in the everyday," in spite of the fact that he believed everybody experiences God anyway, if "unreflexively": "Because...someone who does not recognize the innermost nearness of the incomprehensible mystery...does not know himself. He does not grasp his own greatness and significance, the call of the infinite mystery, and therefore is threatened by the danger of failing to recognize the true magnitude and significance of his fellow human beings--in whom alone the infinite mystery dwells. Not to have such self-knowledge would go against the innermost tendency of every human being. Everyone must know who he or she ultimately is."

Furthermore, the explanation continues, if one fails to consider that "the ultimate determination of humanity" is the "way into the incomprehensible mystery:" "to remain once and for all in the presence of the infinite mystery is the meaning of every human life," this will have incalculable consequences for the way we treat and relate to others. Seeing or failing to see "people in

Fourth--almost redundant--the transcendental and anthropological methodology provides a very "natural" means of relating to the empirical human sciences, sociology and anthropology, genetics and the theory of evolution, for instance. Rahner's method allows him both to critique radically the positivistic conceptualizations about the human subject in these sciences and, simultaneously, to take fully seriously--more seriously, because more holistically, than the sciences are taking it--all genuine scientific discoveries about the human individual and society. In contrast to the human sciences, this definition of human beings in terms of an essential transcendentality rules out a positivistic view of human individuals. For no matter how clearly they "grasp" themselves, they always know themselves to be rooted in and tending towards the absolute mystery of all being. Accordingly, Rahner actually defines the human being as the undefinable being which possesses itself in consciousness. In his words: "He is, as we could readily 'define' him, that indefinability which is conscious of itself" (F, p.216; G, p.215). In other words, while the empirical sciences might define the human subject as a being that *has* self-conscious knowledge and freedom the same way it has other properties, transcendental anthropology posits rather that the person is *a priori* self-presence, freedom and transcendence personified. Rahner's methodology is able to do all this because in its view of the human being it represents an "open," "inclusive anthropology," and not an abstract, self-enclosed, "exclusive anthropology," as some critics have alleged, according to O'Donovan.[53]

---

this way would also have immediate political and social consequences. Wherever this ultimate greatness and destiny of the individual is not seen and acknowledged, there is a danger that the individual may be eliminated as being not productive enough, not important and valuable enough, unusable and useless; or that a still 'usable' person may be 'used' as mere material for 'higher' ends, for example a happier future" (*Understanding Karl Rahner*, pp.14f.).

[53] Cf. Leo O'Donovan, especially his subsection titled "An Open Humanity," in "Orthopraxis," pp.52-56.

Fifth, Rahner's method automatically takes into account the concrete, existential and historical dimensions of the human individual. This tendency, of course, unavoidably follows upon the method's centeredness around the category of **human experience** in both its *a priori* and its *a posteriori* aspects. While we have at times underlined more the importance of the *a priori* aspect in the experience of human transcendentality, as the condition for the possibility of metaphysical knowledge, in actuality the two aspects of human experience might fairly be said to receive equal emphasis in Rahner's metaphysical anthropology; the two aspects actually condition each other mutually. This was already pointed out in passing, and is obvious from Rahner's roots in Aquinas, who "teaches that all of our knowledge is rooted in our experience of the finite world" (Dych, p.8).

This insight contains far-reaching consequences for the importance of theology to the world of categorial or historical reality. Rahner himself put it this way:

> What is decisive for a correct interpretation of Christianity is this: being in the world, being in time and being in history are aspects of man which he does not merely *have* alongside of and in addition to his free personhood. They are rather aspects of the free subjectivity of a person as such. Man is not merely also a biological and social organism who exists in time with these characteristics. Rather his subjectivity and his free, personal self-interpretation take place precisely in and through his being in the world, time and history. The question of salvation cannot be answered by bypassing man's historicity and his social nature. Transcendentality and freedom are realized in history. (F, p.40; G, p.51).

This quote clearly confirms Leo O'Donovan's claim that Rahner uses a "twofold method" in which the transcendental and historical moments are "dialectically related."

Clearly, then, the various "aspects" of the human individual's innerworldly and historical existence belong among those "general structures" or "existentials" that are constitutive of human subjectivity as much as the "existentials" of self-presence, freedom, and transcendentality. The decisive value of the subject's historicity is obvious from the fact that our human freedom (to be discussed below), like our self-conscious transcendence, can only be realized in the context of categorial history. Thus Rahner says of the human being that it "as a personal being of transcendence and of freedom is also and at the same time a being in the world, in time and in history" (F, p.40; G, p.51). And vice versa: "without prejudice to the mediation of this self-possession by the experience of sense objects in time and space, this subject is fundamentally and by its very nature pure openness for absolutely everything, for being as such" (F, pp.19f.; G, p.31). Thus Rahner's framework for defining essential human nature may fittingly be called a "systematic polarity between transcendental and categorical experience."[54]

In attempting to outline Rahner's transcendental and anthropological methodology, and list the more obvious results that spring from it, we described our findings mainly in the language and categories of his philosophical anthropology. For Rahner, however, the use of philosophical thought is never an end in itself but always "an intermediate step." Its role is strictly to discover and interpret the essential structures or "existentials" in the human subject which are universally applicable and universally "verifiable" by fundamental human experience. These existentials, therefore, and the language describing them, will provide "the philosophical foundation upon which theology can build" (Dych, pp.6, 7). Obviously, Rahner's philosophical analysis of the subject's experience of its human existence spelled out here was intended to be such a "philosophical foundation" for his work of theology. But while his analysis is carried out consistently and rigorously in the terms of a philosophical or metaphysical anthropology, it is very difficult not to sense alongside it his own transcendental and anthropological theology with its source of convictions deeply

---

[54] Anne Carr, *op. cit.*, pp.23f.

rooted in what was referred to already as his (Ignatian) "experience of God."[55]

This is perhaps not surprising in view of the fact that his "spiritual" booklet, *Encounters with Silence*, and his "philosophy of religion," HW, originated at the same time (1937). And while in HW he explored the conditions under which the human subject might hear a revelatory Word from God, **if God in his absolute, sovereign freedom were to speak such a Word in our history,**[56] in the spiritual booklet Rahner categorically asserts that God has indeed spoken such a word. Thus after pleading with God: "You must make Your infinite word finite, if I am to be spared this feeling of terror at Your Infinity...just say that You love me....But don't say it in Your divine language...say it rather in *my* language...," he says rejoicingly: "O Infinite God, You have actually willed to speak such a word!...You have come to me in a human word. For You, the Infinite, are the God of Our Lord Jesus Christ. He has spoken to us in human language."[57] This statement from one of Rahner's "pious books" illustrates clearly that underlying (or accompanying) his rigorous

---

[55] Cf. "Ignatius of Loyola Speaks to a Modern Jesuit," Karl Rahner and Paul Imhof, *Ignatius of Loyola*, R. Ockenden, tr., (London: Collins, 1979), pp.11-38, especially his opening words about having experienced "God's own self," p.12; cf. also n.#30 in this chapter.

[56] G.A. McCool, for instance, gives this interpretive summary of HW: "If, then, God should determine to communicate His personal revelation to man, he would be compelled to do so by means of some sensible symbol, a 'word', a spatiotemporally perceptible event, which will carry God's message to man...If there is to be a revelation, it will be a unique, historical event." ("Philosophy of the Human Person in Karl Rahner's Theology," *Theological Studies* 22 (1961), pp.543f.)

For a different accentuation in the reading of Rahner's "philosophy of religion" (in HW), cf. J.B. Metz, "Preface" to K. Rahner, HW, J.B. Metz, second revised edition; M. Richards, tr., (N.Y: Herder & Herder, 1963), p.viii.

[57] Karl Rahner, *Encounters with Silence*, J.M. Demske, tr., (London/Glasgow: Sands & Co. Ltd., 1966), pp.15f. These words of "meditation" go back to 1937 and were first published in German in 1938.

"philosophical" questioning is that Christian conviction which he wants to enable his modern readers to embrace with intellectual honesty. (Nor was the writing of "spiritual works" merely a sideline activity to his more "scholarly" works. The fact that "his spiritual-practical publications nearly equal the number of scientific, scholarly ones,"[58] is eloquent testimony to the importance Rahner attributed to these works).

For Rahner, "anthropocentricity" and "theocentricity" are two sides of one reality. This relationship is not static but dynamic, as seen in his concept of the "supernatural existential." Obviously, if for Rahner human-centeredness and God-centeredness are strictly interchangeable, then one may not expect his philosophical reflection on human subjectivity to be carried out, as it were, in disregard of the Christian theological tradition and what it says about God and the human being. Rather one can assume that all his philosophical elaborations on human subjectivity were accompanied (if at times tacitly) by his theological understanding of the human subject.

Accordingly, it can be argued (with Metz) that Rahner's transcendental anthropology is inextricably and always bound up with Christology, with the Christian understanding of the Incarnation of the divine *Logos*. In fact, Rahner's whole "anthropologically-oriented theology" has to be understood in the light of its Christological center. This center, says Metz, is what gives Rahner's great diversity of theological explorations their unity or "inner form," because "in the end result, his theological statements always center on one thing, namely, the Word of the intractable mystery of God spoken in Jesus Christ as forgiveness and love, in and towards which man affirms himself, when believing, hoping and loving he accepts the painful darkness of his existence." Metz continues: "Rahner has developed this anthropocentric theology in relation to many individual questions and treatises--the Trinity, grace, eschatology, salvation

---

[58] Karl Rahner, *The Practice of Faith: A Handbook of Contemporary Spirituality*, K. Lehmann, A. Raffelt, eds. and "Introduction", (N.Y: Crossroad, 1983), p.ix.

history,...And also to Christology." As evidence of the latter he cites Rahner himself:

> Christology is the end and beginning of anthropology, and this anthropology in its radical realization, namely, in Christology, is in eternity theology; it is first of all that theology which God spoke in speaking his Word as our flesh in the emptiness of the ungodly and sinful; it is that theology which we, believing, pursue when we do not think that we could encounter God in bypassing the man Christ and man in general.[59]

The ultimate criterion, therefore, for what Rahner means by "anthropology" is found in Christology. Thus when he fully affirms modern anthropocentric thought, insisting that the human being with his or her transcendental and historical experiences and not an abstract dogma from past history, must be the starting point in theology, he does so because God himself has, so to speak, sanctioned our humanness and made our experience into the starting point of theology by his loving act of communicating himself in the Incarnation. In addition, the political theological implications in this "anthropological theology" are unmistakable in this Christological statement, for the human individual clearly cannot come before God except in loving his or her neighbour; cannot come alone but only in solidarity with all of humanity.

When Rahner, after establishing a general philosophical anthropological framework with its corresponding categories, engages in a "theological application" of his findings, he is not moving into a different realm of reality (e.g. "religious" reality) at all. Rather he invites the reader to take the logical "next step" within the same territory of his or her familiar experience of human existence. And that is, simply put, to examine the teachings and beliefs of Christianity in the light of experience and see whether these teachings are not saying exactly what is already "known" from experience, at least unthematically. The heart of Christian belief for Rahner is the claim that the infinite, seemingly frightening and incomprehensible mystery we

---

[59] Metz, "Foreword: An Essay on Karl Rahner," Karl Rahner, SW, W. Dych, tr., (N.Y: Herder & Herder, 1968), p.xvii.

experience is perhaps not distant at all, but instead a personal God, who is our absolute future coming toward us and wants to communicate himself to us in his infinite love as Christianity's teaching says.[60] Put another way, since a purely philosophical analysis of our human experience reveals that we are unanswerable and ever-growing questions before the absolute transcendence (in which we somehow share), Rahner, in switching to a theological mode of reflection on the same experience, invites us to consider whether the claims of a so-called history of salvation and revelation do not in fact correspond to, or make sense in the light of, our existential experience and thus provide an answer to the question we and the absolute mystery are to ourselves. In theological terms, Rahner invites the modern individual to ask the fundamental theological question: is there sufficient "experiential" reason or grounds for one to accept the Christian interpretation of human existence as the ultimate truth about oneself? (cf. Dych, p.10).

In order to answer this question, however, the individual needs to consider at the same time the systematic theological question about what Christianity actually believes, and the fundamental theological question whether Christianity's claims make sense in terms of one's own experience.

This approach would of course require that all the major doctrines of the Christian faith be examined for their relevance and validity in the light of today's transcendental anthropological self-understanding and vice versa. Since persons of today experience themselves as transcendental beings of freedom, and hence as a radically open subjects, and since the doctrinal expressions of faith throughout the Judeo-Christian history represent statements about particular events and experiences in time (which happened or were perceived this way, but could have happened or been perceived differently), it follows that these

---

[60] For example, Rahner develops the idea of the incomprehensible mystery not being far off but, as Christianity says, absolutely near in a transcendental framework in *Foundations* (pp.126-133) in connection with the "supernatural existential."

"expressions" are not seen as static and unchangeable truths but rather as historical formulations marked and conditioned to a certain extent by their times and places, and therefore open to reformulation within the horizon of thought in every age. Rahner has made great efforts to guide the modern individual in examining the various Christian dogmas for their validity in view of the transcendental anthropological experience of existence. In view of the central role which Christology has played in his transcendental and anthropological interpretation of the many dogmas of theology (as suggested by Metz), it is sufficient to illustrate briefly his methodological procedure with respect to Christology.

Christianity's appeal to the saving significance of particular events in history reaches its high point when it declares the historical Jesus to be the center of its faith. His life, ministry, death and resurrection form the foundation of this faith. Jesus is believed to be the Christ and hence Christologies or theologies about him emerged. However, these Christologies may not replace the historical person behind them who is the real focus of our faith. As people living far removed in time, we cannot, of course, reconstruct the life and person of Jesus as he was with absolute reliability and without the help or hindrance of the many Christologies that have developed in time. Thus, if our faith in Jesus Christ is to stand up before today's critical-scientific reason, Rahner would suggest, according to Dych, that a twofold effort has to be made. First, we must always endeavour to go beyond the Christological formulations to the man Jesus himself. This requires above all the use of exegetical studies of the biblical records about him, if we are to avoid "mythologizing" the center of our faith. Second, a continual effort must be made to "translate" the theological meaning of the ministry and life of Jesus so that faith in him will "make sense" to people of every age, race and religion within their horizon of understanding (cf. Dych, p.11).

What is involved here methodologically is this: Rahner is convinced that Christology needs to be carried out in two ways or steps today. On the one hand, one needs to look at "the past, the history of Jesus and what has been said about him in scripture and in the subsequent tradition of the Church." On the other hand, one must analyze "the present in order to develop a conceptual framework within which this past can speak to the present and actually be heard and understood in it. This framework is called 'transcendental Christology'; it is not in addition to what [one] can know *a posteriori* from historical Christology, but the *a priori* horizon or framework within which the theological significance of those facts is expressed" (Dych, p.12).

As this explanation of the "transcendental method" makes abundantly clear, there is nothing abstract or ahistorical about the concept of transcendentality. On the contrary, it is employed in order to prevent both our understanding of past theological tradition and our response to this tradition, conditioned by our modern historical situation, from becoming "mythologized" in an ahistorical way. This helps us to understand Rahner's own interpretation (cited above) of transcendental theology as his attempt, with the help of philosophy, at making intelligible to our age those historical salvific events that always preceded the reflective efforts of transcendental theology (cf. TI IX, p.100). Hence, in keeping with this methodological principle, "transcendental Christology does not attempt to prove what happened, but to understand what happened in its universal significance." One could in fact say that transcendental theology presupposes as "factual" history the "events" around which Christian faith centers and which it says it has experienced. Transcendental theology is seeking a hermeneutical instrument by which it can render intelligible for us today the meaning and significance of the history of which Christian faith speaks. The word "transcendental," Dych writes, means that it "focuses on those necessary or universal structures within which all concrete human history takes place." He continues:

> Through discovering the common ground for the concrete history of Jesus and our own collective and individual histories today, transcendental Christology can express the universal significance of Jesus' particularity. Since, for example, in our philosophical reflection we have come to

understand human existence as an openness which is simply unlimited and undetermined, and to which meaning must come through the actualities of history, the history of Jesus can be understood as the fullest actualization of that meaning and the fulfillment of the human potential for self-transcendence. Likewise, if we experience in ourselves human hopes which Christian faith says have been fully realized in the human Jesus, then his history touches ours at the deepest levels of our experience (Dych, p.12).

What is said in this statement in a rather compressed form will be spelled out in a bit more detail in the discussion of Rahner's category of the "supernatural existential." There is no need, therefore, to elaborate on it further here--except for one comment: as Dych's statement makes plain, the cardinal reason why Jesus' life and work has such a uniquely universal significance consists in the fact that in his own historical existence all that which in metaphysical anthropology is seen as the constitutively most inherent human destiny (total self-presence, free historical self-realization, unreserved loving self-transcendence toward others) finds its unparalleled actualization. The obvious "incarnational" direction of this interpretation of Jesus' existence (and of all human existence) is surely full of political-theological implications.

The "Supernatural Existential": Incarnate Grace

Most of Rahner's methodological reflections on the experience of human existence occur in something of a twilight zone between the "philosophical" and the "theological" modes of thought, and it is quite impossible to tell always which mode prevails in a given discussion. This may be because Rahner's philosophy of human existence is ultimately rooted in his "prior" experience of God so that even his most rigorous metaphysics[61]

---

[61] That this commitment to intellectual rigour need not in any way go against Rahner's profound "pastoral" motivation follows from his conviction that "in fact the strictest theology, that most passionately devoted to reality alone and ever on the alert for new questions, the most scientific theology, is

is influenced and modified (however indirectly) by his "spirituality." And, vice versa, all his theological deliberations are by definition always permeated or underpinned by the categories that form his philosophical framework of thought.

Rahner has, however, discovered another "existential" that inheres as deeply in our humanness as do the existentials of self-presence and free personhood, and that is the "supernatural existential." In his elaboration of this human structure or existential Rahner changes his metaphysical-anthropological considerations over to the mode of a specifically Christian-theological anthropology. The reason for this is of course that under this category Rahner undertakes to show that grace is experienced transcendentally. Since grace is ultimately God's free self-communication, it is "supernatural." Therefore, the "supernatural existential" constitutes what one might call a primarily "theological"-anthropological existential which Rahner, as theologian, claims to be an essential given, at least in the form of an offer, in every human being.

A handy summary of Rahner's understanding of the supernatural existential can be found in *Foundations*.[62] The central thesis of his treatment there is that **"man is the event of God's absolute self-communication."** The intent is to impress upon the reader that God's grace as his self-gift to the individual is as much an *a priori* transcendental human experience--at least by way of an offer--as is our sense of ourselves as subjects and as free. Moreover, to view the human being as "the event of God's absolute self-communication" is not qualitatively different from saying that "Transcendence is reality and man is only a transcendental subject because this transcendence exists" (Weger, above), considering that transcendence is for Rahner equivalent to God. But the former is a "theological" anthropological

---

itself in the long run the most kerygmatic theology" (cited by Metz, "Foreword: An Essay on Karl Rahner," p.xiii.).

[62] Cf. particularly the section, "The offer of Self-Communication as 'Supernatural Existential'," F, pp.126-133.

statement. The supernatural existential has in common with the other existentials that it is so intrinsic to the essential human subject that any verbal conceptual communication (including "the explicit teaching of revelation formulated officially by the church") must appear "extrinsic" or secondary by comparison (F, p.126). In practical terms, even though in one sense the only way for Christian teaching to reach the individual of today is via the church and its conceptualized profession of faith, Rahner wants us to realize that it is not simply a matter of the church's imparting its message from the "outside" through concepts only. "Rather," says Rahner, the church's message "appeals to reality, which is not only said, but also given and really experienced in man's transcendental experience. Hence it expresses to man his own self-understanding, one which he already has, although unreflexively" (F, p.127).

Rahner further stresses the real and universal givenness of the supernatural existential "to absolutely all men," even though it is and remains ever a free and unmerited gift, accepted or rejected freely by human individuals. And it does not cease to be **supernatural**, says Rahner, by the fact that it "is present in *every* person" (F, p.127), for the offer to the free human subjectivity to fulfill in it its unlimited transcendentality is an offer to "essentially transcend...the natural." And the means offered for performing the act of transcending "the natural" is the loving and gratuitous self-communication of God himself (hence a "supernatural" means). Moreover, the claim of the presence of grace as God's self-communication in absolutely every person is not invalidated by the fact that some people may in freedom choose to reject it. If it is rejected by the free subject, it remains, nevertheless, constitutively present in this subject as the offer to fulfill its supernatural potentialities. Rahner observes a parallel here between the inevitable and persistent presence (irrespective of the free human response) of the "natural existentials" and the "supernatural existential," saying:

> Just as man's essential being, his spiritual personhood, in spite of the fact that it is and remains an inescapable given for every free subject, is given to his freedom in such a way that the free subject can possess himself in

the mode of 'yes' or in the mode of 'no,' in the mode of deliberate and obedient acceptance or in the mode of protest against this essential being of his which has been entrusted to freedom, so too the existential of man's absolute immediacy to God in and through this divine self-communication as permanently offered to freedom can exist merely in the mode of an antecedent offer, in the mode of acceptance and in the mode of rejection (F, p.128).

More light is shed upon Rahner's understanding of the supernatural existential when he says elsewhere, on the one hand, that it belongs to the humanness of every individual "prior" to any justifying grace, because "man is already subject to the universal salvific will of God,...*is* already redeemed and absolutely obliged to tend to his supernatural end." On the other hand, it "is a real modification of man, added indeed to his nature by God's grace and therefore supernatural, but in fact never lacking in the real order."[63] This "graced" existential is so profoundly inherent to our humanness that even in the event of rejecting the offer of grace we are for ever affected by this "supernatural destiny," as our rejection (if persistent) amounts to a state of perdition.

Furthermore, God's free self-communication is not only a gift received but is itself at the same time the "condition" for enabling the person to receive the gift in a way that will not "reduce...God himself to the level of man" (cf. F, p.128). As mentioned already, this ability to accept God's offer of himself in a way that "elevates" the human subject to the supernatural level (which God in his universal saving will gives as his offer to every individual), brings with it the "obligation" to accept God's offer. Otherwise the person must ever bear the absence of the self-gift of God which he or she refused.

It needs to be emphasized that in his elaboration of the "constitutional structure" of the supernatural existential, Rahner is not developing a dualistic view of human subjectivity. For the supernatural existential as "God's offer of himself...to all men,"

---

[63] Rahner & Vorgrimler, "Existential, Supernatural," *Concise Theological Dictionary*, p.163f.

"has the characteristics which all the other elements in man's transcendental constitution have." That is why the supernatural existential is able to provide the "answer" to the question encountered by the "natural" existentials in perceiving the absolute transcendence as infinitely remote and unapproachable, as the following words by Rahner show:

> The antecedent self-communication of God which is prior to man's freedom means nothing else but that the spirit's transcendental movement in knowledge and love towards the absolute mystery is borne by God himself in his communication in such a way that this movement has its term and its source not in the holy mystery as eternally distant and as a goal which can only be reached asymptomatically, but rather as the God of absolute closeness and immediacy (F, p.129).

The exact relationship between the "natural" transcendentality and the "supernatural" transcendentality (worked by grace) cannot, therefore, be disentangled easily and unambiguously in human subjectivity. The reasons for a persistent ambiguity in the relationship are several, according to Rahner. "God's self-communication in grace as a modification of our transcendentality is not reflexive and cannot be made reflexive" because a) "on the side of the addressee of this self-communication" one finds "the unlimited nature of the subjective spirit already in its natural state." This makes it difficult if not impossible to tell where exactly the "radicalizing effect" of supernatural grace sets in. b) "On the side of God's self-communication" one is faced with "the unfulfilled state of this self-communication," i.e., "it has not yet become the [beatific or immediate] vision of God," its ultimate goal (F, p.130). c) This relation is further blurred by the sin factor (both as personal guilt and original sin; cf. F, p.133).

For these reasons we cannot say or establish more concerning "the transcendental experience of God's self-communication in grace, or...the dynamism and the finalization of the spirit as knowledge and love towards the immediacy of God" than that **"in grace the spirit moves within its goal (because of God's self-communication) towards its goal (the beatific vision)"** (F, p.130). Thus, even though the supernatural existential cannot reflexively and "objectively" be isolated and identified in the human subject (any more than the essential transcendental mystery that we are to ourselves can be so identified), nevertheless, it can be transcendentally experienced in faith. This original experience of God's ongoing self-communication in the subject may serve as the final authenticating touchstone with which to test the veracity of Christianity's express formulations of its profession of faith. (Only) if the modern subject finds this faith to be speaking meaningfully to its innermost experience of its human existence is it obligated to respond in freedom to that faith message (cf. p.132).   As with the other essential human existentials, the existential of God's supernatural self-communication involves a radically "incarnate" or historical dimension. Without prejudice to its abiding "supernatural" quality, it can only be realized and humanly perceived via particular innerhistorical worldly realities:

> If God's self-communication is an ultimate and radicalizing modification of that very transcendentality of ours by which we are subjects, and if we are such subjects of unlimited transcendentality in the most ordinary affairs of our everyday existence, in our secular dealings with any and every individual reality, then this means in principle that the original experience of God even in his self-communication can be so universal, so unthematic and so 'unreligious' that it takes place, unnamed but really, wherever we are living out our existence (F, p.132).

While from this perspective no part of categorial reality can be excluded from being a possible medium or vehicle for experiencing God's loving self-communication, Rahner leaves, however, no doubt as to his conviction that ultimately history and transcendence come together above all in the experience of realized loving intersubjectivity, as his closing comment on the supernatural existential indicates:

> He [the human individual] remains a subject who actualizes the subjectivity of his gratuitously elevated transcendence in his *a posteriori* and historical encounter with the world of persons and of things, an encounter which is never completely at his disposal. And **he actualizes it in his encounter**

with a human thou in whom history and transcendence find their one actualization together and in unity, and there he finds his encounter with God as the absolute Thou (F, p.133; my emph.).

The idea about the possibility of experiencing God's gracious self-communication as conditioned by, or identical with, our intersubjective encounters is humanly "comprehensible" via a metaphysical anthropology--it is certainly not in conflict with our constituent "social-historical existential." However, it can only be clearly confirmed to the extent it is enacted in the life of an actual person in history. Accordingly, it is in his Christological reflections where Rahner discovered that it is impossible "that we could encounter God in by-passing the man Christ and man in general" (cited above). (The political theological significance of this idea, particularly in terms of its implications for a universal Christian solidarity, is evident). It is in this obvious rootedness in the event of the Incarnation that the concept of intersubjectivity or solidarity receives a specifically "theological" dimension. This expressly theologically conceived notion of solidarity is even more evident in Rahner's discussion elsewhere of "monogenism," when he speaks of a solidarity-in-salvation in humanity, saying:

> Even without the presupposition of a biological monogenism, mankind forms a true unity. All men have their origin in the one God with his one plan for the history of mankind and his universal salvific will, through which all individuals are already members of the one mankind in the sight of God. They are *de facto* interdependent on one another in the one spatio-temporal history. All are concretely ordained to the one Christ. All have the same goal, the kingdom of God.[64]

Rahner holds this divine "ordination" of humanity to God's kingdom to be a more powerful existential than the solidarity-in-perdition to which all are subject by virtue of their "membership of the human race," in consequence of which the "human being

---

[64] Karl Rahner, "Monogenism," *A Concise SM*, p.976.

is...lastingly, inescapably and really conditioned by that human denial in regard to God...call[ed] original sin."[65]

What became apparent already from a philosophical analysis of the experience of human existence (i.e. the subject's ultimate dependence upon the absolute mystery, as the ground of the possibility for all of its activities and relationships), is in the end boldly affirmed as a truth "revealed" in the historical Jesus. For the notion that the transcendental subject can experience the absolute mystery as a close and loving being via loving encounters with other free subjects in history is finally derived from God's incarnate revelation in the life and ministry of Jesus of Nazareth. This is so because, as will be seen later on, for Rahner human freedom and knowledge (including self-knowledge) are only possible in their concrete loving interhuman actualization in history. And human freedom, love of neighbour and love of God have never been as fully and radically realized as they are in the person of Jesus. This is why Christianity professes Jesus to be the unsurpassable and irreversible self-communication of God to humanity.

Thus Fiorenza's assertion that Rahner's concept of the supernatural existential has a basic Christological foundation is well taken. He says that for Rahner the full measure of human nature is discernible "only in relation to God's revelation in Christ."[66]   This, by extension, has also consequences for Rahner's theological view of history and society, a view already

[65] Rahner & Vorgrimler, *Concise Theological Dictionary*, p.164.

[66] Schüssler Fiorenza, "The Kantian Problematic," p.xliv. The author suggests that Rahner developed the concept of the "supernatural existential" in dialogue with modern existential philosophy, and used it to explain "this transcendental orientation to God." From its vantage point, "Man's relation to God is not an abstract or 'natural' openness to God, but is the result of God's historical calling of man to himself in Christ and thereby constituting the historical nature of man. The fullness of human nature therefore culminates not extrinsically, but intrinsically in Christ. Rahner's anthropology is thus not a pure philosophical or transcendental anthropology, but is an anthropology only in relation to God's revelation in Christ."

encountered in his HW, the central thesis of which, according to Metz, is that "man must listen in on history in order to encounter there the 'word' that founds history, this word to which the perceptive reason of man has always been questioningly attuned."[67] This implies that the 'essence' of history (and society) is by no means self-evident, but is in fact first determined or "revealed" by God's communication of himself in history, i.e., is "knowable" only in the "doing" of human love and freedom in concrete social history. This is not, however, to minimize the radical importance which Rahner attributes to the "almost naive" human being in his theology, mentioned above. Rather, God's revealing Word and natural knowledge of God ought to be seen as "related not by chronological succession but by mutual conditioning," as O'Donovan observes,[68] adding these words from Rahner's early work:

> Thus the Word of revelation and natural knowledge of God mutually condition each other. The revealed Word presupposes a person who really, despite the sinful lying and lostness which idolizes the world, knows something about God; and on the other hand this concealed knowledge of God only breaks through human hardness of heart and becomes really conscious of itself when it is released by the Word of God who reveals God's self as utterly beyond the world (TI I, p.98).

Obviously, there is at work in this early work by Rahner a kind of insight that anticipates the later concept of the "supernatural existential."

This perspective with its reference to the historically "realized" Word of revelation as the condition for our true knowledge of God has, of course, far-reaching significance for our theological understanding of the meaning and role of the historical church. In a word, the church (founded through God's communication of himself in the life and work of Jesus) only is and has salvation insofar as it exists or realizes itself "sacramentally" and freely for

---

[67] Cf. the reference to Metz in my note #56 above in this chapter.

[68] Leo O'Donovan, "Orthopraxis," p.58.

the salvation of the world.[69]   The church by definition cannot be an end in itself. It is a "real sign" of the gracious self-communication of God to humanity.[70] This too will be seen to have weighty implications with respect to the sorts and limits of sociopolitical engagement that is to be expected of the church.

That Rahner's Christological-anthropological understanding of interhuman relations is not to be mistaken for the I-Thou dimension of bourgeois Christianity of which Metz has spoken becomes apparent at the latest in the "Brief Creedal Statements" in his *Foundations*. In the Christological creed, titled "A Brief Anthropological Creed," he states among other things: "A person really discovers his true self in a genuine act of self-realization only if he risks himself radically for another." It goes on to say, that such an act amounts to "grasping" God "who in his existentiell and historical self-communication" made human love possible by making "himself the realm within which such love is possible." In other words, the conditions for the possibility of metaphysical knowledge of self and of God, from the theological perspective of the "supernatural existential," is nothing less than that the human person live her or his life in loving outreach toward the neighbour (and thereby toward God). And yet this is made possible only by the antecedent, historical self-

---

[69] This follows from Rahner's definition of the meaning of the church's "self-realization" in the world from *Handbuch der Pastoraltheologie* I, p.122, n.1, as cited by Neumann:
"The word 'self-realization' has to be understood in its *formal* sense. It does not imply any 'introvertedness' on the part of the Church, as if its activities were ultimately centered upon itself. The Church exists in order to worship God, serve the salvation of humankind, and be available for the world. All *this* constitutes precisely its self-realization, just as man realizes himself precisely when he loves God and so comes away from himself" (Cf. Neumann, *op. cit.*, p.389; italics his; my tr.).

[70] Dych, *op. cit.*, p.14f. The author discusses here the ways in which the concept of "real symbol" applies both to Jesus and to the church in their relation to the salvation of the world.

communication of God as both the means and the goal of such love.

Rahner insists that this love cannot be confined to the private sphere: **"This love is meant in both an interpersonal and a social sense, and in the radical unity of both of these elements it is the ground of the essence of the church."**[71] Since this love constitutes for Rahner the center of the gospel--the gospel being the chief or sole criterion for sociocritical engagement--and since in its necessarily interpersonal and social expressions it inevitably implies the concrete church as its innerhistorical "home," it is not surprising that Rahner's explicit political theological reflections are related to his ecclesiology.

All of this, of course, is related to Rahner's basic concept of "the unity between love of God and love of neighbour," a concept that will be considered below. That all true love of neighbour and love of God is radically related to the person of Jesus Christ as the concrete historical realization of God's loving and irreversible self-communication to humankind is clear from what has been said above.

I cannot further pursue what possibilities and advantages Rahner's transcendental and anthropological methodology holds out for translating other theological doctrines into the modern horizon of thought for apologetics, for missionary outreach or ecumenical relations. Dych's succinct summary captures this well and will suffice here:

> Rahner's use of transcendental categories has given him a common framework within which to link the past with the present, and also to link the variety of religions and cultures in our own contemporary world, and, finally, to unify the "religious" and "secular" moments within our single human existence.[72]

This method serves then to eliminate a host of dualisms, as well as much of the outdated "ghetto language" of theology, which

---

[71] F, p.456; G, p.460.

[72] Dych, *op. cit.*, p.14.

posed such an unnecessary hindrance for giving an account of Christian hope before a modern anthropocentric world.

It has become abundantly clear by now that in order to be perceptible to essentially historical human beings, Christianity's hope has to be given concrete expression within history. This already follows from the essential nature of the transcendental human subject. This nature necessitates that God should speak his "word" of self-communication into that history in human terms. There is therefore inherent to Rahner's transcendental and anthropological methodology a radical world-directedness or groundedness in history which cannot be over-emphasized. Again Dych articulates the matter well in saying:

> Because human beings are historical and social beings, transcendental structures of knowledge and freedom must be actualized in the world and in history....there is no actual knowledge of God and no free response to him except when actualized in the world and in history. Humanity's transcendental essence comes to be and achieves actuality in time and space; it has no existence of its own apart from the concrete world and concrete history. Hence Rahner emphasizes that humanity is indeed transcendence and spirit, but only in and through the particularities of our individual and social world and collective history.[73]

This inexorable "world-directedness" of Rahner's anthropological theology is not something that he also emphasizes "alongside of" his "supernatural" or theological understanding of the human individual (described by Weger as "the heart of Rahner's theology," pp.86-111). Rather the world-directedness receives its most radical affirmation precisely through God's gift of himself in a particular historical event (or person) to absolutely every human being in history, at least as an abiding offer. For in this gracious act, transcendental theology demonstrates to us, we discover a singularly holistic understanding of the human subject, in relation to itself, history, the world, and reality as such. Spiritual subjectivity in Rahner's theology is conceived of as at once more concretely historical and more radically transcendent

---

[73] *Loc. cit.*

than in modern transcendental philosophy. I have already touched on the social and political significance of this "fuller picture" of the human subject: it prevents us, for instance, from seeing or treating fellow men and women from a strictly utilitarian perspective for utopian ends.

It is apparent, therefore, that whether we look at Rahner's methodology in general or more specifically at his notion of the "supernatural existential," there is in his thought an inner dynamism that demands that human beings be concerned with reality beyond themselves, with society, history, the world, and through these with God. Ultimately, human beings must realize themselves in self-transcendence because God first transcended himself in loving self-communication in Jesus Christ. The failure to do so constitutes the human sin of selfishness.

Nor is the inner dynamism of Rahner's method merely a later addition (even if one leaves room for subtle "developments" along the way). "The world of historicity, relativity, intersubjectivity, and personalism," argues O'Donovan, belongs to the "root" of "his anthropology" and does not simply constitute a later "application" of it.[74] Lehmann has likewise pointed out that although one may speak of certain "phases" in the development of Rahner's theology, these do not constitute drastic "reversals" (*Umbrüche*) but fit into a basically continuous theological work of a lifetime.[75]

---

[74] Cf. Leo O'Donovan, "Orthopraxis," p.54.

[75] Lehmann, *Rechenschaft*, 40*. On p.39*f. The author speaks of there being three discernible "phases" in Rahner's theological work, and mentions an "intensification" during the third phase (late 1960s) of the thematization of "the *'a posteriori'* elements in theology, especially of the historically concrete reality in its [absolute] uniqueness." The transcendental theological "primacy" is preserved even though the "realm of the transcendent" is broadened. The "limits" of transcendental theology become visible as well, and so one observes in his Christology of this phase that the accentuation shifts more to the historical Jesus.

But Lehmann adds: "Doubtlessly, his conversation with J.B. Metz has also contributed, from a completely different angle, to the differentiation of

In summary, then, Rahner's transcendental and anthropological method of theology is obviously not incompatible with the emphases and functions of the new political theology as outlined by Metz. On the contrary, when considering its roots in Ignatian spirituality, its pastoral motivation, its Thomistic and modern philosophical foundations--the latter serving as the philosophical "instrument"[76] which in turn is radicalized by the "supernatural existential"--Rahner's theological starting point is open to all the major political theological categories or emphases discussed above. This is of course not yet to suggest that if *materially* the same categories can be discerned in Rahner and Metz, they are in fact given identical interpretations or applications by each theologian. It may make a significant difference, for instance, that Rahner's theology as a whole appears to be heavily slanted

---

[Rahner's] transcendental starting point. Clearly, one witnesses a heightened effort concerning the mediation of the transcendental and the categorial-historical dimensions, whereby of course the transcendental dimension, for many reasons and to some extent rightly, maintains its predominance (cf. e.g., *Sacramentum mundi* IV, 987ff., and STh IX-XIII)." The matter of the relation between these categories in Rahner's work thus remains unresolved: "Of course, the final word has not yet been spoken on this subject, since important inquiries are still outstanding." As significant, but insufficiently noted evidence, including from phases one and two, Lehmann mentions the very extensive "'Theology of the Symbol' (STh VI, 275-311) [in which] such a mediation is found. The range of these efforts reaches from his theological dissertation to the essays on the 'heart-of-Jesus-theology' and the Ignatian Exercises and up to the already mentioned third phase" (trs. mine).

[76] With respect to the relationship in Rahner between philosophy and theology, besides the above-mentioned methodological reflections by Rahner (TI XI, pp.68-114), cf. especially his "The Current Relationship between Philosophy and Theology," TI XIII, pp.61-79.

On the question of the primacy between philosophy and theology, O'Donovan argues that there is no doubt but that Rahner gives priority to the latter: "The starting point is not philosophical but decidedly theological or, more accurately still, religious. Correspondingly, Rahner's reflections on the relations between theology and philosophy have consistently placed the latter within the former, as a moment in theology's effort to seek a living understanding of faith" ("Orthopraxis," p.58).

towards an "incarnational" interpretation of reality. By contrast, we noted that Metz's theology is heavily weighted in favour of an apocalyptic-eschatological approach. These differing accentuations may have far-reaching implications.

Furthermore, having identified a natural tendency in Rahner's theological starting point or mode of operation towards giving categories like human experience, historicity, intersubjectivity or solidarity, and a metaphysics-of-praxis-of-love a central role in his theological work is not to deny that Metz may have exercised a significant influence, for example, on the pace in which or the degree to which these categories were developed by his former teacher. The fact, however, that Rahner's transcendental theological method has been shown to be inherently suited for providing the modern individual with effective means to deal both with her or his own personal faith crisis and to address the public issues of today critically, yet constructively, augurs very well indeed for the thesis that his is also a political theology in a real, if qualified, sense.

3. Human Freedom and Responsibility within an Eschatological Horizon

Since there is substantial overlap in Rahner's treatment of human transcendence and freedom, our inquiry into the latter may be relatively brief. Moreover, because certain key aspects of human freedom, both individual and collective, are dealt with under the category of Rahner's eschatology, these themes may be considered jointly.

Consistent with his twofold method, and analogously to his approach to transcendentality, Rahner understands human freedom as an "existential" that involves an *a priori* and an *a posteriori* moment. The first moment refers to that fundamental constituent by which human beings *are* free beings, prior to any initiative of their own. To be human is unavoidably to be a radically free being. The second moment refers to that dimension of our existence which we create as we realize ourselves freely within our categorial existence. In this latter sense, freedom entails not only a gift but a responsibility, and when considering that human beings are inherently also historical and social beings, this has implications for their participation in the social and political world in which they live. The two moments, however, cannot actually be separated since they are like two sides of a coin, but neither can the two sides be conflated into one.

As with transcendentality, so human freedom in both its transcendent and categorial dimensions inevitably leads to God, since freedom is only possible because of its rootedness in God as absolute freedom. In Rahner's words:

> Since in every act of freedom which is concerned on the categorical level with a quite definite object, a quite definite person, there is always present, as the condition and possibility for such an act, transcendence towards the absolute term and source of all of our intellectual and spiritual acts, and hence towards God, there must be present in every such act an *unthematic* *'yes' or 'no'* to this God of original, transcendental experience (F, p.98; G, p.105).

He then affirms the rootedness in God of every act of freedom even more plainly: "Subjectivity and freedom imply and entail that this freedom is not only freedom with respect to the object of categorical experience within the absolute horizon of God, but it is also and in truth, although always in only a mediated way, a freedom which decides about God and with respect to God himself." Thus God is encountered by the human being "in a radical way everywhere as a question to our freedom...unthematic...in all the things of the world, and therefore and especially in our neighbor" (F, pp.98f.; G, p.105). Freedom, as the last statement shows, clearly has a social dimension.

This transcendental-categorial interpretation of human freedom has implications for our investigation. First, it demonstrates Rahner's critical affirmation of the modern anthropocentric notion of human "emancipation," of radical autonomy from heteronomous determinants: freedom is not primarily the ability to do or not do certain moral acts, but rather to do oneself, or quite literally to "create" oneself in all dimensions of one's subjectivity, including the historical and social dimensions, in short, the whole categorial world in which the subject lives. Second, we note a critical limiting dimension in this definition. Because every free human act is enveloped by God's absolute freedom, is made possible by God's prevenient grace (in the terms of the supernatural existential), human freedom is "limited" or penultimate freedom. This entails a critique of the false or atheistic notion of autonomy in modern philosophy, in response to which, as we have seen, Rahner largely fashioned his transcendental anthropocentric theological method.

Paradoxically, however, this "limiting" affirmation of a total human dependence upon and orientation towards God gives genuine human autonomy an infinitely greater depth than immanentist absolutizing modern philosophy can conceive of. Rahner's theological treatment of human freedom perfectly parallels the critical affirmation and radicalization of the anthropocentric modern philosophical concept of human emancipation found in Metz's political theology. For both theologians, the problem is not that modern persons want too much freedom, but that they attempt to attain the freedom they are rightfully meant to have in the wrong way: without faith in a transcendent God (Metz). And without faith ultimate autonomy is unattainable. Hence Rahner's theology of freedom also displays the twofold function of a negative-critical and a positive-apologetic theology, which is central to political theology as defined by Metz.

The transcendentalist view that every free act has lasting value and "eternalizes" human beings who thus actualize themselves (or refuse to do so), already places the whole conception of human freedom in an "eschatological" framework. Every free action throughout our lives, necessarily realized within categorial and temporal reality, is of ultimate, eternal significance; it represents in a real way an "existentiell" consummation, i.e. a final fulfillment. From this perspective, death is not something that happens at the end of our lives, but we actually "die" every moment as we posit ourselves in our free action as a yes or no before God. Again, this view allows Rahner to take human freedom (and responsibility) more seriously than modern thought does. Freedom is not the ability to "revise" our actions arbitrarily and endlessly. Rather it is a matter of our self-realization by realizing our various historical possibilities, thus positing our nature both "individually and as members of the human race."[77]

This radicalized conception of freedom entails of course a heightened human responsibility. For if salvation is not seen in the sense of a death-bed conversion, but of a lifelong train of actions of self-realization in freedom, then it is of greater importance, whether or not the individual realizes his or her personal and social nature conscientiously at every moment. To emphasize this point is of course not a matter of salvation by work righteousness. For Rahner knows human freedom to be "profoundly wounded" by sin and in need of healing by God's forgiving grace in Christ (cf. TI VI, p.195). Moreover, as we have already noted, he holds all free human decisions to have been "caused" by the "original" prevenient grace of God.

Human "guilt" or sin in transcendental theology is seen fundamentally as a "closing oneself to [the] offer of God's absolute self-communication." And the human being can only grasp the monstrosity of this guilt "in the process of forgiveness to which the person opens himself" in free acceptance (F, p.93; G, p.100). The individual's freedom is not absolute freedom, because it is affected by both original sin and by the "free 'independencies'" of other people in a limiting way. However, at the same time, the person's "freedom itself" (i.e. his or her ultimate freedom and responsibility to decide about and eternalize his or her destiny) cannot be eliminated by these factors (cf. *Concise Theological Dictionary*, p.181).

Prevenient grace, however, which also (even more powerfully) affects human freedom, and which is indispensable for human freedom, in no way diminishes the subject's options for ill or good. We grasp the radical nature of human freedom in Rahner's theology, when he argues that a person, during his historical

---

[77] Rahner & Vorgrimler, "Freedom," *Concise Theological Dictionary*, p.181.

existence, "is still exercising his freedom in the openness of two radically different possibilities,...[and] cannot say that absolute loss as a conclusion and outcome of his free guilt is not a possibility with which he has to reckon," even though (as asserted by the Bible and tradition) "the world and the human race as a whole will find a blessed and positive fulfillment in Jesus Christ by the power of God's grace" (F, pp.443f.; G, pp.425f.). (Rahner deals with this apparent conflict between the two assertions by saying that the first claim may not be of equal "rank" with the second claim, and that it must be left to the counsel of God to determine how the human individual's freedom can be absolutely binding in light of his universal saving will.)

Although this self-realization in life radically concerns the unique human individual, there is also an inevitable "communal" side to freedom. Thus Rahner says, "the question of salvation cannot be answered by bypassing man's historicity and his social being. Transcendentality and freedom are realized in history" (F, p.40; G, p.51). This point is even more stressed later on in the book:

> As existing in an interpersonal world, a person arrives concretely at his own self-interpretation, however much it comes from within and enters within, only within the self-interpretation of his interpersonal world, and by participating in and receiving from the tradition of the historical self-interpretation of those people who form his interpersonal world from out of the past and through the present into the future...A person always forms his own secular self-understanding only within the community of persons, and in the experience of a history which he never makes alone, in dialogue, and in experience which reproduces the productive self-interpretation of other people...In his religious experience, too, man is always an interpersonal being, and this extends to the ultimate uniqueness of his subjectivity. The historical self-interpretation of one's own religious existence is not a solipsistic affair, but takes place necessarily in and through the historical experience of the religious self-interpretation of one's own world, of one's own 'religious community' (F, p.160; G, pp.163f.).

This inevitable social-historical dimension in the human being's self-perception and self-actualization requires a complete deprivatization of his or her relation (in freedom) to God and the neighbour. But all of this is not simply rooted in an abstract philosophy of transcendence which claims that human self-transcendence is only possible via intramundane communication; it is ultimately based on the principle and practice of love, and thus on Christology since genuine love is exemplified and made possible only in Jesus Christ. For Rahner, a self-realization in freedom, a coming before God, is only possible in the realization of love. As he puts it:

> The original relationship to God is...love of neighbour. If man becomes himself only in the exercise of love towards God and must achieve this self-mastery by a categorial action, then it holds good...that the act of love of neighbour is the only categorial and original act in which man attains the whole of concretely given reality and finds the transcendental and supernatural [*gnadenhafte*], directly experienced experience of God (TI VI, pp.189f.; STh VI, pp.228f.).

The only incarnate measure of a perfectly free self-realization in love is of course that of Jesus: "This man Jesus is the perfect man in an absolute sense precisely because he forgot himself for the sake of God and his fellow man who was in need of salvation, and existed only in this process of this forgetting" (F, pp.250f.; G, p.248). Here only do we learn how genuine human freedom is achievable: through acts of love in which we realize ourselves without seeking our own realization.

There is an inevitable "eschatological" dimension in everything relating to freedom. Both human freedom and eschatology have to do with genuine openness toward the future. Eschatology, says Rahner, "is the doctrine about man insofar as he is a being who is open to the absolute future of God himself....Eschatology is not really an addition, but rather it gives expression once again to man as Christianity understands him: as a being who ex-ists from out of his present 'now' towards his future" (F, p.431; G, p.414). Since, then, Christian eschatology is really a transposition of all of theology into the "key" of "man's futurity,"--the human being's basic transcendentality towards God as his absolute future (cf. F, p.457)--only a few comments on Rahner's eschatology are needed before examining it for its political theological relevance.

In his "Brief Future-Oriented Creed," Rahner gives this formulation: "Christianity is the religion which keeps open the question about the absolute future which wills to give itself in its own reality by self-communication, and which has established this will as eschatologically irreversible in Jesus Christ, and this future is called God" (F, p.457; G, p.460). As this formulation readily reveals, Rahner's eschatology embodies a tension between a "realized" and not yet realized eschatology. This tension has decisive critical significance both for the individual and for society. Another fundamental aspect of Rahner's eschatology is the tension between individual consummation and collective consummation, as his section on eschatology shows (cf. F, pp.431-447). It is, however, really only one eschatology with an individual and a historical-social moment. And according to Rahner, it cannot be reduced to either of these moments and neither pole can cover the other adequately.[78]

The main objective in examining both Rahner's theology of freedom and his eschatology is to assess their political theological significance. Having introduced each of these theological dimensions briefly in a somewhat "theoretical"

---

[78] Karl Rahner, "Eschatologie, theol.-wissenschaftstheoretisch," *Lexikon für Theologie und Kirche* III (1959) p.1095. It is significant for our study that even in this scholarly reflection on eschatology Rahner was guided by what we may call a practical "political theological" concern about the modern individual and society. For if eschatology were translated into the "existential-ontological analysis and reflectedness...," he says, it "would enable the human being with today's outlook on the world [*Weltbild*] to accept more easily in faith the eschatological message and to synthesize its cosmology with his general philosophy of life [*Daseinsverständnis*]" (my tr.).

This early article contained a certain "public" dimension as well. The "situation" is diagnosed as being in dire need of an updated eschatology because it is a scientific, rationalistic, future-self-and-world-planning situation, which plans to achieve this change of all human relations "through modern militant-political world heresies of an innerworldly utopianism" (cf. p.1095; my tr.). These tendencies can and should be counteracted by an "updated" eschatology.

format, we may now turn to consider some of the practical consequences that flow from them for Rahner's work. We will consider Rahner's teachings on human freedom and eschatology in the historical context in which he first developed them, for practical-pastoral reasons.

As in the case of the above-mentioned development of an individual ethic in the late 1940s and early 1950s, the immediate context for much of what Rahner has to say about human freedom (and about eschatology) is the Christian church. This is readily evident from Rahner's articles in the *Handbook of Pastoral Theology*, all of which somehow deal with the self-realization of the church in the world: by being a fundamental sacrament after the pattern of Christ, the "original" sacrament (*Ursakrament*). His early ethical reflections on individual responsibility over against a collectivist mentality is directly related to his teaching on human freedom. Of course, all his teachings in this regard are also directly relevant to any individual or modern society as a whole.

Considering the totalitarian or "monolithic" tendency in the early postwar Catholic church (not to mention the fascist political atmosphere characterizing the times around W.W.II), Rahner's essays on individual freedom in the institutional church are a supreme example of a *theologia negativa* in terms of their critical function. But in arguing for the freedom of every individual member to exercise their spiritual charisms, these essays did more than bring to bear the gospel message just on the church itself. They represented simultaneously and inevitably a message to society at large.

As early as 1955, Rahner reflected upon "Freedom in the Church" and "The Dignity and Freedom of Man" (TI II, pp.89-107; pp.235-263). In the latter article, although defining the person as essentially a social being (the "orientation of man to a 'thou' in love and mutual service already belongs to the nature of man from the very start"), Rahner asserts the person's freedom before both the state and the church, saying: "The state exists for man and not vice versa" (pp.255f.; STh II, p.269). As for the institutional church, it must guard, not rob, the individual's freedom: "The Church is an indispensable shelter of freedom in the world; she teaches, lives and defends the dignity and hence the inviolability of individual man: that he is a person, has eternal destiny and has freedom" (p.258; p.272). (The original German *"Hort der Freiheit"* is stronger, more active, than "shelter of freedom.") Again, while fully recognizing the need for historical structure in the church, he pleads for freedom of the spirit: "Side by side with the [legitimate] official function...there is and must also be the charismatic and prophetic in the Church which cannot be officially organized right from the start...It is written: 'Do not extinguish the Spirit'" (p.262; p.276). Thus Metz's concept of the church as the "asylum of freedom" is rooted in Rahner and not the other way around.

This was, however, only the beginning of Rahner's lifelong preoccupation with ensuring that there would be room in the necessarily formalized church for each of its members to freely exercise his or her charisms, and thus freedom for the Holy Spirit to work through each believing person. For example, he uttered the warning cry in 1962, on the eve of Vatican II, "Do not Stifle the Spirit" (TI VII, pp.72-87; STh VII, pp.77-90), as the conservative forces in the church threatened to suppress ecclesiastical renewal. This warning cry is in a sense axiomatic for all of Rahner's theological work.[79] For instance, he did not hesitate to voice vigorously and publicly his protest when in 1979, Cardinal Ratzinger and the Bavarian minister of education conspired against Metz's appointment to a well deserved teaching post in Munich, lamenting that "church leaders rarely admit their mistakes," and that there is in fact less "sensitivity to basic human rights...within the church" than in secular society.[80]

---

[79] In his "Foreword" to *Theology and Discovery:...*, W.J. Kelly, ed., (Marquette Univ. Press, 1980), Rahner recalls that his life's goal has been to point out "that our time calls also us theologians sleeping under the broom tree of orthodoxy like Elijah in old days:...Arise, a long journey lies ahead of you."

[80] R. Delaney, "Theologian tells cardinal, 'Church leaders rarely admit their mistakes'," *National Catholic Reporter*, 16, No.5 (1979), p.1.

In two other related instances, Rahner registered his solidarity with liberation theologians. Gregory Baum writes: "In November 1977, Karl Rahner joined a group of German theologians [including Metz] who protested against the ecclesiastical campaign to discredit the theology of liberation...in Latin America..." on the eve of the Latin American Bishops' Conference at Puebla, Mexico.[81] Vorgrimler says Rahner had many conversations with liberation theologians and "showed solidarity" with them, supporting their "work for integral liberation of the people," "though he sometimes found that [their] practical zeal needed to be based on deeper theoretical reflection." Vorgrimler continues: "When he was already fatally ill he supported the theologian Gustavo Gutiérrez, whose existence in the church and therefore whose physical existence was threatened, in a letter to the bishops of Peru."[82]

The fact that Rahner's *theologia negativa* is primarily applied to the church of course does not diminish its true political theological dimension. For that is also the approach of a large segment of the Metzian theology, namely to be a corrective above all to Christian theology and the church.

These negative-critical and positive-apologetic functions in Rahner's theology, however, were not limited by any means to having merely an indirect influence on the secular world. This is demonstrable with special clarity in his eschatology. And although Rahner's is a "historical eschatology" (TI IV, p.343), (in contrast to Metz's "apocalyptic eschatology," which largely sees its role as an "interruption" of evolutionary time and progress), its results are rather similar insofar as it confronts the Marxist ideology of a future man-made *utopia*. For it is precisely in the name of that absolute future which wills to communicate itself to us that Rahner, in his public dialogue (together with Metz, in 1966) with the Marxist Garaudy, opposes the immanentist or

---

[81] Gregory Baum, "German Theologians and Liberation Theology," *The Ecumenist*, 16, No.4 (1978), p.49.

[82] Vorgrimler, *Understanding Karl Rahner*, p.114.

self-absolutizing *utopia*, which is willing to sacrifice every present generation to the "Moloch" of a humanly conceived and controlled future.[83]

Perhaps the concept of human "solidarity" is not developed (or made explicit) to the same degree in Rahner as we have found it to be in Metz, but when in the name of the absolute future that is coming toward us, and on the basis of the unity of love of God and love of neighbour, he defends not only each respective human generation but makes plain to representatives of dialectical materialism "why even *that* man preserves his dignity and intangible significance who can no longer make any tangible contribution to the approach to the intramundane future," then there is more than just a pointer toward a practical universal solidarity. It amounts to a solidarity that is enacted in practical terms.

When Rahner proceeds to stress that such love is no purely abstract ideal but must necessarily be realized historically, he is in fact enjoining on his dialogue partners the necessity of concrete historical engagement on behalf of their fellow men and

---

[83] Karl Rahner, "Marxist Utopia and the Christian Future of Man," TI VI, cf. pp.59-68, esp. pp.65f. Here Rahner states:
"Christianity even taken as the thematically explicit religion which sees God as the absolute future, has great significance for intramundane society and its goals. By its hope for the absolute future, Christianity defends man against the temptation of engaging in **the justified intramundane efforts for the future** with *such* energy that every generation is always sacrificed in favour of the next, so that the future becomes a Moloch before whom the man existing at present is butchered for the sake of some man who is never real and always still to come" (his italics; my emphs.).
For a similarly frank dialogue with Marxism, cf. also K. Rahner, "The Theological Problems Entailed in the Idea of the 'New Earth'," TI X, pp.260-272, or STh VIII, esp. p.587; for his relatively late comments on Christian-Marxist relations, cf. *Karl Rahner. Erinnerungen im Gespräch mit Meinold Krauss*, (Herder, 1984), pp.87f.
There is a close relation between Rahner's argumentation and that observed in Metz on the same subject. Metz, as we have seen, also defended the human person against a "depersonalizing" utopia by means of the "eschatological proviso."

women, including the least among them. Because, "if...this man who is to be loved cannot exist except as someone who makes projects with a view to his future, then this means that the love of God understood as the love of neighbour cannot exist without the will to *this* man and hence also to his intramundane future" (TI VI, p.66). On the other hand, of course, his concepts of transcendentality and freedom will not allow a reduction of the human being to nothing but tangible innerhistorical or chemical processes. His plea for the historical enactment of Christian love amounts to an "orthopraxis" in the sense of making Christian teaching come true.

Rahner's efforts at giving an account of the Christian faith and hope (and his personal experience and struggle with them) extends of course beyond his dialogue with Marxists to his extensive interaction with natural and human scientists. Thus he tried to translate the basic Christian convictions into an evolutionary frame of thought in "Christology within an Evolutionary View of the World" (TI V, pp.157-192), and he wrestled with the question of human self-manipulation in "The Experiment with Man," and "The Problem of Genetic Manipulation," (TI IX, pp.205-224; pp.225-252), to name but a few examples. To this could be added Rahner's extensive public lecture tours during W.W. II, which he undertook with a view to cultivating and defending a Christian concept of the human person against the Nazi ideology. (Cf. Vorgrimler, ed., *Bilder eines Lebens*, p.46.)

In whatever area of human knowledge or practice he encounters a "positivistic" outlook on life (the church, Marxism, natural and human sciences, theology), Rahner invariably opposes or "dissolves" it through the same anthropocentric concept of human transcendentality and freedom, ultimately and fundamentally rooted in God's absolute future, with which he confronts Marxism.[84] Since human persons are perceived as

---

[84] Rahner's frank critique of "the weak points and the inhumanities in Marxism" was by no means a one-way conversation. For, according to Vorgrimler, his conversations with Marxists contributed toward "his important

beings of radical freedom and responsibility, they can never adequately or fully define themselves, because they are rooted in and tend toward absolute freedom, the absolute future. Nevertheless, persons must realize themselves in the multiplicity of possibilities and dimensions within history. And such an intramundane engagement has abiding significance. Says Rahner: "a history that is constructed by man himself as event and as the end product of his activities has a final and definitive significance..." because "precisely this 'world in its worldliness',

---

distinction between absolute future and future within the world." When either of these futures is neglected, it is at the expense of the other. This is implicit in the following interpretive statement by Vorgrimler (*Understanding Karl Rahner*, pp.113f.):

"He said that it was the task of Christianity to show humanity as being on the way to an absolute future, a future which cannot be planned and cannot be made, but comes of itself and consummates all things--humanity, history and the world: the absolute future which is only another name for God. But he had learned from Marxists that there must be a connection between the two futures, without Christianity being mere consolation with the beyond. Therefore Rahner emphatically said that a man misses his absolute future--God-- if he does not work with all his power for the human realization of the future within the world. Rahner never naively assumed that people can realize the kingdom of God on this earth. He knew that the kingdom of God is promised to all men, living and dead, and that therefore the kingdom of God cannot by-pass the dead. The kingdom of God presupposes the transformation of all that exists. But he was equally convinced that no one can enter the kingdom of God who does not make his own contribution towards changing existing circumstances in the direction of the divine promises, of freedom, justice and peace."

The tension between every historical reality and the promised eschaton, as well as the criterion that results from it for all human activity toward transforming the world, are reminiscent of Metz's eschatological reflections. For him, too, eschatology is irreversibly inaugurated in Christ but cannot be identified with any historical situation. Rather it relativizes all intramundane reality and all human ideals and the "eschatological promises" serve as the criterion for the Christian's innerworldly activity. Moreover, these "promises" serve to activate, not assuage, Christian engagement in the world for Metz as for Rahner.

which as such retains all its secularity, nevertheless, still in itself and as such, at basis exhibits a secret Christianity" (TI X, p.271).

Because of the basic future orientation of human nature (and hence of history and the world) which must be actualized in the present, the Christian religion has to keep open the question about the absolute future coming toward us. This requires a balancing act between waiting for the kingdom of God as the absolute future coming toward us (and the world) in its own time, and humanity's active engagement in the building of the innerworldly future, even though Christians have no definite and concrete plan, "no recipe" according to which to build this world. The particular and the universal moments of history are thus taken equally seriously by Rahner. The particular act of the individual has absolute significance for the totality of human history, while its uniqueness cannot be reduced to being merely a moment of this totality. Because the human person is not only unique, however, but also by definition a member of humanity as a whole, this universal whole requires a final consummation independent of the personal consummation at each person's (lifelong) individual death or "dying." That is why a twofold consummation, an individual and a collective eschatology, is indispensable for dealing holistically with the totality of the human being. On this point Rahner is absolutely emphatic.

> All eschatological assertions have the *one* totality of man in mind, which cannot be neatly *divided* into two parts, body and soul. All eschatological assertions merely repeat, transposing into terms of fulfilment, what dogmatic theology says about the one man in question. Hence eschatology cannot but be marked by the same two-fold dualism which is unavoidable in anthropological assertions about man who is always one. **It must be a universal and an individual eschatology, because man is always both individual and member of society and neither can be completely absorbed by the other, nor can everything be said about man in one statement alone** (TI IV, p.341; my emph.; his italics).

He develops the topic further still:

> Eschatology is concerned with the fulfilment of the individual as individual spirit-person which comes with death as the end of the individual history.

Eschatology is also concerned with the fulfilment of humanity in the resurrection of the flesh as the end of the bodily history of the world. But in each case it is concerned in different ways with the *whole* man. It cannot be read as two sets of statements about two different things, each of which can simply be taken separately. And yet the two sets of statements do not simply mean the same thing... (*Loc. cit.*).

In light of this holistic and eschatologically oriented theological anthropology (the "bipolarity" of which Rahner says, in his 1959 article on eschatology in *LThK*, refers as far back as Benedict XII), it is easy to see how Rahner's theology constitutes a radical criticism of any immanentist self-absolutizing view of reality. Any such view remains unsatisfactory in failing to take into account the totality of human beings: their bodily and spiritual, categorial and transcendental, individual and social, present as well as past and future dimensions. If these are not all taken into account, they leave a less than complete picture of the concrete present human individual (or of the whole present generation of humankind).

Rahner's criticism, however, is above all a constructive criticism, since he not only fully affirms the absolute need for a responsible innerhistorical human engagement, but actually radicalizes it by insisting that this task is only possible when reality in its totality is taken seriously. And this infinite task requires that the human individual and society accept in freedom finite existence and reality as the arena in which the absolute future freely wills to give itself to them. This absolute horizon alone is sufficient in order to accommodate the totality of being, without which the whole human being (or society or history or world) cannot be saved through its transcendental-historical self-realization. This theological truth, of course, is made visible in its irreversible establishment, ultimately, in the event of the Incarnation of the *Logos* in Jesus of Nazareth.

In summary, the discussion of the "characteristics and dynamics of Rahner's theology" (the title of this chapter) presents considerable evidence in support of the thesis of this book. A look at the early context of his work revealed that, even though Rahner does not and could not use formal political theological terminology and reasoning because of historical conditions prevailing during much of his writing career, his work was nevertheless based on a careful situation analysis and served the functions (both key to the new political theology) of a critical and an apologetic theology in relation to the ecclesiastical and political needs of its time with remarkable results.

This was no mere accident, as our cursory look at his transcendental and anthropocentric theological method has shown. This method itself was carefully designed in dialogue with and (pastoral) response to the framework of thought of the modern world. Both its inner epistemological dynamic, its pastoral-practical motivation and its Ignatian spirituality of finding God in all things tended more than a little towards a critical affirmation of the totality of the human being, even if the new ecclesiastical and theological atmosphere of pluralist thought, symbolized by the church of Vatican II and beyond (including the new political theology), was to influence Rahner's formal adoption of, for example, the Metzian theological categories, at least to an extent. To say the least, there is nothing in the transcendental theological methodology, if its various moments are all properly considered, that would inherently prevent it from serving the function of giving an account of Christian faith, hope and love before modern society, as Metz's theology aspires to do. On the contrary, we found many pointers that suggest Rahner's method promises results which compare favourably indeed with those of a formal political theology.

Our findings in relation to Rahner's conception of freedom and responsibility, as well as eschatology, tended to be in the same direction as those in the area of his method. Enveloped by absolute freedom (God), human beings are nevertheless "condemned" to the active task of a free lifelong self-actualization within time and space--which requires a constant openness toward that future that is always a gift before it becomes human initiative--so that refusal to accept this mandate means not only the rejection of particular options, but also the absolute loss of their very selves. Clearly, then, Rahner's concept of freedom is marked by a dynamic and public characteristic that is inherent in his methodology itself. But this characteristic is heightened even more when he places it in a Christological framework, saying true freedom can only occur in the act of love of neighbour. Thus, paradoxically, free self-actualization can only be achieved, after the manner of Jesus, by forgetting oneself in loving outreach toward those around us, and through them toward God.

Our findings also show that the inner dynamic of Rahner's theology holds out considerable potential for developing an active universal solidarity (including with the dead and those yet to come), and therefore potential for developing a narrative theology in the sense of an active and public Christian discipleship (as defined by Metz). Since the political theological dynamics or dimensions established in Rahner thus far are more implicit than explicit (due to some extent to the "atmosphere" in which he began his work), a further and closer examination of his theology in the more "open" context after Vatican II is warranted. Does the changing context in the church, the emergence of political and liberation theologies visibly influence or alter the style and/or content of his theology? Can a transcendental theology do justice to both poles in the "unity of love of God and love of neighbour?" We have noted an extensive implicit political theological dimension in Rahner, but what does he say explicitly about political theology now that it is on the scene? These are among the central questions considered in the next chapter.

Chapter 3

Political Theological Content in Rahner's Work

Our investigation concerning the inner dynamics of Rahner's transcendental theology has shown that, methodologically speaking, there is nothing which would prevent it from moving in the direction of the Metzian political theology as outlined above. On the contrary, there is substantial overlap between the characteristics of these theologies (which is not to declare them to be identical on all points). Both are deeply rooted in and assign a crucial place to the experiential side of life, and both consider ongoing situation analysis indispensable for doing theology. Both theologies are fundamentally motivated by a desire to translate the message of Christianity into modern categories of thought and choose the methodologies that seem best suited for the task.

This chapter seeks to prove our thesis by looking at the content of Rahner's theology. Of course, we should keep in mind that a distinction between "method" and "content" is somewhat artificial and only partly possible at best. This distinction, in the most simple terms, is aimed at making a comparison between the "dynamics" of Rahner's theology (established in the preceding chapter) with the "political theological" statements of "content" in his actual writings.

We will first explore what precisely Metz means by his designation of Rahner's transcendental theology as a paradigmatic "'biographical dogmatic theology' or 'theological biography'" (FHS, p.220). Second, for Rahner the situation co-determines the course of theology. Therefore, we may expect his transcendental theology of the (individual) subject to be influenced and/or altered by the changing context that accompanies, or is symbolized by, the Second Vatican Council. We will see if this is indeed the case.

Third, it has been noted in passing that the twofold love commandment is at the very heart of Rahner's theology. For example, we have seen that for him genuine freedom is attainable only through the act of agape love (of neighbour/God). The need to reach out in loving mutual service to a "Thou" belongs from early on to Rahner's definition of the human being. This theological view surely implies an irrepressible drive toward that public "praxis" which is not just the mutuality between equals within bourgeois society (or Christianity), but a praxis which only in the process of its self-realization discovers what it means to be free and responsible human beings. In other words, a discussion of the place and role of the double love commandment in Rahner's theology promises significant results for our assessment of its political theological contents.

The concluding section of this chapter will focus on the "explicit" political theological dimension in Rahner's work.

1. Experience-Based Transcendental Theology: Faith Crisis of the Modern Individual

The category of "experience" is pivotal for the new political theology. For example, we noted Metz's claim that his entire theological work hinges on his prototypal personal crisis experience as a youthly soldier. This crisis would thereafter colour all of his thinking about God. All his theology would be, as a result, a theodicy: talk of God would have to be "justified" in the face of all the suffering in the world. And in this experience, too, he first learned the beginnings of resolute solidarity thinking. There can be no individualistic hope: the individual may hope for self only in his or her hope for others.

The new political theology holds that theological reflection has to be related to experience. Metz believes accordingly that only the realm of experience lends itself to a "narrative theology."

Only original experience can be narrated in a way that will invite the listener to venture forth into a possible similar religious experience. He is convinced that the only hope for responding to the widespread and growing modern crisis of faith lies in a narrative, and not argumentative, theology. Metz discovered this from the Jewish tradition and found it confirmed in the basically "narrative" structure of the Christian Gospel. Hence, he argued, all theology, if it is to invite the praxis of discipleship, as the Gospel clearly and persistently does, must be in this sense a "narrative theology." Only the retelling of the experience-rooted memories both old (including the Christian dogmatic tradition) and new may hope to touch modern persons in the present experience of their existence, inspiring hope and action.

How does "transcendental theology" relate to experience, in this technical sense of a political theological category? We have found considerable evidence of a fundamental relatedness to experience of Rahner's theological work in terms of its origin, method and goal. His bold attempts at making the theological tradition speak to the critical issues of today were seen to be based on, and preceded by, careful and perceptive analyses, both implicit and explicit of each situation. His transcendental method, we have learned, was born from contemporary experience. The very transcendental and anthropological theological method, which defines "man as the being (*Wesen*) of absolute transcendence towards God," must at the same time be considered a concretely "historical" method since it resulted from Rahner's sympathetic response to the way people in the modern era experience themselves.

Because Rahner's theological methodology emerged from experience, in the wider sense of that word, it is not surprising that we found the dynamic of his theology to be straining toward addressing the modern individual and society precisely within the experience of the crisis of their everyday existence. This is borne out by the fact that Rahner spent a lifetime reflecting on issues and problems directed to him by the very people and society that he addressed.

There is still another way in which Rahner's theology is both rooted in and tending towards experience: his personal (Ignatian) experience of God,[1] and the resulting need to lead his modern readers to the same intimate experience of God in all things. This is the dominant objective of all his efforts at theologizing. This is necessitated by the very nature of theology as understood by Rahner. Theology is by definition secondary to its subject matter: all theology must be "talk about God," Rahner holds, and "talk about God contains God only if it derives from God." But God is more than the origin of theology, he is also its goal: "All speech of God is ultimately a leading back into the silent mystery [God]."[2]

This is a very dynamic understanding of theology. Experience of God becomes here a precondition for doing any theology proper and the motivation for telling others of it with a view to inviting them to also open themselves up to such experiences. Theology, or speaking about one's original experience of God, however, assumes a decidedly secondary position since it must not be confused with the thing itself, i.e., the content of that

---

[1] Vorgrimler speaks about "the foundational experiences of [Rahner's] theological life." These "foundational experiences," Vorgrimler suggests, are identified in Rahner's own words in his essay, "Ignatius of Loyola Speaks to a Modern Jesuit," in which he has Ignatius say: "I have experienced God, the nameless and inscrutable, silent and yet near one, in the trinity of his coming towards me." Vorgrimler comments: **"This testimony**, which you place on the lips of Ignatius, the founder of your Order, **is [really] the biographical testimony of your theology."** Cf. "Ein Brief zur Einführung," *Wagnis Theologie...*, *Ibid.*, ed., (Herder, 1979), p.13.

On the centrality of this experience of God, both as his own starting point and his uppermost pastoral concern towards others, in all of Rahner's theology, cf. Lehmann in note #27 in chapter II; and on the accessibility of this experience to everybody, cf. Vorgrimler *Understanding Karl Rahner*, pp.11-14.

[2] Karl Neumann, *Der Praxisbezug der Theologie bei Karl Rahner*, (Herder, 1980), p.410f.; my tr. "Die Rede von Gott hat Gott nur, wenn sie von daher kommt" (cf. STh VIII, p.184). "Alles Reden von Gott ist schließlich Rückführung ins schweigende Geheimnis [Gott]" (cf. STh IX, pp.113-126).

experience.[3]   This perspective on theology rules out a "privatistic" interpretation of human self-transcendence and in fact contains an inevitable drive to reach out toward others. Far from being opposed to practical involvement in the public arena of life, Rahner's spiritual and transcendental theology implies or even requires it. Such involvement is its logical conclusion. In this regard, McCool speaks of a "dialectical spiral in Rahner's thought" which "moves from experience to system and back to experience again," as can be discerned from his writings on all central Christian doctrines.[4]

Nobody has captured this aspect of Rahner's work more succinctly and poignantly than Metz in an excursus entitled "Theology as Biography?"[5]   Metz observed that Rahner's theology can boast the achievement of reuniting dogmatic theology with life as it is experienced today. Hence, to describe transcendental theology as "theological biography" is not to

---

[3] *Ibid.*, p.109. Concerning the secondary position of theological reflection or speech, according to Rahner, says Neumann, "Experience impels towards the word, towards its articulation...The word, speech, however, is merely the objectivation of the original experience, not this experience itself; it can merely foreshadow experience" (my tr.).

W.V. Dych also speaks to the relation between experience and its reflection, saying: "Rahner seems to me to emphasize that there is a 'more' or a 'fullness' in experience which is intrinsically 'inconceivable' on the level of reflection, and intrinsically 'ineffable' on the level of expression, and that this 'more' or this 'fullness' must be constantly returned to as an intrinsic moment in theological method." "Method in Theology According to Karl Rahner," *Theology and Discovery*, p.44.

[4] Gerald A. McCool, ed., *A Rahner Reader*, (Seabury, 1975), p.xxv.

[5] Cf. FHS, pp.219-228. This "Excursus" is an adapted version of a paper Metz wrote in 1974 "as a tribute to Karl Rahner on the occasion of his seventieth birthday..., entitled 'Karl Rahner--ein theologisches Leben. Theologie als mystische Biographie eines Christenmenschen heute'" (FHS, p.228, n.1).

It is noteworthy that this *laudatio* is markedly less critical of transcendental theology than the one presented by Metz for Rahner's sixtieth birthday. While the earlier *laudatio* ends with a list of penetrating questions (cf. n.#7 in the Introduction), this one closes with only one mildly critical observation regarding a not fully developed sociocritical theology.

reduce it to being a "narrative theology" only. Rather, as is evident from his alternative designation, "biographical dogmatic theology," Metz's argument is quite clearly that it represents a corrective to the historical separation of narrative and "argumentative" (dogmatic) theology, thus bridging the chasm between them by integrating once again the two into an organic whole. It is a matter of "creative mediation" between these two aspects of theology and not of reducing one to the other.[6]

The term "biography" here is not to be confused with a "literary reflection of subjectivity" (FHS, p.220). It has rather a technical meaning for Metz: "Theology is biographical when the mystical biography of religious experience in the concealed presence of God is written into the doxography of faith." Or again:

> Biographical theology introduces the subject into the dogmatic consciousness of theology....'Subject' is not a term that can be exchanged at will in this context for any other. It is man involved in his experiences and history and capable of identifying himself again and again in the light of those experiences. Introducing the subject into dogmatic theology therefore means raising man in his religious experience and biography to the level at which he becomes the objective theme of dogmatic theology. In other words, it means that dogmatic theology and biography can be reconciled with each other and that theological doxography and mystical biography can be brought together (FHS, p.220).

These definitional statements not only are helpful for a better understanding of Rahner's transcendental theology but also

---

[6] Metz says as much, claiming that modern Catholic theology suffers from a "deep division...between theology as a system and religious experience, doxography and biography and dogmatism and mysticism." This resulted in a one-sidedness in which "Religious experience, the articulation of Christian history in the presence of God and the idea of mystical biography became more and more overshadowed by doxography," and so it was difficult for theology's contents to gain "public" relevance. Moreover, "Dogmatic theology," he says, "became an increasingly objectively atrophied form of teaching and often functioned as a systematized fear of contagion from life that was not understood" (FHS, p.219).

provide a better grasp of the sense in which political theology wants to be a narrative theology. Narrative here is not a matter of writing theology in a style that lends itself to "light reading." Even the most scientific lexicon theology may function as "narrative" theology in the sense Metz uses the concept. What makes Rahner's work a narrative theology is that its diverse themes cover all the peculiar dilemmas and struggles which the contemporary modern individual faces at work and in society. Not sensational events or problems but mostly the "average" experiences of ordinary people are the focus of this theology. Rahner has simply tried to respond to "the excessive number of claims made on him by life's questions and experiences" (FHS, p.224). Hence he deals not only with many different themes, as a random look at the pages of his bibliography reveals, but he also deals with them in a "variety of ways...with so many different questions in theology, the Church and public life" (FHS, p.224).

Life and life's experiences are given such a central position in Rahner's theology that Metz speaks of a reversed "system" in which--in contrast to scholastic theology--his "canon is life itself...life as it imposes itself" in all its "uncomfortable" dimensions. The richness and multiplicity of his work is not an attempt at being fashionable. It is a "systematic" effort at bringing "doctrine and life together within the context of the modern world" (FHS, p.224).

Rahner's is a bold theology, a "mystagogy for all without any fear of popularization or contagion from dull, ordinary everyday life and its religious experiences that can hardly be deciphered," says Metz (p.221). Rahner can confidently introduce the human subject with his or her everyday experiences into dogmatic theology, because he knows that all relevant Christian theology has always done the same; that "the classical questions of theology... are [but] the everyday questions of a previous period" (p.224).

In this qualified sense, Rahner's theology is "biographical" in several ways. First, it narrates the story of his own ordinary life which knew no sensational high points or drastic changes.

Second, by extension, it simply tells the story of all such routine, mundane lives facing the same odds in their attempts to lead a Christian existence. Metz, therefore, can describe Rahner's "theological work...as biographical dogmatic theology or the mystical biography of the Christian believer today" (FHS, pp.222f.) in a paradigmatic sense. But he emphasizes that Rahner's biographical theology is radically unique among its prototypes:

> It is above all a biographical dogmatic account of the simple, one might even venture to say the average, Christian, the mystical biography of an undramatic life. It is the biographical dogmatic theology of a markedly antibiographical type. In this respect, then, it is quite different from the comparable theological work of Augustine, Newman or Bonhoeffer, whom I included among his ancestors (FHS, p.226).

Far from being a disadvantage, argues Metz, it is this quality of simplicity which makes Rahner's theology "present and contemporary in a very specific way" (p.226). For here lies the explanation why Rahner was able to reach and touch so many people both within Christianity and beyond, despite his difficult linguistic style (cf. p.227).

In his reference to the dimension of simplicity which marks Rahner's work, Metz reverses in effect his earlier charge of "elitism" relating to the concept of anonymous Christianity (cf. FHS, pp.159f.). He now says "Rahner himself has a distinctly proletarian aversion to everything elitist or esoteric." For the "so-called elitist theologumena" (among others his "theory of anonymous Christianity") "have been determined by precisely the opposite intention" (FHS, p.227).

There is a third way in which Rahner's work is a "biographical dogmatic theology." While the individual subject is its immediate focus, Rahner's theological doxography represents at the same time "the biography of a whole people, the average, everyday collective routine religious experience of the Catholic people..." (FHS, p.221). Or, as Metz states further on, Rahner's "work is quite simply a theologically substantial report about life in the light of contemporary Christianity" (p.224). He draws the circle even wider in calling this transcendental theology "basically a concentrated and shortened biography of human history in the presence of God" (p.227).

Metz holds that this experience-rooted biographical dimension is so pervasive in Rahner's work that it is neither possible nor necessary to establish it in individual theological themes. But the "narrative, mystical biographical element" is unmistakably present, he says, in Rahner's treatment of Christology, soteriology, eschatology and historical theology. Moreover, a closer look reveals that even his theology of the Trinity, which raises the "strongest suspicion" as to its "biographical" content, is marked by a deep relatedness to human experience. Metz says:

> in [Rahner's] introduction to a treatise that he wrote on the triune God, [God is seen] as the transcendental ground of the history of salvation. He claimed that the mystery of the Trinity was the ultimate mystery of our own reality and that it could also be experienced in that human reality. This experience provided us with a methodological principle that could be applied to the Trinity. The Trinity, Rahner insisted, was a mystery with a paradoxical character that had an echo in man's own existence (FHS, pp.225f.).

Among other things this means that "man's experience as withdrawn from himself" into absolute mystery is rooted for Rahner in the incomprehensibility of God. On the other hand, must not human experience teach us that, if transcendent human persons can only realize themselves in the tangible world of history, the absolutely transcendent triune God can also be expected to enter worldly history, thus adopting it as salvation history? The inverse, of course, is also true: if the eternal and pre-existent *Logos* has decided to enter into concrete world history, then human beings may not hope to attain salvation by bypassing categorial reality.

Our discussion leaves no doubt that Rahner's theology is integrally experience-related and is therefore an exemplary narrative theology as specified by the new political theology. Metz in fact concludes his excursus by saying that his "consideration of Rahner's theological approach as a paradigm, [shows it] is the type of theology to which the narrative structure of the Christian faith most closely corresponds" (FHS, p.227). This testimony should carry even more weight since it comes from perhaps the boldest and most respected (by Rahner himself) critic of transcendental theology.

The question of the sociopolitical relevance of Rahner's work could be raised, however, since, according to Metz, he is seen largely to "narrate" the story or experiences of the human individual. Metz observes that there is a certain "orientation towards the subject" or a "predominance of anthropology...as opposed to history or society" in Rahner. But Metz's position is that a "total approach to a practical fundamental theology" ought to include "a theological biography of Christianity in which the twofold mystical and political structure of that theology, in other words, **the social pattern of Christian faith**, was more consistently taken into account and made the moving force of theological reflection" (p.227). But this critical suggestion wishes mainly to correct a perceived imbalance. It does not deny the very valuable service rendered by this theology to life in modern society. Metz emphatically recognizes this in his rhetorical questions:

> Who, after all, is in greater need of a biographical form of dogmatic theology than the Christian who finds it very difficult to feel part of theological teaching as a whole, to be affected by it or be involved in it and to identify himself or his own experience with the mysticism of that theology...? And where would he find greater need of it than in modern society, in which his identity is called into question, the death of the subject and the end of the individual are proclaimed, the experiences of the individual can no longer keep pace with the advances of technology in a world that has a stabilizing effect on expectations that conform to the system and at the same time banishes or reduces to nothing all hopes and dreams that call society into question? Modern society after all prefabricates man's pattern of life and produces a weariness with human identity that eats away at man's soul (FHS, p.221).

Rahner's transcendental theology, then, in its penetrating analysis of the human person's condition, also goes well beyond the individual realm of existence as it takes into account and affects the social situation at the same time.[7]

In order to demonstrate the presence of the experiential-narrative dimension in Rahner's work, we have emphasized here more what Metz calls its "mystical" or "biographical" element. It is important, therefore, to remind ourselves once more that Rahner does not stress this dimension at the expense or to the exclusion of its twin dimension, the "dogmatic" element. These two dimensions find a balanced integration in Rahner. To say it with Metz, "Doxography and mystical biography are merged into one another" (p.226). Rahner's work can only be correctly understood if both dimensions are seen in their polarity. However, perhaps because Rahner's theology represents a corrective of scholasticism, the balance--if anything--is tilted towards the experiential side. With respect to this "balance," Metz comments:

> The basic theme of his work can only really be heard if one listens to all the variations. His system is not without stories, his doctrine is not without communicated experiences and his doxography is not without mystical biography--none of the first can be understood without reference to the second (FHS, p.225).

The results of our study of Rahner thus far show conclusively that his theology is profoundly related to human experience. It is clear from our discussion of Metz's analysis of "narrative theology" that this "dialectical" relation between "experience" and "system" (McCool) has indeed the characteristics of "narrative

---

[7] Fischer, *op. cit.*, cf. p.27. That Rahner's practice in his theology of speaking about the human individual in the singular should not be taken too literally is supported by this comment by Fischer: "Already in his relatively early reflections, such as 'Meine Nacht kennt keine Finsternis,' 'Von der Not und dem Segen des Gebetes,' among others, one can detect in Rahner a strong tendency, toward interpreting and capturing the modern faith-crisis as a global 'Nacht der Sinne und des Geistes' [Night of the Senses and the Spirit]...**The nights of the senses and the spirit as destiny of individual man (or woman) can [therefore]... just as easily become the destiny of peoples, yes fundamentally of 'all' humankind**" (my tr. & emph.).

theology." Metz's perception of Rahner's theology concerning its narrative-experiential value is accurate; this can easily be verified, to take a random example, by examining Rahner's argumentation in his 1970 essay on the relation between "horizontalism" and "verticalism" (cf. TI XIV, pp.295-313). There we witness a superb example of modern individual and collective experience being converged into one. And the experience of concrete "love of neighbour" becomes the key to understanding what is meant by the existence of God and "love of God" for moderns. Only after uncovering the historical roots of "the sudden appearance of this radical horizontalism in the Church" (p.298)--, a) in the post-Enlightenment "historicist" "tendency to "*demythologizing*" the Christian tradition, b) the rationalist mentality of today's believers that stems from the natural sciences, and c) the modern trend of seeing in the newly discovered responsibility for the world the quintessence of the meaning of human life--does he proceed to examine the theological validity of this movement of thought and ask what the church's response to it should be. But although our complex modern experience is subjected to a critique by the church's response to it, the response itself is in turn substantively co-determined by that experience of life.

The profound and consistent rootedness of Rahner's theology in human experience, in the technical sense indicated by political theology, has been sufficiently demonstrated for our purposes, although it would be easy to supply ample additional material as proof.[8]

---

[8] As random examples that would bear out Metz's claim that all Rahner's theology is deeply rooted in experience, we could adduce statements like: "Precisely because the original reference towards God is of a transcendental kind and hence does not fall into any category but is given in the infinite reference of the spirit of man beyond every mere object of his personal and material surroundings, the original experience of God (as distinct from his separating representation in an individual concept) is always given in a 'worldly' experience. This, however, is only present originally and totally in the communication with a 'Thou'" (TI VI, p.246).

The main question that still remains is, how, if at all, are Rahner's "biographical dogmatic theology" and political theology's "narrative theology" different from each other? This question will be considered below. For now we may simply say that the two theologies will evidently differ somewhat materially as their "contents" represent responses to differing situations. But their formal functions would certainly overlap widely, if they are not in fact the same. As an example in support of this supposition, we may recall how, when faced with a comparable challenge, e.g., the threat from a Marxist utopianism to liquidate the human individual in order to speed up the achievement of an ideal communist society, both theologies respond with a resolute defense of the dignity of every present human individual or generation. And both theologies make their defense on the basis of Christian eschatology as grounded in the memory of the life and death of Jesus Christ.

One difference that Metz himself has suggested is that in transcendental theology the biographical theology of the person predominates over "the social pattern of Christian faith." An important comment on this issue is omitted from the original version of Metz's adapted "Excursus" discussed above. It says that, although Rahner has written a masterful mystical biography of the afflicted modern individual, he falls short in that he has "more intuited than developed...that threat to human identity which in history [*Lebensgeschichte*] takes the form of a social

---

Likewise, when Rahner wants to illustrate the possibility of genuine existential love for Jesus today, he uses the analogy of marital love and the risks and difficulties involved in it (cf. his passage entitled "Love for Jesus," *The Practice of Faith*, p.140). Or again, in *Von der Not und dem Segen des Gebetes* (pp.43f.) he illustrates our love for God by way of our experience of human love.

Finally, we could mention, how he employs the most ordinary human experiences, as witnessed in a little pamphlet, *Everyday Things*, M.H. Heelan, tr., Hans Küng, ed., (London and Melbourne: Sheed and Ward, 1965), with chapters such as: "On Work," "On Getting About," "On Sitting Down," "On Seeing," "On Laughter," "On Eating," "On Sleep."

and political history of suffering."[9] This comment is puzzling
at best in view of the fact that Metz himself has recognized in
the same *laudatio* the supreme social relevance of Rahner's
biographical theology, calling it even "a concentrated and
shortened biography of human history in the presence of God."

It is true, of course, that Rahner's transcendental and
anthropological theology does not take one specific historical
crisis, like *Auschwitz*, as the central experiential turning point the
way Metz does. Nevertheless, Rahner's work as a whole is
extremely sensitive to the cumulative crises that confront the
modern individual, church and society. Moreover, if Vorgrimler's
observation is correct that Rahner's public lectures during the
war were aimed at upholding a Christian view of humanity over
against the Nazi ideology, then the latter could hardly be said to
be doing theology "with his back turned to *Auschwitz*" (as Metz
has alleged).[10]

2. A Changing Context: Vatican II

Having argued that the pre-Vatican II conservative atmosphere
in Catholicism might have influenced Rahner's earlier theological
work, it stands to reason that the post-conciliar, more open
atmosphere should have had an impact on his later work as well.
We would come away with a distorted picture, however, were we

---

[9] Metz, "Karl Rahner--ein theologisches Leben," *op. cit.*, p.310; (my tr.).
In German (expanded):

"Rahner hat die mystische Biographie dieses in seiner lebensgeschichtlichen
Identität bedrängten modernen Menschen geschrieben. Mehr gefühlt nur als
entfaltet ist dabei freilich jene Identitätsbedrohung, die sich in der
Lebensgeschichte als soziale und politische Leidensgeschichte ausdrückt."

[10] Cf. Metz, "Christians and Jews after Auschwitz," EC, pp.17-33. Cf. also his *Im
Angesichte der Juden*. Here Metz says of Rahner's theology, "even in this theology,
in my opinion, the best Catholic theology of this time, *Auschwitz* did not figure" (p.5).
Then more generally: "With our backs to *Auschwitz*, we went on praying and
celebrating the liturgy" (p.8; my tr.).

to look strictly for the influence which this changing context exerted on Rahner's theology, without also considering his substantial role in bringing about the changes that made the watershed event of Vatican II possible in the first place. We shall remain attentive to both of these "dialectical" factors in the following considerations.

Mention has been made already of Rahner's significant role in paving the way for the Council through his provocative writings during the decade before it took place. This preparatory work was possibly more important than his outstanding contribution during the Council sessions proper.[11] As one of the most knowledgeable interpreters of scholastic theology, his reinterpretation of it found a ready channel through which to influence the Catholic leadership the world over when he uncovered the original intentions or the "inner dynamic" of that great but insulated body of dogma so familiar everywhere.[12]

Rahner's efforts at finding an intelligible language for the modern individual and society; his consciousness-raising concerning the individual's freedom and responsibility in the world; and his attempts to differentiate between the lasting kernel and the historically conditioned dimensions in the church's teaching, for nearly three decades before the Council took place, all helped significantly in the process of preparation for the event. Then, immediately before the sessions and by request of certain cardinals, he read and annotated the schemata intended by

---

[11] Lehmann says in this respect: "Rahner's influence rests however not only on the type of collaboration during the council, but [shows itself] also already in the worldwide pre-conciliar reception of his theological thought, which helped to set the mood [or cultivate the 'spirit'] of this Church gathering." *Rechenschaft*, p.19*; (my tr.).

[12] *Ibid.*, p.15*; On the matter of scholastic theology serving as a means for the rapid dissemination of Rahner's thought, Lehmann says: "'Scholastic theology,' as the starting point of many of Rahner's reflections, is probably one of the reasons why his thought patterns could achieve such an astounding power for their international expansion: every theologian, from his studies of traditional theology, was familiar with the problems it was faced with and so was better able to follow new developments" (p.19*; my tr.).

the central commission for the Council.[13] His status in relation
to the Council becomes apparent also by his "behind the scenes"
activities, including numerous lectures before German, French,
Dutch, Austrian and Belgian bishops, cardinals and theologians,
as well as his lively interaction with the Latin American
delegation.[14]

Rahner's performance during the Council sessions proper is
presented in considerable detail in Vorgrimler's biography, which
includes a collection of Rahner's private letters to the former
during that time.[15] Vorgrimler's discussion shows that although
it may be impossible to measure with precision the degree of
influence exercised by Rahner on many or all of the sixteen
documents passed by the Council, his influence can hardly be
overestimated. He clearly played a key role in the shaping of
many conciliar documents.[16] Most significant for the thesis of
this book is the fact that Rahner was instrumentally involved in
the elaboration of "The Pastoral Constitution on the Church in
the Modern World," from its inception to its conclusion.[17] This

---

[13] Vorgrimler, *Understanding Karl Rahner*, p.96.

[14] *Ibid.*, p.97. Vorgrimler even states: "His real work took place outside of the
official meetings." Cf. also p.99.

[15] For Rahner's correspondence to Vorgrimler between 1959 and 1965, cf.
"Appendix," *Ibid.*, pp.141-184.

[16] Although it is impossible to establish Rahner's direct influence on the
Council documents with certainty (partly because there were other renewal
theologians all along who also helped pave the way for and influenced the
outcome of the Council), it is reported that "no trace of Rahner's influence can
be found in four texts....In all the rest...we can see traces of Rahner's
theology." Because "without doubt, Rahner's publications on church and
sacraments, episcopacy and primacy, revelation and tradition, the inspiration
of scripture and the diaconate were as important for bishops as for
theologians" (*Ibid.*, p.100).

[17] A.P. Flannery, ed., *Documents of Vatican II*, (Wm.B. Eerdmans, 1975),
cf. pp.903-1014. Concerning Rahner's involvement in the elaboration of this
text--which eloquently contrasts the Catholic church's attitude toward the

schema occupied much discussion time during the final sessions. And when it became the focus of the Council in 1964 and 1965 (along with a number of other texts), Vorgrimler says "Rahner was in great demand." He continues: "Rahner's involvement was significant, particularly on the inerrancy of scripture (in the schema on revelation) and in setting the basic theological trend and giving an account of the Christian view of man in the text on the church in the modern world."[18]

Although Rahner proved himself to be a great team worker with supporters of church renewal at the Council, he nevertheless occupied a unique and leading position among theological advisors.[19] Yves Congar, for instance, thinks that the idea of "Two Sources" of revelation was rejected because of Rahner's influence--even though Rahner was not on the committee responsible for this schema--and calls the day that rejection took place "the end of the Counter Reformation."[20] Thus, while

---

world with that of the turn of the century--cf. Vorgrimler, *Understanding Karl Rahner*, p.98.

[18] Vorgrimler, *Ibid.*, p.99.

[19] For a glimpse of Rahner's outstanding performance at Vatican II, cf. the sketch of an apparently typical scene during the proceedings of the Council by his fellow *peritus*, F. Wulf S.J., *Bilder eines Lebens*, (1985), p.65.

[20] Yves Congar, "Erinnerungen an Karl Rahner auf dem Zweiten Vatikanum," *Ibid.*, p.65.

Congar, moreover, points out that Rahner's informal comments sometimes had an amazing impact. For example: one of thirteen 'modi', prepared by the theological commission, related to the papacy. "Rahner commented about it: 'If one wished to prevent the Protestants from ever gaining access to a theological understanding of the 'primacy,' then of course one could not have done anything better than this'." Congar adds: "I need not add, that this modus was rejected by the commission" (p.68; my tr.). Thus, according to Congar, although Rahner was not officially appointed to work with the commission for ecumenism, a contribution by him in this area was thereby not necessarily precluded.

Another similar testimony to Rahner's position at the Council could be cited from Cardinal König's "Der Konzilstheologe," where he says: "He was the

Lehmann's observation that "the history of Karl Rahner's influence upon the Second Vatican Council has yet to be written"[21] is undoubtedly correct, E. Klinger's claim that "Rahner's understanding of the meaning of dogma is a 'dogma' of the Vatican II church [and] his teaching concerning the existence of man and the church is a teaching of the church of the Council..."[22] would seem to be valid.

One further observation is in order, before turning to consider the possible influence of the Council's changing theological climate upon Rahner's thinking. It relates to the fact that Rahner did not merely help prepare for and actualize the Council; he remained a keen observer until the end of his life of how the decisions of Vatican II were or were not being implemented. His bibliography abounds in articles about the meaning of the Council. He reflects not only on the possible failure by the church to carry out its resolutions but also on the need for going beyond the demands of the conciliar texts.[23] For our purposes

---

mediator in the background, the never tiring inspirer [*Anreger*], not seldom the energetic defender of new ideas. His influences within this tapestry have yet to be investigated" (*Ibid.*, p.64; my tr.).

[21] Lehmann, *Rechenschaft*, p.19*; (my tr): "Die Geschichte des Einflusses Karl Rahners auf das Zweite Vatikanische Konzil wäre erst noch zu schreiben."

[22] E. Klinger as cited in *Bilder eines Lebens*, p.68; (my tr): "'Rahners Auffassung vom Dogmatischen ist ein 'Dogma' der Kirche des Zweiten Vatikanums. Seine Lehre von der Existenz des Menschen und der Kirche ist eine Lehre der Kirche des Konzils...'"

Elsewhere, Klinger makes a similar point in saying: "Karl Rahner was not just *peritus* at the Council. He counts also among those preparing its way. In him it has found a creative defender of its own cause, the cause, to be a true defender of the human being." Thus, this *Festschrift* for his 80th birthday is intended to pay proper homage "to one of the most important teachers of its [the Council's] theology." "Vorwort," *Glaube im Prozeß. Christsein nach dem II. Vatikanum*, E. Klinger, *et al*, eds., (Herder, 2. Aufl. 1984), p.5; (my tr.).

[23] The following examples will suffice: "The Second Vatican Council's Challenge to Theology;" "Theology and the Church's Teaching Authority after the Council," TI IX, pp.3-27; pp.83-100; "On the Presence of Christ in the Diaspora Community According to the Teaching of the Second Vatican

here, this signifies that, if additional elements should make their appearance in his theology in the post-conciliar period, these might have been evoked by the new intellectual climate or they could simply represent old aspirations of his which could only find realization when their time had come.[24]

The fact that Rahner is considered to be one of the key figures at Vatican II who were chiefly responsible for its success in bringing about renewal in the Catholic church does not necessarily mean, of course, that the final outcome of this great gathering did not, or would not, in turn, significantly affect his own theology. We will presently see some evidence that it did present challenges to his theology. But in order to better appreciate these challenges, it will be helpful to enumerate some of the actual changes precipitated by the Council.

Council;" "The Teaching of the Second Vatican Council on the Diaconate;" "On the Theological Problems Entailed in a 'Pastoral Constitution'," TI X, pp.84-102; pp.222-232; pp.293-317; "Basic Theological Interpretation of the Second Vatican Council;" "The Abiding Significance of the Second Vatican Council," TI XX, pp.77-89; pp.90-102; and "Vergessene Anstöße dogmatischer Art des II. Vatikanischen Konzils" (not tr. to my knowledge), STh XVI, pp.131-142.

Besides these specific reflections on the Council, Rahner frequently refers to it in essays whose titles may give no hint at the subject of the Council.

On going beyond the Council, we can refer to Rahner's comments on the status of the conciliar documents in *The Shape of the Church to Come*, p.13. Here he comments that, besides being "too general" to provide individual norms for us today, "in the positive decisions of the council...there is much that is already obsolete--in the decree on the liturgy, for example."

[24] That this is not just idle speculation can be illustrated from certain comments by Rahner in his correspondence during the Council. For instance, he sees it as entirely possible that some of his thoughts on renewal (of the diaconate, specifically) may be rejected by the then imminent Council. Should this really happen, then he "must wait. If we do not win here, we shall at the next Council." *Understanding Karl Rahner*, p.144.

Rahner himself mentioned the most notable achievements at the end of his life.[25] This Council, he said, was the first Council of a world church which wants to be, and has started to become, a world church, rather than being a European church that is exported into all the world. Vatican II has effectively put an end to the neoscholastic period of theology in making room for pluralism in the church and in theology. Along with beginning to transform the "church for the people" into a "church of the people" by assigning a higher value to the laity, it has also conceded greater initiative and importance to local bishops everywhere.

If all these areas leave much to be desired still, Rahner is concerned but not too distressed, because, he asks, did not the Council of Trent also take a hundred years to prevail? Although things may happen faster today, "one should not assume too quickly," he reminds those who seem impatient with the church, "that within ten years the conciliar measures should have been visibly realized." In any event, he himself has no doubt that "the Second Vatican Council was so decisive that the church cannot return to a pre-conciliar situation."[26]

It was, however, not merely the failure to implement and carry further the Council's teachings in the world church that would

---

[25] Cf. *Karl Rahner. Erinnerungen im Gespräch mit Meinold Krauss,* (Herderbücherei, 1984), p.100.

[26] *Loc. cit.*; (my tr): "Man darf nicht so rasch denken..., daß konziliare Maßnahmen in zehn Jahren sich schon merklich ausgewirkt haben müßten.... Das Zweite Vatikanum war ein Konzil, hinter das die Kirche nicht mehr zurück kann."

Elsewhere we learn that for Rahner Vatican II signifies the beginning of a whole new era in the history of the Christian church, i.e., the third era that exhibits "beginnings of a real world Church," whereby "the Church...finds itself on a pilgrimage from a culturally more or less monocentric Church of Europe and North America toward a culturally polycentric world Church," as Metz interprets in reference to STh XIV (cf. Metz, *Theologie im neuen Paradigma: politische Theologie, op. cit,* pp.8 and 14, n.26; (my tr.).

give Rahner cause for worry.[27]   In some ways it was also the very "successes" of that historic event that would seriously challenge his theological thinking. In an atmosphere of theological pluralism, it was no longer possible to simply divide theologians into "conservatives" and "progressives." Given the increased freedom for academic pursuit, approved by the Council, it happened that "former allies now took up positions which Rahner could not accept either from the Right or the Left without opposition.... The situation became more baffling [and] the road more troublesome."[28]   Before, Rahner had to concern himself mainly with uncovering the original meaning of the great theological tradition and its inherent message for our times. But now he felt suddenly compelled to engage in what he called a battle on two fronts (*Zweifrontenkrieg*). Things were changing so drastically that, in a sense, he suffered the feeling of a reversal of roles. He was, so to speak, "overtaken" by the new developments. In his words:

I now feel like someone, who suddenly has to defend the actual central positions of a traditional kind in the church...It can of course happen that one switches from the Left to the Right, not because oneself is changing one's position, but because others are changing theirs.[29]

---

[27] A good illustration of how the failure to implement and advance further the impulses of the Council in present Catholicism is seen in Karl Rahner, "Vergessene Anstöße dogmatischer Art des II. Vatikanischen Konzils," in: STh XVI (1984), pp.131-142. Thus he says, for instance, about the conciliar idea of a true episcopal worldwide collegiality: "The Council thus posits a task for itself, which it does not realize: to demonstrate, in theory and praxis, that the worldwide episcopacy governs the Church and how it does so" (p.137; my tr.).

[28] Lehmann, *Rechenschaft*, p.20*; (my tr): "Frühere Bundesgenossen vertraten nun Thesen, die [Rahner] weder von rechts noch von links ohne Widerspruch hinnahm....Die Lage wurde unübersichtlicher, der Weg noch mühsamer."

[29] As cited by Lehmann in *Bilanz*, p.178; (my tr): "'Ich komme mir jetzt (aber) vor als einer, der plötzlich die eigentlichen zentralen Positionen traditioneller Art der Kirche verteidigen muß...Man kann ja aus einem 'Linken'

Rahner's response was not resignation, however; he attempted to learn to live with the challenges of a pluralistic age. Of course, this did not mean adopting a "liberal," quasi-democratic approach to matters of theology. It meant engaging in respectful but vigorous dialogue with those whose positions differed from his own; this included a posture of learning as well as teaching. One such example is Rahner's two-year discussion with Hans Küng concerning the latter's book *Infallible?*. Rahner's dialogue often crossed over into other disciplines besides theology, e.g., his conversations with Marxists, scientists, journalists, the young and so on.[30]

The most extensive, and for our purposes most important, dialogue is Rahner's exchange with the political theology of Metz. The fact that this dialogue is mostly a friendly conversation rather than a confrontational debate and that for the most part it is implicit rather than explicit, does not necessarily diminish its intensity. And if the new political theology, along with some other theologies, is to a certain extent only thinkable because of Rahner's courageous pioneering work in theology and the church, then this need not mean that it cannot pose a fundamental challenge to a transcendental and anthropological theology. At any rate, once on the scene, political theology was to remain, as it were, a lifelong travelling companion to Rahner's theological thought. What Lehmann said in 1970 about the then last two volumes of STh (VIII and IX) surely applies also to most of the other volumes that were yet to follow, namely, that

---

ein 'Rechter' werden, indem nicht man selbst, sondern andere ihre Positionen wechseln.'"

[30] The crossing over toward a wide range of disciplines of Rahner's theology, and its reception, is well attested, on the scholarly level, in the numerous *Festschriften* in his honour, (beginning with *Gott in Welt* [1964], with its *tabula gratulatoria* containing "more than 900 names from all over the world" [cf. Vorgrimler, *Understanding Karl Rahner*, p.102] and ending with *Glaube im Prozeß: Christsein nach dem II. Vatikanum* [1984]), and on a more popular level, in, e.g., *Conversations...1965--1982* and *Bilder eines Lebens* (1985).

in them he was continually wrestling, implicitly, with the fundamental intention of the "political theology" of Metz.[31]

The emergence of the new political theology must itself be seen as one of the fruits of Vatican II. At the heart of the political theological critique of transcendental theology is clearly the more public social dimension of theology. The validity of this interpretation is confirmed both by the several points of Metz's criticism of transcendental theology and by Rahner's statements of his perception of that criticism that have been cited above. Therefore, if Rahner felt compelled to rethink his earlier work so as to integrate the "social dimension" more consciously into his theological thinking, then he obviously felt pushed forward by the very movement of renewal which he had helped to create. This is not to diminish Metz's role in the process of making this concept a theological reality. The idea of Rahner learning this particular "lesson" from the Council (and Metz!), however, is modified by the fact that he was one of the key movers of the constitution of the church in the modern world, passed by the Council.

Rahner did indeed learn this lesson, as can be seen by his remarks about a dimension in the theological interpretation of love which was formerly not there. What it consists of becomes apparent as he discusses "the new relationship between "horizontalism" and "verticalism" which has emerged in our particular epoch."[32] He explains that the abiding and "indissoluble unity in the midst of distinction between love of God and love of neighbour" notwithstanding, "nowadays...there is a need for a shift of emphasis" between these two aspects of

---

[31] *Ibid.*, pp.178f. With respect to this issue, Lehmann says: "Again and again Karl Rahner has risen to meet the needs of the Church and still more the challenges to theology in the last number of years. The last two volumes of STh (VIII and IX [TI: IXff.), e.g., grapple constantly, if implicitly, with the fundamental tenets of the 'political theology' of his student and friend Johannes B. Metz" (my tr.).

[32] Karl Rahner, "The Church's Commission to Bring Salvation and the Humanization of the World," TI XIV, pp.295-313, cf. esp. pp.308-310.

love. This is so because in our times it is no longer self-evident what is meant by the existence of God, and faith "is now lonely, no longer sustained and protected by public opinion," and so must start ever afresh and, one might say, deliberately. And it is above all in the self-transcending act of reaching out in "love for a Thou" that "the faith of the individual in God is kindled." In our post-Enlightenment intellectual climate, there seems to be no more effective medium available for generating faith in God (and humanity, of course) than practical love of neighbour. In Rahner's words:

> It is in this love of neighbour that the outward movement of man from himself is achieved most radically in knowledge and freedom. And it is only in the love of neighbour as thus conceived that it becomes clear for the man of today what is meant by God and the existence of God--clear in a sense in which it never needed to be made clear at all in earlier ages (TI XIV, pp.308f.).

The present age, however, brings with it not only special challenges but also distinct advantages, and is therefore to be welcomed. For the "experience of God" that comes about as a result of such practical love, he says, "has a clarity and radical depth in the life of a man such as it did not have in earlier times, when...there was a constant temptation to make a mere external indoctrination concerning the existence of God a substitute for this authentic experience of God" (p.309).

Thus, because of today's special circumstances, Rahner explains, to assign a certain "priority" to "horizontalism" over a "verticalism" does not necessarily contradict the basic truths of Christianity's self-understanding. The church should therefore boldly encourage modern men and women to engage themselves whole-heartedly in society-directed love, even though this dimension of love is in a sense secondary to love of God.[33]

---

[33] *Ibid.*, p.307. Rahner always holds fast to an ultimate primacy of the love of God, despite "the mutually conditioning relationship of horizontalism and verticalism." This is evident from statements like the following one: "in the unity which we recognize here it is obvious that the verticalism which

Rahner especially emphasizes that the church today should proclaim a love of neighbour "that transcends the immediate circumstances of your own private life which are constantly suspected of being tainted with egoism!" (p.309). The church may confidently make this "shift of emphasis" demanded by our times because a genuine "horizontal" love will lead to the clearest grasp of "what is meant by God and love for God." At the same time, in proclaiming the message of love of neighbour, says Rahner, the church "would simply be preaching that ultimate and essential truth which she has all along been attempting to bring home to man" (p.309). Thus, if the modern situation constitutes an unprecedented challenge to Christianity, it brings with it also uniquely new possibilities: the truth of Christian love assumes a clarity and concreteness, if it is enacted, which formerly it could not achieve.

While Rahner concedes that the present world situation demands that priority be given to the dimension of the twofold love commandment which is ordinarily subordinate, it is nevertheless a conditional concession. The condition is as follows:

> If a horizontalism were to seek nothing else than to awaken and disseminate the conviction that Christians must recognize and put into effect their responsibility for the world in a far more radical manner than formerly, taking this at last [sic] as the task for the hour, then a horizontalism of this kind can only be praised as a characteristic of this particular epoch, this particular age of the Church (TI XIV, p.310).

Having made this admission, Rahner hastens to add that taking our broadened Christian responsibility for the world utterly

---

orientates us towards God, in so far as it can and must be distinguished from the horizontalism that orientates us towards man, has a higher dignity and of itself implies a more radical duty on man's part." This is no arbitrary preference, however. Rather, it has a position of primacy because it is "only through the grace of God that we are set free in such a way as to be able to use and enjoy the world, and open ourselves unreservedly to our neighbour without becoming enslaved by the social and material environment of ours, without having to idolize it in order to be able to endure it" (p.312).

seriously does not absolve us or the church from tending to all the complex duties which belong to the life of the church: worship, theology, and "the cultivation of an interior religious orientation to God" (p.310). Or still more plainly: "Even a Christianity that is radically aware of its responsibility for the world should still pray, still pursue theology, still rejoice in God and his peace, thank God and praise him." For, on closer analysis, this balance between action, reflection and meditation is most necessary exactly for those most deeply committed to their tasks in and for the world, states Rahner (p.310).

When turning to the question of what the church can contribute to the humanization of the world, Rahner exhibits a similar cautiously balanced position. On the one hand, he fully affirms that today "love of neighbour means not merely an attitude but concrete action" in which we reach out toward others in unselfish, sacrificial ways (p.310). On the other, he reminds us that the actual concrete planning for, and realization of, the humanization of the world cannot be the "direct" responsibility of the official church, but is the proper task of the secular world. The church's role is rather a "critical" one in that it must explain to the modern individual, insofar as possible, what implications his or her responsibility for the world have with respect to "eternal salvation or perdition" (p.311). In other words, the church's contribution is here seen to be an indirect one, the criterion being that the goals pursued "be inspired by ultimately Christian motivations." It may collaborate with agents of the secular world under the following condition:

> In her official life the Church can even go on to give help to secular institutions in their efforts when this seems desirable or profitable, and when the immediate goals of these are unequivocally designed to serve the dignity and freedom of man, and can on these grounds be recognized as Christian too. The Church *as an official* Church, however, is not the immediate or proper subject for realizing in the concrete the humanization of the world (TI XIV, pp.311f.).

The proper role of the church is primarily that of being a living example of respect for "the freedom and dignity of man" (p.312).

It is obvious by now that Rahner's acceptance of the (post-conciliar) view of the increased importance of the sociopolitical aspect of life is by no means an uncritical one. To begin with, only after some careful introductory remarks on how this horizontalism really borders on the "heretical," even on "apostasy,"[34] does he turn to search for the "kernel of validity" in the new doctrine. Moreover, he takes care to remind us again in closing that the concession can only be a temporary measure made in respect of particular conditions. But even this horizontalism dare not become an immanentist end in itself. It must stand in the service of the central proclamation of the church. Without creating a false dualism of the "secular" versus "sacral," the church must give the world over to itself, because only then will the church "herself be free to undertake what is

---

[34] *Ibid.*, p.295. Here Rahner begins his search for the kernel of truth in "horizontalism" by pointing out that in its present reductionistic tendency it may well be "more than heresy;" that in traditional terminology it "should be called apostasy," because it will lead to "an elimination of Christianity." Specifically, says Rahner, "We mean here the view that that which constitutes the true essence of Christianity, the true heart and center which alone is signified in all its doctrines, the true task of the Church, consists in something which can simply be called 'love of neighbour' or (because this term has perhaps too individualistic or pietistic a ring for the upholders of this movement) 'commitment at the level of social politics and criticism of society', 'responsibility for the world'."

In other words, he is speaking about a "pure horizontalism." This "radical horizontalism" which he says (p.296) is tantamount to apostasy is "that doctrine and that interpretation of life which regards Christianity, its doctrines and in truth the task of the Church as properly speaking consisting in one thing alone: a responsibility for mankind, for human society. 'God' is reduced to a mere cipher...It stands for mankind itself, its unassailable dignity, the future which it still has to strive to achieve for itself."

On how a "horizontalist" theology needs to relate to the whole of Christian revelation and theology, cf. Rahner's opening remarks in "On the Theology of Revolution," TI XIV, pp.314-316.

her own true saving function which she alone can fulfil." This function is quite simply to be a living reminder to the world that although "it is true that salvation itself is achieved by man in the whole scope of life as pervaded throughout by the moving power of God's spirit," it must nevertheless be recognized

> that the whole human existence, and so the entire world in all its dimensions, ultimately reaches out to the life of God; that there is no horizontal dimension which is *entirely whole and complete* in itself without a vertical one; that it is only through God's grace that we are set free in such a way as to be able to use and enjoy the world, and open ourselves unreservedly to our neighbour without becoming enslaved by this social and material environment of ours, without having to idolize it in order to be able to endure it....

Rahner elaborates further on the "salvific function" of the church as he continues:

> All this must be offered and communicated to the world ceaselessly in the physical sign of God also, in the power of his grace as the innermost *entelecheia* of the world itself. And over and above all this God himself must be adored in spirit and in truth. The historical embodiment of his self-utterance in the death and resurrection of Jesus Christ must be accepted and celebrated ever anew precisely because this self-utterance of God takes place in the *world* as such. All this is included in the salvific function of the Church (TI XIV, p.312; italics his).

Rahner insists on this central, if indirect, function of the church even if this may raise suspicion of creating "an impotent and ineffectual ideology," because he is convinced that modern society needs reminding that "the ideological superstructure has effects which redound upon that which constitutes its real basis....that the so-called ideological factor is itself a part of the reality such that without it even the other factors in man could not exist." Society today needs to understand that "even in his so-called natural state [a person] is incapable of existing without culture." Ideology is not, then, "a luxury" which the human being can do without. Therefore, "the salvific function of the Church, even in its vertical orientation to God, has a direct significance for the task of man in his own sphere" (pp.312f.).

We made the claim a bit earlier that in the post-conciliar theological climate Rahner learned the "lesson," especially from political theology, of the essential importance of the social or "public" dimension of the Christian faith and life. However, the question that presents itself to us, in the light of the evidence presented here, might well be: has Rahner really learned that "lesson"? Is he not in the end evading the issue again in his insistence upon the "indirect" approach and upon fulfilling all the complex duties emerging from Christian revelation--even maintaining an ultimate primacy with respect to the duty of love and the worship of God? To be sure, as has become amply evident, Rahner's acceptance of the "shift" of the present emphasis towards the "horizontal" dimension in the life of the church (and society) is no uncritical adaptation to current trends. But it can nevertheless be maintained that he truly adopts this dimension and integrates it into his own theology, perhaps as a combination of a "corrective" to his earlier individual-oriented work and/or a "fulfillment" of the inherent (if latent) world-directedness in it which needed a proper atmosphere in order to emerge fully. By way of analogy, we could say that Rahner now extrapolates the "kernel" of truth from the doctrine of "horizontalism" just as he was formerly seen to extract it from traditional dogmatic theology. Thus one might cautiously say that Rahner's way of adopting the impulses from new theological movements "from the Left" represents a certain kind of political theology to political theology itself in that it is criticizing these movements sympathetically, much like sociopolitical theology had criticized his transcendental theology beforehand.

It is important, however, to note that his charge against the new horizontalist theology as being "more than heresy" is not directed against "political theology" as such. For he specifically acknowledges that there is a place for the "serious upholders of a so-called 'political theology'," who "have nothing to do with this radical horizontalism" criticized by him (TI XIV, p.297). This does not mean that he has no criticisms with respect to the new political theology represented by Metz (as will be seen below), but it does mean that he admits that there is a "perfectly orthodox" form of it, as was seen above.

The fact that Rahner is seen to adopt a posture of courageous dialogue towards the new post-conciliar theological movements, including the Latin American liberation theology[35] is, of course, entirely consistent with his lifelong endeavours in defense of freedom in the church. One might even say that Rahner's basic theological position of openness toward the *Deus semper maior* dictates that he should always maintain an attitude of critical "learning," even when the "new" aspects of political theology may be personally irritating to him at times.[36] He lives up to his maxim that "one should never stop thinking too soon," even when this is unpleasant.

The more precise relation of Rahner's later work to the new political theology cannot be pursued further here; this will be dealt with further on. Our inquiry thus far holds out good

---

[35] We have already made reference to Vorgrimler's mention of Rahner's interaction at the Council with those who would become Latin American liberation theologians (particularly Brazilians), and his intervention on their behalf later on. That his theology has become a source of perspective for these theologians is evident for instance from G. Gutiérrez's "classic" *A Theology of Liberation*--foundational for the whole movement--in which he refers extensively to Karl Rahner. Another most eloquent "testimony" to this effect is the congratulatory letter to Rahner on his 80th birthday from the National Bishops Conference (and theologians) of Brazil. It says in part: "...the Brazilian bishops and theologians, who are...meeting in Brasilia with the Doctrinal Commission of Bishops for a workshop, would like to congratulate you and are giving thanks to God for the fruitful theological contribution which you are rendering in the Church and in the world.

"We appreciate in a special way those contributions which your theological, pastoral and spiritual work gives us and through which you are helping us to grasp our Church's mission in the world, above all in regards to human dignity and with respect to a Christian response to the problems of our modern times." (*Bilder eines Lebens*, p.147; my tr.) For specific examples of ways and areas in which Rahner affirmed and/or criticized liberation theology, cf. L. Boff's and J. Sobrino's reflections, *Ibid.*, pp.146-150.

[36] Cf. G. Sporschill, ed., *Karl Rahner. Bekenntnisse* (Herold, 1984), p.37. Here Rahner tells of how Metz's repeated use of the "fairy tale" of "the hare and the hedgehog" (cf. FHS, pp.161f.) against his transcendental theology did anger him.

promise, however, with respect to our central thesis as outlined at the outset. There appears to be much and substantial overlap between the work of Rahner and the "new political theology" sketched out above. But there may also be considerable differences between them.

3. Love of God and Love of Neighbour

It is not by accident that Rahner chooses as his criterion for assessing new theological movements the category of the twofold love commandment. It forms the very center of his theological work[37] --perhaps of all genuine theology deserving of the name.[38] According to Rahner, for example, the fundamental "existential" of human freedom can only be known and achieved by an act of interhuman love. The following statement shows that this holds true also with respect to freedom in relation to God: "Human freedom is always freedom with regard to a categorial

---

[37] Cf. Neumann, *op. cit.*, p.114. Thus Neumann mentions that Rahner finds that "Love becomes 'in the NT the most fundamental and central 'root word' [*Stichwort*], even if in the history of theology this has scarcely been unambiguously carried forward'." Therefore, "in this respect theology has yet to catch up to the NT" (my tr.). This is obviously what Rahner sets out to accomplish.

[38] Cf. Helmut Peukert, "Kommunikative Freiheit und absolute befreiende Freiheit. Bemerkungen zu Karl Rahners These über die Einheit von Nächsten- und Gottesliebe," *Wagnis Theologie*, p.274. According to the author, "Not only the Christian [but] already the Jewish tradition comprehends the relationship to God in terms of radical love," for it is central to this tradition that "the commandment of love of neighbour, too,...is the sum total of all the rules of conduct toward the other person" (my tr.). However, Peukert adds, historically it seems to be the hallmark of Christianity to equate the two commandments and to intertwine them inextricably.

object and an inner-worldly Thou, even when it begins to be directly freedom before God."[39]

The centrality of human-divine love in Rahner's theology is made explicit, when he says: "The original relation to God is the love of neighbour." He then explains: "If man becomes himself only through the love of God and must achieve this by categorial action then, in the order of grace, the act of neighbourly love is the only categorial and original act in which man reaches the whole categorially given reality and thus experiences God directly, transcendentally and through grace."[40] It is readily obvious from these observations that a brief inquiry into the formal meaning of this category of Rahner's theology--before assessing the implicit and explicit political theological dimensions of his theology in more detail in the subsequent section--is both well warranted and promising for the thesis of this book.

Before taking a closer look at the subject at hand, it is well to take notice of the pastoral-practical dimension that is involved here. As with all of his work, so his reflections on the precise relationship between love of neighbour and love of God are undertaken in response to a specific situation. The immediate occasion for Rahner's "foundational" "Reflections on the Unity of the Love of Neighbour and the Love of God" was a Cologne audience of Catholic social workers, before whom he delivered a lecture on this topic in 1965, just after Vatican II. But in this lecture, Neumann says, Rahner was in fact (in his usual way) taking hold of the "hidden trend of the times" and gave it a Christian interpretation, finding for it the much needed key concept, i.e. "at the dawn of such a new epoch, 'love of

---

[39] Karl Rahner, *Grace in Freedom*, (N.Y: Herder & Herder, 1969), p.217f. Rahner adds: "For even such an act of a direct Yes or No to God does not envisage immediately and solely the God of original transcendental experience and his presence as revealed in this, but first the God of thematic categorial reflection, the notional God" (p.218). (Cf. also TI VI, p.241.)

[40] *Ibid.*, p.218.

neighbour' might easily be the root-word which really moves people and the key-word for today."[41]

What the "epoch" in question consists of emerges from Rahner's opening analysis of the situation at the time of that lecture. The people of this epoch find it difficult to build a bridge toward the transcendent God as "there is talk of the end of metaphysics" and the "transcendental philosophy of the pure subject, with openness to the Absolute" (in its modern "anthropocentric" meaning) is also questioned again; all religion and cult have become deeply suspect for many in a time which questions all ideologies and seeks "to demythologize everything" until all that remains is we "ourselves in solitude as the only real bottomless abyss," or "the incomprehensible something which is experienced as the absurd something which one would like to honour in silence, or as the honest and bitter minimum of everyday duty in the service of others, if one is still inclined to act and talk about an 'ideal' at all."[42] This, then, is the stark situation that presents itself to Christianity and in which it has to proclaim the gospel message. And because it must make the gospel comprehensible to persons precisely where they live and how they understand themselves, concludes Rahner, the challenge to Christianity consists in demonstrating to modern individuals "that the *whole* truth of the gospel" is still contained, at least in germ, in that vestige of what they can believe in and act upon, namely, "in the love of one's neighbour" (TI VI, p.233). In order to demonstrate this, love would have to be inclusive of the whole reality to which the Christian trilogy of faith, hope and charity is pointing. If this can be shown to be so, "then **love could be the valid topical word for today** which calls the whole of Christianity in the man of tomorrow into the concreteness of life

---

[41] Cf. Neumann, *op. cit.*, pp.115f.; the longer quote is from K. Rahner, TI VI, p.249. Having said this, Rahner warns that it is only valid if the love of neighbour is taken in its inclusive meaning, i.e. in such a way that it "contains the whole of Christian salvation and of Christianity."

[42] Karl Rahner, TI VI, p.233.

and out of the depth into which God (and not ourselves) has immersed it by his offer of grace, the grace which is He Himself." The validity of this supposition requires "that it can really be said seriously that the love of God and the love of neighbour are one and the same thing, and that, in this way and in this way alone, we understand what God and his Christ are, and that we accomplish what is the love of God in Christ when we allow the love of our neighbour to attain its own nature and perfection" (TI VI, pp.233f.). In the rest of the lecture, Rahner tries to establish that, and how, this is in fact the case by examining scripture and theological tradition, both in its classical and modern forms.

But before we proceed to delineate the central points of his thinking on the topic (as presented in this "foundational" essay on the subject), we should first point out that the topic itself is not at all new at this moment of Rahner's development. Rahner, early on, defined the human being as a being who is oriented toward mutual service with respect to a "Thou." Likewise, there is a portion in his postwar sermons of 1946[43] that treats of the love of God and the love of neighbour in a comparative fashion. Some key insights of his 1965 lecture are already present in those early meditations, although he had to develop further and radicalize his thinking on the matter.[44] Then, in a 1957 lecture,

---

[43] Karl Rahner, "Das Gebet der Liebe," *Von der Not und dem Segen des Gebetes*, (Herderbücherei: 12th ed., 1985), pp.39-52. The meditations of this "spiritual" booklet are his *Fastenpredigten* in war-ruined Munich of 1946.

[44] Cf. *Ibid.*, pp.43f. For example, the key insight of his 1965 lecture, that genuine love of neighbour is unlimited and is simultaneously directed toward the whole of reality, is clearly present in that early work, when he says: "...And remarkably: the person who loves thus, truly loves the other person, has escaped from the dungeon of his (or her) limitation, from which he (or she) fled, not into another such dungeon. In this movement of love toward the other unique person, he (or she) discovers not just the worth of the loved being, but somehow the whole world in its mysterious, blissful depth. Or perhaps better still: When a human person thus lovingly goes out of himself (or herself) and goes over to the other one, then such an act of love already

Rahner observed that just as the multiplicity of assertions about the Christian faith are ultimately "reducible" to (because rooted in) the mystery of God's self-communication, so in Christian ethics there is necessarily such a "reduction" of the many commandments to the one all-encompassing love commandment.[45] Rahner's 1961 essay "The 'Commandment' of Love in Relation to the other Commandments" (TI V, pp.439-459), explored this theme in a systematic manner.[46] In it much of the stage is prepared for his 1965 lecture on the strict unity of the two loves. We learn that there are many commandments and yet only one commandment (of love) that encompasses the whole law and the prophets (Mt 22:34-40; Rom 13:10; 1 Jn 4:8,12,20f.). But this love commandment, in contrast to all other commandments, Rahner shows, is not really a "commandment," since it does not ask for certain achievements of the human being but requires the person herself or himself. In Rahner's words:

> One may speak of a commandment of love as long as one does not forget that this law does not command man to do something or other but simply commands him to fulfill himself, and charges man with himself, i.e. himself as the possibility of love in the acceptance of the love in which God does

---

contains 'image and likeness' of that love, which reaches out toward everything--toward God."

Thus, while Neumann (cf. p.115) may be right in saying that in the early stages of Rahner's thinking on the Biblical love commandment he tended to give priority to its "love of God" dimension, this quote from 1946 already shows clearly an awareness of a "mysterious more, that lives in the genuine love of one person for another..." (p.44; my tr.).

[45] Neumann, *op. cit.*, p.107. By using the term "reducible," I intend the meaning of Neumann's term *Rückführung* and not its possible negative or minimizing meaning. The love commandment is so vast that it can gather into itself all other ethical precepts, thereby actually "widening out" their meaning instead of narrowing them down.

[46] *Ibid.*, cf. pp.108f.

not give something but gives Himself. Can this commission still be called a commandment? (TI V, p.456).

This thought on the nature of the love "commandment" is already found in his 1946 meditations.[47]

This interpretation of the love commandment entails a dynamic and basically always unfinished relation between the moral agent and this fundamental precept. If the person is asked to love God and the neighbour with all her or his being and might, then nobody can "possess" this love all at once and in all its fullness. Nobody can claim at a given point to have "arrived" at the goal of being perfectly loving. One can only be on a "pilgrimage" toward her or his ever growing love. How could one ever claim to have completely fulfilled one's obligation to love God and the neighbour perfectly, any more than one could claim to have perfectly realized all one's potential?

In his post-conciliar lecture concerning the strict unity between the two loves, Rahner confronts the challenge of demonstrating that "love of neighbour"--the only thing the modern individual may still grasp and believe in--can really be that "key-word" in which the whole essence of Christianity is yet encompassed. This challenge is compounded by the apparently contradictory assertion, which Rahner has always maintained, that

> The love of God is the totality of the free fulfillment of human existence. It is not, in the last analysis, the content of an individual commandment, but is at once the basis and the goal of all individual commandments. **And it is what it must be only when God is loved for his own sake**--when love for him is produced and experienced not with a view to human self-assertion and interior self-fulfillment...but when human beings, ultimately without self-seeking, go out of themselves, forget themselves because of God, and really lose themselves in the ineffable mystery to which they willingly surrender.[48]

---

[47] Cf. n.#44 in this chapter.

[48] Karl Rahner, *The Love of Jesus and the Love of Neighbor*, R. Barr, tr., (N.Y: Crossroad, 1983), p.70.

How, then, can Rahner say just as categorically that "the original relation to God is the love of neighbour" (as cited already)? How can the love of neighbour by itself constitute the fulfillment of "the whole truth of the gospel"? This claim could only be made if it were possible to show that the genuine act of neighbourly love already unfailingly contains in itself, simultaneously, all that is meant by the love of God. We need to remember that love of God, and only that love, is ultimately the person's self-realization.

In the 1965 lecture, Rahner begins the demonstration that this is indeed the case by recalling the "declarations of scripture" on the subject. Matthew 25:34-46 and 1 John 4 are key among the many texts he cites from the gospels and the epistles. In the eschatological passage about the Judgment in Mt 25, it is evident that for the "Synoptic theology of love," "love of neighbour is given...as the only standard by which man will be judged....In addition, there is that puzzling saying in the Synoptic tradition that what is done to the least of his brethren is done to Jesus." This text, argues Rahner, surely implies that "the unity of *this* Son with man," if we consider Jesus' "absolutely unique position" as the Son of God in whom the kingdom of God is present among humankind (TI VI, p.234). Rahner's inference from this is not surprising: these considerations will lead us "back again to the doctrine of the mysterious unity of the love of God and of neighbour and to its Christological radicalisation" (p.234).

In John's theology, this love for one another, made possible by God's first loving us concretely in Christ, is even more radical. For John, "the consequence of this is that God who *is* Love (1 Jn 4:16) has loved us, not so that we might love him in return but so that we might love *one another* (1 Jn 4:7,11)" (p.235). In short, Rahner extrapolates from this epistle, that if the invisible God cannot be reached by a love of "gnostic-mystic interiority alone," then it follows that we can only love **the 'God in us'** by **mutual love**" (p.235).[49]   Scripture, then, substantially supports Rahner's thesis of the unity of the two loves, even if this needs to be translated into, and spelled out further in our modern philosophy of life.

Similarly, he finds a certain measure of support for his position in the theological tradition. Classical theologians, while aware that so-called acts of charity may originate from ambiguous motives would readily see the love of God to be "implicit" in "every act of charity towards our neighbour." But "scholastic theology would probably deny that conversely every act of the love of God is formally also a love of neighbour" (p.237). The "demonstration" that this is indeed the case, however, is of great importance in that it, if true, implies an unavoidable requirement of reaching out in active love towards others. It is then not possible to be a genuine Christian privately, given the centrality of love (human and divine) in the Christian life, and given the dynamic nature of love.

Reservations to accepting the idea of a radical unity between the "two loves" are by no means limited to scholastic theology. As Rahner sees it, it is still widespread even in the present:

> Most theologians of today would still shrink from the proposition which gives our fundamental thesis its ultimate meaning, its real clarity and inescapable character, viz. that wherever a genuine love of man attains its proper nature and its moral absoluteness and depth, it is in addition always so underpinned and heightened by God's saving grace that it is also love of God, whether it be explicitly considered to be such a love by the subject or not (TI VI, p.237).

---

[49] Rahner spells out this idea further in a rhetorical question: "Or may we take the words of St. John absolutely seriously, so that the 'God in us' is really the one who alone can be loved and who is reached precisely in the love of our brother and in no other way, and that the love of neighbour encounters the love of God in *such* a way that it moves itself, and us with it, closer to the brother near by and attains both itself and the peak of perfection in the love of this brother, i.e. specifically as love of neighbour, and brings us to God and his love by the love of our neighbour?" (TI VI, p.235.)

This has, of course, ramifications for what is known as his idea of "anonymous Christianity," as well as for Christianity's relationship to other religions.

The remainder of his lecture is dedicated to demonstrating that, and how, this thesis finds support not only in scripture and tradition, but also in the modern human self-understanding developed in the disciplines of transcendental philosophy, ethics and theology.

When Rahner says that all genuine love of neighbour is simultaneously love of God, he understands love "as an unconceptualised transcendental horizon of action" which is more than "reflected" or "explicit" love of neighbour because the latter presupposes the former. The difference has to do with the qualitative difference between the two respective "objects" of love. Thus the love in which God is explicitly the "object"--, e.g., in relating oneself directly to God in prayer, trust and love--deals with an object of "higher dignity" than the object in the conscious act of love of neighbour (238). Yet genuine interhuman love, in so far as it reaches its ultimate depth, is also necessarily love of God, since "the neighbour, through God's love for him, is 'one' with God." Moreover, all radical love of neighbour is also love of God by reason of Rahner's doctrine of the "supernatural existential," which considers all interhuman love, as indeed all moral action, to be rooted in an "inescapably given transcendental horizon, which is given gratuitously by God's always prevenient saving grace" (cf. pp.238f.).

The radical unity of love of neighbour and love of God, in the area of morality is illustrated by Rahner's understanding of human freedom. For him, human freedom finds its genuine expression only in the subject's holistic self-realization through the loving relation towards a Thou, the concrete manner and meaning of which is modeled in Jesus. In terms of morality, the commandment to love one's neighbour does not refer to a "regional" act but relates to "the sum total of the moral as such" (TI VI, pp.239f.), because love is fundamentally bound up with human freedom. But within the whole world of "thous," human freedom and love reach their true goal solely in relation to another human thou--if only for the reason that love for God cannot be realized directly but only via the categorial mediation. According to Rahner, in the great seemingly arbitrary multiplicity that forms our surrounding world,

> the true and proper surrounding of man is his **personal environment**. This environment of persons is the world through which man finds and fulfils himself (by knowledge and will) and...gets away from himself. From a personal and moral point of view, the world of things is of significance only as a factor for man and for his neighbour (p.240).

This insight has a fundamental significance as it shows how deeply Rahner's whole framework of thought is centered around interhuman love. However much his theology of love may be rooted in his foundational transcendental epistemology (SW) and philosophy of religion (HW),[50] human "knowledge" (i.e. "self-possession"), in turn, culminates for him or is ultimately meaningful only in free and loving outreach toward fellow men and women, as the following statement attests:

> Knowledge (being itself already an act) attains its proper and full nature only in an act of freedom and therefore must lose itself and yet keep itself in freedom in order to be completely itself, it has a fully human significance only once it is integrated into freedom, i.e. into the loving communication with the Thou. **The act of personal love for another human being is therefore the all-embracing basic act of man which**

---

[50] This comment should not be interpreted as suggesting that Rahner's foundational philosophical works were devoid of the idea of love as the central basic act of human individuals. As Neumann (*op. cit.*, p.114) points out, Rahner tried to appropriate into his treatment on love the New Testament position of "love" as the most central key-word (which he felt current theology had long since largely neglected to consider sufficiently). But this attempt on Rahner's part was not new with him: "He attempted this already in principle in *Hörer des Wortes* (chap. 8: 'The free Hearer' ['Der freie Hörende']). Then more pointedly in the chapter, 'Freedom is the Empowerment of Love for Dialogue' ['Freiheit ist dialogisches Vermögen der Liebe']. Love is here (as already in HW) no regional and particularized potential in the human person, but the fundamental act of freedom itself" (my tr.).

gives meaning, direction and measure to everything else (TI VI, p.241; my emph.).

Rahner makes explicit the inherent logic of his methodology when he infers from this assertion that "the essential *a priori* openness to the other human being which must be undertaken freely belongs as such to the *a priori* and most basic constitution of man and is an essential inner moment of his (knowing and willing) transcendentality." This "basic constitution," he says, is experienced in concrete relationships with concrete people. Therefore, the one (moral or immoral) fundamental act in which persons truly reach conscious self-possession and make a final decision about themselves, Rahner submits, is "the (loving or hating) communication with the concrete Thou in which man experiences, accepts or denies his basic *a priori* reference to the Thou as such" (p.241). The act of loving interaction with the neighbour is the only pivotal act that "assembles" a person's self-knowledge and in which the self is realized with finality. This entails "that the whole incalculable mystery of man is contained and exercised in this act of love of neighbour," says Rahner, and continues: "it means that all anthropological statements must also be read as statements about that love which is not merely a 'regional' happening in the life of man but is the whole of himself in which alone he possesses himself completely, meets himself completely and falls into the ultimate abyss of his nature" (p.242).

This centrality of interhuman love in relation to "everything else" in a person's life, should not, however, be confused with a facile reductionism. The other dimensions in life and in the world remain (as do the other commandments) indispensable dimensions and values. But they have a subordinate position so that "everything else is a moment, presupposition, initial stage or the result of *this* [act of loving communication with the Thou]" (p.242).

Rahner then concludes his investigation concerning the thesis of the radical unity of the love of neighbour and the love of God with a resounding affirmation, stating:

The categorised explicit love of neighbour is the primary act of the love of God. The love of God unreflectedly but really and always intends God in supernatural transcendentality in the love of neighbour. It is radically true, i.e. by an ontological and not merely 'moral' or psychological necessity, that whoever does not love the brother whom he 'sees', also cannot love God whom he does not see, and that one can love God whom one does not see only by loving one's visible brother (TI VI, p.247).

This interpretation of the twofold love commandment, translated in this lecture into the modern horizon of experience and thought, is of course firmly based on Christological considerations. It presupposes Jesus Christ throughout. For although the above elaboration on the unity of love of God and love of neighbour can only be understood in its relatedness to ordinary human experience, it remains "theoretical" in the sense that nowhere in human life, except in "the man Jesus," can it ever be said that the neighbour has been loved with such an "eschatological" perfection that God too was loved with all one's heart and mind and might. And, vice versa, nowhere but in Jesus is God loved with that complete abandon which necessarily finds expression in genuine love of neighbour (cf. p.247).[51]

Although we have attempted to capture the radical degree to which Rahner asserts the unity of love of neighbour and love of God, it might still be possible to infer from our discussion thus far, that one or the other of these loves takes a secondary position, depending on which one is accentuated more in a given situation or argumentation; that one is merely the consequence or "test case" of the other. It would be wrong to conclude this because "love of God and love of neighbour" really "stand in a relationship of mutual conditioning,...of mutual inclusion," as he

---

[51] The relation of the love of neighbour to Christology is discussed, for example, in Karl Rahner, *The Love of Jesus and the Love of Neighbor*, *op. cit.*; a specially poignant excerpt from it, "Love for Jesus," is found in: *The Practice of Faith: A [Rahner] Handbook of Contemporary Spirituality*, K. Lehmann, A. Raffelt, eds., (N.Y: Crossroad, 1983), pp.136-142.

argues in another context.[52] And yet, despite this radical unity, a certain irreducible creative tension between the poles of this unified love remains. Both sides of the coin, so to speak, are absolutely indispensable in order to make up the one single coin. One cannot, therefore, infer (one-sidedly) from this unity of the twofold love that love of God is really only an outdated "mythical" name for love of neighbour, as secular humanism is prone to do. The radicalness of both their abiding distinctness and unity is yet again expressed as follows:

> There is no love for God that is not, in itself, already a love for neighbor; and love for God only comes into its own identity through its fulfillment in a love for neighbor. Only one who loves his neighbor can know who God actually is. Only one who ultimately loves God (whether he or she is reflectively aware of this or not is another matter) can manage unconditionally to abandon himself or herself to another person, and not make that person the means of his or her own self-assertion.[53]

This dynamic relationship within this radically unified love of neighbour and God has, among other things, a decidedly **relativizing** effect. It "relativizes," delimits or serves as the criterion for a Christian's interpersonal and social involvement. It serves to rule out certain involvements as well as to prevent one from absolutizing any situation or person or state (of maturity of love) within a person this side of eschatological consummation. The "indirect" nature of social involvement by Christians that flows from this, has been touched on in our discussion on "horizontalism" versus "verticalism".

Since truly self-forgetful love of neighbour ("in both an interpersonal and a social sense"; F p.456) is only possible as a result of the always prevenient loving self-communication of God, this love really grows out of, and inevitably tends towards, the hidden kingdom of God which is drawing near. That is why Rahner, in the opening remarks to his 1965 lecture, cautions his

---

[52] *Ibid.* (*The Practice of Faith*), p.136.

[53] *Loc. cit.*

audience not to equate all socially effective help by definition with acts of charity (the latter invariably includes love of God for Rahner). Such efforts may well be the result of strictly secular social organization, without necessarily springing from sound love (cf. TI VI, p.231). Rahner bases this distinction on 1 Cor. 13, where "the Apostle" says "it is completely possible to give all one's goods to the poor and yet lack charity." He takes this to mean that "no matter how important and wonderful, and how 'useful' sociopolitical action may be, it alone does not yet represent what is precisely the decisive factor of this undertaking; by this kind of action alone--without this mysterious love--" (which it is beyond human beings to recognize with certainty, he warns the *Katholische Fürsorgeverein für Mädchen, Frauen und Kinder*) "your 'Association' would sink to the level of a function of secular society and would become *that* which belongs to the age of a world which passes away" (TI VI, pp.231f.).

The importance of the presence of this genuine love for God and love for neighbour--really but "two names" for "the same reality" where "the one does not exist and cannot be understood or exercised without the other" (p.232)--in human action cannot be overestimated. For it is decisive for discovering one's true self and for realizing oneself in the sense of "eternalizing" oneself.[54] Put another way, the presence or absence of true love towards others is the deciding factor for our entering (or failing to enter) into God's kingdom. That is to say, "such love...where it truly exists and remains and *thus* really supports the social efforts between men...is not the function of secular society but itself constitutes a completely new society of men even where it has no name; it allows the eternal kingdom of God to begin in secret and is the miracle of the birth of eternity" (p.231). Here is where the criterion for the Christian's commitment to "horizontalist" causes, mentioned earlier, is clearly rooted.

---

[54] *Foundations...*, p.456. Here the author, in one of his brief creedal statements, also stresses the impossibility of grasping the actual meaning of "God" other than in such an act of love whereby a person "risks himself radically for another"--a profoundly praxis-oriented notion.

This theology of love is directly related to Rahner's ecclesiology. Where such a love in "both an interpersonal and a social sense" is present, "and in the radical unity of both of these elements it is the ground and the essence of the church."[55] It is precisely on the dynamic existence of such pristine interhuman love that the "completely new society," mentioned a moment ago, is founded. This society, renewed and inspired by such love represents, of course, (to that extent) the presence of the kingdom of God, founded by his irreversible loving act of self-communication. From this ecclesiological vantage point, the church is then co-extensive with the existence in society of love of neighbour and love of God. And because it is impossible for human agents to discern with certainty the presence of such love, Christians must be open to the possibility of the true church extending far beyond its officially recognized boundaries.

Now it is one thing to have established the "nature" of a genuinely Christian twofold love. But it is another thing to consider how a Christian comes by this love. Rahner, in his discussion of a person's "love for Jesus," comments that a mature love is not obtained all at once, but requires careful cultivating and nurturing, realizing all the while that it is ultimately "the gift of God's Spirit." It cannot be seized violently or commandeered, but must be received in a patient and prayerful attitude. The nurturing of this love involves a process that is marked by a "tender interiority...to which it need not be afraid to admit." And although one may never claim to have fully acquired it, even one's "aspiration to such a love is already its beginning."[56]

---

[55] *Loc. cit.* Cf. his subsection, entitled "The Church as the Place for Love of God and of Neighbor," F, pp.398f.

[56] *The Practice of Faith, op. cit.*, p.142; on this point cf. also F, p.310. Here we learn how central the love of Jesus really is in relation to all other neighbourly love. This is because: "A person can love him as a true man in the most proper and vital meaning of this word. Indeed because of who the God-Man is, this love is even the absolute instance of a love in which love for a man and love for God find their most radical unity and mediate each other mutually. Jesus is the most concrete absolute, and therefore it is in love for him that love reaches the most absolute concreteness and absence of ambiguity which it seeks by its very nature. For love is not a movement

This realization is essential for its political theological significance. For it is related to the Metzian "eschatological proviso" that prevents any given moment in the history of "humanization" from declaring itself to be the absolute end. In Rahner's concept, "love" is a dynamic process that is and remains "on the road," a pilgrimage. For no one but Jesus can claim to love God (and the neighbour) with the fully "consummated" perfection which is demanded of her or him by God's highest "commandment" to humankind.

Anticipating that critics might suspect his interpretation of the love commandment of not going beyond the individualistic bourgeois mutuality (which Metz rejects as having nothing to do with genuine Christian solidarity), Rahner explicitly advocates a "social" understanding of the category of love of neighbour, supported strongly and widely by parallel biblical "social" categories, when he says:

> The commandment to love one's neighbour was not given to make our social or private lives bearable or agreeable, but to proclaim everyone's concern in everyone else's possibility of salvation. It goes without saying that concepts like 'people (of God)' in salvation history, 'covenant', 'Body of Christ', 'Prayer for one another' etc., presuppose this kind of intercommunicative existence. The reality and experience of this intercommunicative existence which is so important for salvation is made concrete in the absolute quality and unfathomable depths of the love for one's neighbour, in the puzzling experience that in the fate of any individual we are confronted and put face to face with the fate of all human kind, and that this experience cannot be explained away rationalistically as abstraction, induction or the seeing of all 'cases' in a single 'case.'[57]

This forms the basis for his inference "that the concept of neighbourly love to which we refer must not be understood in an introverted and 'private' sense, but, in an original sense, gains

---

towards an abstract ideal, but towards concrete individual and irreducible uniqueness, and this very love finds in its Thou the absolute expanse of incomprehensible mystery."

[57] Karl Rahner, "One Mediation and Many Mediations," TI IX, pp.176f.

'political' dimensions" (TI IX, p.177, n.36; where he makes reference to Metz).

The whole of Rahner's theology is somehow summed up and, in a sense, modified in what he says about Christian love. It would simply be impossible to properly understand any of Rahner's transcendental philosophy (e.g. his ontology, epistemology, his concept of human freedom) without seeing its fundamental and inextricable relatedness to his dynamic understanding of love as outlined here. Thus the above definition of the human person as "that essence of absolute transcendence towards God insofar as man in his understanding and interpretation of the world respectively 'preapprehends' (*vorgreift*) towards God," need be no idealistic abstraction once it is realized that the only way to actualize this transcendence is via acts of loving outreach toward the concrete neighbour and, as Rahner makes plain, that in our age this outreach must necessarily adopt a social dimension. For "by reason of its enormous numbers, its concrete unity and in its new social forms," he said in 1965, "mankind must learn to love completely anew or go under" (TI VI, pp.248f.).

Given its centrality to all of Rahner's theological thought,[58] if it can be shown that his understanding of the radical unity of love contains substantially and fundamentally political theological content, then this would support the claim that his theology as a whole may legitimately be seen as a "new political theology" in its own right.

A number of political theological consequences clearly flow from Rahner's understanding of the double love commandment. First, since it is based on careful situation analysis and so forms a response to specific current needs, the thesis about the radical unity of the twofold love brings with it a great propensity for "praxis" in the political theological sense. For in keeping with critical theory (critically adopted by Metz), this concept of love gives priority to praxis, holding that knowledge (of self or of God) is not possible apart from practical loving commitment to neighbour, including on the social level. Second, this concept of love also and inherently leads to a courageous dialogical openness toward "the other" in the secular world, similar to the openness called for by the new political theology. And like the latter, it points out (without false diplomacy) the weaknesses of

---

[58] Rahner's conception of the radical unity of love of neighbour and love of God forms the beginning and the end of his whole theology, but especially in its political theological dimension. This view is supported by the political theologian Helmut Peukert (*op. cit.*, p.281), who says: "I consider this thesis of Karl Rahner's to be one of the more important and fruitful ones of the newer theology, which indeed has 'epochal significance' for the understanding of Christianity today." One reason it has such importance is that it eliminates the false dichotomy between a "functional" and an "essential" Christology. And this has great political theological significance in that Christology then inevitably presupposes practical commitment (accompanied, of course, by theoretical reflection). And Christology requires here by definition a public or social consciousness and therein a consciousness of God. For, says Peukert, **"The absolute affirmation of the other concrete human person as the one to whom one owes the possibility of one's own self-actualization [*Selbstseins*] is, simultaneously, the affirmation of God as absolute love, which in that person manifests and really communicates itself for everyone"** (my tr.).

a purely secularist socialism or horizontalism. Thus it serves the function of a negative-critical theology very well.

Third, this timely "catch-word," as defined by Rahner, serves as the basic criterion for Christian political theological involvement in a self-critical sense. Fourth, this category demonstrates a great sensitivity toward the real problems of belief in God in modern individuals. Therefore, it performs the other cardinal political theological function of a positive apologia for the essence of the Christian faith. In this area, too, Rahner displays admirable courage in his willingness to "prune away" all excess traditional baggage, so that the individual might be spared any unnecessary hindrances and be faced solely with the essentials of the Gospel message.

Fifth, the category of love holds out, of course, great potential for interhuman solidarity, including with the oppressed[59] and the already dead. To love the other person as other in such a way that God is thereby affirmed in his absolute love as well means to affirm every person, even the ones that history has trampled under, as being absolutely loved. One particular mark of this absolute love is that it is not limited by death or anything else. "This," says Peukert, "is the kernel of the faith in the resurrection of the dead." He continues: "therefore, to love the other person, means to approach God as that reality, which saves the other person even in death. That is why Karl Rahner's thesis on the unity of love of neighbour and love of God at its heart opens up the possibility of a theology, that is tenable even after *Auschwitz*."[60]

---

[59] Cf. Jon Sobrino, who cites these words from a letter by Rahner to Cardinal J. Landazuri Ricketts of Lima two weeks before his death: "The voice of the poor must be made audible." Sobrino adds: "To have grasped that is a guarantee of the fact that Karl Rahner has comprehended the kernel of liberation theology" (*Bilder eines Lebens*, p.146; my tr.).

[60] Peukert, *op. cit.*, p.283; (my tr.). The (extended) German reads: "Den andern unbedingt zu bejahen, und zwar so, daß darin Gott als die absolute Liebe bejaht wird, heißt, einen jeden, auch den in der Geschichte Vernichteten, als absolut geliebt zu bejahen. Das ist der Kern des Glaubens an die

Sixth, Rahner's theological understanding of the twofold love also unquestionably qualifies as political theology on the basis of being presented in the form of "narrative theology," in the sense specified above. He succeeds superbly in writing modern experience, both individual and collective, into the crucial dogma concerning love of God and love of neighbour, which penetrates all other "dogmas."

Seventh, in spite of the strong evidence for the fact that Rahner's reflections on the subject integrate high levels of political theological content--not just implicitly but explicitly proclaiming that in our "epoch" new forms of active "social" outreach are called for--his theology of neighbourly love might still be questioned as ultimately too much confined to intercommunication on the interpersonal level only, and thus cannot properly account for the social or structural dimension.[61] This objection is probably valid to a certain extent, insofar as Rahner's statements on the matter cited thus far hardly go beyond general statements of principle. However, another important dimension of his thought responds to this objection. Wherever genuine interhuman love is expressed, there the church is present for Rahner (cf. F, p.456; also pp.398f.). Therefore, his most concentrated elaborations on the "social" or "public" realm

---

Auferstehung der Toten. Deswegen bedeutet, den anderen zu lieben, auf Gott als die Wirklichkeit zugehen, die den andern auch im Tode rettet. Und deswegen eröffnet die These Karl Rahners über die Einheit von Nächsten- und Gottesliebe in ihrem Kern die Möglichkeit einer Theologie, die auch nach Auschwitz verantwortbar ist."

[61] *Ibid.*, p.282. Here Peukert sensitively lists some of the probable objections to "Rahner's transcendental analytical approach" on the part of an "empirical-practically oriented theology." The latter holds, among other things, that the individual is unavoidably ensnared in and alienated by the social-historical structures. Therefore: "Under alienating social conditions only a socially relevant political praxis can create the presuppositions for real freedom." But Rahner's theology, these "empirical theorists of interaction" would object, is too much confined to the "realm of intimate interaction" to be able to achieve such a "structural relevance." For Peukert's critical response cf. n. #64 below (my tr.).

of human life are found in his ecclesiology, broadly speaking. This will be discussed somewhat further in the next section. Suffice it to say here that his SCC (origl. 1972), described by Neumann as a capsule statement of his practical theology,[62] is seen as comparing rather favourably to Metz's EC (origl. 1980) in the practical relevance of its theological diagnosis of the church's relation to the world structures of today, according to one reviewer.[63]

One final comment on the objection, made by Metz himself on some occasions, that Rahner's theology of freedom and love appears to neglect the historical-structural aspect too much needs to be made here. A counter question poses itself, namely, what criteria does a theology that concentrates mainly if not exclusively on the socially oppressive structures have to offer to ensure that the individual in mass society will have room to become and remain the subject of her or his own history?[64] Is

---

[62] Neumann, *op. cit.*, p.385, n.49: "Das Bändchcn *Strukturwandel der Kirche* ist eine knappe praktische Theologie. Auf den ersten Teil 'Wo stehen wir?' folgt als zweiter Teil 'Was sollen wir tun?'"

[63] Cf. J. Topel's "This Bourgeois Church" (a Review of Metz's *The Emergent Church*), *National Catholic Reporter* (Sept.18, 1981), p.15, where the reviewer criticizes Metz's theology of being "too formal and abstract," adding that Metz's "evocation of the church as basic community [in EC] lacks even the specificity which Karl Rahner could achieve in *The Shape of the Church to Come.*"

[64] Peukert, *op. cit.*, pp.282f. In reference to P. Freire, Peukert counters the objections of the empirical-practical theorists by asking "how such a socially transformative praxis orients itself." His own view is that, "if this praxis does not, in turn, want to create alienating conditions, in which the subjects are unable to become themselves, then it will have to orient itself, by way of mediation or directly, via the free self-determination of the affected persons"-- the recognition of which is precisely the strength of Rahner's theology.

That this is not just a matter of theoretical speculation, for the sake of clinging to an abstract individualism, can be seen in the area of Rahner's moral theology where he wrestles with the problem of "Nuclear Weapons and the Christian" ("Die Atomwaffen und der Christ," STh XV, pp.280-297; not translated to my knowledge). There he insists that, no matter how complex the

this perhaps what Rahner had in mind, when in his response to Metz's criticism he maintained that "political theology" has a need for certain aspects that are covered by his transcendental theology?

Perhaps, too, we have here a reminder that, no matter how strongly and legitimately we may affirm a political theological dimension or function in all of Rahner's theology, it may not simply be "reducible" to being nothing more or other than a "political theology" (which one-sidedly stresses only the so-called "horizontalist" dimension of Christian life). As we have noted in passing, Rahner would remind such a theology that there are many more and equally important aspects with which the church needs to concern itself, things such as prayer, liturgy, and theology itself.

4. Rahner's "Explicit" Political Theology

We could make the following distinction. "Implicit" political theology serves the function of political theology while its "form" may appear to be unrelated, i.e., it is not cast in the language or categories of political theology. "Explicit" political theology is manifestly related in both form and content to the political theological characteristics presented in chapter one.

---

issues of our moral situation, and no matter how "dependent" one is upon one's "[social] environment," the Christian individual can never abdicate his or her ultimate responsibility before God. In his words: We do not grasp sufficiently, "that the decision-of-conscience of every person occurs ultimately always in solitude and in immediate responsibility before the inscrutable God, and therefore, in spite of all admitted dependency upon the historically given situation that precedes the individual, he (or she) may not continuously excuse himself (herself) on the basis of this dependency and let others *de facto* make the decisions for him (her). **The dignity of the human person consists precisely in his or her responsibility before God, which cannot be delegated to others**" (pp.281f.; my tr.).

Is this dimension of ultimate personal responsibility possible in a strictly social-theoretical theology?

Such a distinction is problematic, however, because the dividing line is so tentative and fluid that the distinction is practically inoperative. It belongs to the very make-up of the "new political theology," even in its most radical form as "apocalyptic interruption" of the sameness of "evolutionary" progress thinking, that its message and activity necessarily remain "indirect" ones, because it is fundamentally governed by the "eschatological proviso" that belongs to all political theology

It could therefore be argued, in view of its own definition, that even if our investigation were to reveal that the whole political theological dimension in Rahner's work is at best an indirect dimension, this need not yet (at least not wholly) disqualify the claim of this book. In fact, this might actually confirm the claim as being the more accurate. There are nevertheless "degrees" by which a theology may conform more or less implicitly or explicitly to the standards of the new political theology. This would seem to be supported from Metz's own critical comments about transcendental theology, when he observes that Rahner has produced an excellent narrative and sociocritical theology of the individual who is threatened by the social and technological dynamics of today, but has more "intuited" than "developed" a theology that squarely addresses the evils resulting from the social and political structures as such.

If such a nuanced assessment were at all meaningful, one could claim that all of Rahner's transcendental and anthropological theology has political theological "implications," but that only some of his work could be designated "expressly" as political theology strictly speaking. And in that case, we would concentrate in the following pages mainly on this more "explicit" dimension of his work, in a qualified sense.

All of Rahner's theology--including his early work, his "spiritual" meditations and prayer collections,[65] his rigorously

---

[65] It may come as a surprise at first that theology-as-prayer can be or should be classed as "political theology" at all (i.e. from the perspective of our conventional notions of prayer). But it will likely be more surprising for many readers to learn that in Rahner's understanding of prayer, it is more "political"

scientific writings (viz. lexicon work), his "dogmatic" and "moral" theology, his public lecture itinerancy and his career of essay publishing, etc.--has been shown to largely meet the cardinal criteria of the new political theology in that (implicitly at least) it serves the negative-critical and positive-apologetic functions of that theology. Therefore, we need not further elaborate on that dimension here but may instead turn directly to examine his work for its "explicit" political theological content. It will be remembered that by Metz's very definition of political theology, it must include such "indirect" subject matter as the church's function of critic of society through its own exemplary transformation through self-criticism, no matter how "explicit" it wants to be.

Even though we find unquestionable overt "political theological" argumentation in Rahner--in the sense of displaying an emphatically "public" agenda and advocating deliberate and practical transformation of unjust structures and institutions--his theology may not easily and completely conform to such fairly general definitions of "political theology" as, for instance, those given by Matthew Lamb, when he says: "I call 'political' all theologies which acknowledge that human action, or praxis, is not only the goal but the foundation of theory..." The envisioned supremacy of praxis over theory is emphasized even more when Lamb states further: "Political theology is part of a contemporary enlightenment seeking to establish transformative praxis as the control of both theory and empirical technique."[66]

(in its inherent drive toward the concrete realization of what is "prayed") than is the more reflective-scientific theology. We glimpse this aspect when Rahner says:

"For in the end all abstract theology winds up in a vacuum if it cannot rise from mere words about a particular topic **to prayer, wherein that which has previously only been spoken about may yet happen.**" Cited by K. Lehmann: K. Rahner,, *Prayers for a Lifetime*, K. Lehmann & A. Raffelt, eds., (N.Y: Crossroad, 1985), p.xiii (my emph.).

[66] Lamb, *Solidarity with Victims, op. cit.*, pp.103 and 107, respectively.

Evidently, in view of his assertion that all human knowledge (and freedom) is ultimately rooted in acts of love, Rahner would accept Lamb's emphasis on the primacy of "praxis," provided only that the latter's definition takes into account that for Rahner the always "prevenient" praxis of God "reveals" what humankind ought to strive for, and how it may strive for it. This obviously has strong implications for the importance of "theoretical" or dogmatic theology in relation to praxis. It may be pointed out in this connection that for Rahner, in a sense, "theory" rather than "praxis" is given a certain position of priority (Neumann); that for him "there are no [neutral] facts, whether of oppression or of liberation, without the commitment which interprets them" (O'Donovan).

Thus when Lamb further says "...political theology reverses the primacy of theory over praxis. Where Aristotle subordinated *praxis* and *poiesis* to disclosive theory, political theology subordinates theory and production to praxis,"[67] Rahner's theology does not (nor is it certain that Metz's theology does) unqualifiedly conform to such a definition. But this may merely raise the question as to whether a theology is more genuinely "political" when it one-sidedly exalts "praxis" over against theory or when it strives for a balance between theory and action.

The question may remain open here whether Rahner actually achieves such a relative balance or not. But that he is troubled when he senses the "theoretical" aspect to be underrepresented is evident from his above remarks on liberation theology, which he otherwise strongly defended.

We need to demonstrate that Rahner's work indeed has an overt political theological dimension. Since Rahner's political theological reflections usually fall within his discussion of

---

[67] *Ibid.*, p.106. In attempting to place "praxis" in a position of "control" over theory and technique, the pendulum swings to the opposite extreme instead of aiming for a healthy medium between theory and praxis. In the light of this tendency--although perhaps understandable as a corrective--is it any wonder that Rahner hesitates to adopt it uncritically?

ecclesiology, we will focus on a couple of his relatively short statements on this "sociocritical" function of the church.[68]

His succinct "structural" analysis of the church within the present world and the corresponding challenges he sees for post-conciliar Christianity, presented in SCC,[69] resulted from Rahner's uneasiness with the lack of a clear vision or direction on the part of the German synod which met in 1972. His suggestions to the synod are based on a penetrating analysis of the social and ecclesiastical situation in West Germany, not only in the first part, "Where do we stand?," but throughout. This analysis quite naturally leads to a reflection on the practical tasks of the church in that situation both at present and in the future, at home and abroad.

The synod, said Rahner, suffered because its participants were overwhelmed by the great many individual issues it was trying to cover. It was lacking in that:

> The synod must have in mind a basic conception, a basic trend for its efforts, ultimate norms of selection for its work. Otherwise, at most, some good individual results may be expected from the synod; but the hope would have to be abandoned that the synod might in principle show to the

---

[68] I realize that it might be problematic to speak of "political theology" as one dimension within theology in the light of Metz's claim that all true theology has to be fundamentally political theology. Nevertheless, this position stands in tension with Rahner's argument, cited above, to the effect that "political theology" needs to be supplemented by certain results of "transcendental theology."

Until this tension is resolved, then, it must be permitted to speak of political theology in terms of one dimension or genre in theology--perhaps analogously to the way one speaks of dogmatic, biblical or moral theology. Surely none of these designations is aimed at less than the "whole" of theology, but each gives it its particular accentuation.

[69] Its Original title, *Strukturwandel der Kirche als Aufgabe und Chance*, is much more descriptive of the book's content and ethos. For one thing, it intimates that the changes which the church must undergo are fundamental changes, affecting its very "structure." For another thing, it implies very clearly that this transformation implies not only arduous tasks but also holds out new opportunities, fresh hope and promise of exciting new developments, which is most indicative of the attitude Rahner exhibits throughout the book.

German Church a way through the next decades and compel it by legally binding directives to proceed in this way and no other (SCC, p.12).

Apart from the SCC, many of his more expressly "political theological" essays in his *Theological Investigations* are also primarily cast in an ecclesiological framework.[70] Perhaps as good as any are his 1968 lecture, "The Function of the Church as a Critic of Society" (TI XII, pp.229-249) and his 1974 lecture, "Transformation in the Church and Secular Society" (TI XVII, pp.167-180; loosely based on SCC). Certainly other relevant "political theological" writings could be adduced, but these will be adequate.

In view of the close connection between Rahner's ecclesiology and his more concrete political theological thought, a treatment of his political theology could include a definitional statement of his formal concept of the church. However, it is not strictly necessary when we realize how fundamentally "anthropocentric" his concept of the church is. Thus much of what was said about the human individual's transcendent, free self-actualization, applies by way of analogy to the community of the Christian church as well. As with a person, the central task of the church is its own free self-realization within the world and society. The church "is called to adore God, work towards the salvation of humankind, to exist for the sake of the world. *All* of this is precisely its self-realization, just as the human person realizes himself or herself precisely by loving God and thereby comes away from himself or herself."[71]

Furthermore, as with individual persons, the church cannot actualize itself except through concrete acts of love toward the neighbour and God, as all its members, individually and

---

[70] It should not be overlooked, however, that Rahner's "ecclesiology" is by no means limited to those essays which explicitly deal with the subject of the church. As we have seen earlier, it is also actively present in his thought when he engages in dialogue with Marxist representatives, or with humanists and scientists.

[71] As cited by Neumann from *Handbuch der Pastoraltheologie*; my tr.

collectively, respond in free acts of consent to the invitation to
enter into that "realm" which God has created by his loving act
of communicating himself irrevocably to humankind in Jesus
Christ.

The central insights in SCC are not entirely new. They closely
parallel his 1954 lecture, "A Theological Interpretation of the
Position of Christians in the Modern World." Both deal with such
key concepts as the church rapidly becoming a "little flock," i.e.
the church living in a "diaspora." Both state that the church's
only hope resides not in a desperate struggle for its self-
preservation but in a bold "missionary" offensive towards its new
mission field in Europe's "neopaganism."

In these essays, Rahner reminds us from the start that the
sociocritical function of the church is but one among many. He
therefore alerts the audience in his 1974 lecture to the fact that
he will not focus on "all the real, essential services which the
Church can perform in secular society, in the light of its nature,
its mission and its life" (TI XVII, p.171). Some of these services
are:

> In the future as in the past, it will continue to be of the greatest importance
> for secular society that the Church believes in the living Lord of all history,
> and in the blessed end of this history which he has promised; that, contrary
> to all the hopelessness which this history continually reiterates, the Church
> goes on hoping; that it prays for, and feels responsible for, the poor and the
> oppressed, for people who have not had their fair share of things in this
> world, and for the dead; that the Church stands in the way when people
> want to turn history into a mere tale of victors and survivors; and that in
> the world the Church continually upholds with vital force a position from
> which both proved tradition and the tempting future can be quite soberly
> and critically called in question, and in the face of which no tangible
> historical reality can claim to be God, either theoretically or practically. **All
> this and much more besides is of vital importance for secular society
> too.** (TI XVII, pp.171f.; my emph.).

In taking up the subject of the church's role of exercising
criticism and transformation within secular society, then, Rahner
is only dealing with *one* of its multiple functions--which, like her
other functions, follows from her nature--and this not even the

most central one. For he adds at the end of that list: "And, of course, this is more important than anything which we can now mention as being the result for secular society of the changes in the Church determined by a particular period" (p.172).

After having put into perspective the relative worth of that function in the whole of the church's life, however, Rahner makes a strong case for it. The approach he uses in his deliberations is instructive in itself. He consistently emphasizes that the church's critical function towards society must always start with self-criticism. Only if the church is willing to undergo the structural transformations needed to keep up to date in continually changing situations in history, can it hope to have any critical influence on secular society at all. But what is the source of the criteria for such self-criticism? Insofar as it is a sociological institution, the church as well as secular society has to be subjected to critique. But, says Rahner, "only a Church with a clear and unambiguous creed and dogma can be subjected to this critique. The dogma is itself the necessary prior condition for a critique." This is so because constructive criticism of any institution is possible only when it is directed at its understanding of its own nature. (And "dogma" is the church's "articulation of her awareness of her own nature." TI XII, p.232; also n.6). If the church is true to her self-understanding, it must conduct ongoing, sometimes confrontational self-criticism (for even Peter and Paul confronted one another), "because her own understanding of her own nature is always wider, freer, and more exalted than that which is *de facto* realized in the form which she assumes in history, and is in fact wider in scope than that which we have already formulated to ourselves about her at the level of speculation and theory" (TI XII, p.233). Therefore, if we may put it boldly, the church (while taking seriously "sociological" criticism from within and without) must insist upon carrying out its own "theological" self-critique, because a purely descriptive or immanentist critique would fall short of the radical demands from the transcendental critique which inheres in its doctrine about itself.

Rahner's understanding of the church is dialectical. He keeps the church's nature with both its abiding and its historically conditioned aspects in a constant, creative tension. On the one hand, the church as the visible community of God's irreversibly imparted grace in Christ, is that fellowship which

> is constantly being guided by the Holy Spirit...in order that she may not depart from the truth of Christ in any *definitive* doctrine, and in order that in her that hope and that love may always be manifested in history and in adequate ways...without which the Church would not be what she must be, and, moreover, must always remain, through the eschatologically victorious grace in Christ (TI X, pp.304f.).

This is not to deny that the pilgrim church in history is actually "a Church of sinners," even "a sinful Church," in which "wrong decisions, wrong developments, denials of the Church as such" are to be registered. Thus there is built into this abiding element of the church a dynamic factor demanding that it be a continuously "reforming church" (cf. TI X, p.305).

On the other hand, says Rahner, we must remember "that *the Church has something more to do* than merely to preach the enduring truth of the gospel....Over and above this she must *act in and upon history, and the necessity of such concrete action in history also belongs to her own intrinsic nature.*" If this is correct, he continues, "*then the necessity and the power of recognizing the situation in which she has to act and so to realise herself likewise belongs to her own intrinsic nature, or to the full realisation of this*" (TI X, pp.307f.; italics his).

One further comment with regard to the specifically "pastoral" category will be helpful for understanding Rahner's sociocritical theological statements. In his discussion "On the Theological Problems Entailed in a 'Pastoral Constitution'" (from which the last quotations were taken: TI X, pp.293-317), Rahner takes some pains to explain the exact nature of a "pastoral instruction," compared with official proclamations of universally binding doctrinal teachings. In contrast to the latter, the former cannot claim the same universally binding authority, because it represents that cutting edge of the church's existence by which it continually responds to ever new and concrete historical situations. As such, "pastoral instruction" is more tentative in nature than is "'doctrine' (with eternal validity)." Therefore, what Rahner says about Vatican II's Pastoral Constitution is surely also enlightening with respect to all his public or "pastoral" theology:

> This document is manifestly concerned to throw light upon the concrete contemporary situation in which the world, the Church and the individual Christians live and have to accomplish their tasks, and over and above this, with the instructions, recommendations, admonitions, warnings and encouragements which the Church of herself addresses to Christians and to all mankind in order that they may all shape their lives aright in this situation which they have to endure.... (TI X, p.295).

These "pastoral" statements have neither the binding power of eternally valid doctrines or binding laws or norms, nor are they as noncommittal as mere public opinion informed by secular social science. One might venture to place such pastoral instruction at the crossroads between the two.

This is important background information if we are to understand why Rahner argues, as he does in his chapter, "Church of Concrete Directives" (SCC, pp.76-81), that even the official church can be expected to make concrete pronouncements with regard to the life of society (cf. p.77). These pronouncements are not on par with those official teachings about the abiding essence of the church but rather on the level of directives or counsel. Ultimately, of course, the latter is inspired by the gospel, too, and derives its "standards" and "authority" from that same source.[72] Besides making it much easier for the church to get involved in the vital social concerns of the day, this

---

[72] Thus Rahner can say: "Certainly the first point to be recognised about such '*instructions*'...is that in principle it has a doctrinal basis. For what could be the starting-point for such instructions, from which they could derive **their standards** and the authority which they do ultimately claim to have, if not **the message of the gospel**, the doctrine of the faith which the Church upholds and proclaims in virtue of her teaching authority?" (TI X, p.295; my emph.; on the gospel as the only guide for social criticism, cf. also TI XII, p.235).

qualified distinction between different modes of ecclesiastical pronouncements obviously also has a self-relativizing effect upon the church as such (and by extension upon the given positions taken by secular social institutions). For even though what is immediately "relativized" is its "pastoral teaching," the entire "essential" ecclesiology is necessarily affected by the church's response to its historical situation.

In line with this, in a passage in his 1968 lecture,[73] Rahner identifies and develops a number of such gospel criteria. a) The gospel teaches that the church mediates salvation to the individual person necessarily in the context of, and never in isolation from, "history, society, the people of God." Rahner stresses that "as the subject to whom God's grace-bestowed will is addressed, the individual is always aimed at as the member of a community of mankind, and always and necessarily this also has a social manifestation" (p.238). b) From the gospel we learn that salvation is not restricted to the "explicitly sacral" sphere alone, but the realm in which it occurs "is identical with the sphere of human existence in general." That is why the church as "the mediatrix of salvation" may not "adopt an attitude of indifference towards this total sphere of human existence which also always involves social structures." That is why it is demanded of the Christian as such "that he shall commit himself to the world..." (pp.239f.).

c) Another gospel principle is provided by that future orientation which knows that "God himself...wills to be the infinite future of man, infinitely transcending all that man could ever plan or fashion for himself" (p.239). We are already familiar with this idea and the relativizing effect it can produce from our earlier discussion of Rahner's critique of Marxist utopianism. But it is important to note that, as with Metz, so for Rahner, the relativization of "this-worldly" goals and achievements of human beings resulting from this principle "far from diminishing their importance, actually increases it" (p.240).

---

[73] Karl Rahner, "The Origins of the Perspective Provided by the Church as Critic of Society as Found in the Gospel Itself," TI XII, pp.235-241.

d) Furthermore, the already familiar principle of the unity of love of God and love of neighbour, is rooted in the gospel. It must be fulfilled "in a world that is constantly sinful, a world of injustice and self-alienation on man's part," and "implies an attitude of protest and criticism of society," once it is realized that such love is no mere natural inclination or "private" interpersonal matter, but "is an act which has to permeate all social dimensions of human life, and...implies soberly and realistically giving others their due and respecting their freedom in the social sphere as well" (pp.240f.).

e) Finally, since "the gospel is always and essentially a gospel of the Cross," and since "Christian theology is always a theology of the Cross," it is herein that the church discovers another crucial "insight" concerning its critical function in society. Even though, as Rahner asserts, "the death of Christ is certainly not the death of a social revolutionary...," the Cross is no "private" affair. For "this death of his did take place in the social and public life of Israel, and in a hostile confrontation with the social forces and institutions then prevailing" (p.241). His Cross was thus a "public" one, "a political event." Therefore, since the only way of being a Christian is that of "following our crucified Lord in the assent of faith and hope to all the futility of human existence," and this not just in the "purely cultic" or in private interiority alone but "in the hard down-to-earth secular sphere of the Christian's worldly life" as well, then, clearly, this orientation by the Cross has a liberating effect upon Christians in the way in which they can abandon themselves in order to take up the task (inherent in being a Christian) of seeking "social change in the struggle against all the forces in society that cling onto their own selfish interests," and this "without any assurance of success" (p.241).

It is not easy to reconcile Rahner's emphasis on the gospel as the sole source of norms for social involvement--especially in the light of the last two "gospel criteria," of love of God/neighbour and of the cross--with the comments he made in relation to the "theology of revolution," arguing that in view of the fact that "concupiscence" is an abiding factor in human history, constantly preventing "man from achieving an absolute transformation of the world solely on the basis of the single and central idea of love," "the Christian will not commit himself to the declaration that the application of force, or **even one which may lead to human killing**, is immoral and unChristian in any possible situation in society" (TI XII, p.248). It is indeed difficult to harmonize this statement with the logic of his own observation in the context of the double love commandment, saying that the genuine love of neighbour it asks of us, is also necessarily love of God, **since "the neighbour, through God's love for him, is 'one' with God"** (TI VI, p.238). Is not therefore every act of aggression against the neighbour also an act against the God of love in the neighbour? Elsewhere, too, Rahner professes plainly: "that we not only should, but indeed *can* love even our 'enemies', and as long in fact as they remain 'enemies'," or that "love of neighbour requires us to treat no one as an enemy in the ultimate meaning of the word..." (cf. SCC, pp.40 and 74, respectively).

It may be significant to add in this connection also that in his more recent reflections on "Nuclear Weapons and the Christian,"[74] Rahner is not only led personally to reject as absolutely immoral all nuclear warfare and armament but also to question whether there ever was a just or justifiable war. He says, the fact that the long-term consequences of a prospective nuclear war, for the entire human family, are "qualitatively" more horrendous, **"still does not mean, that there ever has been a conventional war, or can be even now, which for the Christian conscience, rightly, would not present a problem."** Does this perhaps mean that in his later years Rahner has revised his 1968 position on the moral admissibility of human killing by Christians?

Before turning to some samples of the social criticisms Rahner envisions for the church, we can draw attention to another predominant methodological dimension in his "political theology." It has already been mentioned in passing and so need

---

[74] "Die Atomwaffen und der Christ" (STh XV (1983), pp.280-297; article not translated to my knowledge; this tr. and emph. are mine).

not be dealt with at great length here. It is his frequent and extensive situation analysis.

After all that we have said about the absolute importance for Rahner of always keeping in the back of our mind the unchanging dogmatic deposit (here of ecclesiology) and the fact that ultimately only the gospel itself gives whatever "authority" the church's "pastoral" counsel or warning has in relation to society, Rahner takes equally seriously the crucial role played by the situation in which this counsel is given. This is evident both from what he says on the matter and from the considerable space he regularly devotes at the opening of his reflections to a close analysis of the environment which the church is to criticize. Moreover, it would not be hard to demonstrate that his very choice of which gospel values to lift out appears to be co-determined by the contextual factors that press in upon the church today. For example, the fact of today's discontinuity between the church and secular society, in radical contrast to the times when society was thought to agree with and offer support to the church (cf. TI XVII, p.169; also TI XII, pp.236f.), elicits the question of where salvation takes place and what the church's role in it is; whether it is a private or a public matter. Obviously, according to the gospel, it is the latter.

Similarly, consequences are drawn from the fact that the church lives today in a "pluralistic" secular society. It follows from this that the church must learn to tolerate, even welcome or cultivate a plurality of theologies not just because this pluralism of world-views increasingly permeates the church's own ranks anyway, but also because a plurality of approaches is required in order to be able to evangelize the various groupings in society around it (TI XVII, p.170; also the appropriate chapters in SCC).

Rahner draws one more inference for the church from the fact that in our predominantly secular society the church has a "minority status"--a situation which he sees as being the result and intention of Christianity, to be welcomed insofar as it allows the church to do better its own proper work (TI XII, p.237). Because of this fact, the ordinary church member takes on a growing importance in the life of the church. This will inevitably lead to a certain "democratization" in the church and to the recognition of the so-called "'grass roots' of the Church's people" (TI XVII, p.171; cf. also "A Declericalized Church" and "Democratized Church," in SCC). Likewise, and in view of the prospective developments in the church, it will soon become necessary for the church to consider ordaining married men and women as priests. The final criterion for this is noteworthy, insofar as it is a perfect blend of being determined both by **church dogma** (in the wider sense: its supreme "law" is to carry on its salvific work in the world: *"Salus animarum suprema lex"* SCC, p.111) and **the situation** (if insufficient numbers of willing candidates for the celibate priesthood can be found, then the church can obviously ordain alternative candidates, so as not to neglect the essential work).

The church's primary means for exercising its "critical function" towards secular society are the ongoing reforms of its own inner structures. Therefore, our elaborations on the church and the criteria by which it determines this function are already a vital part of political theology itself. Because it would be no exaggeration to say that for Rahner by far the greater part of the church's influence upon its surrounding world derives from its own exemplary way of being or living before or within that world, and only a comparatively minor part assumes the form of overt criticism. That is why he devotes so much attention to examining the church's own life and structural organization in his reflections on the church's critical function toward society.

Perhaps the best illustration of this is found in his SCC, where the first 120 pages are devoted to a penetrating analysis and critique of the life and structures of the church herself in order, finally, in the remaining 10 pages, to reflect on the outward looking "sociocritical church" (pp.123-132). Of course, the "internal" critique of the church is not carried out in isolation from the world. Instead, much of the inner-ecclesiastical critique is applied to the church, as it were, from the perspective of "looking in" from outside through the eyes of secular society. Thus the major part of SCC shows how seriously Rahner takes the notion that the situation co-determines the essence of the church.

The fact that Rahner places such a high premium on the church's example as the primary vehicle of sociopolitical critique represents in itself a structural change within Catholicism. In the past, he recalls, the church normally relied on the power of a homogeneously Christian society for its own propagation. This can no longer be done as a result of the changes in all areas of life in the modern situation. Therefore, the church that tended often towards domination in the past must become "a Church concerned with serving." After all, "the Church with all its institutions is itself a means for [human beings] and they are its end" (SCC, pp.61f.). Rahner points out why and whom the church should serve, and admits that historically it has often not served in imitation of the "folly of the cross" as it should have, but mainly with a view to its own gains for itself (viz. to gain new members in order to strengthen itself and for the purpose of self-preservation). The complete reverse should be the case. It ought to serve others in order to win "new churchgoing Christians," not primarily from the motive of "saving those who would otherwise be lost," but in order to acquire "witnesses as signs making clear for all the grace of God effective throughout the world." Moreover, "The wish to bring people into the Church...must be a determination to make these churchgoing Christians **serve everyone**, even those who are ready to accept their services but nevertheless despise and oppose them; the poor too, the old, the sick, those who come down in the world, the people on the edge of society, all those who have no power themselves and can bring no increase of power to the Church" (my emph.). Rahner then picks up a motif of the church's function as *Hort der Freiheit* of the individual person that he expressed as early as 1962, when he continues: "The Church has to stand up for justice and freedom, for man's dignity, even when this is to her own detriment," as when it forfeits "an alliance...with the ruling powers..." (SCC, p.62).

A restructuring of the church is thus clearly demanded, because: "Concrete and living Christianity today and particularly tomorrow can no longer be passed on simply by the power of a homogeneous Christian society...by administration from the top, by religious instruction as part of the compulsory education received by every child," says Rahner later in the book, "but must be carried into the future through the life and witness of a genuine Christian community living out what Christianity really means" (SCC, p.117).

Another reason for his emphasis on the effect of the church's example has to do with the insight that, in spite of all that distinguishes it from secular society,[75] the church is to a large extent a social institution. And on this level it has much in common with other concrete social institutions. Both kinds of societies (ecclesiastical and secular) need a minimum of "shared basic convictions" (in spite of modern pluralism) in order to be able to exist and function. The methods used by each type of institution for achieving and maintaining those foundational convictions may differ somewhat but the difficulties and temptations involved in the process are similar enough that each can learn from the other. For instance, one such basic dynamic, common to both church and secular society, is the tension between freedom and institutionalization; between the administration and the "grass roots" (cf. TI XVII, pp.173-180). That is why it does not seem "far-fetched" to Rahner "to seek for models for secular society in the Church." But he hastens to remind the reader that this is really not at all new: "We can read of Christianity's early period: 'See how those Christians love one

---

[75] According to Rahner, what distinguishes the church is that it must take the uniqueness and freedom of every individual utterly seriously, in contrast to "any other society. For a secular society has to cater for what is common to all men, and merely to ensure that man's uniqueness is accorded the necessary scope." ("On the Structure of the People of the Church Today," TI XII, p.220; cf. also TI XVII, pp. 173, 179.)

From these similarities and differences Rahner deduces that secular society cannot and should not emulate ecclesiastical society in all matters, but both societies have enough in common so that the church's example can serve as an effective reminder for secular society to fulfil its highest mandate as well as it is able.

another'." Although circumstances are different, is it not the same principle today? Thus he asks, "might it not later also be said of us: 'See how they really live *together*, in liberty and without coercion?'" But the church will acquire a certain "exemplary significance for secular society" only when its "out-of-date patterns of inter-human relationships will cease to be cultivated when they have been abandoned everywhere else" (TI XVII, p.180).

When Rahner finally turns to address the "social and sociocritical commitment of the Church in all her members and particular groups," which he says must be included among "what is the most important thing to be done in the German Church of the future," he addresses the topic "with fear and trembling" (SCC, p.123). For he is aware of the danger that is involved in "all the talk and appeals about the world-responsibility of Christians and the Church" since Vatican II, which has caused some people to fear that the church may be reduced to a mere "humanitarian institution" with a purely "horizontalist" tendency in the future (123). We have already noted Rahner's views on a pure humanism or horizontalism elsewhere. He reaffirms that stance but affirms also that "nevertheless in the light of the nature of the Church and of Christianity itself **this world-responsibility is part of the Church's task**"[76]

This is not only obvious as a result of Vatican II. It is also rooted in the love commandment. Since love of neighbour and love of God are "radically dependent on each other," one being "mediated" by the other, and since today's society can and must be transformed so as to afford greater justice and freedom to the individual, Rahner concludes:

> The task of Christian love of neighbour (and of the virtue of justice implicit in this) can no longer be restricted to private, personal relationships. **Love of neighbour in such a society acquires also (not only!) a sociopolitical**

---

[76] SCC, p.123; my emph. It is "a part" of Christianity's task, even though "the nature, task and mission of the Church are [radically] distinguished from a humanism concerned only with the present world."

character, becomes necessarily also the will to a better society; it is not mere feeling, not only private relationship between individuals, but is [also] aimed at changing social institutions--or it is not what it ought to be (SCC, p.123; my emph.).[77]

Furthermore, the sociocritical world- responsibility of Christianity emerges also from the fact that not only human individuals are sinful but "actual social conditions and institutions are also marked by sin." Thus, Rahner suggests that to want to reduce the drama of redemption to the "private, inner world" of individuals alone so as "to be played between the redeeming God of freedom, love and justice, and sinful man, ...corrupt[s] Christianity and the unity of the living and historical person at least as much as the attempt to reduce Christianity to a purely humanitarian and social commitment" (SCC, p.124). In other words, a mentality of radical privatization would also be tantamount to "apostasy" as is the other extreme. In any case, Christians have the responsibility to change sinful social conditions. On this score, Rahner finds, neither the officeholders nor the members of the church are sufficiently conscious "of the task, imposed by Christian love, of criticizing and changing society" (SCC, p.125). What is perhaps worse, is that in our sinfulness, we tend towards proclaiming only mild and general criticisms about the lack of freedom and justice in society. And this only serves "to quiet our conscience" (p.125).

The present global situation, as Rahner sees it, requires the Christian church to take very radical measures because "the contrast between the modern industrial nations and the underdeveloped peoples really amounts to a global revolutionary situation," even if individual (rich) nations may not feel this. By "revolutionary" Rahner does not imply "bloodshed and violence" but that the structural injustices in international relations have reached such a critical level that the "vast social changes" which

---

[77] The "also" [auch] in square brackets, omitted by the translator from the German original (*Strukturwandel...*, p.131), is an important modifier of the sentence in question. (The subsequent statement by Rahner is also mistranslated.)

are urgently required cannot be achieved "in an evolutionary way" (cf. p.125). In this situation of crisis neither church officials nor the laity are exercising their Christian responsibility in finding "plans and models which we could offer boldly and practically for a future society" so that it might be enabled to cope with this situation (p.126).

Obviously, there would not be automatic agreement among individual Christians or groups of Christians as to which proposed plan is the better one. Hence a certain amount of (internal) conflict will be unavoidable as attempts are made to discharge the responsibilities that flow from our duty to love the neighbour. Such conflict is inherent to any attempt at realizing projects in concrete situations because it always involves things which cannot be adequately reflected in advance (p.126). While committed Christians need not be ashamed when conflict arises (for it is preferable to the "graveyard peace" that so often prevails among Christians), the church of this pluralistic age must learn to "maintain the Church's unity and mutual love even in this bitter struggle" (p.126).

When Rahner now turns to make some concrete suggestions on how Christians and the church may seek to bring about change in "the world outside"--after reminding the church again that its credibility depends on creating greater freedom in its "internal life"--he draws attention to frequently forgotten issues. There should be room for such "spectacular declarations" as those represented by student demonstrations. The "institutional Church" may offer the students financial support, even if it does not officially subscribe to the political stance they represent (p.127).[78] But these spectacular, "organized efforts" are not the

---

[78] Rahner stresses the need for flexibility and pluralism of positions, while in no way advocating total anarchy, saying: "A student parish, for example, can certainly commit itself politically (which does not mean party politics) in a particular direction, even though this direction seems to some bishops objectively wayward, as long as the student parish does not proclaim heretical fundamental principles or cease to be a community open to *all* Catholic students who want to live with it" (SCC, p.127; his italics). A Protestant student may well wonder why not stretch this "openness" further so as to

only way of discharging one's sociopolitical responsibilities. For example, "the question of the immigrant workers" is receiving far too little attention both from regular parishes and from basic Christian communities. The German Catholic charitable organization, Caritas, is however a laudable one, exactly "because it makes less noise than quite a number of other organizations which behave as if the Church had hitherto done nothing in the social field" (SCC, p.128).

Interestingly enough, Rahner's concrete proposals on how to realize our sociocritical task better toward the world around us include a section in which he urges Christian individuals and small groups (particularly the basic communities) to focus their efforts on those tasks that cannot be done properly by the large institutions of church or state.[79] Institutionalization often brings in its wake a "depersonalization." Even if institutions can and do satisfy someone's material needs, "he still lacks what he needs most of all: the person of the other human being." That is why Rahner sees here a unique "social task for the basic communities," as this task falls "between the wholly private sphere" and that social life that can be institutionalized. In other words, these basic communities are the ideal setting for translating neighbourly love into social work, because with them neighbourly help does not become cold "material aid" (as with institutions) nor is it reduced to "mere spontaneous sympathy" (as with individual persons), but they can realize this neighbourly love in such a way that it has a human face. For "only there can the appropriate aid and personal encounter be one" (SCC, p.129).

By emphasizing the community approach to holistic sociopolitical commitment, Rahner has no intention of downplaying the important role which institutions have to play

---

invite participation from other denominations (or other religions).

[79] "Christians today," says Rahner, "are only too much inclined to leave to official institutions of Church and state what they should do themselves and what really they alone can do by way of Christian love and the defence of justice and freedom" (SCC, p.128).

in this regard. These enter in, for example, when the question of helping the Third World comes up. And this, he says, forms "a part of the sociopolitical commitment of Christians, their groups, and the Church" today (p.129). Not only is aid to the impoverished two thirds of the world desperately needed but it would be in the best, "even the material interests of the highly industrialized nations" (SCC, p.130). But it is really "a matter of Christian love," says Rahner, and much more ought to be and could be done than is in fact being done in this respect. For even the most cursory assessment of the world ought to suffice to make it obvious "that we are in a global revolutionary situation (which is not the same as revolution)," he suggests. "For the social situation of this one world as a whole is characterized by such massive injustice and material peril for the greater part of mankind that it would be impossible to find any institutions capable of removing these things in an 'evolutionary' way and in accordance with principles recognized on all sides in society" (p.130).

In order to tackle the problem of the Third World effectively, according to Rahner, it is not enough to simply increase our "personal contributions" or the amount of taxes used by the state for "development aid." Rather, he adds, "for once at least we ought to go beyond all this and **enter into a mental and material solidarity** with those Christians [sic] and non-Christian groups which are working for radical changes in the social and economic structures in their own underdeveloped countries" (SCC, p.130; my emph.). And we need not be too squeamish either about the "headings" with which they designate their programs or goals, he submits, because:

> Revolution must not be understood either in the style of the French Revolution or of the Russian October Revolution and is certainly not something which always and in every situation is bound to be contrary to the Christian conscience or the Sermon on the Mount (SCC, p.131).

This statement concerning the meaning and moral admissibility of "revolution," is too vague to be very helpful. Of course he has explained in this chapter that although it means very drastic social change, it may not necessarily mean "bloodshed and violence, which is or can be immoral" (p. 125).

If the proviso is that the structural changes supported by Christians and Christian groups be nonviolent, or put in the positive, that they occur always within the framework of love of neighbour (including the enemy: **"love of neighbour requires us to treat no one as an enemy..."** SCC, p.74), then of course "revolution" need not offend against the Sermon on the Mount. More than that, the values of this Sermon represent in fact, according to **peace church theologians,** the most "revolutionary manifesto" there ever was. In a like-named chapter in *The Original Revolution*, John Howard Yoder argues:

> What was wrong with the Zealot path [that defies the ethics of the Sermon on the Mount] for Jesus is not that it produces its new order by use of illegitimate instruments, but that the order it produces cannot be new. An order created by the *sword* is at the heart still not the new peoplehood Jesus announces. It still...preserves unbroken the self-righteousness of the mighty and denies the servanthood which God has chosen as His tool to remake the world.[80]

In other words, the values laid down by Jesus in this Sermon aim at creating in the midst of secular society a counter community, which by its very existence and lifestyle of servanthood will serve as the most radical and effective transformative agency imaginable for remaking the old social order.

Returning to Rahner's treatment of the critical function of the church within society, is all that he has said so far not still very abstract and insignificant? Rahner is the first to recognize that he has still "said almost nothing" about a concrete engagement by Christians in relation to the Third World. Moreover, perhaps all practical and realizable things we might come up with would finally amount to only a "drop in the ocean." But even if this

---

[80] Cf. John H. Yoder, *The Original Revolution*, (Herald Press: 1971) p.24; for a brief description of how this new peoplehood functions as a transformative agent, cf. pp.27-31, but esp. p.29; cf also his chap. 2: "The Political Axioms of the Sermon on the Mount," pp.34-54).

were so, then this would still "not dispense the Christian from the duty of providing at least this drop" (131). As a nonutopian possibility of making a difference in the poor hemisphere, Rahner suggests that sizable youth groups might send volunteers to assist with development work, or Christian parishes could adopt and support local development organizations in developing countries, and so on.

These concrete proposals on how the church might begin to discharge its "sociocritical" duties in our age will possibly not go as far as many political theologians would expect they should. And Rahner himself seems to share that feeling. Nevertheless, it seems obvious that whether one thinks the Christian sociopolitical commitment today should go farther than this or not, the evidence presented here positively supports our claim that not only does Rahner's theology have an implicit political theological dimension but it also shows an openness in principle toward developing an explicit political theological dimension and that he in fact deliberately developed this latter dimension, to some extent at least. It is important to remember in this connection that in view of our earlier definition of the category of an "explicit" political theological dimension, it is not limited to only sociocritical pronouncements[81] (which Rahner affirms and himself produces) but includes all of those ecclesio-theological reflections carried out with a view toward concretely transforming the church so as to effect change in secular society indirectly. This interpretation is warranted by the very indirect

---

[81] Elsewhere, Rahner (in 1968) is careful to establish that to be a critic of society is not the same as political action. In his words: "it must first be emphasized that the thesis concerning the function of the Church as a critic of society is not intended to conjure up the idea of a Church actively engaged in politics." It may not "deprive secular society and the institutions belonging to it of its political decision making...[and] the Church cannot act as a higher authority to manipulate or control this autonomous secular society" (TI XII, p.233).

nature of political theology as defined and used by Metz.[82] For
him, too, the idea which is central to his "mystical and political
theology" is that the church's most effective way of witnessing
to the gospel before the world consists in the church's concrete
life of "discipleship."

Our overall findings in this chapter concerning the actual
political theological content in Rahner's work confirms
abundantly what we had come to expect as a result of the
dynamics inherent in his theological starting point. Thus it is not
surprising that a theology which has fashioned for itself a
methodology that tries to mediate between a holistic Christian
spirituality and the anguished experience of our modern scientific
and technological existence should produce a supreme "narrative"
theological account which encompasses all levels of human
experience. Moreover it is only a logical step further for a
theology which has learned from the model of the incarnation of
the divine *Logos* that the only possible way for human self-
realization is to transcend oneself in free acts of interhuman love,
that it should proceed to draw consequences for all dimensions
of human existence, personal and social, spiritual and categorial.

---

[82] Cf. the following comments about the church in Metz's definitional
article on "political theology": Under the heading, "the Church as the place
and institution for socio-critical freedom," he speaks of "the Church in action
(in preaching, worshipping and sacraments) and in its central task of
reconciliation and forgiveness [which] may take the direction of social
criticism." Besides illustrating that Metz does not have a one-dimensional view
of the church, it also makes clear that this "social criticism" is above all a
criticism by example. Thus it makes visible: "how the ecclesiastical institution,
conscious of its own provisional status, does not repress critical freedom but
makes it possible...; how criticism is part of the public life of the Church; how
partial identification with the institution is to be positively treasured; how
rights and freedom in the Church are not merely constitutional problems, but
elements of the process of attaining knowledge in the Church's theology; and
so on." ("Political Theology," *Encyclopedia of Theology: The Concise
Sacramentum Mundi*, K. Rahner, *et al*, eds., (N.Y: Seabury, 1975), pp.1242f.)

That Metz puts a supreme value on the church's sociocritical contribution
via its example is also evident throughout his FoC.

In other words, it is natural that a theology based on the transcendence of the individual in acts of love should proceed to address the person's (and the church's) social responsibilities as well. Finally, it seems also natural that a theology which played a significant role in the preparation for and execution of far-reaching transformations in both the teachings and the structures of the Catholic church that reverberated throughout the world (in Vatican II), should proceed to concern itself also with the problems in modern society, including the structures of injustice, corruption and unfreedom. This is the more logical as Rahner has defined the church as existing primarily for the salvation of the world.

5. Some Afterthoughts

In closing, we address here one critical observation by Metz about Rahner's transcendental theology. It is significant in that it tacitly confirms that Metz's objections are not made primarily on the basis of the "contents" of transcendental theology, what it does or does not say, but on whether or not it manages to remain relevant to the issues of the day. According to this observation, Rahner's theology was most "dramatic" and relevant earlier on, but became gradually less vibrant and relevant as its erstwhile struggles were being won. In Metz's words:

> I am of the opinion that Rahner's transcendental theology can only be continued without a break if it is criticized and corrected with the help of experiences and a praxis that are not derived from the theological system hitherto in use. Rahner's transcendental theology continued to be dramatic and in that respect free of the suspicion of being tautological, as long as it was a corrective, in other words, as long as it was engaged in controversy with a theological opponent. In the initial stages of Rahner's transcendental theology, that opponent was neoscholasticism. The first crisis of identity began to appear in Rahner's theology, however, when this opponent finally collapsed in exhaustion in the strong arms of transcendental theology (FHS, p.13, n.15).

Concerning the first part of this critical statement (made in 1977), it can be credibly claimed that Rahner's post-conciliar theological work has indeed "criticized and corrected [itself] with the help of experiences and a praxis" within the new prevailing intellectual and ecclesiastical climate, which he has taken no less seriously than he formerly took the neoscholastic "theological system."[83]   What is less certain is that Rahner made such a clean break with that system "hitherto in use" (as the statement suggests he should have) in his struggle with these experiences that were extrinsic to the classical theological system. It is noteworthy in this connection that R. Johns, who otherwise thinks highly of Metz's political theological thought, applies to it a criticism which has often been levelled against Rahner, when he says: **"Because of a residue of scholastic content in his thought**..., sociopolitical analysis is not made sufficiently relevant to concrete, practical action in the church and society in Metz's work."[84]

---

[83] We have referred to K. Lehmann on this matter already. One could add to this the observations of K.H. Neufeld and R. Bleistein, eds., *Rahner Register. Karl Rahner zum 70. Geburtstag*, (Benziger, 1974; covering vols. I-XI), p.18. These authors assert both a basic continuity in Rahner's theological work and an intense wrestling with the post-conciliar theological movements. On the one hand, after Vatican II, Rahner engages in "a slower, more painstaking search for new ways [in theology]" than in his earlier work. "Nor does Rahner avoid the questions posed by modern theology: he grapples with the questions of the theology of revolution, political theology, futurology etc."

On the other hand, they say that in Vol.X we witness "parallel to a further development of scientific-theoretical questions above all a series of concrete projections toward and proposals for the future. **In all this [however], one can discern the unmistakable "philosophical beginnings" of the Rahnerian style of doing theology as again looming visibly in the foreground"** (my tr. and emph.). Anyone familiar with the subsequent volumes of STh (or TI) could readily apply these comments to them as well.

[84] Johns, *op. cit.*, p.vi (my emph.). This comment need not, of course, be seen only in terms of a negative critique (as it is meant by Johns), but can also be considered as a positive compliment. Perhaps it is precisely this "residue

For the rest of this critical statement, one would have to ask just when did this transcendental theology cease to be a "corrective," and to be "engaged with a theological opponent," and did it ever really see neoscholasticism as an opponent to be overcome, and, if so, did this "opponent" ever completely collapse under the weight of transcendental theology? The likely answer is that it may have experienced a lull here and there, between "battles" so to speak, but Rahner felt neither during the Council[85] nor for the rest of his life[86] that his theological position had won the day. And if it might be argued that the new vision embodied within the transcendental theology during and after the Council had managed to win a partial victory over the opposing conservative forces of church and theology, then its "spare energies" were soon to be in full demand in the dialogue with the new theological movements that quickly emerged within the post-conciliar pluralistic milieu. We have already mentioned

---

of scholastic content" which confers upon Metz's political theology a greater depth in comparison with other expressions of it.

[85] We have already noted that Rahner would not allow the synod of the German church to rest on the laurels of the achievements of the Council (cf. SCC, p.13). To him the Council is only "the beginning of a beginning," (as Metz himself cites Rahner in his article, "Theology Today: New Crises and New Visions," *CTSA Proceedings*, 40 (1985), p.2.

[86] Rahner never felt Vatican II had completed the tasks that needed doing. This is obvious from the many essays he wrote expressly on the subject (including "Vergessene Anstöße dogmatischer Art des II. Vatikanischen Konzils," STh XVI, pp.131-142, near the end of his life) as well as his frequent critical comments on it in other contexts.

Nor did Rahner ever look on his own transcendental theology as "having arrived," as is evident from his opening comments to his series, STh (cf. "Preface" to TI I, p.xxii), where he wants to impress upon "young theologians...the conviction that Catholic theology has no reason to rest on its laurels...." It is also evident from his words of response on his 80th birthday, saying that the intention of his theology has all along been "to hint from afar that our time calls also us theologians sleeping under the broom tree of orthodoxy like Elijah in old days: *Surge, grandis tibi restat via*--Arise, a long journey lies ahead of you." ("Foreword," *Theology and Discovery, op. cit.*).

Rahner's feeling of being engaged in "a battle on two fronts," in the wake of the Council, in which he had imperceptively moved (or been moved) from being on the theological Left to being on the Right.

Thus, from our vantage point (fifteen years later), it would not be hard to document the claim that Rahner's transcendental theology never was short of "theological opponents" towards whom it tried to play the role of a "corrective" influence.[87] To what extent it owed this continual state of alertness towards the ever new challenges to the "nudgings" of critical statements such as this one by Metz, and to what extent it was inherent to its own inner dynamic, may remain a moot question here. But if allowing the "praxis"--i.e., the "corrective" insights which theology reaps from its engagement with the challenges of each new situation--and experiences that are extrinsic to the traditional theological system to modify deeply one's current theological work saves it from becoming "tautological," then Rahner's work can (in retrospect) surely be exempt from the indictment of this critical statement on the basis of its own standards. And to that

---

[87] These "opponents" (or at least controversial causes) range from such new theological (or ideological) movements as "horizontalism" or the "pure humanism," discussed earlier, to his intervention (along with others) on behalf of Liberation Theology generally, and of Gustavo Gutiérrez in particular.

Perhaps even more to the point is his vigorous public defense of Metz's "perfectly orthodox" political theology--ironically just two years after this critical statement was made by the latter. At issue in this case is precisely the resurgence of a kind of conservative "neoscholastic" attitude or "a symptom of a backward movement in the Catholic Church," according to Rahner himself (cf. *Conversations*, p.234), which Metz had thought had collapsed already. (For Metz's grateful recognition of this gesture by Rahner, cf. "On My Own Behalf," EC, pp.119-123.)

extent it cannot be denied to approximate the characteristics of a new political theology.[88]

---

[88] Metz is not beyond changing and updating his own theological position, as can be seen not only from the adjustments of his political theology (mentioned above in reference to N. Ancic), but also from a statement like the following one: "For many, the last Council seemed to belong to the past even before it was concluded. **I myself was once of this opinion. I was mistaken.** The question: how to be faithful to the inheritance of the Second Vatican Council is a life-and-death question for the Church" ("Theology Today: New Crises and New Visions" (1985), *op. cit.*, p.1; my emph.). Obviously, Rahner would have agreed wholeheartedly with this last statement, and in fact shared that agenda with Metz.

Chapter 4

Conclusion

Karl Rahner's "Political Theology"

1. Between Rahner and Metz

Our study has shown clearly that the areas of similarities or overlap between the works of Rahner and Metz is considerable indeed. But it is also apparent that the theological thinking of each theologian refuses to be fully encompassed by that of the other. We need to explain more precisely these similarities and differences.

Our claim is that Rahner's transcendental theology is also a political theology, despite its irreducible "otherness" from Metz's work. This requires, of course, that a definition of "political theology" be found which justifies such a claim. Will Metz's definition of the "new political theology," as sketched out above, be able to accommodate the unique aspects in Rahner's theology, or will the latter require an amplification of Metz's political theological framework? The answer to this question can be given only after the relationship between the works of Rahner and Metz has been more precisely established. But it is conceivable in principle that the uniquely Rahnerian theological elements are not only compatible with Metz's definition of political theology, but even "fill in" some of the political theological landscape which Metz has not managed to cover in his own work, despite his inclusive definition. Stated more provocatively, it is thinkable that Metz might not have fulfilled the mandate of his own definition and that Rahner might have fulfilled aspects of it which Metz himself has not.

It is, of course, also conceivable that Rahner's unique emphases simply cannot be fitted into Metz's definition. If this were the case, and if we still wished to maintain our thesis about Rahner's whole work also being political theology, we would then have to offer a definition of political theology which would justify our claim. Without wanting to prejudge the case, it would seem there is nothing in Rahner's transcendental and anthropological theology that necessarily violates the definition-in-principle which Metz gives, but that the ethos or mode of each theologian's work is markedly different. More will be said about this below. David Tracy, for instance, in commenting on the relationship between their theologies, speaks of a "profound unity-in-difference" between "these two major theologians."[1]

What, then, are some of the areas which these two theologians have in common, and what is unique to each of them? Summarizing the above findings and focusing on the major categories of the new political theology, the following points stand out:

1. Rahner's theology is deeply rooted in contemporary experience, and this on all levels, from the individual to the collective and from the scholarly to the liturgical and popular levels. Metz has extensively acknowledged this rootedness in experience. This interpretation is not a notion imposed on Rahner by a great critic of his work, as can be seen from Rahner's own words, in which he specifically acknowledges the correctness of Metz's political theological interpretation of the Christian love commandment as spelled out in *Followers of Christ*:

'If Christianity is love of God and the neighbour, if love of God today can only be realized in a mysticism of the experience of the nearness of God, and if love of neighbour can only be realized by perceiving a social and political task which everyone has, then what Metz says is, I think, clear:

---

[1] David Tracy, "A Response to Fr. Metz," *Theology and Discovery, op. cit.*, (1980), p.185.

that Christianity, particularly today, has a mystical and a social component. I say 'particularly today', because without the mystical component a merely external indoctrination does not do justice to the existence of God and Christianity and its content. And I would say that precisely today, a social and political or a social element is particularly significant because the person of today will not find true love of neighbour which comes from God and bears witness to God credible if it is limited to an intimate sphere between human beings and does not perceive the real sociopolitical and socio-critical task.[2]

This line of reasoning has already been seen elsewhere in Rahner's reflections. But here we are given irrefutable evidence about an explicit convergence between Rahner and Metz on the necessity for theology to take contemporary human experience, particularly sociopolitical experience, with utmost seriousness--and with no apparent deviation from the ethos of Rahner's own transcendental theology.

There is possibly a difference in the role assigned to experience by Rahner and Metz. Rahner brings "experience" to bear even in those areas of human existence that are not of immediate interest to political theology, strictly speaking, as for example when he reflects on such mundane experiences as "on getting about," "on eating," "on laughter," "on sleeping," etc.[3] But surely, the fact that Rahner's theology is more inclusive in its relation to human experience should not detract from its political theological validity.

However, the difference in the kinds of "experiences" which each theologian selects for treatment and reflection can assume considerable importance. For instance, Rahner has attempted at some length to address Christianity's message to the "evolutionist" world-view (developed over the last century and a half). It is hard to imagine, in view of Metz's increasingly central emphasis on the need for an apocalyptic "interruption" of modern

---

[2] As cited by Vorgrimler, *Understanding Karl Rahner*, p.127. For a fuller discussion of this question, cf. also *Conversations*, pp.181-185.

[3] Karl Rahner, *Everyday Things*, *op. cit.*

evolutionary time consciousness, that he would be interested in addressing that particular segment of modern consciousness, pointing out the "affinity between the evolutionary world-view and Christian faith," as Rahner does.[4] This not insignificant difference may well be symptomatic of what is at the heart of the persistent refusal of each other's works to be fully reconcilable in the dynamics and/or direction they adopt. One immediate consequence of this observation is obviously that the fact that both transcendental and political theology have a deeply "experiential" base need not rule out major differences in how such experience is processed by each. In other words, it still leaves room for these theologies to largely overlap (materially) and yet at the same time be abidingly different (in modality).

2. There is also considerable agreement between Rahner's thought and political theology's position on the need for a **deprivatized theology**. Or one could even say that Rahner argues at least as vehemently as political theology for **a "de-ghetto-ized" church**, a church that exists primarily for the salvation of the world. This is most obvious both in his understanding of the radical unity of love of neighbour and love of God and from his ecclesiology. While there is no denying that Rahner may have been stimulated by Metz's thought to develop further and express more clearly the outward-directedness of his theology (as Lehmann and Vorgrimler suggest), it can be shown that this change is not superimposed upon his work but that it was already inherent in his very methodology (although it may include a certain development in this regard). Thus O'Donovan has pointed out that if Rahner's critics had "let his text truly live, in either its development or its imaginative power," they would have discovered that his "inclusive rather than exclusive" anthropology "contain[s] the seeds for the very developments about which his critics have rightly been exercised," namely:

----

[4] Cf. Leo O'Donovan, "Orthopraxis," p.54f. As an example of Rahner's efforts at addressing the evolutionary philosophy of life, cf. "Christology within an Evolutionary View of the World," TI V, 157-192.

Rather than being individualistic, Rahner's thought has shown a steady development towards 'a richer understanding of the world itself. It is now clearer than ever that the world is not merely the world of discreet *sensa* but is also the world of historicity, relativity, intersubjectivity, and personalism.' This emphasis on the social and historical aspects of human life qualify his anthropology as dialogic rather than individualist; it is inclusive at its roots and not simply by application.[5]

O'Donovan further clarifies the dynamic nature of Rahner's anthropology. After showing how Rahner developed an "increasingly critical sense...with respect to human self-understanding, to the organization of secular society [and] to the Church itself" (cf. *The Dynamic Element in the Church* and SCC), O'Donovan states: "the freer criticism in each case is a fruit of Rahner's theological anthropology and not a mere accretion to it."[6] These comments are not intended, of course, to belittle a possible external influence in this regard upon Rahner. The intention is rather to attempt a fair and balanced interpretation of his transcendental and anthropological theology, letting it speak for itself when possible.

3. Rahner's understanding of the radical unity of love of neighbour and love of God, his ecclesiology and his concept of the supernatural existential--which never loses sight of the fact that God's grace stands abidingly as his self-offering to humanity and creation through the incarnate *Logos*--also form the basis in transcendental theology for stressing a theology of **solidarity**. Such a theology necessarily breaks out of the constraints of a framework of bourgeois interpersonal mutuality, which political theology also rejects. This stress on worldwide solidarity, which requires Christian individuals and groups to work towards a radical transformation of structures of injustice and unfreedom everywhere, is for Rahner simply the logical outcome of the commandment to love one's neighbour. But it is also inherent in

----

[5] *Ibid.*, p.54.

[6] *Loc. cit.*

such biblical metaphors as "covenant," "people of God," "body of Christ" and others.[7]

But, according to Rahner himself, such a notion of intersubjectivity or solidarity-in-radical-mutuality was already inherent in his foundational philosophical conception of the human being as transcendent *Spirit in the World*. This concept intended to be a certain "correction" of the Marechalian interpretation of transcendental Thomism, to the effect that the idea of the human spirit coming to conscious self-possession only through the *conversio ad phantasmata* "may precisely not be translated as 'turning to the sensorial' but as 'turning toward history, toward [one's] free self-realization, toward fellow men and women'."[8] From the fact that Rahner's conception of love

---

[7] Rahner recognizes the "corrective" value of political theology, saying: "To the extent that political theology is directed against this tendency to restrict salvation to the private sphere it represents a genuine concern of the Church" (TI XII, 237, n.13).

But this is not a new insight, as he observes in his text: while the church is the "mediatrix of salvation to individual man in God's sight...the Church has never interpreted this salvation in an individualistic sense as a matter of man's merely private interior life" (p.237).

[8] Karl Rahner, *Glaube in winterlicher Zeit. Gespräche mit Karl Rahner aus den letzten Lebensjahren*, P. Imhof, et al, eds., (Düsseldorf: Patmos Verlag, 1986), p.61; my tr. German (expanded): "...in dieser Arbeit [*Geist in Welt*] [wird] 'Geist' thematisiert...als Transzendenz, die nur zu sich selber vermittelt werden kann durch die '*conversio ad phantasmata*,' was eben nicht übersetzt werden darf mit 'Hinwendung zum Sinnenbild,' sondern mit 'Hinwendung zur Geschichte, zum Freiheitsvollzug, zum Mitmenschen'."

This would eventually culminate in the emphatic "interpersonal" epistemology which is witnessed in TI XIII, 127: "The only way in which a man achieves self-realization is through encounters with his fellow man, a fellow who is rendered present to his experience in knowledge and love in the course of his personal life, one, therefore, who is not a thing or a matter, but a man." The preceding self-interpretation by Rahner of his early work, therefore, challenges the following claim by Vorgrimler: "In his early days Rahner had in fact formulated his philosophy of religion, the stages in the knowledge of God, 'objectively' in terms of a movement of the human spirit towards things, towards objects. Rahner owed his encounter with a philosophy

(not to mention his conceptions of history and of freedom) was already explicitly present in sections of HW, it follows that the notion of solidarity was inherent in this early work as well. We also find it dynamically at work in Rahner's interpretation of Romans 8 in a sermon from 1957. Even though his focus is decidedly anthropocentric, he extends the notion of solidarity in redemption not only to humankind as a whole but to all of creation, as the Pauline text would require.[9] His conception of the human person as essentially a free and knowing being, living in mutuality with other such beings, later culminates in the following statement:

> Freedom is always the freedom of a subject who exists in interpersonal communication with other subjects. Therefore it is necessarily freedom vis-a-vis another subject of transcendence, and this transcendence is not primarily the condition of possibility of knowing *things*, but is the condition of possibility for a subject being present to himself and just as basically and originally being present to another *subject*. But for a subject who is present to himself to affirm freely vis-a-vis another subject means ultimately to love (F, 65; his italics).

Although Rahner's solidarity thinking clearly shares a global outlook with Metz's, specifically advocating a practical solidarity with the impoverished segments of humanity, he argues at the same time that there is a rightful place for an "immediate love for Jesus," and "the tender interiority of this love, to which it need not be afraid to admit, [and which] is the fruit of patience,

---

and theology of intercommunication primarily to Metz" (*Understanding Karl Rahner*, p.126).

[9] K. Rahner, *Biblische Predigten*, (Herder, 1965), pp.108-113. This meditation on Romans 8:18-23 is entitled "Die Schöpfung ist entworfen, daß sie zu uns paßt" ("Creation is conceived in such a way that it suits us"), and is dated July 7, 1957.

prayer, and an ever renewed immersion in Scripture."[10] This nuance in emphasis may represent something of a difference between Rahner and Metz, although the latter's stress on there being both a social and a mystical component to salvation could hardly exclude a personal spiritual dimension. Besides, Metz not only admits of a New Testament emphasis upon the individual's calling by God, but also that his theology's involvement with social structures is undertaken precisely for the sake of the human person's salvation. Also, at the center of Metz's "fruitful conflict" with a Marxist utopianism stands his effort to prevent a "depersonalization" of human existence.

An exhaustive treatment of the question of solidarity thinking, and whether and how Rahner and Metz differ on it, would have to include their respective views on original sin (with its implications of a solidarity in perdition) and on redemption in Christ (his life, death and resurrection representing God's irreversibly victorious salvation of the world and all humankind). This cannot be done in detail here. But another difference seems to be lodged here. For while Metz shares with Rahner the view that in Christ God has irreversibly "accepted" the world as a whole, he feels some of Rahner's remarks on this topic are "almost incomprehensibly optimistic."[11] It is not surprising that Metz's solidarity thinking as rooted in his war experience as a

---

[10] *The Practice of Faith*, p.142. In this regard, cf. also *Glaube in winterlicher Zeit*, p.128, where he warns young people not to limit themselves merely to a one-sided social and political engagement: "They should be sure to bring their religious life into an inner synthesis with this engagement [that is so in vogue, but possibly already receding]. After all God is, [and] there is such a thing as a personal relationship to him, and there is a personal divine judgment by way of the personal death of each individual. These things cannot be ignored because of a sociopolitical and sociocritical commitment" (my tr.).

[11] The words are Vorgrimler's, but are meant to convey Metz's thinking on the matter as they are found in the section in which the critical relationship between Rahner and Metz is discussed (cf. *Understanding Karl Rahner*, p.128).

young soldier (which he was to translate into the larger tragedy of *Auschwitz* and beyond to all human injustice and suffering) clashes with the following expression of hope by Rahner, who says:

> For me the history of humanity, despite all the disastrous things which have happened to men, even despite Auschwitz and all the catastrophes which perhaps we must still fear as a result of the exhaustion of natural resources and nuclear madness, is a history of salvation, a universal history of the power of grace and divine love, a history in which we can hope for all *human beings* and not just a few.[12]

This and other such statements of "faith" and "hope" (cited by Vorgrimler in the same context) give rise to several questions. Is Rahner (and his God) immune to the real, "wordless suffering" in the world, or is he simply practicing the biblical faith and hope which knows it must do what it can but must also leave much of the problematic of evil and suffering to God's inscrutable wisdom and judgment (cf. Rom. 8:28ff.)? Conversely, is there not a contradiction between Metz's confession of God's absolute acceptance of the world and his simultaneous fear of a possible universal failure of God's salvation when he "is afraid of a complete questioning of the history of God with humankind"?[13] For what does this total questioning do with the ultimately victorious "white rider," who was seen with the eyes of faith in the apocalyptic vision of the book of Revelation 19:11-16?

We are touching again on the central nerve of the irreducible difference between Rahner and Metz, whereby the former leans more towards a historical or sacramental (cultic?) interpretation of reality, while the latter tends more towards an apocalyptic or "prophetic" reading of the human situation. Speaking in eschatological terms, one might contrast their differing tendencies

---

[12] As cited by Vorgrimler, *Ibid.*, p.129; his italics. Vorgrimler gives several more similar quotations from Rahner (pp.128ff.).

[13] *Ibid.*, p.130.

as follows: Rahner's outlook on reality is more (not only)[14] that of a historical or "realized" eschatology, whereas Metz's is more inclined towards an apocalyptic eschatology bent upon interrupting the innerworldly succession of things and events. Rahner can be characterized with an "always-already" position and Metz with a "not-yet" position with respect to God's fulfillment of his promise of salvation, according to some theologians.[15]   Neither of these "tendencies" or characteristics are necessarily more or less "orthodox" than their counterparts, nor can either position claim stronger or weaker support from traditional theology or Scripture. We will come back to this later, but we can state here that these two differing orientations may ultimately not be fully reconcilable.

Obviously, the problem alluded to here will not be solved by easy answers. The reason for citing it is not to offer a solution, but rather to indicate that the convergence between Rahner and Metz is by no means complete. The question to keep in mind is simply whether the differences between Rahner and Metz which do emerge are of such a nature as to make Rahner's thought "anti" or "non-political theological" as such. This is not the case with the difference just cited, as can be seen when these highly "optimistic" statements are juxtaposed with alternative and/or accompanying statements made by Rahner on the same subject

---

[14] Lamb's observation is relevant here in pointing out that Rahner's is by no means a one-dimensional "always-already" eschatology, when in his "Response to Fr. Metz" he says, one could read Rahner's "transcendental theology, not as disclosive of an 'always already' achieved Christian identity, but as imperatives impelling us towards personal and social transformations of a world 'not yet' truly human and 'not yet' truly Christ-like" (*Theology of Discovery*, p.181).

[15] On the basic characterization of Rahner's and Metz's theological positions as "always already" vs. "not yet" positions, respectively, cf. Lamb's & Tracy's "Response(s) to Fr. Metz," *Theology and Discovery*, pp.179-183 and 184-187.

matter. Rahner does not absolve human responsibility in the least from doing what it can.[16]

4. Much of what we have said up to here relates also to the topic of "praxis." The fact that Rahner's theology as a whole, but particularly in its so-called "pastoral dimension," has a strong practical orientation was established above. We even found that a good case can be made to the effect that Rahner's transcendental theology goes a long way in meeting the praxis orientation which political theology critically adopts from critical reason. We showed that Rahner gives the concrete social situation a tremendously important status in co-determining the essential truth about the church and Christianity and in co-determining principles about how Christians should live in and for the world. In this, Rahner does not substantially differ from Metz, who proposes to engage in his frank dialogue with the secular world "in the light of Catholic theology" (ThW, p.13, n.1). And a bit later on, in FoC, he holds that the communal praxis of discipleship is to measure its own verbal and enacted life story always against the story of its founder.

As far as the relationship between theory and praxis is concerned, however, we saw that Rahner does not fit into the kind of political theology that would assign to "praxis" a status of "control" over "theory" as defined by Lamb. On the contrary,

---

[16] Consider for instance this statement by Rahner for a balanced emphasis on active engagement and waiting on God: "I'm all for the courageous struggle for a better economy, for a better social future and I believe that a person who is really convinced of this must take responsibility for this social obligation before the judgment seat of God. When all is said and done, believers cannot and must not allow people who do not believe in this absolute future to get the better of them. I would say that if the world is destroyed by atomic weapons or slips further into economic misery, that would be all too horrible and frightful. And everyone is obliged before God's eternal judgment to do everything in his or her power to prevent such things from happening. One day we must give a reckoning for this. But if a people or humanity were to fall into the abyss, then I would still be firmly convinced--and I hope to keep this conviction--that even such an abyss always ultimately ends in the arms of the eternally good, eternally powerful God" (*Understanding Karl Rahner*, p.129.).

we found that, if anything, Rahner may in fact lean in the opposite direction of giving a certain priority to "theoretical" or doctrinal theology over against the "practical" aspect.[17] Mention has already been made of the reservations Rahner has with respect to insufficient "theoretical reflection" by some liberation theologians.

Metz is emphatic that the only Christology that can be "known" or truly understood is one which comes from an engaged practical discipleship. But that this is not intended as an extremist or one-sided emphasis on "praxis" to the exclusion of theory or dogmatic reflection seems to me obvious from the fact that he derives this insight from his reading of the gospels (for which he has a certain preference over Paul's epistles), and from Jewish story tellers.[18]   His appreciation and respect for the dogmatic tradition is evident also from the fact that these (dogmatic) stories are to be included in the repertoire of "narrative theology" today. There is obviously a difference, at least in emphasis, between Rahner and Metz in terms of the

---

[17] Incidentally, this primacy of "theory" over "action" may actually claim Scriptural support. For Paul writes in 1 Thessalonians (5:21; JB): **"think before you do anything."** While in itself such a citation may not be all that significant, the context in which it is found makes clear, however, that Paul encourages critical evaluation of new experiences and movements in church and society.

[18] It would be interesting to examine why Metz is more attracted to the gospels than to Paul's writings. Does he feel less akin to the latter for reasons similar to those for which he criticises Rahner, i.e., because the latter embodies more of an incarnational-sacramental view of salvation (e.g. Rom. 8:28-39)?

As for Metz's "learning" an apocalyptic eschatology from Jewish story tellers, therein lies perhaps both his genius and his vulnerability. For while the "triumphalist" strand of Christian eschatological thought undeniably can benefit from the Jewish reminder that the Messiah has not "arrived" yet (in a certain sense at least), to what extent may one adopt this attitude of faith before it becomes "unbelief" against all that the New Testament and Christian tradition affirm?

theoretical versus the practical dimensions in theology. Tracy is surely right in contrasting them as follows:

> Where Rahner will emphasize the cognitive identity crisis of the contents of faith of Christianity in modernity and thereby develop a transcendental program of theology, Metz will insist upon the political-ethical crisis of subjects and institutions of Christian identity today and thereby develop a political theology dependent upon the *intelligible* logos of *praxis*.[19]

No doubt, these words aptly depict a certain tendency in each theologian. However, they should not be pushed too far. In terms of active engagement, Rahner is supremely a theologian of praxis. He too is keenly aware that Christianity's message is credible only insofar as it is embodied in the lives of Christians in the church. And while his is superbly a "transcendental program," it will be remembered that for Rahner the free self-realization and the achievement of self-possession (or knowledge

---

[19] Tracy, *op. cit.*, p.184; his italics. This prevalence of the "cognitive" dimension in Rahner is also envisaged in M. Lamb's list of Metz's five "suspicions" with regards to a predominant "metaphysical conceptuality" in transcendental theology (cf. "A Response to Fr. Metz," *op. cit.*, p.179f.; on Rahner's concern about a "deficit" in metaphysics in Metz, cf. note #45 below). While Lamb's analysis of the aim of Metz's "political hermeneutics of suspicion" in relation to transcendental theology is perhaps accurate, the assessment of Rahner's work as "idealistic," "disclosive," "illusory," and passive (because "concepts do not move") is highly inadequate, which the writer cannot fail to realize (in part at least) as the rest of his article shows. Thus Lamb indicates further on that Rahner's theology was neither inactive nor idealistic, saying: "Rahner loved the Church enough to challenge official policies when those contradicted the demands of fidelity to the ongoing *traditio* or handing on of the faith. Nor was it in the cheap grace of a romantic idealism that Rahner gained insight into how anthropocentrism is profoundly theocentric. That insight concretely emerged within the darkness and despair of a human and historical identity-crisis, the apocalyptic dimensions of which can only be glimpsed in the many histories of suffering spread across two World Wars" (p.182).

On how transcendental theology can also be seen as an engaged, vulnerable hare, instead of a hedgehog trying to win the race by stealth, cf. note #52 below.

of any sort) by the human subject via self-transcendence are ultimately possible only in loving outreach towards other subjects.

5. Finally, the twin categories of "narrative" and "memory" form perhaps the most illuminating source for appreciating the unity-in-difference of these two theologians. Is there a significant difference in the way in which Rahner's transcendental theology may claim to be a "remembering narrative theology" in comparison to that specified by Metz's political theology from the early 1970s onward? Metz himself attests that Rahner's theology can indeed claim to be superbly a "narrative theology" (and hence a political theology as well). He calls it the best paradigmatic narrative theology of our time. The only shortcoming he observes in this regard is the fact that the anthropological factor of the subject, rather than the societal one, appears to be the more central "moving force" of the human "story" it narrates so masterfully.

Our own cursory survey of selected writings by Rahner confirms Metz's claim in the sense that in his pre-conciliar writings Rahner did not (and perhaps could not) make the social experience as central as he might have. But this dimension certainly takes on considerable proportions, and is explicitly declared to be indispensable, in his post-conciliar writings. In the light of Rahner's explicit and frequent recognition of the necessity of the "social component" alongside the "mystical component" today, it is indeed "all the more surprising," as Vorgrimler observes, "that Metz criticized Rahner and his theology of transcendence" so persistently.[20]   In Rahner's

---

[20] *Understanding Karl Rahner*, p.127. Vorgrimler specifically refers to FHS, chap. 9, esp. pp.161ff., the famous fairy tale about the hare and the hedgehog, told by Metz "against the grain." Vorgrimler had formerly seriously challenged Metz about the "unfairness" of accusing Rahner of "conjuring tricks." Cf. H. Vorgrimler, ed., *Wagnis Theologie* (Freiburg i.Br: Herder, 1979), p.258, where he says among other things:
"To apply the fairy tale to these two theologies is perverse precisely because this presupposes two hedgehogs, whereas transcendental theology is simply just one. To accuse Rahner of 'conjuring tricks' is a serious matter, seeing that

above-cited response to Metz's criticism (in FHS) of his work on this very point, he claims that his has actually been a "political theology from its inception:"

> For it has always been clear in my theology that a "transcendental experience" (of God and of grace) is always mediated through a categorical experience in history, in interpersonal relationships, and in society. If one not only sees and takes seriously these necessary mediations of transcendental experience but also fills it out in a concrete way, then one already practices in an authentic way political theology, or...a practical fundamental theology.[21]

This claim is supported by all his theological writings and not only his later ones.

The fact that Rahner can be said to concentrate his efforts primarily on the "retrieval of the contemporary meaning of the classical doctrines" from the history of Christianity[22] (Metz would speak here of a focus on "argumentative" theology), does not of course detract from its value as "narrative" theology. According to Metz, both aspects are indispensable and need to complement one another. And Metz lauds Rahner's theology precisely for having achieved a balanced blending of the doctrinal and the existential-mystical aspects, saying: "Doxography and mystical biography are merged into one another" (FHS, p.226). Moreover, Metz's greater emphasis on narrative theology--with a pervading emphasis on the history of suffering rather than on the full range of Christian tradition--is never intended in opposition to argumentative or doctrinal theology but merely as a corrective to the traditional overemphasis on a too abstract or ideal dogmatic system.

---

the analogy does not fit front or back" (my tr.).

[21] Rahner, "Introduction" to J. Bacik, *op. cit.*, p.x. For the expanded context of these comments, cf. the Introduction above.

[22] Tracy, *op. cit.*, p.184.

To argue that Rahner's transcendental theology is fundamentally and simultaneously also a narrative theology is not necessarily to say that it does not significantly differ from Metz's narrative political theology. This will be seen presently. But first a few words about the memory-concept are in place.

Directly related to the category of narrative theology is the sibling category of "remembrance." The "memory" at issue is the "dangerous memory" first of the death and resurrection of Jesus Christ, but then also of all true suffering and truly victorious life that springs from the suffering of Christians and humankind throughout the ages. When these "memories" are recited aloud in stories and in living action, they will form an unlimited source of inspiration, hope and energy towards their re-enactment in each new situation of injustice and unfreedom. They will be a genuine "danger" to the present structures of violence and oppression.

The question which emerges for us is whether transcendental theology can claim to include at its core this *memoria passionis et resurrectionis*. The answer is in the affirmative, even when "memory" is defined as seeing history from the perspective of the victims rather than the victors. For in our discussion on the "explicit" political theological dimension in Rahner, we noted that he urged the German church finally to "enter into a mental and material solidarity with those Christians [sic] and non-Christian groups" of the Third World who suffer from injustice and lack of freedom. Obviously, the many instances cited above in which Rahner actively and vigorously protested and at considerable personal risk against injustice and unfreedom in the institutional church and in society at large show that transcendental theology indeed "remembers" the genuine freedom wrought by the Son (cf. Jn 8:36), or the freedom guaranteed in Christ's body by the Holy Spirit as Paul speaks of it (cf. 2 Cor. 3:17; 1 Thes. 5:19; also Rahner's "Do not Stifle the Spirit," TI VII, pp.72-87; later, *Ich protestiere*).

The "memory" of Christianity in general, both past and present, runs through Rahner's transcendental theology in a uniquely powerful way, and is crucial in shaping every step of the way. Aside from Lehmann and Fischer, nobody has brought this out as eloquently as Metz, who explicitly stresses that the "memoria" in question includes the whole dogmatic deposit of the Christian faith.

To say this is, of course, not to say that this memoria is brought to bear in exactly the same way on present-day experience in both political theology and transcendental theology. Nor is it to say that exactly the same sufferings or experiences are "remembered." But neither is it to say that, if these theologies tap different reservoirs of the deposits of the vast Christian "memory" of sufferings (and the victories that are achieved therein), or use different methods to gain access to them, then one or other theology must be to that extent "wrong" or unorthodox, must be more or less a **political** theology. Quite clearly, it is possible for them to be "political theologies" in ways that differ from one another.

In this area of memory and narrative, perhaps more clearly than anywhere else, there exist significant differences. Tracy has sketched these perceptively, when he says:

> Where Rahner will concentrate his theological energies upon a method of retrieval of the contemporary meaning of the classical doctrines, Metz will retrieve above all the "memories of the suffering of the oppressed" throughout the centuries and the powerful negations of the present status quo as those negations are embedded in the apocalyptic texts of the New Testament. Where Rahner will re-express the mystagogical experience of the Christian, Metz will develop a political theology which is at the same time mystical-political theology.[23]

Obviously, these characterizations cannot serve undialectically as "objectivistic" statements about either theologian's work. They merely serve to denote certain tendencies in each of them. With that proviso, however, these characterizations deserve to be taken seriously. But while the differences envisaged here are irreducible differences, they are nevertheless "differences [which are] yet grounded in a joint emphasis upon the *subject* as *subject*

---

[23] *Loc. cit.*

and upon the identifiably religious, Christian, indeed mystagogical resources of the tradition," writes Tracy. He adds, pointing out their common rootage despite their irreconcilable otherness: "Rahner's emphasis upon the "always-already" reality of redemption and Metz's emphasis upon the negations of the present and the "not-yet" are both grounded in the narratives which function as normative for us all, the passion-narratives of the New Testament."[24]

Then, accepting Metz's challenge that theology should "concentrate upon narrative," Tracy very concisely but ingeniously qualifies this argument by attempting to answer the question: "what do our classical narratives--the gospels--disclose of the reality of the always-already and of the not-yet of Christian *praxis* and thought? What finally do these narratives narrate?"[25]

Tracy's "answer" shows, more by way of an informed allusion than detailed exegesis, how both of the characteristic tendencies which mark the works of Rahner and Metz, respectively, are co-present in the original gospel narratives. Rahner's predominant tendency towards a position of an "always-already" view of salvation thereby resonates more closely the tendency found in Luke-Acts and John, a position in which one might cautiously say eschatology is less apocalyptically and more incarnational-sacramentally oriented: the eschatological kingdom of God is viewed as already "realized eschatology" in God's gracious self-communication in the *logos*-become-flesh.

By contrast, Metz's political theology with its increasingly apocalyptic interpretation of all redemptive reality in history as being primarily an "interruption" of the evolutionary modern consciousness, being more of a "not-yet" than an "already" in relation to the promised kingdom of God, represents a tendency found more prevalent in Mark and Matthew. Put differently, in and between the gospel narratives themselves a certain tension

---

[24] *Ibid.*, p.185.

[25] *Loc. cit.*

exists "between a fulfillment of the eschatological Kingdom of God in the ministry, passion, and resurrection of Jesus Christ and an as yet unfulfilled hope for the end-time and for all, the living and the dead, in that Kingdom." This, in Tracy's view, roughly corresponds to the tension that can be observed between Rahner and Metz. The differing "tendencies" in the gospel narratives can be prototypically illustrated by referring to Jesus' final cry on the cross as recorded by each evangelist. In Tracy's words:

> The prophets and apocalyptic-minded among us, like Metz, are likely to resonate to one temporary end of the story of the crucified one: the frightening and shaking "not-yet" cry of Jesus in Matthew and Mark, "**My God, my God why have you forsaken me**" (Mt 27:46; Mk 15:34)? The more "ordinary" Christian--a type which the gospel also honors and for whom it demands that attention must be paid--is more likely to overhear the trusting words of Luke's crucified Jesus, "**Father, into your hands I commend my spirit**" (Lk 23:46), and its disclosure of the reality of fundamental trust. The mystics and all those who honor authentic religious manifestations of cosmos from chaos, all those who, like Rahner, sense the ground of all in the ultimate mystery and radical grace are likely to turn to the words in the narrative of John's exalted as crucified one: "**It is accomplished**" (Jn 19:30).[26]

This perceptive, though rather stylized, depiction of each theologian and of their respective associations with the corresponding dimensions of the gospel narratives is undoubtedly accurate. Tracy's observations are especially helpful in pointing out that even the original gospel narratives are variegated almost to the point of mutual contradiction. Thus it is difficult for any one Christian theologian to tap all of their riches. Therefore, the undeniable and perhaps irreconcilable difference in accentuation in Rahner's and Metz's theologies seem to harken back to a similar unity-in-difference among the New Testament evangelists themselves. These considerable differences need not signify, however, that one theologian has a less "narrative" theology than the other. By extension, this surely means that if narrative theology--provided it is rooted soundly in the original gospel

---

[26] *Ibid.*, pp.186f.; my emphs.

narratives, whether reflecting more of an "incarnational" mode or an "apocalyptic" mode--qualifies it ipso facto as a political theology, then Rahner's surely is one. His narrative work can claim to be a political theology of the Lukan or Johannine (incarnational or sacramental) style, if not of the Matthean or Markan (apocalyptic) style. As we saw with the experience dimension earlier, so we see now with memory and narrative that these concepts play no less a role in transcendental theology than in Metz's political theology, but perhaps different areas and types of memory and narrative are found to be prevalent in Rahner. In the same way and to the degree that these concepts are employed with distinction, then, Rahner's is a political theology with a distinctly incarnational approach to the narratives, whereas Metz's thought obviously tends towards an apocalyptic appropriation of the memory of the gospels and Christian tradition.

Tracy's depiction of Rahner and Metz with the help of certain emphases in the gospels, while very effective in lifting out the unique colours of each, could easily become a distortion, a caricature, if it were pushed too far. A closer look at each of the gospels would surely reveal a fairer blend of the incarnational and the apocalyptic elements, of fulfillment of promised salvation and unfulfilled hope in the final salvation of all, of suffering as symbolized by the Cross and victory or exaltation of which the emblem is the Resurrection. In the same way, a closer analysis of the theologies of Rahner and Metz reveals that these emphases are just that and may not be taken to the extreme. For although Rahner is certainly not an "apocalyptic" theologian in the same way as Metz, his eschatology serves a similar "denying," "interrupting," or relativizing function, for example, in relation to Marxist utopianism as is served by Metz's theology. Likewise, it would not be difficult to find embedded in Metz's theology emphases of a sacramental, institutional, and incarnational nature.

This has been amply documented above from ThW.[27] If it might be objected that this dimension in Metz later gives way to his growing emphasis upon the apocalyptic aspect of theology, it ought to be remembered that he created his narrative theology partly in order better to do justice to the historical-as-realized salvation and so to counter accusations from the theological Right that his theology was too exclusively future-oriented (cf. Johns). He introduced this category in order to help the contemporary generation which he felt was suffering under a growing "forgetfulness" of its doctrinal and confessional Christian "past" (cf. Ancic).

One more observation with respect to Tracy's "typologization" of the transcendental and political theologies is in order here. While it is perfectly acceptable, even unavoidable to an extent, to characterize the gospels and/or theologians by their prevalent emphases, neither the incarnational or apocalyptic "tendency" could exist independently from the other without becoming a distortion of Christian teaching or praxis. Tracy acknowledges this:

> Yet whatever classical route of spirituality or theology individual Christians take, none of us can forget that the Christian narrative must finally be remembered in its entirety: as a whole of real negation and real exaltation, of real suffering and active love, as a proclamation and manifestation of the Crucified and Risen One who lived, lives, and will live; as a narrative which has not ended and will not end until all the living and the dead are touched...; as a narrative which discloses the tense and paradoxical presence of both the utter reality of the "always-already" graced state which is ours and, at the same time, the reality of the "not-yet" negating all present

---

[27] This incarnational dimension did not disappear by any means in Metz with ThW. Besides being re-channelled into the active "narrative" of discipleship (in FoC, and elsewhere), it is found operative for instance in passages like "Invoking Grace in the Senses;" "Invoking Grace in Freedom;" and "Invoking Grace in Politics," in the chapter, "Toward the Second Reformation," in EC (pp.48-66). While appreciative of the courage of the Protestant Reformers, he finds Protestantism's narrow stress on the spoken word (the sense of hearing mainly) too restricting and prefers the holistic, more inclusive emphasis of Catholicism.

securities; as a narrative which disallows *any* assumption that the reality of
the "not-yet" is not as real as the "always-already" presence of God in
creation, covenant, and the radical, universal grace of Jesus Christ at the
heart of the lived tension of Christian identity and Christian theology.[28]

Obviously, therefore, to the extent that Rahner and Metz each
tend toward one typological frame of reference or the other--and
there is no question that their works represent lastingly diverging
approaches to the same classical theological tradition(s), despite
the vast and profound areas of converging theological
thought each of thcm stands in need of correction and/or
supplementation. Both theologians have recognized and
acknowledged this.

In short, the central tenets of the works of Rahner and Metz,
in terms of goals, inner dynamics and critical sociopolitical
effect, obviously converge. But the differences are also
undeniable and indeed quite certainly unbridgeable. No doubt the
differences are in part related to the specific terminology and
categories through which each theologian filters his theological
content. But the underlying differences have more to do with a
certain personal-theological temperament--i.e. sacramental-
incarnational vs. prophetic-apocalyptic leanings, which account
for the uniquely different emphases in their attempts to face up
to the challenges of the modern situation on the basis of the one
Christian gospel and tradition--and less with methodology per se.

Some hold that only one point resists fuller convergence,
namely, the question of the sociopolitical dimension, which Metz
in his theology stresses so tenaciously and on which he
persistently registers a "deficit" in Rahner's theology. However,
the real difference between these theologians and their theologies
lies deeper than this. It has ultimately to do precisely with the
fact that at the roots of their theologies Rahner and Metz have
adopted two fundamentally different orientations. Their
fundamental theological outlooks are as disparate from each other
as the cultic-sacramental-incarnational is from the prophetic-

---

[28] Tracy, *op. cit.*, p.187; his italics.

apocalyptic world-view. Metz is not only or primarily troubled by the fact that transcendental theology appears to take the individual subject as its focus (political theology does this too to some extent); he is troubled rather because he feels the affirmative incarnational approach is highly inadequate in the face of the tremendous moral, political and religious crises that confront Christianity in *Auschwitz* (and all it stands for) and in the sufferings of the Third World. Thus he concludes with the telling rhetorical questions with which he rounds off the above-cited critique of Rahner's transcendental and anthropological theology:

> Therefore, should not the transcendental theology of person and existence be translated into a type of 'political theology'? And finally, does not a radical transcendental-existential theology undervalue the rank of eschatology? Can the eschatology really be extrapolated out of the existential approach of theology? Or does not every anthropologically oriented theology which does not want to leave the world and history out of the sight of operative and responsible faith flow into an eschatologically oriented theology? Is [not in fact only] the eschatological horizon broad enough to communicate (*vermitteln*) unabridged the faith and the historically arising world?[29]

This one question, asked from so many angles, is charged with meaning as soon as one realizes that the eschatology advanced here is not an incarnational eschatology stressing the "always-already" dimension of the Kingdom of God irreversibly "realized" in Jesus Christ (which Rahner has developed, if we may stereotype him this way for argument's sake). Rather, it is an **apocalyptic** eschatology, behind which resonates the theodicy question, which Metz says pervades all his theology ever since

---

[29] Metz, "Foreword [to SW]: An Essay on Karl Rahner," *op. cit.*, p.xviii. The words inserted in the quote in brackets are crucial. Dych mistranslated that sentence, which reads thus in the original German: "Ist nämlich nicht erst der eschatologische Horizont umfassend genug, daß in ihm Glaube und geschichtlich entstehende Welt unverkürzt vermittelt werden können?" (The emphasized words are omitted from the translated text; cf. note #7 of the Introduction for the context and source of this quote.)

his unspeakably tragic battlefield experience as a young soldier. The massive scale of evil and suffering witnessed in the world requires an appropriate and proportional redress from theology if it is to be believable in its God-talk. Is a basically "optimistic" transcendental theology, which is content to challenge the free human individual to transcend himself or herself into God and neighbour, in fact able to rise to the occasion and produce such an "impatient," yet "inclusive" eschatology?

The specifically "apocalyptic" dimension, which can be detected in this "eschatological" questioning of transcendental theology, was of course to be refined by Metz in his subsequent writings. Reference was made already in chapter 1 to what we might call his "theology in an apocalyptic key." Metz gradually came to stress emphatically that there is not and cannot be "hope" for the Christian, unless it is "hope for all." But especially, German Christian believers may not claim saving hope for themselves, if it is not also hope for the Jewish victims of *Auschwitz*, which figuratively stands for all the downtrodden in history and in that sense is valid for all Christians. In other words, Metz's critique of the transcendental and anthropological theology of the mid-1960s from the angle of "eschatology" quite certainly involves the "not-yet" element as Tracy has depicted it, namely, a theological position which takes utterly seriously--is perhaps even dominated by--the reality of the "as yet unfulfilled hope for the end-time and for all, the living and the dead," in spite of the kingdom of God having drawn near in Jesus Christ. That this apocalyptic dimension is in fact there in this early criticism, seems evident from the way Metz phrases his words in recognition of Rahner's meritorious achievements:

> Such questions, coming out of Rahner's program, need not be solved against him, but rather in dialogue with him. **For finally Rahner's theology in all the truly great and enduring things it has given us is properly characterized by one overriding "tendency": the ever new**

initiation into the mystery of God's love and the service of the hope of all men.[30]

These are not just polite words toward his mentor. Rather, it is a genuine recognition that Rahner's work shares with apocalyptic political theology a keen concern to be in "the service of the hope of all men," despite the "incarnational bent" of transcendental theology towards a basic perception of the "mystery of God's love" as having already been irreversibly established in Jesus Christ, so that the eventual acceptance of that mystery by all humanity is viewed as a foregone conclusion; so the actual realization of it can confidently be left to God's inscrutable counsel as he waits out every person's free decision. And that is why the "corrective" to the Rahnerian focus proposed by political theology--actually partially contained within its own recesses--may be attempted in dialogue with, rather than opposition to him.[31] In other words, Metz's acknowledgments are a genuine endorsement of Rahner's theology to the effect that despite some serious shortcomings (as Metz perceives them), this transcendental theology is nevertheless, in its own way, rendering a contribution to modern society, which has been seen to be the constant concern of the new political theology also, namely, the attempt (undertaken in so many ways) to somehow open up the human subject of the post-Enlightenment scientific, technological society for the absolute mystery--God.

To be sure, their approaches differ. Rahner's approach can be said to tend more towards addressing the "intellectual crisis," while that of Metz consists increasingly in his effort to lead the church towards exercising its service of "apologetics" within modern society by its way of life, by praxis rather than more subtle argumentation. However, both are motivated by a profound

---

[30] *Loc. cit.*

[31] Metz explicitly made this claim in 1980 about Rahner's theology: "we can often find support for objections to his theories in the broader context of his own thinking" (cited by M. Lamb, "A Response to Fr. Metz," *op. cit.*, p.181).

pastoral concern for translating Christianity's message into the horizon of modern individuals and society: "the ever new initiation into the mystery of God's love and the service of the hope of all men."

2. Rahner's Comments on Political Theology

Rahner and Metz both would seem to be in basic agreement with an assessment of a far-reaching, though qualified, compatibility between their theologies. Thus, when responding to my original thesis proposal, Metz (and Rahner) agreed that his work represents more of a logical continuation of what characterizes the latter's transcendental and anthropological theological thought than a break-away from it. A letter from Metz reads in part:

> Prof. Metz and I have read your exposition with interest and are in agreement with it. Already the opening observation, that Metz's theology stands not *'in opposition to'*, but rather *'in conversation with'* Karl Rahner, is well taken. Karl Rahner also commented on this observation with approval when Prof. Metz informed him of it. As for the position of the proposal [*zur Konzeption*], I have nothing critical to say in this short reply. Therefore, please let our approval be sufficient to you. We have the impression that [your research project] will turn out to be a good work...[32]

The profound "unity-in-difference" between Rahner and Metz -- here accepted by the authors themselves according to this letter -- is discernible also in Rahner's occasional comments later on in

---

[32] My tr. In the original the letter, written by Metz's assistant, Dr. Werner Kroh (dated March 20, 1984), reads: "Prof. Metz und ich [haben] Ihre Exposition mit Aufmerksamkeit und Zustimmung gelesen. Bereits die Eingangsbemerkung über Metz' Theologie, die nicht *'in opposition to'*, sondern *'in conversation with'* K[arl] Rahner steht, trifft die Sache gut. Auch K[arl] Rahner hat sich über die Bemerkung affirmativ geäußert, als Prof. Metz ihm davon berichtete. Zur Konzeption kann ich in der Kürze gar nichts Kritisches sagen. Begnügen Sie sich deshalb bitte mit unserer Zustimmung. Wir haben den Eindruck, daß es eine gute Arbeit werden wird..."

his life about Metz's work. Rahner dealt with Metz's criticisms indirectly by silently integrating some of them into his post-conciliar writings.[33]   And his later direct comments on political theology generally and Metz's work specifically are baffling at first glance because these range from complete disclaimers to complete acceptance. For instance, how is one to reconcile the apparent contradiction between Rahner's 1979 statement: "I am not a representative of political theology..."[34]   and his 1966 assertion that "theology must always be 'political' theology" (in a qualified church historical sense)?[35]

---

[33] In his indirect debates with the "fundamental intentions" of the Metzian theology, says Lehmann, "Rahner does not abandon...the terrain of his own thought, but rather demonstrates in this largely hidden, friendly dispute how capable of expanding, how effective and flexible his own thought can be. The 'gathering-in' (*Einbeziehung*) e.g. of the themes of 'political theology' into the larger totality of theological reflection in a certain sense takes the cutting edge off of its critical questions (which is then sometimes interpreted to mean, that political theology has not been 'understood' at all), represents in fact, however, simultaneously a quiet theological correction" (Lehmann, *Bilanz*, cf. pp.178f.; my tr.).

[34] In a radio interview about "the political theology of... Metz," Rahner presents this disclaimer about his own work: "I am not a representative of political theology." Then he goes on to affirm of Metz: "but I believe that the kind of political theology which Metz represents is thoroughly orthodox..." It is so sound that even if a bishop were to "have pertinent objections" (provided he did not have to fear open heresy), he ought not to prevent Metz from teaching it. (*Conversations*, p.234.)

[35] Cf. TI IX, p.189: "The theologian is aware that, since the necessary setting for the individual's salvation is the Church as the unity of mankind and its history *theology must always be 'political' theology*. He is aware that he may only look at the salvation of an individual as one which is not achieved fully except within the absolute future of the whole of mankind, as the ultimate result of the love of all the others in the absoluteness of God. In other words, the salvation of an individual soul does not consist in escaping from the history of humanity but in entering into the latter's absolute future, which we call the 'kingdom of God'" (his italics).

This apparent inner tension in Rahner surely relates to his qualified reservations about the new political theology. For while Rahner expresses frequent agreement, and on occasion even defends political theology when it is attacked, there are and remain areas in his thinking which resist uncritical integration into Metz's theological thought. This is quite evident from Rahner's persistently stated reservations on the matter. We have an advantage over Lehmann, who in 1970 had relatively few overt statements by Rahner on the issue on which to base his comments. In his "conversations" and "interviews" during his later years, Rahner has repeatedly commented on political theology. Nevertheless, it will become evident that Lehmann's assessment concerning the relationship between these theologians has remained fairly accurate, even in the light of later remarks from Rahner.

It will be helpful to list some of the cautiously-stated positive evaluations of political theology by Rahner. In 1979 Rahner characterized Metz's work as "perfectly orthodox" and developed "within Catholicism." But this did not mean, he added, that he and Metz agreed on all details; Metz had, in fact, "vigorously attacked" his transcendental theology. Basically the same observations recur in a 1979 radio interview.[36] In 1980, when asked if Metz's theology was "a child or grandchild of [his] thought," Rahner refers the questioner to Metz, who "is convinced that real political theology is his own invention and does not come from me," adding, "so political theology strictly speaking could not have been inherited from me, though I have nothing against that."[37]

Rahner also had some negative comments. In 1981, after some observations on the meaning of love of neighbour today as

---

[36] Cf. note #34 above. It may be noted that the hypothetical "objections" to political theology of which Rahner speaks in that radio interview are an indirect reference to Cardinal Ratzinger's rejection of Metz as professor at Munich.

[37] *Conversations*, pp.269f.

involving "also... political responsibility," he states categorically: "I never developed any political theology." Then follows this disclaimer: "I suppose I do not quite understand what it is that my friend and former student Metz is developing and championing under that label."[38]   What does this comment mean? Implausible as it may seem at first, might one perhaps question Vorgrimler's assertion that Rahner "understands" Metz's political theological thought perfectly well,[39] in the sense that a strongly "incarnational" frame of thought might have genuine problems laying hold of the "frequencies" of an "apocalyptic" thought pattern (and the reason for advancing it)? Put another way, is it not possible that from Rahner's theological vantage point certain dynamics of thought in the fundamental apocalyptic theology of Metz are as nearly "incomprehensible" as the latter says Rahner's theological "optimism" is?[40]

This seemingly real impossibility of a final convergence of their differing thoughts does not necessarily imply that the transcendental mode of theological thought is therefore "apolitical" theology. The following statement by Rahner attests to the fact that transcendental theology is keenly aware of a wide range of "social" responsibilities for Christians:

> But I am thoroughly convinced that the true Christian of the present should not only be a respectable person in the realm of sexuality and in money matters, but also must deal with horrendous societal and political issues....I

---

[38] *Ibid.*, p.269.

[39] In Vorgrimler's words: "Though Rahner sometimes said that he did not know what was meant by the 'political theology' of his friend Metz, in reality he knew very well." Vorgrimler then gives a quote from Rahner's later writings to prove his point. *Understanding Karl Rahner*, pp.126f. This quote, to be sure, proves Rahner's "factual" understanding of Metz's work, but does not necessarily prove that an incarnational theology does, or ever could, "understand" the movements of an apocalyptic political theology.

[40] *Ibid.*, cf. p.128. Here Vorgrimler gives several quotes from Rahner to illustrate the, for Metz, "almost incomprehensibly optimistic" dimension in the work of the former.

am also thoroughly convinced that church teaching and formation would have to be structured very differently than it is, from bottom to top. There is no question in my mind that the German bishops are in the right in their campaign against abortion legislation, but I admit that I would like to see the bishops and the whole official Church put the same energy into many other areas.[41]

Elsewhere he specifies the "peace question" as another "area" in which theology should use all available means towards the sensitizing of society about the moral unacceptability of nuclear war under any circumstances.[42]

To return momentarily to Rahner's comment of not "understanding" Metz's thought: he is surely saying thereby that he has disagreements with political theology as developed by the latter. Metz's critique of Rahner's theology is crystal clear to the latter, as his response to FHS demonstrates. According to Rahner, "Metz insists on going beyond my own theology to a societal situation of man and the [sic] Christian praxis, precisely because this praxis is not merely the carrying out of an abstract Christian theory," and that "every concrete mystagogy must...from the very beginning consider the societal situation and the Christian praxis

---

[41] *Conversations*, p.269. The fact that Rahner "understands" perfectly well (in terms of the factual contents, at least) what political theology is about, can be seen from his summary of Metz's FoC. The climax of that summary has been cited already above, and its reference was given in n. #2 of this section.

[42] *Glaube in winterlicher Zeit*, p.192: Theology "has the task to sensitize the social conscience with all its means towards the realization, that a nuclear war--regardless under what conditions--is absolutely immoral." Rahner is doing precisely this in his essay, "Die Atomwaffen und der Christ," STh XV, pp.280-297.

When asked what he would like to say to US president Reagan, he gives related examples, saying: "That I am not in agreement with the way in which he speaks about nuclear armaments...I would say to him once more like the American bishops did and remind him that one of them refuses the payment of one half of his taxes, and another encourages the workers to abandon the nuclear factories, etc." (p.191; my tr.).

to which it addresses itself."[43]   Rahner, however, does not believe this dimension is absent from his own "mystagogy"; his work was such a "political theology from its inception," he contends.

The concluding comments in the same response show also an area of criticism which Rahner has with respect to political theology. He maintains that transcendental and political theology need and complement each other, but points out a "deficit" in the latter in its "metaphysical" foundation. For, says Rahner, "...such a political theology is, if it truly wishes to concern itself with God, not possible without reflection on those essential characteristics of man which transcendental theology discloses."[44]

This is not the only time Rahner draws attention to a lack of metaphysical grounding in, among others', Metz's approach.[45]

This "a-metaphysical" approach to theology, Rahner suggests elsewhere, runs the danger of developing a less than adequate conception of God. In an unusually strongly worded critique (in 1982) of the modern theology "of the world," Rahner expresses the view that it all too quickly tends to make God into a mere

---

[43] Cf. Introduction above.

[44] *Loc. cit.* Still, Rahner is confident that these theological approaches are "not necessarily contradictory." Otherwise, he "gladly recognize[s] that a concrete mystagogy must, to use Metz's language, be at the same time 'mystical and political'."

[45] *Glaube in winterlicher Zeit*, pp.57f. Rahner says: "Metz wanted or wants to do fundamental theology that comes 'after' theology. In contrast, Joseph Ratzinger wants to carry out fundamental theology 'before' the actual theology." He then explains: "Lets put it this way: that, which in classical philosophy, starting with the pre-Socratic philosophers up until today, was done under the name of 'metaphysics,' has to somehow affect the theological process. And exactly this is what Thomas has done exceptionally well. Therefore, at least in that sense one should attempt to learn from him. If the young theologians do not know what to do with this Thomist legacy, then this reflects badly--not on Thomas, but on today's theologians."

"God of the gaps."[46]   It is surely significant that Metz is mentioned in the context of this powerful reproach to world-directed theology. These critical observations (although certainly not to be seen as a charge against Metz's own theology as such) may yield some helpful insights concerning Rahner's persistent hesitancy about accepting Metz's political theology in all of its details.

The direct focus of Rahner's attack is Ernesto Cardenal's declaration in Frankfurt, in a lecture which Rahner attended, "that in Nicaragua the kingdom of God has come, that there are no more prisons there and that all the people there love one

---

[46] *Ibid.*, p.61. After asserting that his early epistemology aims not at conscious self-possession through turning toward sensory reality but through our historical free self-realization in relation to the neighbour, Rahner has this to say "to this theological 'turn' (*Wende*) to the world:"

"I have stressed repeatedly, and I think one should say this still more clearly today: in its turning to the world, modern theology all too often does not see that it is presuming (*vereinnahmt*) all too quickly that God is a 'stand in' (*Lückenbüßer*) for the human being, his (or her) good luck and his (or her) so-called 'self-realization'; and this is the basest and most shameless thing one can do before God! I once gave a talk in Salzburg about the '*Unverbrauchbarkeit der Transzendenz*' (The Inexhaustibility of Transcendence). In it I emphasized that God does not 'exist' for the human being, but rather the human being exists for Him, and that we are true Christians only when, with Jesus, the crucified One, we let ourselves fall in self-capitulation and without condition into the inscrutable mystery of God. All this modern nonsense about self-realization and also the presumption of God for politics, Third World and similar things are from the devil! Of course we should do much more for the Third World and be more critical towards our Western European bourgeoisie. **I have nothing against liberation theology or political theology.** But did Johann Baptist Metz not let Ernesto Cardenal pull the wool over his eyes a bit (*doch ein wenig 'einseifen'*)?" (My tr. and emphs.)

Quite evidently, this unusually intense statement may not be interpreted as a charge that Metz's theology itself actually contains the distortions it mentions. But it is revealing in that it suggests that Rahner believes Metz's theological approach is not free of (latent?) tendencies in that direction.

another..." (he wants nothing to do with this sort of "nonsense").[47]

In reading Metz's 1980 *laudatio*[48] on the occasion of Cardenal's reception of a peace medal in Germany, one can understand Rahner's uneasiness to some extent. Metz's overall tone is very "affirmative" indeed. He seems to really believe that a *Kultur des Friedens* ("peaceable culture") can spring up from a revolution that cost 40,000 lives in Nicaragua to achieve its objective. This statistic was given to a gathering of Mennonite relief workers and missionaries of Southern Africa, which I attended in Lesotho in 1983, by Hildegard Goss-Mayr of the International Fellowship of Reconciliation. And in order to affirm the candidate for the *Friedenspreis* (peace award), Metz is willing (as observed above) to reinterpret the Sermon on the Mount so as to make it fit (cf. pp.76f.) Elsewhere, however, he has argued--against Bismarck--this Sermon should be the norm also for political life (cf. EC). Besides being questionable exegesis, such reasoning is also unsound in the light of practical sense, as suggested by this statement signed by some 20 bishops from all over Latin America concerning the importance of the means of social change:

> In the process of bringing about change itself, nonviolent action is already implanting the values towards which this change aspires. **Peace is not implanted through war. One does not build up by destroying. With nonviolent action, the hope for a just and humane world is not negated by the very actions which seek to transform society.**[49]

---

[47] *Ibid.*, pp.61f.; my tr.; German (slightly expanded): "In Frankfurt war ich selbst dabei, als Cardenal erklärte, daß in Nicaragua das Reich Gottes angebrochen sei, daß es dort keine Gefängnisse mehr gebe, daß alle sich liebten....Mit solchem Unsinn will ich nichts zu tun haben!"

[48] It was first published as "Paradigma für eine politische Kultur des Friedens"; here, in *Unterbrechungen* (pp.74-84), as "Ernesto Cardenal--ein produktives Ärgernis" ("Ernesto Cardenal--a Productive Stumbling Block").

[49] *Evangelical Nonviolence: Force for Liberation*, 1977, p.31; my emph.; cf. also Dom Hélder Camara, *The Spiral of Violence*, (London: Sheed and Ward, 1971).

In fairness, however, Metz himself is not entirely without criticism towards Cardenal. Thus in his closing comments he warns, among other things, that the initial euphoria over the "successful revolution" cannot last (cf. esp. pp.83f.).

All Rahner seems to be saying is that Metz's political theology, with its emphasis upon human social accountability and commitment, is exposed to the peril of an excessive "horizontalization" of theology, of reducing God to the interhuman historical level of reality, as this statement from the same context (as that on Cardenal) indicates:

> One may not overlook the danger that modernity tends towards the just mentioned fundamental heresy, allowing God to play merely the role of a stand-in [*Lückenbüßer*] in those cases in which the human person cannot manage alone. I want nothing to do with such a pseudo-humanistic and horizontalistic theology. Of course, many of the younger theologians, like Johann Baptist Metz or Peter Eicher, accuse my theology of being too aprioristic and too transcendentalistic. In it, they say, the encounter with the concrete God of the history in which we live, is short-changed. My answer to this: in principle, my theology at least keeps this perspective open and in no way denies it.[50]

It would be all too easy to conclude from these critical comments that Rahner's main objection to political theology is that it is insufficiently grounded in metaphysical reflection as to be able to withstand the immanentist tendencies of modern secularist thought; that this is why political theology, despite all its rightful insistence upon deprivatization and sociocritical commitment has need of being supplemented with reflections on the essence of

---

[50] *Glaube in winterlicher Zeit*, p.62; my tr. German: "Man darf nicht die Gefahr übersehen, daß die Moderne zu der erwähnten fundamentalen Häresie neigt, Gott nur noch die Rolle eines Lückenbüßers für solche Fälle spielen zu lassen, in denen der Mensch nicht mehr allein zurechtkommt. Mit einer solchen pseudo-humanistischen und horizontalistischen Theologie will ich nichts zu tun haben. Natürlich werfen manche der jüngeren Theologen, wie Johann Baptist Metz oder Peter Eicher, meiner Theologie vor, sie sei zu aprioristisch und zu transzendentalistisch. In ihr komme die Begegnung mit dem konkreten Gott der Geschichte, in der man lebt, zu kurz. Meine Antwort darauf: Prinzipiell wird bei mir diese Perspektive doch zumindest offengehalten und keineswegs geleugnet."

the human individual and the relation to God a la transcendental theology. But to conclude this would be to mistake the symptom for the cause. The criticism by Rahner of an insufficient "philosophical" foundation in the world-directed theological movements (also in Metz to some extent) should not be belittled. It is fundamental. But the prior reason for this critique is surely what we have called Rahner's "theological temperament" of a predominantly incarnational, "always-already" attitude about God's loving and saving self-communication to humankind--an attitude which knows this so firmly that even two world wars cannot shake this certainty,[51] because Rahner "has experienced God."

These findings, when seen against the background of the above discussion of Rahner's conception of the unity of love of neighbour and love of God and the explicit political theological dimension of his work, allow us to clarify some of the apparent contradictions in Rahner's overt remarks on political theology. Thus when Rahner categorically says, as he does on more than

---

[51] Cf. Lamb, "A Response to Fr. Metz," *op. cit.*, p.182. Perhaps what I have called Rahner's incarnational-sacramental theology is seen nowhere more clearly at work than in his "spiritual performance" or response to his own experience of human depravity and suffering in both World Wars. Lamb has formulated this well, saying: "Only a mind and heart steeped in the mystery of the Crucified would have the audacity to think of humanity as 'Spirit in the World' and 'Hearer(s) of the Word' through the din and carnage of Germany in the late 1930s and 1940s."

This is quite a different reaction than Metz's "theodicy question," noted above as his response to the horrors he experienced in W.W.II. Rahner's response can only be understood in the light of his 'mystical' experience and concept of God as "a God who loves 'unfathomably' beyond all human understanding," as Vorgrimler says. Vorgrimler recognizes this connection between Rahner's "optimistic" response to tragedy in history and his experience of God, and realizes that it need not mean Rahner was unaware of human pain and suffering, as these comments show: "This image of God--which arose out of an experience of God--certainly does not belittle human suffering. Rahner was aware of torture and despair. But [and this Vorgrimler--and Metz--find "incomprehensible"] he always pointed to what lay 'behind' and 'afterwards', and so it was that he sometimes talked about human life, its drama, history and tragedy, as though it were past" (*Understanding Karl Rahner*, p.128).

The reason for pointing out these things is not to pass judgement on the defensibility or indefensibility of such a response, but simply to indicate the source of it.

one occasion, that his theology is not a political theology, one motive may be--since these disclaimers are normally coupled with a reference to Metz as the founder in a formal sense of this discipline--that he will simply not encroach upon the creation of one of his leading students. Another motive obviously relates to the irreducible and abiding differences between their theologies due to varying personal and theological temperaments. It may remain an open question here whether a political theology with a prophetic-apocalyptic accentuation is able or not able to accord the proper and rightful place in its horizon to all those aspects that are important to Rahner. But as a number of his statements indicate, Rahner will clearly not rest content with world-directed theologies until they have safeguarded certain unnegotiable aspects from his own work. That is why he reminds the young people of Germany for instance to balance their social and political engagement with an effort to cultivate a personal relationship with God. And that is why his Ignatius utters similar reminders to modern-day Jesuits.

Rahner not only has nothing against theology being political (in a holistic sense of this term), he even categorically asserts that "theology must always be 'political' theology" (TI IX, p.189) and that his transcendental theology has been such a political theology "from its inception." For Rahner, all theology must be "political" theology. This follows from the very nature of the church, which can only realize itself as it exists for the salvation of the world. And it is implicit in many biblical categories like covenant, body of Christ, the people of God, and in the summons to love God and neighbour simultaneously. It is given in the ideas of original sin and even more powerfully in the notion of redemption in and through Jesus Christ. And it is unavoidably envisaged in the conception of the free human self-realization in history which can only happen through concrete acts of interhuman love.

Therefore, when properly qualified, Rahner does not hesitate in the least to have his work characterized as being a political theology from beginning to end. The process of qualification must include the use of our reflective capacities examining the

Christian faith memory and must take into account the concrete existential situation of both the individual and society today. And although Rahner's theology can without presumption be called a narrative theology, based upon and of necessity leading to praxis- -albeit "narrative" and "praxis" with an accent on realization rather than on interruption--he does not overly concern himself with whether theory or praxis assumes the primary position. For neither of these aspects can function soundly without the other.

Rahner goes the second or even third mile with current secular and theological movements, in order to lead the church to a situation analysis as a basis for its directives for planning its agenda for life during the next decade and beyond. He nevertheless asserts unabashedly: "The Church therefore is concerned from first to last with God" (SCC, p.86). In other words, his theology, although strongly praxis-oriented, clearly begins and ends with revelation in the sense of being informed by the "ideal" that is manifested in God's always "prevenient" loving self-communication in Jesus Christ. Perhaps Rahner is not overly concerned about the primacy between theory and praxis, or about starting with "revelation," because he has no doubt that Christian "praxis" will inevitably follow when human individuals truly encounter the absolute mystery.

It ultimately comes down to this: Rahner does not and cannot consider himself a political theologian in the formal sense. This discipline was forged by Johann Baptist Metz "within Catholicism" from the mid-1960s on. Rahner has serious reservations about some aspects of this new fundamental theology. But he affirms and defends its general direction as being "perfectly orthodox." While in no way wanting to claim this theology for himself, Rahner expends considerable energies in discerning its true intentions and even in advocating it in a courageous though qualified way as being indispensable for our time. In fact, it hardly overstates the case to say that Rahner critically accepts and in a sense takes Metz's political theology one step further by suggesting that it integrate into itself those indispensable aspects of theology which may be underrepresented in it. Insofar as this happens, Rahner is fully prepared to call his own transcendental and anthropological theology also a political theology.

3. An Incarnational-Sacramental Political Theology?

But if Rahner's work can be called a political theology only in this qualified sense, is it still compatible with Metz's definition of the "new political theology"? The answer is yes, without thereby minimizing the real differences between their theologies. Why should it make Rahner's transcendental theology any less "political" if it is not written in the "apocalyptic" key but rather in the "incarnational" or "mystical" key, in the Ignatian sense of seeing God in all things? That Rahner's theology can indeed boast of many achievements along the lines advocated by political theology has been amply documented above and need not be reiterated here.

Our claim that Rahner's transcendental theology is at the same time a political theology in a qualified but valid sense of the concept has already been sufficiently established. To draw this conclusion, however, is not to preclude mutually modifying exchanges between these theologians. But in traversing the "furrow" of his own thought again and again in an attempt at coming to terms with political theology and its new emphases, Rahner has perhaps modified political theology as much as it has modified his own thought. This, of course, is not to belittle the very significant influence of Metz upon Rahner in the long and intense process of interaction between them. While one might boldly and perhaps exaggeratedly state that in the course of his grappling with the challenges of political theology, Rahner exercised something of a political theological function within the new political theology itself, not least of all by maintaining or

reasserting old motifs,[52] there is no denying that the categories
and even the terminology of the Metzian theology penetrate his
later theological writings increasingly and pervasively. The fact
that Rahner moves along --often under some protest--only so far
as the whole deposit of Christian theology can be moved along
does nothing to diminish the merits of Metz's courageous
theological work in this regard.

One might invert Matthew Lamb's application of Metz's
famous folk tale about the hare and the hedgehog, when he says
in effect that without the "omnipresent" hedgehog of
transcendental theology, the hare of political theology might
never have started to run.[53]   Taking into account Vorgrimler's

---

[52] The idea that Rahner's restatement of his theology (after examining it
in the light of political theology) serves, in turn, as a critique of political
theology would find support in H. Peukert's (*op. cit.*, pp.282f.) observations
on how the modern "theories-of-interaction" beg the question: "how does such
transformative societal praxis orient itself." Therefore, "if it does not wish to
create renewed alienating and 'thing-ifying' conditions, in which the [human]
subjects are unable to 'become' or realize themselves, then it will have to
orient itself, representatively or directly, on the basis of the free self-
determination of the affected persons" (my tr.).

Perhaps it was this that Rahner had in mind when he suggested that
political theology cannot function properly "without reflection on those
characteristics of man which a transcendental theology discloses" (cf. p.7f. and
n.#13 in the Introduction).

[53] In his "Response to Fr. Metz," M. Lamb says, among other things, that
"Metz warns us that it would be a false and distorted reading of Rahner's
work to view it as a calm conceptual unfolding from *Spirit in the World* to the
last volume of the *Theological Investigations*." In the "classical quality of
Rahner's theology," Lamb says (citing Metz), "we can often find support for
our objections to his theories in the broader context of his own thinking."
Then, after adding that Rahner's theology includes a "not yet" dimension as
well as an "always already" dimension (cf. note #14 in this section), Lamb
concludes: "Without the hedgehog the hare would not have run" (*Theology and
Discovery*, p.181; my emph.).

critique of this folk tale,[54] we might submit that without the
provocative political theological hare, the transcendental
hedgehog (which is really only one, not two) might not have
bothered to recheck his furrow over and over again so
carefully.[55]

---

[54] Vorgrimler at one point severely criticized Metz's folk tale and stood
it on its head, suggesting that Rahner's theology is in fact more endangered,
vulnerable, and may have a farther reaching memory than the political
theological hare. In Vorgrimler's words: "For the transcendental-theological
hedgehog it is not the case, that he 'overlooks the street from both ends' and
for this reason does not even need to set foot on it, nor is it correct that the
hedgehog and his wife are chasing the hare to death through their
'transcendental omnipresence,' while themselves unendangered. Let us stay
with the analogy," continues Vorgrimler. "The transcendental-theological
hedgehog is in reality likewise a hare, who interrupts his running for
reflection, runs back and reassures himself of the right direction by running
down the furrow once more from the beginning. He has double the effort,
compared to the hare of political theology. First, he finds himself in the
middle of history, on the road, endangered, on the side of the victims, exposed
to the new. Second, he undertakes the trouble of traversing the same stretch
of road ever anew, in order to establish if the direction, which had appeared
to him to be the right one at the outset, is really the correct one. The hare of
political theology, by contrast, foregoes this reassurance, drawn forward by the
dawn (*Morgenröte*) of the future across the field in front of him. Does his
'dangerous memory' go back sufficiently far, is the dawn bright enough so as
to allow him to keep the right direction?" (*Wagnis Theologie*, p.258; my tr.
and emph.)
  Since Vorgrimler later dampened this criticism, saying he meant it actually
as "literary criticism," and that it "satisfied" Rahner (cf. *Understanding Karl
Rahner*, p.127), perhaps it represents the latter's own response to Metz's attack
on him via the fairy tale. In any event, a theology that is sensitive enough
about changing situations that it continually re-examines its position is surely
an authentic "praxis theology."

[55] Cf. *Loc. cit.* Vorgrimler has rightly argued that since Rahner checked
his theological pathway over and over again in the light of new developments,
his transcendental theology may fittingly be considered to be not a hedgehog
full of duplicity but rather also a hare struggling to keep abreast of the ever
changing situation (cf. n. #54).

This brief analysis of Rahner's critical statements concerning the new political theology has in one sense revealed nothing substantially new. But it has confirmed the abiding "unity-in-difference" between these theologians until the end of Rahner's life. In the light of this analysis, as well as in that of our analyses of their works in general, the claim can be upheld that both theologians have produced (in effect) political theologies, even though each is marked by certain fundamentally distinct emphases. Both theologies can be shown to be profoundly rooted in the "narratives" that gave origin to Christianity, and within the tradition(s) by which the Christian church has lived throughout its history. And both theologies, each in its own way, have endeavoured to translate the remembered Christian story into the modern horizon of thought. If this claim is valid, it means that there is room for a pluralism of sound alternatives (though of necessity interdependent ones) within the one discipline called the new political theology.

In conclusion, then, the differences between Rahner's transcendental and anthropological theology (with its historical, Ignatian-spiritual, pastoral-practical methodological aspects) and Metz's new political theology (with its predominant agenda of making the church relevant to current social problems) are undoubtedly considerable. We need not here reiterate all the numerous areas of fundamental agreement between them, except simply to point out that for both of them the exemplary life of the church as intended and inaugurated by God in Jesus Christ is the main channel for the two fundamental functions of exercising an ongoing negative-critical effect and carrying out the positive-apologetic or kerygmatic task towards society. And for both of them these responsibilities are ultimately and inextricably rooted in their respective eschatologies regardless of the fact that one advocates a "historical eschatology" while the other develops an "apocalyptic eschatology." Both eschatologies serve to prevent either theologian from ever allowing any situation in church or society to idolatrously absolutize itself; both serve to incite the Christian and/or church to move boldly into the future with an active self-abandon, tempered with an attitude of openness towards and waiting for the absolute future and its coming toward us.

Considerable formal differences exist in the categories, structures and language or terminology of their works. The object of this book, however, was not such a formal comparison per se. Any such contrasting that occurs in it is more accidental than intentional. Our objective was strictly to demonstrate that Rahner's so-called transcendental theology is indeed at the same time--and in the light of the Metzian categories or criteria--**in effect** also a new political theology from beginning to end. This, we believe, has been convincingly accomplished, provided one keeps in mind that Rahner's "political theology" is centered more around the incarnational-sacramental-mystical[56] dimension in the gospel narratives than around the prophetic-apocalyptic[57] aspect in these narratives. When this is realized, then the fact that these two theologies could never be reconciled fully and without a "remnant" of divergence, need not necessarily detract from but may in fact strengthen our thesis. Surely, if both types of narrative are fused into a greater whole in the gospels, then neither type can stand on its own, except perhaps as a corrective for a short duration. Therefore, insofar as Rahner's transcendental and anthropological theology may legitimately be contrasted as

---

[56] Cf. K.J. Egan, "A Response to Fr. [Harvey] Egan," in *Theology and Discovery*, p.168, who writes: "Theologians of the Middle Ages were frequently honored with titles that spoke volumes of the import of such persons as St. Thomas Aquinas, *Doctor Angelicus*, and St. Bonaventure, *Doctor Seraphicus*. Might not the work of Karl Rahner be succinctly remembered were we to accord him the title *Doctor Mysticus*?" On the centrality and extent of the mystical theological dimension in the life and work of Rahner, cf. also H. Egan, "The Devout Christian of the Future will...be a "Mystic." Mysticism and Karl Rahner's Theology," *Ibid.*, p.140.

[57] Asked whether the theologian is ever "prophetic," Rahner replies: "...Certainly, there are today movements in theology that are possibly prophetic or at least make claims to be so. One of my students, Johann Baptist Metz, embodies such a form of theology. He, for example, has elaborated the requirements and imperatives of a political theology...," (*Glaube in winterlicher Zeit*, p.190; my tr.).

an "incarnational-mystical political theology" with the Metzian "prophetic-apocalyptic political theology," both types stand in need of being supplemented by the other--a fact which both authors often recognize. But neither type is invalidated by the other in its claim of being a "new political theology" in its own right--however much in need of completion by its counterpart at any given time.

Although Rahner's theology "leans" in a different direction than Metz's, it may still legitimately be called a "new political theology" because all the theological categories that are seen to be central to Metz's definition of that discipline have been shown to be operative therein, albeit in a different mode. Even though it is fundamentally a transcendental theology, it takes the situation very seriously in its discernment of truth; it is deeply rooted in the experience of modern individuals and society--human individuals can transcend themselves into God only by transcending themselves into the historical situation of other human persons; it inevitably requires that a central place be given to active and universal solidarity, and this on all counts: epistemologically, ethically, theologically. Finally, it is a supremely remembering and narrative theology, although its narrative is probably more "incarnational-sacramentally" oriented than "apocalyptically." But this brand of narrative is no less rooted in the gospel than the apocalyptic version. Consequently, the "praxis" upon which this narrative insists is also tending more towards faithful endurance, no matter how banal or how bleak the situation, rather than towards prophetic denunciation aimed at "denying" or "interrupting" the status quo--though this aspect is by no means absent in his theology, just as the incarnational motif for Metz remains firmly intertwined with the apocalyptic-eschatological dimension in his thought.[58]

Finally, although written in a different key or mode, Rahner's transcendental theology has an all-pervasive eschatological dimension. But does it "become a political theology" in the sense of "a (socio)critical theology," as Metz says every eschatological

---

[58] This is the case even in FHS, cf. p.188 or note #80 in chapter 1.

theology must? Obviously, the answer is yes. Rahner's theological life and work has not only indirectly or implicitly influenced the sociopolitical scene in all areas of human existence around the world, both inside the Christian church and beyond. His outstanding contribution in this regard, i.e. in bringing the church to live up to its calling of being the "fundamental sacrament" (*Grundsakrament*) in a discipleship of Jesus Christ, the "original sacrament" (*Ursakrament*), in the world of today has already been documented. But his theology, which urges the Christian church to remain open towards and receptive to the absolute future, God, who has in one sense only just begun to communicate himself to humankind, has indeed also become a sociocritical political theology in an explicit way--and this from its own inherent inner dynamic (while his dialogue with Metz has surely influenced this process decisively).

The areas of overlap and those of divergence between the political theological impact of Rahner and Metz cannot be determined precisely. The unity-in-difference is substantial and cannot be resolved completely. Perhaps the best illustration of the importance of the fact that each theologian's work is written in a different "key" may be found in their different reactions to the horrors of *Auschwitz* as a symbol of the worst of human degradation and suffering. For the apocalyptic political theology it resulted in a theological reaction marked by the "wordless cry" of the theodicy question, i.e., it throws theology into a fundamental crisis: "we can never return to a pre-*Auschwitz* situation" (*hinter Auschwitz können wir nicht mehr zurück*). The incarnational-sacramental political theology of Rahner, by contrast, as much as it too felt the horrors of W.W.I and II,[59] reacts instead with the unshakable faith that the God whom it has personally experienced so profoundly (that even without the Bible it should never doubt his saving presence) can be found within "all things" and his will to save the world can never be thwarted, regardless of how human history may end.

---

[59] cf. note #51 in this section.

Both are political theologies, very similar in many things, but drastically different in others; both are rooted in the same gospel message. And both need each other very much.

Abbreviations

EC   = *The Emergent Church*

FHS   = *Faith in History and Society*

FoC   = *Followers of Christ*

ThW   = *Theology of the World*

ZThW = *Zur Theologie der Welt*

ME   = *The Mennonite Encyclopedia*

Concise SM = *Encyclopedia of Theology: A Concise Sacramentum Mundi*

F   = *Foundations of Christian Faith*

G   = *Grundkurs des Glaubens*

HW   = *Hearers of the Word*

LThK   = *Lexikon für Theologie und Kirche*

SCC   = *The Shape of the Church to Come*

STh   = *Schriften zur Theologie*

SW   = *Spirit in the World*

TI   = *Theological Investigations*

Bibliography

Note: In the "Primary Sources" sections (1) and (3) of my **Selected Bibliography** I use as my organizing principle a chronological approach. When listing the English translation jointly with the German original, the date of the original source is taken as the decisive one. In the other three sections I follow the standard alphabetical order of the authors' names.

1. Karl Rahner -- Primary Sources

Rahner's writings are listed in the following sources: Bleistein, R. & Klinger, E. (Hgg.), *Bibliographie Karl Rahner 1924-1969*, Freiburg i.Br., 1969; Bleistein, R. (Hg.), *Bibliographie Karl Rahner 1969-1974*, Freiburg i.Br., 1974; Imhof, P. & Treziak, H., "Bibliographie Karl Rahner 1974-1979," in: *Wagnis Theologie. Erfahrungen mit der Theologie Karl Rahners*, H. Vorgrimler (Hg.), Freiburg-Basel-Wien: Herder, 1979, pp.579-597; *Ibid.*, pp.598-622 contains "Karl Rahner: Bibliographie der Sekundärliteratur 1948-1978," by A. Raffelt; Imhof, P. & Meuser, E., "Bibliographie Karl Rahner 1979-1984," in: *Glaube im Prozeß. Christsein nach dem II. Vatikanum*, Klinger, E. & Wittstadt, K. (Hgg.), Freiburg i.Br.: Herder, 1984, pp.854-871; *Ibid.*, pp.872-885; (The last two sources were also published by Herder as: "*Sonderdruck*," 1984, following Rahner's death.)

K. Neumann's *Der Praxisbezug der Theologie bei Karl Rahner* (Freiburg i.Br., 1980, pp.413-419) also contains a bibliography of Rahner's theological writings "to have appeared in book form" and lists his "*Lexikonartikel*" on practical theology.

The follwing works by Rahner have been useful for my dissertation:

Worte ins Schweigen / Gebete der Einkehr, (with brother Hugo Rahner), Herderbücherei, 5. Aufl. 1980. (Meditations written in 1937, publ. in book form 1938.) Engl. tr: *Encounters with Silence*, Westminister, Md: Newman Press, 1960.

Geist in Welt. Zur Metaphysik der endlichen Erkenntnis bei Thomas von Aquin, (Innsbruck 1939), 2. Aufl. bearbeitet v. J.B. Metz, München, 1957. *Spirit in the World*, W. Dych, tr., N.Y: Herder & Herder, 1968. With a "Foreword" by Metz, and an "Introduction" by F. Fiorenza.

Hörer des Wortes. Zur Grundlegung einer Religionsphilosophie, (München, 1941), 2. Aufl. bearbeitet v. J.B. Metz (1963), Herderbücherei (Nr. 403), Freiburg i.Br., 1971. *Hearers of the Word*, M. Richards, tr., N.Y: Herder & Herder, 1969. With a "Preface" by Metz.

Von der Not und dem Segen des Gebetes, (Innsbruck 1949), Freiburg i.Br., 12. Aufl. 1985. This "spiritual" book represents his "Fastenpredigten..., gehalten im zerbombten München des Jahres 1946."

Das freie Wort in der Kirche. Die Chancen des Christentums, Einsiedeln, 1953. Engl. tr: *Free Speech in the Church*. N.Y: Sheed & Ward, 1960.

Das Dynamische in der Kirche, (QD 5), Freiburg i.Br., 1958. Engl. tr. by W.J. O'Hara: *The Dynamic Element in the Church*, (QD 12), N.Y: Herder & Herder, 1964.

Sendung und Gnade. [24] Pastoraltheologische Beiträge, (Innsbruck 1959). Engl. tr: *The Christian Commitment. Mission and Grace*, London & Sydney: Sheed and Ward, 1963, 1970.

With Rahner, Hugo, *Gebete der Einkehr*, Herder, 1962; R. Brennan, tr., *Prayers for Meditation*, N.Y: Herder & Herder, 1963.

"Einführender Essay," in: J.B. Metz, *Christliche Anthropozentrik. Über die Denkform des Thomas von Aquin.*, München: Kösel, 1962, pp.9-20.

Handbuch der Pastoraltheologie. Praktische Theologie der Kirche in ihrer Gegenwart, Vol.I, Freiburg i.Br., 1964 (in it: 5f.; 117-229; 323-343.

Biblische Predigten, Freiburg i.Br.: Herder, 1965.
Contains sermons given by Rahner in the mid-1950s.

Belief Today, London: Sheed & Ward, 1965...1976.

Everyday Things, M.H. Heelan, tr., London: Sheed & Ward, 1965. (Theological Meditations edited by H. Küng.)

"Karl Rahner [**Selbstporträt**]," in: W. Ernest Böhm, ed., *Forscher und Gelehrte.*, Stuttgart: Battenberg, 1966, p.21.

"Marxistische Utopie und christliche Zukunft des Menschen," in: R. Garaudy, J.B. Metz, K. Rahner, *Der Dialog*, Reinbek bei Hamburg: Rowohlt, 1966.

Glaube der die Erde liebt. Christliche Besinnung im Alltag der Welt, Freiburg i.Br., 1966.

With Vorgrimler, H., *Kleines Konzilskompendium. Alle Konstitutionen, Dekrete und Erklärungen des Zweiten Vaticanums in der bischöflich beauftragten Übersetzung*, Freiburg i.Br.: Herder-Bücherei, 1966.

Gnade als Freiheit: Kleine theologische Beiträge, Freiburg i.Br., 1968. Engl. tr. by Hilda Gräf: *Grace in Freedom*, N.Y: Herder & Herder, *et al*, 1969.

Freiheit und Manipulation in Gesellschaft und Kirche, München, 1970.

Kritisches Wort. Aktuelle Probleme in Kirche und Welt, Freiburg i.Br., 1970.

"Orthodoxy and Freedom in Theology," Engl. tr. by John Griffiths, in: *New Concilium* No.66, J.B. Metz, ed., N.Y: Herder & Herder, 1971, pp.90-104.

Strukturwandel der Kirche als Aufgabe und Chance, Freiburg i.Br., 1972. Engl. tr. with an "Introduction" by E. Quinn: *The Shape of the Church to Come*, N.Y: Seabury Press, 1974.

Herders Theologisches Taschenlexikon, in 8 Vols. K. Rahner, ed., Herderbücherei, 1972-1973.

Was sollen wir jetzt tun? Vier Meditationen zu Matthäus und Lukas, Freiburg i.Br., 1974.

"Gnade als Mitte menschlicher Existenz. Bilanz aus Anlaß des 70. Geburtstages," (Interview), *Herder-Korrespondenz* 28 (1974), 77-92.

Ein Brief an K. Fischer, in: K. Fischer, *Der Mensch als Geheimnis. Die Anthropologie Karl Rahners*, Freiburg i.Br., 1974, pp.400-410.

Gott ist Mensch geworden. Meditationen, Freiburg i.Br., 1975.

Encyclopedia of Theology: A Concise Sacramentum Mundi, K. Rahner, ed.; Engl. tr., exec. ed., J. Cumming, London: Burns & Oates, 1975, 1977, 1981, 1986. (From here on: *Concise SM*.)

"Monogenism," in *Concise SM, op. cit.*, pp.974-977.

Grundkurs des Glaubens. Einführung in den Begriff des Christentums, Freiburg i.Br., 1976. Engl. tr. by W.V. Dych: *Foundations of Christian Faith: An Introduction to the Idea of Christianity*, N.Y: Seabury Press, 1978.

Toleranz in der Kirche. Freiheit und Manipulation in Gesellschaft und Kirche. Rückblick auf das Konzil, Freiburg i.Br., 1977.

With J.B. Metz , *Ermutigung zum Gebet*, Freiburg i.Br: Herder, 1977. Engl. tr. by Sarah O'Brien Twohig: *The Courage to Pray*, Search Press Ltd., 1980; N.Y: Crossroad, 1981.

"Kirche in säkularisierter Umwelt. Ein Gespräch mit Prof. Karl Rahner," *Herder-Korrespondenz* 31 (1977), 606-614.

"Rede des Ignatius von Loyola an einen Jesuiten von heute," in: *Ignatius von Loyola*, Freiburg i.Br., 1978, pp.10-38. Also in: *Schriften zur Theologie* XV, 373-408.

"Ich protestiere," in: *Publik-Forum-Sonderdruck*, 8 (1979), pp.15-19. Offener Brief an Kultusminister Hans Maier und Kardinal Joseph Ratzinger. Eine Wortmeldung zur Ablehnung von J.B. Metz. Engl.: R. Delaney, "Theologian tells Cardinal, 'Church Leaders Rarely Admit their Mistakes'," in: *Natioanl Catholic Reporter* 16, No.5 (Nov.23, 1979) p.1.

With Vorgrimler, H., *Kleines Theologisches Wörterbuch*, Herderbücherei, 12. völlig neu bearbeitete Auflage, 1980. Engl. tr. by R. Strachan, *et al*, *Concise Theological Dictionary*, London: Burns & Oates, 1965, 2nd ed. 1983.

"Introduction," in: James J. Bacik, *Apologetics and the Eclipse of Mystery*, Notre Dame, Indiana: University of Notre Dame Press, 1980, p.ix-x. (Rahner speaks here specifically to the relation between his and Metz's theologies.)

The Love of Jesus and the Love of Neighbor, R. Barr, tr., N.Y: Crossroad, 1983. (Appeared in German 1981 & 1982, respectively.)

Karl Rahner im Gespräch, Band 1: 1964-1977; Band 2: 1978-1982, P. Imhof & H. Biallowons, eds., München: Köse 1-Verlag, 1982 & 1983, respectively.

Karl Rahner in Dialogue: Conversations and Interviews 1965-1982, H.D. Egan, tr. (one vol. only), N.Y: Crossroad, 1986.

With Fries, H., *Einigung der Kirchen -- reale Möglichkeit*, Herder, 1983. *Unity of the Churches: An Actual Possibility*, R. Gritsch *et al*, trs., Philadelphia: Fortress Press, 1985.

Gebete des Lebens, Freiburg i.Br.: Herder, 1984. *Prayers For a Lifetime*, A. Raffelt, ed., K. Lehmann, "Introduction," N.Y: Crossroad, 1985 (includes Rahner's "last text, composed on his sickbed, the **'Prayer for the Reunion of All Christians'**").

Karl Rahner. Bekenntnisse. Rückblick auf 80 Jahre, Sporschill, Georg, ed., Wien - München: Herold, 1984.

Karl Rahner. Bilder eines Lebens, P. Imhof & H. Biallowons, eds., Zürich - Köln: Benziger; Freiburg - Basel - Wien: Herder, 1985.

Glaube in winterlicher Zeit. Gespräche mit Karl Rahner aus den letzten Lebensjahren. P. Imhof & H. Biallowons, eds., Düsseldorf: Patmos Verlag, 1986.

Articles from:

Schriften zur Theologie & *Theological Investigations*

The following articles are found in Rahner's *Schriften zur Theologie* (= STh), volumes I-XVI, Einsiedeln - Zürich - Köln: Benziger, 1954-1984. In English tr.: *Theological Investigations* (= TI), volumes I-XX, N.Y: Crossroad, 1961-1981.

"Theos im Neuen Testament," STh I, 91-167; "Theos in the New Testament," TI I, 79-148.

"Probleme der Christologie von heute," STh I (1954), 169-222; "Current Problems in Christology," TI I (1961), 149-200.

"Die Freiheit in der Kirche," STh II (1955), 95-114; "Freedom in the Church," TI II (1963), 89-107.

"Würde und Freiheit des Menschen," STh II, 247-277; "The Dignity and Freedom of Man," TI II, 235-263.

"Die ewige Bedeutung der Menschheit Jesu für unser Gottesverhältnis," STh III (1956), 47-60; "The Eternal Significance of the Humanity of Jesus for our Relationship with God," TI III (1967), pp.35-46.

"Über die Erfahrung der Gnade," STh III, 105-109; "Reflections on the Experience of Grace," TI III, pp. 86-90.

"Die ignatianische Mystik der Weltfreudigkeit," STh III, 329-48; "The Ignatian Mysticism of Joy in the World," TI III, pp.277-93.

"Zur Theologie der Menschwerdung," STh IV (1960), 137-155; "On the Theology of the Incarnation," TI IV (1966), 105-20.

"Theologische Prinzipien der Hermeneutik eschatologischer Aussagen," STh IV (1964), 401-28; "The Hermeneutics of Eschatological Assertions," TI IV (1966), 323-46.

"Theologie der Macht," STh IV, 485-508; "The Theology of Power," TI IV, 391-409.

"Weltgeschichte und Heilsgeschichte," STh V (1962), 115-135; "History of the World and Salvation-History," TI V (1965), 97-114.

"Die Christologie innerhalb einer evolutiven Weltanschauung," STh V, 183-221; "Christology Within an Evolutionary View of the World," TI V, 157-92.

"Das 'Gebot' der Liebe unter den anderen Geboten," STh V, 494-517; "The 'Commandment' of Love in Relation to the Other Commandments," TI V, 439-59.

"Über die Einheit von Nächsten- und Gottesliebe," STh VI (1965), 277-298; "Reflections on the Unity of the Love of Neighbour and the Love of God," TI VI (1969), 231-52.

"Kirche der Sünder, STh VI, 301-320. "The Church of Sinners," TI VI, 253-69.

"Sündige Kirche nach den Dekreten des Zweiten Vatikanischen Konzils," STh VI, 321-47; "The Sinful Church in the Decrees of Vatican II," TI VI, 270-94.

"Kirche und Parusie Christi," STh VI, 348-67; "The Church and the Parousia of Christ," TI VI, 295-312.

"Vom Offensein für den je grösseren Gott," STh VII (1966), 32-53; "Being Open to God as Ever Greater," TI VII (1971), 25-46.

"Löscht den Geist nicht aus," STh VII, 77-90; "Do not Stifle the Spirit," TI VII, 72-87.

"Der Christ in seiner Umwelt," STh VII, 91-102; "The Christian in his World," TI VII, 88-99.

"Friede auf Erden," STh VII, 133-36; "Peace on Earth," TI VII, 132-35.

"Gedanken zu einer Theologie der Kindheit," STh VII, 313-29; "Ideas for a Theology of Childhood," TI VIII (1971), 33-50.

"Die Frau in der neuen Situation der Kirche," STh VII, 351-67; "The Position of Women in the New Situation in Which the Church Finds Herself," TI VIII, 75-93.

"Über die evangelischen Räte," STh VII, 404-34; "On the Evangelical Counsels," TI VIII, 133-67.

"Theologie der Armut," STh VII, 435-78; "The Theology of Poverty," TI VIII, 168-214.

"Die Herausforderung der Theologie durch das Zweite Vatikanische Konzil," STh VIII (1967), 13-42; "The Second Vatican Council's Challenge to Theology," TI IX (1972), 3-27.

"Kirchliches Lehramt und Theologie nach dem Konzil," STh VIII, 111-32; "Theology and the Church's Teaching Authority after the Council," TI IX, 83-100.

"Die praktische Theologie im Ganzen der theologischen Disziplinen," STh VIII, 133-149; "Practical Theology Within the Totality of Theology," TI IX, 101-14.

"Der eine Mittler und die Vielfalt der Vermittlungen," STh VIII, 218-35; "One Mediator and Many Mediations," TI IX, 169-84.

"Christlicher Humanismus," STh VIII, 239-259; "Christian Humanism," TI IX, 187-204.

"Experiment Mensch," STh VIII, 260-285; "The Experiment With Man," TI IX, 205-24.

"Zum Problem der genetischen Manipulation," STh VIII, 286-321; "The Problem of Genetic Manipulation," TI IX, 225-52.

"Über die Gegenwart Christi in der Diasporagemeinde nach der Lehre des Zweiten Vatikanischen Konzils," STh VIII, 409-25; "On the Presence of Christ in the Diaspora Community According to the Teaching of the Second Vatican Council," TIX (1973), 84-102.

"Die Lehre des Zweiten Vatikanischen Konzils über den Diakonat," STh VIII, 541-52; "The Teaching of the Second Vatican Council on the Diaconate," TI X, 222-32.

"Über die theologische Problematik der 'Neuen Erde'," STh VIII, 580-92; "The Theological Problems Entailed in the Idea of the 'New Earth'," TI X, 260-72.

"Zur theologischen Problematik einer 'Pastoralkonstitution'," STh VIII, 613-36; "On the Theological Problems Entailed in a 'Pastoral Constitution'," TI X, 293-317.

"Überlegungen zur Methode der Theologie," STh IX (1970) 79-126; "Reflections on Methodology in Theology," TI XI (1974), 68-114.

"Die Zukunft der Theologie," STh IX, 148-157; "The Future of Theology," TI XI, 137-46.

"Gotteserfahrung heute," STh IX, 161-176; "The Experience of God Today," TI XI, 149-165.

"Theologische Überlegungen zu Säkularisation und Atheismus," STh IX, 177-96; "Theological Considerations on Secularization and Atheism," TI XI, 166-84.

"Bemerkungen über das Charismatische in der Kirche," STh IX, 415-31; "Observations on the Factor of the Charismatic in the Church," TI XII (1974), 81-97.

"Die gesellschaftliche Funktion der Kirche," STh IX, 569-590; "The Function of the Church as a Critic of Society," TI XII, 229-49.

"Zum heutigen Verhältnis von Philosophie und Theologie," STh X, 70-88; "The Current Relationship Between Philosophy and Theology," TI XIII, 61-79.

"Institution und Freiheit," STh X (1972) 115-32; "Institution and Freedom," TI XIII (1975), 105-21.

"Die zwei Grundtypen der Christologie," STh X, 227-38; "The Two Basic Types of Christology," TI XIII, 213-23.

"Grundsätzliche Bemerkungen zum Thema: Wandelbares und Unwandelbares in der Kirche," STh X, 241-61; "Basic Observations on the Subject of Changeable and Unchangeable Factors in the Church," TI XIV (1976) 3-23.

"Heilsauftrag der Kirche und Humanisierung der Welt," STh X, 547-67; "The Church's Commission to Bring Salvation and the Humanization of the World," TI XIV, 295-313.

"Zur Theologie der Revolution," STh X, 568-86; "On the Theology of Revolution," TI XIV, 314-30.

"Kirchliche Wandlungen und Profangesellschaft," STh XII (1975) 513-28; "Transformations in the Church and Secular Society," TI XVII (1981), 167-80.

"Nachfolge des Gekreuzigten," STh XIII (1978) 188-203; "Following the Crucified," TI XVIII (1983) 157-70.

"Zur Situation des Glaubens," STh XIV (1980) 23-47; "On the Situation of Faith," TI XX (1981), 13-32.

"Grundkurs des Glaubens," STh XIV, 48-62; "Foundations of Christian Faith," TI XIX (1983) 3-15.

"Priestertum der Frau," STh XIV, 208-223; "Women in the Priesthood," TI XX (1981) 35-47.

"Die Verantwortung der Kirche für die Freiheit des einzelnen," STh XIV, 248-64; "The Church's Responsibility for the Freedom of the Individual," TI XX, 51-64.

"Basisgemeinden," STh XIV, 265-72; "Basic Communities," TI XIX, 159-65.

"Theologische Begründung der kirchlichen Entwicklungsarbeit," STh XIV, 273-83; "Theological Justification of the Church's Development Work," TI XX, 65-73.

"Theologische Grundinterpretation des II. Vatikanischen Konzils," STh XIV, 303-18; "Basic Theological Interpretation of the Second Vatican Council," TI XX, 77-89.

"Die bleibende Bedeutung de II. Vatikanischen Konzils," STh XIV, 303-18; "The Abiding Significance of the Second Vatican Council," TI XX, 90-102.

"Strukturwandel der Kirche in der künftigen Gesellschaft, STh XIV, 333-54; "Structural Change in the Church of the Future," TI XX, 115-32.

"Einheit der Kirche -- Einheit der Menschheit," STh XIV, 382-404; "Unity of the Church -- Unity of Mankind," TI XX, 154-72.

"Die unverbrauchbare Transzendenz Gottes und unsere Sorge um die Zukunft," STh XIV, 405-21; "The Inexhaustible Transcendence of God and our Concern for the Future," TI XX, 173-86.

"Die Atomwaffen und der Christ," STh XV (1983), 280-97.

"Rede des Ignatius von Loyola an einen Jesuiten von heute," STh XV, 373-408.

"Utopie und Realität," STh XVI, (1984), 42-56.

"Die Theologische Dimension des Friedens," STh XVI, 57-62.

"Realistische Möglichkeit der Glaubenseinigung?," STh XVI, 93-109.

"Vergessene Anstöße dogmatischer Art des II. Vatikanischen Konzils," STh XVI, 131-142.

"Perspektiven der Pastoral in der Zukunft," STh XVI, 143-59.

"Südamerikanische Basisgemeinden in einer europäischen Kirche?," STh XVI, 196-205.

328Rahner and Metz

2. Karl Rahner -- Secondary Sources

A. Vargas-Machuca, ed., *Teología y mundo contemporáneo*, Madrid, 1975. (A *Festschrift* for Rahner's 70th Birthday published in Spain.)

Baum, Gregory, "Truth in the Church: Küng, Rahner and Beyond," in: *The Ecumenist*, 9 (1971) 33-48.

_____, "German Theologians and Liberation Theology," in: *The Ecumenist* 16 (1978) 49-51.

Bradley, D.J.M., "Rahner's *Spirit in the World*: Aquinas or Hegel," in: *The Thomist* Vol.41, No.2 (1977), 167-199.

Brandenburg, A., "Theologisches Dokument seiner Zeit. Zu Karl Rahners: 'Grundkurs des Glaubens'," in: *Catholica* 31 (1977) 66-68.

Donovan, Daniel, "Rahner's 'Grundkurs': Frankly Pastoral," in: *The Ecumenist* 16 (July/August, 1978) 65-70.

Dulles, A., "Die Rezeption Karl Rahners in den USA," in: *Orientierung 22 (1984) 242-45.*

Egan, H., "'The Devout Christian of the Future will...be a "Mystic."' Mysticism and Karl Rahner's Theology," in: *Theology and Discovery:...*, 1980, pp.139-165.

Egan, K.J., "A Response to Fr. (Harvey) Egan," in: *Ibid.*, pp.166-68.

Eicher, Peter, *Die anthropologische Wende. Karl Rahners philosophischer Weg vom Wesen des Menschen zur personalen Existenz*, Freiburg/Schweiz, 1970. (With a letter from K. Rahner.)

Fahey, Michael A., S.J., "Continuity in the Church Amid Structural Changes," in: *Theological Studies*, 35 (1974), pp.415-440.

Fiorenza, F., "Introduction: Karl Rahner and the Kantian Problematic," in: K. Rahner, *Spirit in the World*, W. Dych, tr., N.Y: Herder & Herder, 1968, pp.xix-xlv.

Fischer, Klaus, *Der Mensch als Geheimnis. Die Anthropologie Karl Rahners*, Freiburg i.Br: Herder, 1974. (With a Letter from K. Rahner.)

_____, "Als großer Theologe ein engagierter 'Dilettant'. Randbemerkungen zum 70. Geburtstag Karl Rahners," in: *Orientierung* 38 (1974) 44-47.

_____, Review of: "Grundkurs des Glaubens," in: *ThPh* 52 (1977) 67-71.

_____, "Kritik 'der Grundposition'? Kritische Anmerkungen zu B. van der Heijdens Buch über Karl Rahner," in: *ZkTh* 99 (1977) 74-89.

_____, "Wovon erzählt die transzendentale Theologie? Eine Entgegnung an Peter Eicher," in: *ThQ* 157 (1977), 140-142.

Granfield, P.R., "Karl Rahner," in: *Theologians at Work*, N.Y./ London: McMillan/Collier, 1967, pp.35-50.

"Karl Rahner in America," in: *Jubilee* 12 (1965) 22-23.

Gelpi, D.L., S.J., *Light and Life: A Guide to the Theology of Karl Rahner*. N.Y: Sheed & Ward, 1966.

John, Emily Rebecca, *Political Themes in the Thought of Karl Rahner*, Toronto: U. of St. Michael's College, 1983. (M.A. Thesis, unpublished).

Kelly, Wm.J., ed., *Theology and Discovery: Essays in Honor of Karl Rahner, S.J.*, Milwaukee, Wisconsin: Marquette Univ. Press, 1980. With "Foreword" by K. Rahner.

Krauss, Meinold, *Karl Rahner. Erinnerungen im Gespräch mit Meinold Krauss*, Herderbücherei, 1984. *Karl Rahner: I Remember: An Autobiographical Interview with Meinold Krauss*, H.D. Egan, tr., N.Y: Crossroad, 1985.

Kress, Robert, *A Rahner Handbook*. Atlanta, Georgia: John Knox Press, 1982. Kress studied under Rahner from 1954-1958.

Lehmann, K., "Karl Rahner," in: H. Vorgrimler, R. Vander Gucht, eds., *Bilanz der Theologie im 20. Jahrhundert.* (Supplementary Volume:) *Bahnbrechende Theologen*, Freiburg i.Br: Herder, 1970, pp.143-181.

_____, "Laudatio" in: *Karl Rahner 70 Jahre. Geburtstagsempfang im Verlag Herder am 7. März 1974.* Vier Ansprachen. Als Manuskript gedruckt. Freiburg i.Br.: Herder, 1974, pp.11-19.

_____, "Bahnbrecher moderner Theologie. Zum 70. Geburtstag von Karl Rahner," in: *Gehört, Gelesen.* Hrsg. vom Bayerischen Rundfunk, H.4 (1974) 1-8.

_____, "Ein Leben für Theologie und Kirche. Karl Rahner zum 70. Geburtstag," in: *Konradsblatt* 58, Nr.9 (1974) 8-9; dss. in: *Münchener Katholische Kirchenzeitung* 67, Nr.9 (1974) 3.

_____, "Karl Rahner und die Pastoral," in: *Beihefte zum Anzeiger für die katholische Geistlichkeit*, 23. Folge, Februar 1974. I-IV.

_____, "Einführung: Karl Rahner. Ein Porträt," in: K. Lehmann/ A. Raffelt, eds., *Rechenschaft des Glaubens. Karl Rahner-Lesebuch*, Benziger - Herder, *et al*, 1979, 2. Aufl. 1982.

_____/ Raffelt, A., eds., *Karl Rahner. Praxis des Glaubens. Geistliches Lesebuch*, Zürich - Freiburg i.Br., 1982; Engl., *Karl Rahner -- The Practice of Faith: A Handbook of Contemporary Spirituality*, N.Y: Crossroad, 1983.

Macquarrie, John, "Theologians of our Time: V. Karl Rahner, S.J.," in: *The Expository Times*, 74 (1963) 194-197.

McCool, G.A., ed., *A Rahner Reader*, N.Y: Seabury Press, 1975.

_____, "Philosophy of the Human Person in Karl Rahner's Theology," in: *Theological Studies* 22 (1961) 537-562.

Marty, Martin E., Review: "Foundations of Christian Faith...," in: *The New York Times Book Review*, (March 12, 1978), p.15.

Mette, Norbert, "Zwischen Reflexion und Entscheidung. Der Beitrag Karl Rahners zur Grundlegung der Praktischen Theologie," in: *Trierer Theologische Zeitschrift* 87 (1978) (1. Teil) 26-43; (2. Teil) 136-151.

Moltmann, J., "Das Elend der Neuzeit überwinden. Evangelischer Dank an Karl Rahner," in: *Feuilleton*, 5. März, 1974.

Neufeld, K.H., *Rahner-Register. Ein Schlüssel zu Karl Rahners 'Schriften zur Theologie I - X' und zu seinen Lexikonartikeln*, Einsiedeln - Zürich - Köln, 1974.

Neumann, Karl, *Der Praxisbezug der Theologie bei Karl Rahner*, Freiburg i.Br.: Herder, 1980. (Contains helpful bibliography.)

O'Donovan, Leo J., S.J., ed. "A Changing Ecclesiology in a Changing Church: A Symposium on Development in the Ecclesiology of Karl Rahner," in: *Theological Studies*, 38 (1977) 736-62.

_____, ed., *A World of Grace: An Introduction to the Themes and Foundations of Karl Rahner's Theology*, N.Y: Seabury Press, 1980 (with "Glossary").

_____, "Orthopraxis and Theological Method in Karl Rahner," in: *CTSA Proceedings* 35 (1980) 47-65.

_____ & Robertson, J.C., Reviewers, *Foundations of Christian Faith:...* by Karl Rahner; tr. W.V. Dych, N.Y: Seabury Press, 1978, in: *Religious Studies Review* 5 (July 1979) 190-199.

Roach, R.R., "An Excessive Claim: Rahner's Identification of Love of God and Love of Neighbour," Parts 1 & 2 in: *Studies in Religion* 5 (1975/6), 247-57, 360-72.

Roberts, L. *The Achievement of Karl Rahner*, N.Y: Herder & Herder, 1967.

Schoof, T.M., "Karl Rahner," in his: *A Survey of Catholic Theology 1800 - 1970*, N.D. Smith, tr., Paulist Newman Press, 1970, pp.126-31.

Smith, Patricia, *Karl Rahner, Pastoral Theologian: A Study of the Meaning and Dimensions of Pastoral Theology in the Work of Karl Rahner*. Toronto: University of St. Michael's College, 1977. (Ph.D. Dissertation).

Speck, Josef, *Karl Rahners theologische Anthropologie. Eine Einführung*, München, 1967.

Tallon, Andrew, "Spirit, Freedom, History: Karl Rahner's Hörer des Wortes (Hearers of the Word)," in: *The Thomist* 38 (1974) 908-936.

Vandervelde, G., "The Grammer of Grace: Karl Rahner as a Watershed in Contemporary Theology," *Theological Studies*, 49, No.3 (1988), pp.445-459.

Vorgrimler, H., *Karl Rahner. Denken - Leben - Werke*, München, 1963. Engl. tr., E. Quinn, *Karl Rahner: His Life, Thought and Work*, Montreal: Palm Publ., 1965.

_____, ed., *Wagnis Theologie. Erfahrungen mit der Theologie Karl Rahners*, (K. Rahner zum 75. Geburtstag am 5. März 1979), Freiburg i.Br., 1979. (Contains an extensive "Sekundärliteratur 1948-1978," pp.598-622.)

_____, *Karl Rahner verstehen. Eine Einführung in sein Leben und Denken*, Herderbücherei, 1985. J. Bowden, tr., *Understanding Karl Rahner: An Introduction to his Life and Thought*, N.Y: Crossroad, 1986.

Welte, B. "Ein Vorschlag zur Methode der Theologie heute," Chap.XXI in: *Auf der Spur des Ewigen. Philosophische Abhandlungen über die verschiedenen Gegenstände der Religion und der Theologie*, Freiburg i.Br: Herder, 1965, pp.410-26.

Weger, K-H., *Karl Rahner. Eine Einführung in sein theologisches Denken*, Freiburg i.Br., 1978. D. Smith, tr., *Karl Rahner: An Introduction to His Theology*, N.Y: Seabury Press, 1980.

3. Johann Baptist Metz -- Primary Sources

"Theologische und metaphysische Ordnung," in: *ZKT* 83 (1961), pp.1-14.

Armut im Geiste. München: Ars Sacra, 1962; Engl. tr. by J. Drury, *Poverty of Spirit*. N.Y: Paulist Press, 1968.

"Freiheit -- theologische," *Handbuch theologischer Grundbegriffe* Bd. I, hg. H. Fries, (München, 1962), pp.403-414.

Christliche Anthropozentrik. Über die Denkform des Thomas von Aquin, München: Kösel Velag, 1962. With "Einführender Essay" by Karl Rahner.

"Widmung und Würdigung. Karl Rahner, dem Sechzigjährigen," in: *Gott in Welt. Festgabe für Karl Rahner*, Vol. 1, J.B. Metz, *et al*, eds., Freiburg i.Br.: Herder, 1964, pp.5-13. This *laudatio* also appears, condensed, as "Foreword: An Essay on Karl Rahner," in: K. Rahner, *Spirit in the World*, W. Dych, tr., N.Y: Herder & Herder, 1968, pp.xiii-xviii.

"Freiheit als philosophisch-theologisches Grenzproblem," *Gott in Welt* Bd. I, (*Festschrift*; Freiburg, 1964), pp.287-314. Engl. tr. by W.J. Kramer, "Freedom as a Threshold Problem Between Philosophy and Theology," in: *Philosophy Today* (1966?) pp.264-279.

Weltverständnis im Glauben, Mainz, 1965.

"Nochmals: Christliche Anthropozentrik," in: *Theologische Revue* Nr. 1, 61 (1965) 13-16.

"Preface," *The Church and the World*. Vol.6: *Concilium*, J.B. Metz, ed., Paulist Press, 1965, p.1f.; and "Unbelief as a Theological Problem," tr. by T. Rattler, in: *Ibid.*. pp.59-77.

"Gott vor uns," in: *Ernst Bloch zu Ehren*, S. Unseld, ed., Frankfurt: Suhrkamp Verlag, 1965, pp.227-41.

"Verantwortung der Hoffnung. Vier Diskussionsthesen," in: *Stimmen der Zeit, 177 (1966) 451-62.*

"Schöpferische Eschatologie," in: *Orientierung* XXX (1966) 107-9.

"Nachwort," in: Garaudy, R., Metz, J.B., Rahner, K. *Der Dialog. Oder verändert sich das Verhältnis zwischen Katholizismus und Marxismus?*, Rowohlt, 1966, pp.119-138.

"Karl Rahner," in *Tendenzen der Theologie im 20. Jahrhundert. Eine Geschichte in Porträts*, H.J. Schultz, ed., Stuttgart, 1966; 2. Aufl. 1967, pp.513-518.

"Zum Problem einer 'politischen Theologie'," in: *Kontexte* IV (1967) 35-41.

"Religion und Revolution," *Neues Forum* XIV (1967), pp.460-464.

"Theologie der Revolution," *Evangelische Theologie* Vol.12 (1967).

"Friede und Gerechtigkeit. Überlegungen zu einer 'politischen Theologie'," in: *Civitas*, VI (1967) 9-19.

Rendtorff, T. & Tödt H. E., eds., *Theologie der Revolution* (Frankfurt, 1968).

"The Church's Social Function in the Light of a 'Political Theology'," tr. by Th. L. Westow, in: *Faith and the World of Politics*. Vol.36: *Concilium*, J.B. Metz, ed., Paulist Press, 1968, pp.2-18; cf. "The Church and the World in the Light of a 'Political Theology'," Chap. 5 in: *Theology of the World*.

Zur Theologie der Welt. (Mainz: Matthias-Grünewald, 1968; 4. Aufl. 1979). Engl. tr. by W. Glenn-Döpel, *Theology of the World*, Burns & Oates/ Herder & Herder, 1969.

"Der zukünftige Mensch und der kommende Gott," in: *Wer ist das eigentlich--Gott?* H.J. Schultz, ed., München: Kösel, 1969, pp.260-275.

Diskussion zur politischen Theologie, H. Peukert, ed., (München, 1969).

"Political Theology," in: K. Rahner, ed., *Sacramentum Mundi* 5 (N.Y. & London, 1969), pp.34-38.

"Editorial," tr. by M. Hollebone, in: *Perspectives of a Political Ecclesiology*. Vol.66: *New Concilium*, J.B. Metz, ed., Herder & Herder, 1971, pp.7-12.

"Was will die politische Theologie?" in: *Fragen des sozialen Lebens* IX (1971) 35-48.

"The Future in the Memory of Suffering," in: tr. J. Griffiths, *New Questions on God*, Vol.76: *Concilium*, J.B. Metz, ed., N.Y: Herder & Herder, 1972, pp.9-25.

"Erinnerung," in: *Handbuch philosophischer Grundbegriffe* Vol.2, H. Krings, *et al*, eds., München: Kösel Verlag, 1973, pp.386-96.

"Erlösung und Emanzipation," in: *Stimmen der Zeit*, 191 (1973) 171-184. Engl. tr. by M. Lamb & J. Martin, "Redemption and Emancipation," in: *Cross Currents* 27 (Fall 1977) 321-336.

"Politische Theologie," in: K. Rahner, ed., *Herders Theologisches Taschenlexikon* (in 8 Vols.) Vol.6. Herderbücherei, 1973, pp.51-58.

"Karl Rahner--ein theologisches Leben. Theologie als mystische Biographie eines Christenmenschen heute," in: *Stimmen der Zeit*, 192 (1974) pp.305-316. For Rahner's 70th birthday. (Abbreviated also in *Faith in History and Society*, pp.219-228.)

(With J. Moltmann), *Leidensgeschichte. Zwei Meditationen zu Markus 8,31-38*, Freiburg i.Br: Herder, 1974; Engl: *Meditations on the Passion*, 1979.

"Apologetics," in: K. Rahner, ed., *Encyclopedia of Theology: A Concise Sacramentum Mundi*, Burns & Oates, 1975, (4th) reprinted 1986, pp.20-24.

"Political Theology," in: K. Rahner, ed., *Encyclopedia of Theology: The Concise Sacramentum Mundi*, N.Y: Seabury, 1975, pp.1238-1243.

"Zitate von morgen. Zum 'Grundkurs des Glaubens' von Karl Rahner," in: *Süddeutsche Zeitung*, (Nr. 299; Dezember 1976), p.61.

(With K. Rahner), *Ermutigung zum Gebet*, Freiburg i.Br: Herder, 1977. Engl. tr. S. O'Brien Twohig: *The Courage to Pray*, Search Press Ltd.; N.Y: Crossroad, 1981.

Zeit der Orden? Zur Mystik und Politik der Nachfolge, Freiburg i.Br: Herder, 1977; 4. Aufl. 1979. *Followers of Christ: The Religious Life and the Church*, T. Linton, tr., Search Press, 1978.

Glaube in Geschichte und Gesellschaft. Studien einer praktischen Fundamentaltheologie. Mainz: M.-Grünewald, 1977; 3. Aufl., 1980. Engl. tr. by D. Smith: *Faith in History and Society. Toward a Practical Fundamental Theology*. N.Y: Seabury Press, 1980.

"Introductory Address," and "For a Renewed Church Before a New Council: A Concept in Four Thesis," in: D. Tracy, H. Küng, & J.B. Metz, eds., *Toward Vatican III: The Work That Needs to be Done*, Gill and Macmillan Ltd., 1978, p.9f. and pp.137-145, respectively.

"An Identity Crisis in Christianity? Transcendental and Political Responses," in: *Theology and Discovery: Essays in Honor of Karl Rahner, S.J.*, Wm.J. Kelly, ed., Milwaukee, Wisconsin: Marquette Univ. Press, 1980, pp.169-178.

Jenseits bürgerlicher Religion. Reden über die Zukunft des Christentums. München/Mainz: Kaiser/Grünewald, 2. Aufl. 1980. (Forum Politische Theologie Nr.1.) Engl. tr. by Peter Mann: *The Emergent Church: The Future of Christianity in a Postbourgeois World*. N.Y: Crossroad, 1981.

"'Wenn die Betreuten sich ändern': Vision von einer Basiskirche," in: *Reformatio* 29:9 (Sept. 1980) 550-61. Engl., "Base-church and Bourgeois Religion," in: *Theology Digest* 29:3 (Fall, 1981) 203-206. (cf. p.203). (This essay also appears in *The Emergent Church*, chap.6.)

Unterbrechungen. Theologisch-politische Perspektiven und Profile. Gütersloh: Gütersloher Verlagshaus Gerd Mohn, 1981.

Bio-bibliographische Notiz, 1981 (unpubl.; received in private correspondence through Metz's *Assistent*).

"Aufstand der Hoffnung. Das Synodendokument 'Unsere Hoffnung' als Aufruf zur messianischen Erneuerung der Kirche," in *Imprimatur. Nachrichten und kritische Meinungen aus der katholischen Kirche*. E. Bertel, *et al*, eds. (15. Jahrgang, Nr.7, 22. Okt. 1982), pp.309-319.

Im Angesichte der Gefahr. Theologische Meditation zu Lukas Kapitel 21 und zur Apokalypse des Johannes, Bayerischer Rundfunk - Nachtstudio, 19. 12. 1983 (Unpubl., pp.6; kindly given to me by Professor Metz on my visit in 1984).

Den Glauben lernen und lehren. Dank an Karl Rahner. München: Kösel, 1984.

Im Angesichte der Juden. Christliche Theologie nach Auschwitz, (Unpubl. essay, pp.21; also given to me by Professor Metz in 1984).

Theologie im neuen Paradigma: politische Theologie, (Unpubl., undated paper, pp.15; cites 1983 material; also from Professor Metz personally in the summer of 1984). "Political Theology: A New Paradigm of Theology?" in: *Civil Religion and Political Theology*, L.S. Rouner, ed., Notre Dame, IN: University of Notre Dame Press, 1986, pp.141-153.

Gefährliche Erinnerungen. Kleiner Brief zu einem großen Thema, (Unpubl., not dated, letter to "Hans," a former Prisoner of War in Russia. The letter gives important clues as to how Metz's theology is rooted in personal experience; also given to me by Prof. Metz on my 1984 visit with him).

"Theology Today: New Crises and New Visions," *CTSA Proceedings* 40 (1985) 1-14.

"Theologie gegen Mythologie. Kleine Apologie des biblischen Monotheismus," in: *Herder Korrespondenz*, (April, 1988), pp.187-193.

"Anamnetische Vernunft: Anmerkungen eines Theologen zur Krise der Geisteswissen-schaften" in: Honneth/McCarthy/Offe/ Wellmer, eds., *Zwischenbetrachtungen im Prozeß der Aufklärung*, (Jürgen Habermas zum 60. Geburtstag), Frankfurt: Suhrkamp Verlag, 1989, pp.733-738.

"Fehlt uns Karl Rahner? oder: Wer retten will, muß wagen," in: Karl Rahner, *Strukturwandel der Kirche als Aufgabe und Chance*. Mit einer Einführung von Johann Baptist Metz, Freiburg: Herder-Verlag, 1989, pp.9-24.

4. Johann Baptist Metz -- Secondary Sources

Ancic, Nedjeljko, *Die "Politischen Theologie" von Johann Baptist Metz als Antwort auf die Herausforderung des Marxismus*. Frankfurt a.M., Bern: Lang, 1981. pp.377.

Bauer, G., *Christliche Hoffnung und menschlicher Fortschritt. Die politische Theologie von J.B. Metz als theologische Begründung gesellschaftlicher Verantwortung des Christen*, Mainz, 1976.

de Luvallet, H., "La 'theologie politique' de J.B. Metz," in: *RST* 58 (1970) 321-50, (esp. 331).

Egan, Harvey D., Review of: *Faith in History and Society: Toward a Practical Fundamental Theology* by J.B. Metz; tr. by D. Smith, N.Y: Seabury, 1980, in: *Theological Studies* 41, No.3 (1980), pp.591-593.

Fiorenza Schüssler, Francis, "The Thought of J.B. Metz: Origin, Positions, Development," in: *Philosophy Today* X (1966) 247-52.

_____, "The Return of J.B. Metz," in: *New Book Review*, (Dec. 1968) 10-13.

_____, "Critical Social Theory and Christology: Toward an Understanding of Atonement and Redemption as Emancipatory Solidarity," in: *CTSA Proceedings* Vol.30 (1975) 63-110; on Metz and Christology, cf. p.79.

_____, "Political Theology as Fundamental Theology," in: *CTSA Proceedings* Vol.32 (1977) 142-177.

Flüssel, K., "Politische Theologie," in: K. Rahner/ H. Vorgrimler, eds., *Kleines Theologisches Wörterbuch*, Freiburg i.Br: Herder, 1976, 12. Aufl. 1980, p.337f.

Ganoczy, A., *Sprechen von Gott in heutiger Gesellschaft. Weiterentwicklung der 'Politischen Theologie'*, Freiburg, 1974.

Gómez Arango, G., "La 'teología política' según J.B. Metz," in: *Ecclesiástica Xaveriana*, 1973, 68-115.

Heinrichs, J., "Transzendentales-dialogisches-politisches Denken. Thesen zu einer 'transzendentalen Dialogik'," in: *Internat. Dialog-Zeitschrift* 3 (1970), 373-79.

_____, "Sinn und Intersubjektivität," in: *ThuPh* 45 (1970) 161-91.

Jiménez Urresti, F.J., "Crítica teológica a la teología crítico-política de Metz. Reflexiones para la teología del derecho público eclesiástico," in: A. Vargas-Machuca, ed., *Teología y mundo contemporáneo. Homenaje a K. Rahner en su 70 cumpleaños*, Madrid, 1975, 515-43.

Johns, R.D., *Man in the World: The Theology of Johannes Baptist Metz*, Scholars Press (for AAR; no.16), 1976; (author's Dissertation at Duke University, 1973).

Lamb, Matthew L., *Solidarity with Victims: Toward a Theology of Social Transformation*, N.Y: Crossroad, 1982.

Lamb, Matthew L., "A Response to Fr. Metz," in: Wm. J. Kelly, ed. *Theology and Discovery: Essays in Honor of Karl Rahner, S.J.*, Milwaukee, Wisconsin: Marquette Univ. Press, 1980, pp.179-183.

Lehmann, Karl, "Die politische Theologie: Theologische Legitimation und gegenwärtige Aporie," in J. Krautscheidt, H. Marre, eds., *Essener Gespräche zum Thema Staat und Kirche*, Vol. IV, Münster, 1970, pp.90-198. Lehmann's comments on Metz's "Political Theology" deserve more attention than those of most commentators, insofar as he is indisputably also one of the leading authorities with regards to Rahner's theology.

_____, "Wandlungen der neuen 'politischen Theologie'," in: *IKaZ* 2 (1973) 385-399. Engl.: "Metamorphoses of the new 'Political Theology'," in: *Internatioanl Catholic Review* 2 (1973) 247-256.

_____, "Emanzipation und Leid: Wandlungen der neuen 'politischen Theologie'" (Part II), in: *IKaZ* 3 (1974) 42-55. (Continuation of previous item.)

Maier, Hans, "Zur christlichen Anthropozentrik," in: *Theologische Revue* Nr.1, 61 (1965) 9-12.

_____, "'Politische Theologie?' Einwände eines Laien," in: *Diskussion zur 'politischen Theologie'*, ed. H. Peukert. Mainz/ München: Chr. Kaiser/ Grünewald, 1969.

_____, *Kritik der politischen Theologie*, Einsiedeln: Johannes Verlag, 1970.

Peters, Tiemo Rainer, "Johann Baptist Metz: Ein theologisches Porträt," in: *Börsenblatt für den Deutschen Buchhandel*, 19 (1989), pp.81-85; ed. by Börsenverein des Deutschen Buchhandels, Frankfurt.

Schillebeeckx, E., ed., *Mystik und Politik. Theologie im Ringen um Geschichte und Gesellschaft. Johann Paptist Metz zu Ehren*, Mainz: Matthias-Grünewald-Verlag, 1988.

Siebert, R.J., "The Church of the Future--The Church from Below: Küng and Metz," in: *Cross Currents* No.1, Vol.31 (Spring 1981) 62-85.

Topel, John S.J., "This bourgeois church," (a Review of:) *The Emergent Church: The Future of Christianity in a Post-Bourgeois World*, by J.B. Metz, in: *National Catholic Reporter* Sept. 18 (1981) p.14f.

Tracy, David, "A Response to Fr. Metz," in: *Theology and Discovery: Essays in Honor of Karl Rahner, S.J.*, W.J. Kelly, ed., Milwaukee, Wisconsin: Marquette Univ. Press, 1980, pp.184-187.

Ulbricht, Mechthild, *Rationalität und Reich Gottes. Interpretationshilfe zur Politischen Theologie von Johann Baptist Metz.* München, Universität, 1980, pp.179. (Sozialwissenschaftliche Fakultät, Dissertation).

5. Ancillary Secondary Sources

Adorno, Theodor W., "Marginalien zu Theorie und Praxis," in: *Ibid., Stichworte. Kritische Modelle*, 2, Frankfurt/M. 1969, 169-191.

Alves, Rubem, *A Theology of Human Hope*, Washington, D.C: Corpus Books, 1969. (Also available in Portuguese and Spanish.)

_____, *Tomorrow's Child*, N.Y: Harper & Row, 1972.

Aquinas: Selected Political Writings, edited with an Introduction by A.P. D'entreves; tr. by J.G. Dawson. Oxford: Basil Blackwell, 1959; 1965.

Arato, A./ Gebhardt, E., eds. *The Essential Frankfurt School Reader*, N.Y: Urizen Books, 1978; "General Introduction" by Paul Piccone, pp.ix-xxii.

Assmann, Hugo, *Teología desde la praxis de liberación*, Salamanca: Ediciones Sígueme, 1973; Engl. tr., *Practical Theology of Liberation*, Search Press, 1975.

_____, *Theology for a Nomad Church*, Maryknoll: Orbis, 1976.

Aubert, R., "Modernism," in: *Encyclopedia of Theology: A Concise Sacramentum Mundi*, K. Rahner, ed.; J. Cumming, exec. ed. of Engl. tr., London: Burns & Oates, 1975, 1977, 1981, 1986. (From here on: *Concise SM*.)

Augsburger, M., *Pilgrim Aflame* (Herald Press, 1967). Cf. movie, *The Radicals*, produced by Sisters and Brothers, Goshen Indiana (1990). The film, based on Augsburger's historical novel, is about the Anabaptist beginnings. At its center is the life and martyrdom of the Anabaptist leader, Benedictine ex-Abbot Michael Sattler.

Bainton, R.H., *Christian Attitudes Toward War and Peace: A Historical Survey and Re-evaluation*, Nashville - N.Y: Abingdon Press, 1960.

Baum, Gregory, "The Theological Method of Segundo's *The Liberation of Theology*," in: *CTSA Proceedings* Vol.32 (1977), 120-124.

_____, "Political Theology in Canada," in: *The Ecumenist*, Vol.15 No.3 (March/April 1977) 33-46.

_____, *Man Becoming: God in Secular Experience*, N.Y: Herder & Herder, 1970.

_____, ed., *Journeys: The Impact of Personal Experience on Religious Thought*, N.Y., N.J: Paulist Press, 1975.

_____, *Religion and Alienation: A Theological Reading of Sociology*, N.Y., Paramus, Toronto: Paulist Press, 1975.

Bender, H.S.,*et al*, eds., *The Mennonite Encyclopedia*, 4 Volumes, Scottdale, Pa.: Mennonite Publishing House, 1957; for Vol.5, cf. Dyck & Martin, below.

Between Honesty and Hope, Maryknoll, 1970. Documants from and about the Church in Latin America, elaborated and adopted by the Latin American Bishops Conference, held in Bogota, Colombia, in 1968.

Blank, Josef, "Die Praxis ist das Kriterium," in: ders., *Verändert Interpretation den Glauben?*, Freiburg i.Br., 1972, 102-112.

Brockhaus, F.A., *Der Volks-Brockhaus von A-Z*, 14. völlig neu bearbeitete Auflage, Wiesbaden: F.A. Brockhaus, 1969.

Brown, R. McAffee, *Theology in a New Key: Responding to Liberation Themes*, Philadelphia, Pa: Westminster Press, 1978.

Camara, Dom Hélder, *Church and Colonialism*, W. Sweeney, tr., London and Sidney: Sheed & Ward, 1969.

_____, *Dom Helder Camara: The Violence of a Peacemaker*, by Jose de Broucker, Maryknoll: Orbis Books, 1970.

_____, *Spiral of Violence*, London: Sheed & Ward, 1971.

_____, *Revolution through Peace*, A. McLean, tr., N.Y., *et al*: Harper & Row, 1971. Original: *Revolutiao Dentro da Paz*.

Cochrane, Arthur, *The Mystery of Peace*, Elgin, IL: Brethren Press, 1986. Foreword by J.H. Yoder.

Cone, J.H., *A Black Theology of Liberation*, Philadelphia & N.Y: J.B. Lippincott, Co., 1970.

Cox, Harvey, "Political Theology for the United States," in: *Projections: Shaping an American Theology for the Future*,1970, pp.41-49.

Donovan, Daniel, *The Church as Idea and Fact*, Wilmington, Delaware: Michael Glazier, 1988.

Durnbaugh, D.F., *The Believers' Church: The History and Character of Radical Protestantism*, Scottdale PA - Kitchener, Ontario: Herald Press, 1968 & 1985.

Dyck, C.J., ed., *An Introduction to Mennonite History: A Popular History of the Anabaptists and the Mennonites*, Scottdale, PA: Herald Press, 2nd ed. 1981.

Dyck, C.J. and Martin, Dennis, eds., *The Mennonite Encyclopedia*, Supplementary Volume 5, Scottdale, Pa.: Herald Press, 1990; contains circa 1,000 new articles on important topics and updates materials in vols. 1-4.

Eller, Vernard, *War and Peace: From Genesis to Revelation*, Scottdale, Pa.: Herald Press, 1973 and 1981.

_____, *The Most Revealing Book of the Bible: Making Sense out of Revelation*, Grand Rapids, Michigan: W.B. Eerdmans, 1974.

_____, ed., *Thy Kingdom Come: A Blumhardt Reader*, Grand Rapids, Michigan: W.B. Eerdmans, 1980.

Evangelical Nonviolence: Force for Liberation, 1978. Issued by some 20 Bishops from various Latin American countries at a conference in Bogota, Colombia.

Flannery, A.P., ed., *Documents of Vatican II*, Grand Rapids: Michigan: W.B. Eerdmans, 1975.

Freire, Paulo, *Pedagogy of the Oppressed*, M.B. Ramos, tr., Herder & Herder, 1970.

Friedmann, Robert, *The Theology of Anabaptism*, Scottdale, PA: Herald Press, 1973.

Galilea, Segundo, "Liberation as an Encounter with Politics and Contemplation," in: *Concilium* Vol.6, No.10 (1974) 19-33.

Günther, Henning, "Walter Benjamin und die Theologie," in: *Stimmen der Zeit*, 191 (1973) 33-46.

Guenther, Titus, *Torres and Camara: Violence and Nonviolence from a Mennonite Perspective*, M.A. Thesis at U. of St. Michael's College, Toronto, 1977 (unpublished).

Gutiérrez, G. *A Theology of Liberation*, Maryknoll: Orbis Books, 1973.

Haight, Roger, S.J., *An Alternate Vision: An Interpretation of Liberation Theology*, N.Y., Mahwah: Paulist Press, 1985. The "Appendix" contains: "Sacred Congregation for the Doctrine of the Faith: Instruction on Certain Aspects of the 'Theology of Liberation'" (Vatican City, 1984) and Haight's "Interpretation..." of the same.

_____, "The Mission of the Church in the Theology of the Social Gospel," *Theological Studies* 49, No.3 (1988), pp.477-497.

Hengel, Martin, "'Politische Theologie' und neutestamentliche Zeitgeschichte," in: *Kerygma und Dogma* 18 (1972) 18-22.

Herzog, Frederick, "Political Theology in the American Context," in: *Theological Markings*, Vol.1 (Spring 1971), 28-42.

_____, "Political Theology," *Christian Century*, LXXXVI (22?) (July, 1969) 975-78.

Hillerbrand, H.J., "The Origins of Sixteenth Century Anabaptism: Another Look," *Archiv für Reformationsgeschichte* LIII (1962), pp.152-180.

Höflich, E., "Heilsverkündigung als politische Gewissensbildung. Eine Antwort auf Hans Meiers Polemik gegen die politische Theologie," in: *Frankfurter Hefte* (Dez. 1969), p.851.

Kee, A. ed., *A Reader in Political Theology*, SCM Press, 1974.

_____, ed., *The Scope of Political Theology*, SCM Press, 1978.

348 *Rahner and Metz*

Keeney, William, *Lordship as Servanthood: Thirteen Lessons on the Biblical Basis for Peacemaking*, Faith & Life Press - Herald Press, 1975; *La estrategia social de Jesús*, Miguel Llop, tr., Barcelona: Ediciones Evangélicas Europeas, 1978.

Kerans, Patrick, S.J., "Theology of Liberation," in: *Chicago Studies*, (Summer 1972), pp.183-195.

Klaassen, Walter, *Anabaptism: Neither Catholic nor Protestant*, Waterloo: Conrad Press, 1973; Spanish, *Entre la Iglesia del Estado y la Religión Civil*, Ediciones SEMILLA, 1988.

_____, *The Just War: A Summary*, Peace Research Reviews, Vol.VII No.6, Dundas: Ontario, 1978; Spanish tr. by Milka Rindzinski, *La Guerra Justa: Un Resumen*, Ediciones CLAR A - SEMILLA, 1991.

_____, ed. *Anabaptism in Outline*, Scottdale, PA - Kitchener, Ontario: Herald Press, 1981; Spanish tr. by C.A. Snyder, *Selecciones Teológicas Anabautistas. Fuentes Primarias Seleccionadas*, Herald Press, 1985.

_____, "Sixteenth Century Anabaptism: A Vision Valid for the Twentieth Century," *The Conrad Grebel Review*, Vol.7, No.3 (Fall, 1989), pp.241-251.

Koontz, Ted J., "Church-State Relations," in: *The Mennonite Encyclopedia*, Vol. 5, C.J. Dyck & D. Martin, eds., Scottdale, Pa.: Herald Press, 1990, pp.159-162.

Lamb, Matthew, "The Theory-Praxis Relationship in Contemporary Theologies," in: *CTSA Proceedings*, 31 (1976) 149-178.

Lehmann, Karl, Art. "Erfahrung," *Sacramentum Mundi* I (1976) 1117-1123.

Lehmann, Paul, *The Transfiguration of Politics*, N.Y, *et al*: Harper & Row, 1975. (Subtitle: The Presence and Power of Jesu of Nazareth in and over Human Affairs.)

Littell, F.H., *The Anabaptist View of the Church*, Boston: Beacon, 1958.

Lotz, J.B., *Transzendentale Erfahrung*, Freiburg i.Br., 1978.

Marty, Martin E., *A Short History of Christianity*, Philadelphia: Fortress Press, 1959, 14th Printing and 1st Fortress Press Ed. 1980, 3rd Printing 1986.

McCann, Dennis P., "Liberation Theology," in: *The Westminster Dictionary of Christian Ethics*, J.F. Childress & J. Macquarrie, eds., Philadelphia: The Westminster Press, 1986, p.349f.

Mennonite Encyclopedia, The, Vols. 1-4, cf. Bender, H.S., *et al*, eds.; Vol. 5, Dyck, C.J. & Martin, D., respectively above.

Míguez Bonino, José, *Doing Theology in a Revolutionary Situation*, Philadelphia: Fortress Press, 1975.

_____, *Christians and Marxists: The Mutual Challenge to Revolution*, Grand Rapids, Michigan: W.B. Eerdmans, 1976.

_____, *Room to be People*, Philadelphia: Fortress, 1979.

Moltmann, J., *Crucified God: The Cross of Christ as the Foundation and Criticism of Christian Theology*, SCM Press, 1975.

_____, "Political Theology," *Theology Today* 28 (Apr. 1971) 7-9.

_____, "Political Theology," *Christianity Today* 28 (1971/72) 6-23.

350 Rahner and Metz

_____, "Theologische Kritik der politischen Religion," in: *Kirche im Prozeß der Aufklärung*, J.B. Metz, *et al*, eds., Mainz/ München: Chr. Kaiser/ Grünewald, 1970.

_____, *Following Jesus Christ in the World Taday*, Occasional Papers No.4, Elkhart, IN: Institute of Mennonite Studies; Winnipeg, Man.: CMBC Publications, 1983. And *Dialogue Sequel to Jürgen Moltmann's: Following Jesus Christ in the World Today*, Occasional Paper No.8, (by the same publishers) 1984.

Post, Werner, Art. "Theory and Practice," in: *Concise SM*, 1986, pp.1701-1705.

_____, Art. "Marxismus," in: *Herders Theologisches Taschenlexikon*, K. Rahner, ed., Vol.5, Herderbücherei, 1973,pp.7-13. Engl. tr. in: *Concise SM*, pp.939-943.

Raab, H., Art. "Enlightenment," in: *Concise SM*, pp.427-430.

Redekop, C. & Steiner, S., eds., *Mennonite Identity: Historical and Contemporary Perspectives*, Lanham - New York - London: University Press of America, 1988.

Reimer, A. James, *The Emanuel Hirsch and Paul Tillich Debate: A Study in the Political Ramifications of Theology*, Lewiston, NY: The Edwin Mellen Press, 1989.

Ridemans, Peter, *Rechenschaft unserer Religion, Lehre und Glaubens.* (Von den Brüdern, die man die Huterischen nennt), Cayley, Alberta, Canada: Verlag der Huterischen Brüder Gemeine, 1962.

Ruether, Rosemary, *New Woman, New Earth: Sexist Ideologies and Human Liberation*, N.Y: Seabury, 1975.

Rutschman, LaVerne A., "American Liberation Theology from an Anabaptist Perspective," in: *Mission Focus* 9 (June, 1981) 21-26.

_____, *Anabautismo Radical y Teología Latinoamericana de la Liberación*, San José, Costa Rica: Editorial SEBILA, 1982.

Segundo, Juan Luis, S.J., *The Liberation of Theology*, tr. John Drury, Maryknoll: Orbis Books, 1976. (Cf. G. Baum's discussion of the book above.)

_____, *The Shift Within Latin American Liberation Theology*, A lecture given at Regis College, Toronto (March 22, 1983) 1-20.

Sider, R.J., *Christ and Violence*, Scottdale, PA: Herald Press, 1979; Spanish, *Cristo y la Violencia*, Ediciones SEMILLA - CLARA, 1991.

Sölle, Dorothee, *Political Theology*, tr. and Introduction by J. Shelley, Philadelphia: Fortress Press, 1974. (German subtitle: Auseinandersetzung mit Rudolf Bultmann.)

Stayer, J.M., *Anabaptists and the Sword*, Lawrence, KS: Coronado, 1972.

Sturm, Douglas, "Political Theology," in: *The Westminster Dictionary of Christian Ethics*, J.F. Childress & J Macquarrie, eds., Philadelphia: The Westminster Press, 1986, pp.481-83.

Topitsch, Ernst, "Kosmos und Herrschaft. Ursprünge der 'politischen Theologie'," in: *Wort und Wahrheit* X (1955) 19-30.

Torres, S. & Eagleson, J., eds., *Theology in the Americas*, Maryknoll: Orbis Books, 1976.

Wacker, Bernd, *Narrative Theologie?*, München, 1977.

Weinrich, Harald, "Narrative Theologie," in: *Concilium* 9 (1973) 46-56; tr. by F. McDonah.

West, Charles C., "Marxist Ethics," in *The Westminster Dictionary of Christian Ethics*, J.F. Childress & J. Macquarrie, eds., Philadelphia: The Westminster Press, 1986, pp.368-372.

Williams, G.H., *The Radical Reformation*, Philadelphia: Westminster Press, 3rd. printing 1975. Spanish, *La Reforma Radical*, A. Alatorre, tr., México: Fondo de Cultura Económica, 1983.

Yoder, John H., *The Christian Witness to the State*, Newton, Kansas: Faith and Life Press, 1964.

_____, *Täufertum und Reformation im Gespräch*, Zürich: EVZ, 1968.

_____, "The Original Revolution," in: *The Original Revolution*, Scottdale, PA: Herald Press, 1971, pp.13-33.

_____, *The Politics of Jesus. Vicit Agnus Noster*, Grand Rapids, Michigan: W.B. Eerdmans, 1972. Spanish, *Jesús y la Realidad Política*, Buenos Aires/Downers Grove, IN: Ediciones Certeza, 1985.

_____, "Exodus and Exile: The two Faces of Liberation," in: *Cross Currents* (Fall 1973) 297-309.

_____, copilador, *Textos Escogidos de la Reforma Radical*, Buenos Aires: Editorial La Aurora, 1976.

_____, *Christian Attitudes to War, Peace, and Revolution: A Companion to Bainton*, Elkhart, IN: Goshen Biblical Seminary, 1983.

_____, *When War is Unjust: Being Honest in Just-War Thinking*, Minneapolis: Augsburg Publishing House, 1984.

_____, *The Priestly Kingdom: Social Ethics as Gospel*, Notre Dame, IN: University of Notre Dame Press, 1984.

Zahn, Gordon, *In Solitary Witness: The Life and Death of Franz Jägerstätter*, Springfield, IL: Templegate Pub., 1964; Revised ed., 1986.

General Index